# Diversity Matters

## Understanding Diversity in Schools

### SECOND EDITION

**Lynn Kell Spradlin, Ed.D.**
*Morehead State University*

**WADSWORTH**
CENGAGE Learning™

Australia • Brazil • Japan • Korea • Mexico • Singapore • Spain • United Kingdom • United States

WADSWORTH
CENGAGE Learning™

**Diversity Matters: Understanding Diversity in Schools, Second Edition**
Lynn Kell Spradlin

Publisher/Executive Editor: Linda Schreiber-Ganster

Acquisitions Editor: Mark Kerr

Assistant Editor: Rebecca Dashiell

Media Editor: Ashley Cronin

Editorial Assistant: Linda Stewart

Marketing Manager: Kara Kindstrom-Parsons

Marketing Assistant: Dimitri Hagnere

Marketing Communications Manager: Tami Strang

Content Project Management: PreMediaGlobal

Art Director: Jeniffer Wahi

Print Buyer: Karen Hunt

Rights Acquisition Director: Bob Kauser

Rights Acquisition Specialist, Text/Image: Don Schlotman

Production Service/Compositor: PreMediaGlobal

Cover Designer: Jeff Bane

Cover Image: Jeff Bane, CMB Design Partners, illustrator

For product information and technology assistance, contact us at **Cengage Learning Customer & Sales Support, 1-800-354-9706**

For permission to use material from this text or product, submit all requests online at **www.cengage.com/permissions**
Further permissions questions can be emailed to **permissionrequest@cengage.com**

Library of Congress Control Number: 2010933366

ISBN-13: 978-1-111-34167-1

ISBN-10: 1-111-34167-2

**Wadsworth**
20 Davis Drive
Belmont, CA 94002-3098
USA

Cengage Learning is a leading provider of customized learning solutions with office locations around the globe, including Singapore, the United Kingdom, Australia, Mexico, Brazil and Japan. Locate your local office at **www.cengage.com/global**

Cengage Learning products are represented in Canada by Nelson Education, Ltd.

For your course and learning solutions, visit **www.cengage.com**

Purchase any of our products at your local college store or at our preferred online store **www.cengagebrain.com**

Printed in the United States of America
1 2 3 4 5 6 7 14 13 12 11 10

*To Jordan and Dylan Spradlin. Their example and presence in my life have generated in me a deep appreciation for understanding the many faces of truth and the importance of honor, strength, creativity, and faith in all relationships and endeavors.*

# Brief Contents

# Contents

CHAPTER **12**    Learning from the Stories of People with Disabilities   233

PART **3**    **PROMOTING CHANGE AND ACHIEVEMENT**   **263**

CHAPTER **13**    Understanding the Achievement Gap between Minority
and Dominant-Culture Students: Stratification Effects   264

# Preface

This text is designed to take you on a social justice and diversity education journey. You will find that the thorough foundation of knowledge and presentation of salient diversity concepts and principles in Part I will help you identify cultural issues and societal treatment of marginalized groups. Then you encounter many different minority perspectives and experiences in Part II. Finally in Part III, you will apply the knowledge and insights gained from Parts I and II of the text, to explore oppression theory and effects of oppression on achievement and social-emotional adjustment along with effective strategies designed to advance anti-bias curricula, diversity education, and social justice in schools and communities.

## A Guide for Educators

Educators are continually challenged to find effective ways to address diversity in their classrooms, curricula, and professional development. Over the past few decades, many multicultural and diversity education approaches have been identified and attempted—yet educators continue to struggle to find effective, practical approaches to promote equity and increase minority student achievement. This text presents students and educators with an approach that enriches their own understanding and integration of diverse perspectives and social justice education through first-person narratives and teaches methods for identifying, exploring, analyzing, and synthesizing diversity constructs, curricula, and instruction. Not only is understanding and effectively teaching diversity a mandate for educators in order to meet accreditation, ethical, and professional standards in service of the greater good, but it is also a professional imperative for all educators who enter schools and classrooms to work with diverse student populations.

Without a thorough and competent knowledge of their own cultural selves and the perspectives, values, treatment, and issues of members of diverse cultural groups, educators are not well prepared to perform their professional duties. Achievement gap statistics reveal the harm that ensues when educators do not effectively address diversity-related deficits in instruction and curricula. And while it is understandable that educators may be confused about the best ways to address such a pervasive, ingrained, often unconscious or disguised, complex issue, no harm to students should be seen as acceptable. Once conditions within institutions are accepted, they are maintained, become routine, and even reinforced as permanent features of the structures that operate institutions. As such, without recognition, educators' failings and compromises in the area of diversity become threads in the fabric of the status quo policies and procedures that govern inequitable daily school practices.

Whether these failings stem from educators acting without clear conceptual theoretical frameworks for understanding and advocating for anti-bias curricula, social justice and diversity education or from educators who lack the knowledge and skills that develop with intercultural competence, such professional deficiencies reduce minority student adjustment and achievement. So, while not intending harm, they hurt students in ways that cannot be fully measured by turning them off and out of schools and therefore limiting their knowledge while curtailing their access to and utilization of the educational system and its related economic opportunity arenas to the fullest extent.

## Gaining Understanding from Diverse Personal Narratives

There is no recipe for working effectively with a diverse classroom population. In addition, diversity education involves more than effectively teaching diverse students. It also entails seeing all curricula and instruction through the lens of diversity—identifying knowledge and methods that exclude and distort and teaching in ways that guide and empower students to deeply understand and critically analyze what has come to be known as fact in all disciplines and fields of study. With a basis in prominent research and enriched by the individual voices, perspectives, and experiences of those who hold diverse worldviews, *Diversity Matters: Understanding Diversity in Schools* provides pragmatic and theoretically sound strategies for effective social justice and diversity education.

This text is designed to actively engage you—intellectually and emotionally. It will move you from the realm of understanding (head), through personal valuing (heart), and finally to applying (voice) the information provided. In order to move from the head to the heart to voice, it employs a number of unique elements. One predominant feature in this text is the extensive use of autobiographical personal narratives (first-person stories) to enrich your exposure to various cultural groups. They are used throughout this text to help you experience circumstances, issues, worldviews, and concerns of various persons from different cultural groups in their own voices rather than have you learn about the treatment and life circumstances of diverse peoples through reading about different cultural groups of people as perceived by scholars and other researchers. The diversity education approach presented in this text will (1) increase your awareness of traditions and value systems of culturally diverse individuals; (2) help you explore your own cultural background and related value systems as well as an awareness of the lenses through which you filter shape and view knowledge and relations influence your beliefs; (3) provide you with specific reflection and field experience exercises as well as personal narratives to further develop your understanding of diversity in the United States and how it affects student outcomes; (4) integrate a knowledge of oppression, oppression outcomes, and diverse cultural groups' societal treatment and experience, and (5) provide methods for creating and employing strategies that will improve your intercultural interactions and equitable learning communities.

*Please read the About the Author pages before reading this text. These pages provide you with author information that creates a context for the text as well as the author's pedagogical approach to diversity and social justice curriculum integration.*

*Diversity Matters: Understanding Diversity in Schools* is a text that will not permit you to be a passive reviewer or reader of material. The exercises provided will invite you to actively identify the cultural imprints that have affected your cultural self. Further, you will be guided to explore your academic, racial, sexual-orientation, ethnic, gender, ability, and social-class roots and relative status in society. This enhanced self-awareness will provide you with comparison points to use as you begin to discover differences and similarities between yourself and members of other cultural groups. It is this knowledge, this heightened awareness of self and others, that will help you create an openness to considering information that conflicts with your own worldviews. As noted by others (for example, Covey, 1992[1]), being more self-aware allows us to more fully understand the way we approach life and the people we encounter. As we become more aware of how we see ourselves, how we are treated, and perhaps how others see us, we will become more able to understand how others may see and feel about their treatment, others values and experiences, and their worldviews. Without such self-awareness, we are likely to "project our intentions on others behavior and call ourselves objective" (Covey, 1992, p. 67).

In addition to increasing your awareness and understanding, the text has been created in a way that will prepare you to create a personal activism plan that will produce an equitable and enriched learning environment. You will find that when you design ways for you and your students to productively acknowledge yourselves to one another and make clear your individual values and dispositions, your learning environment will produce fewer misconceptions and hidden agendas that would otherwise damage effective communication and achievement.

## Text Structure and Organization

Realizing that teacher and student identities are formed and often entrenched in many layers of experience, a significant focus for diversity education needs to

[1] Covey, S. (1992). The seven habits of highly effective people: Powerful lessons in personal change. *Emergency Librarian, 20*(1).

address the influence of significant others, culture, environment, and social context on interaction patterns and learning conditions. *Diversity Matters: Understanding Diversity in Schools* provides information on the following six cultural factors as they relate to each cultural group presented in this text:

1. The group's historical and current treatment in the United States
2. The initial terms of incorporation of the group into U.S. society
3. Shared values and traditions of the group
4. The group's view of spirituality, including humans' orientation to nature
5. The group's acculturation issues, including experience with exclusion and alienation
6. The group's potential language differences, strengths, and challenges

In addition, each group's strategies for coping with oppression and potential barriers in learning relationships between group members and dominant-culture teachers are also discussed. These factors are explored throughout Part II (Chapters 5–12). They are also reflected in the many autobiographical personal narrative stories and suggested reflection and field experience exercises found in Parts I and III of the text. Throughout the text, you will find thorough descriptions of historical and current conditions to enrich your understanding of diverse views as well as analysis that explains and applies prominent theoretical constructs and models suggested for your use to produce effective intercultural communication, curriculum design, and instruction. Further, you will find detailed presentations of the lived experience of those from diverse cultures told in their own voices. These engaging stories are used to give you an inside view of what it is like to be marginalized based on race, social class, gender, sexual orientation, disability, and culture. You become privy to the worries, struggles, and triumphs of various people as they engage in sometimes alienating and discouraging experienced in U.S. schools. You will hear from students, parents, guardians, and teachers alike as they navigate within the U.S. school system, with all its problems and opportunities for growth and development. You can expect to feel very present in the process of this exploration.

To make the most of this text, keep track of your thoughts and feelings in a reflection journal in which you identify, compare, and contrast the ways in which each chapter's set of autobiographical personal narratives illustrates the six cultural factors and how those circumstances may differ from your own knowledge and experiences in the world. In addition to the integration of narratives and illustrations, the chapters also include the following elements:

Chapter Objectives

Chapter Summary

Questions for Review

Reflection and Field Experience Exercises

Important Terms

Enrichment (suggested autobiographies and readings)

Connections on the Web

## New to this Edition

Features new to this edition include:

- New Questions for Review at the end of each chapter
- Updated content to include the latest research, current legislation, and more connections to popular culture
- Updated end-of-chapter resources, including Connections on the Web, Enrichment, and References
- New personal narratives/voices from a wider range of members within each cultural group explored in the text
- New diversity education concepts that are highly relevant to educators including: self-fulfilling prophecy, student resistance to diversity education, cultural lenses, Maslow's hierarchy on needs as it relates to school climate, cultural consciousness, pedagogical content knowledge, the digital divide, middle-class myths, effects of the sexual objectification of women and girls, hate language in schools, universal design, ally characteristics, and deculturalization

## Major Changes to Each Chapter:

### Chapter 1:
- New diversity terminology exercise and rationale for emphasizing the understanding of diversity terms at the beginning of the diversity education process
- Expanded information on oppression (birdcage metaphor—Frye), privilege (Sullivan), male student disadvantage, and student resistance to diversity education including the need for courageous conversations (Singleton)
- Introduction of the following new concepts: cultural lens, aversive racism, assimilation
- Exploration of affirmative action including different types and definitions
- New stereotype exercise
- New web links

### Chapter 2:
- New personal narratives
- New/revised exercises
- New web links

### Chapter 3:
- New personal narratives
- Introduction of Maslow's hierarchy of needs to expand the understanding of school climate effects on student development and achievement
- New exploration of the following concepts: incivility, bullying, and mobbing (Ferriss)
- New school climate dimensions (Center for Social and Emotional Education)
- New methods for assessing school climate

- New school climate assessment that explores student experiences
- New web links

**Chapter 4:**
- Introduction of the following new concepts: social influence, cultural consciousness, and pedagogical content knowledge
- Exploration of teacher expectation effects on achievement and student self-fulfilling prophecy
- New "my best teacher" personal narratives
- New web links

**Chapter 5:**
- New personal narratives including narratives from Chief Seattle and Chief Luther Bear
- Updated population statistics
- New web links

**Chapter 6:**
- New personal narratives including individuals from Hmong and Vietnamese cultural group members
- Updated population statistics
- New web links

**Chapter 7:**
- New personal narratives
- Updated population statistics
- Exploration of the history of the term *Hispanic*
- Added new web links

**Chapter 8:**
- Exploration of hip hop cultural influences (Dyson, Ludacris, JayZ)
- New personal narratives including hip hop lyrics and poetry (Langston Hughes)
- Updated population statistics
- Discussion of 2000 and 2008 presidential election
- Introduction of the following new concepts: Juneteenth, NAACP, HBCU, Jim Crow laws, school segregation
- New pop culture and Sojourner Truth content
- New exercise with a video link to *A Class Divided* (Jane Elliott)
- New web links

**Chapter 9:**
- New personal narratives
- Expanded exploration of the rural experience
- Introduction of the following new concept: the digital divide

- Definition of the middle class and exploration of associated middle class myths
- Updated population statistics
- New pop culture references
- New SES exercises
- New web links

### Chapter 10:
- New personal narratives including adolescent female voices
- New exploration of the following concepts: sexual objectification, women's pay disparities, and effects on family income and poverty rates
- Updated population statistics
- Exploration of media influences and added pop culture references
- New web links

### Chapter 11:
- New personal narratives including a fraternity member narrative
- Updated population statistics
- New Exploration of the following terms: *closeted, coming out, marriage inequality,* and *hate language in schools*
- Definition of the following terms: *bisexual, transgendered, transsexual,* and *intersexual individuals*
- Discussion of seminal and contemporary Homosexual Identity Development models
- New web links

### Chapter 12:
- New personal narratives
- New Exploration of the following concept: universal design
- New web links

### Chapter 13:
- Introduction of the following new concept: deculturalizaton (Spring)
- New web links

### Chapter 14:
- Revised exercises
- New web links

### Chapter 15:
- New exploration of the following concepts: pluralism, homeostasis as it relates to resistance to change.
- Inclusion of an ally development model; defined allies and identified ally characteristics
- New web links

## Ancillaries

### For Instructors

*Electronic Instructor's Manual and Test Bank.* The Instructor's Manual contains resources designed to streamline and maximize the effectiveness of your course preparation, including a section on establishing a facilitative environment for teaching and learning diversity, focus questions, discussion points, and supplemental resources for each chapter. The test bank contains multiple choice and short-answer questions.

### For Students and Instructors

*Companion Website*  The book-specific website at www.cengage.com/education/spradlin offers students a variety of study tools and useful resources such as related links for each chapter, critical-thinking questions, glossaries, flashcards, and more.

Protected materials such as an electronic version of the instructor's manual and presentation slides are available for download by instructors.

## ACKNOWLEDGMENTS

Throughout the text, numerous researchers and theorists are given credit for their contributions to this book. Others, cited within the text, have generously shared their stories and in so doing, have turned theory and research into personal, lived experience.

In addition to those cited, so many others have contributed to this text. I thank reviewers of the first edition and the following reviewers of the second edition for their insightful comments: Dennis N. Banks, SUNY Oneonta; Alina McLennan Davis, Valencia Community College; Dr. Debra Hopgood, Eastern Illinois University; Christine Olson, Central Florida Community College; William M. Reynolds, Georgia Southern University; and Isis Silva, Broward College.

Finally, I'd like to acknowledge the support and recommendations of my editor, Rebecca Dashiell, and the superb work performed by Dewanshu Ranjan and his production team at PreMediaGlobal.

# About the Author

Dylan A. Spradlin

**Lynn Kell Spradlin, Ed.D.** Dr. Spradlin serves as the Adron Doran Distinguished Professor for Educational Leadership in the College of Education at Morehead State University. She teaches counselor and teacher education courses in the Foundational and Graduate Studies in Education Department and coordinates a partnership with the Fayette Co. Public Schools. In this position she also works with the College of Education Leadership Team to advance the unit's diversity education goals in addressing national accreditation standards. She is a certified high school English, theatre, and speech teacher, a certified school counselor, and a licensed professional counselor. In addition, Dr. Spradlin has published extensively in the field of diversity education. Her many national and regional diversity presentations, school consultations, and collaborations with school districts and universities across the country widen her perspective and bring relevance and practicality to her work.

## Author's Message

Over the past 15 years, I have come to understand effective strategies that engage students while integrating diversity in curriculum. A common need expressed in educational institutions is the recruitment and retention of diverse faculty members and students. Educators' missions almost always include the following goal: *To provide the best educational opportunities possible to enable students to successfully address the concerns of a diverse society. To meet these objectives, we emphasize a deep knowledge of and respect for diversity and effective intercultural communication.*

However, as an African American female educator, I do not at first experience the warm and welcoming reception one might expect from colleagues and students who have worked with diversity concepts in the past but not explored oppression theory effects on student adjustment and achievement. Even though most schools espouse the wish to recruit and retain diverse educators and students, that does not mean they are willing to do anything differently in effort to accomplish said goals. In fact, in many cases, academic institutions are entrenched in the performance of their practices and have come to accept them as the only way of conducting business that they either consciously or not resist all efforts to change them. In so doing, they reject and exclude those they have said they seek to recruit and retain because those who are recruited are by definition different—having different views, different perspectives, different experiences in the world and different ways of working and accomplishing goals.

Griffin (1997) identified "common student reactions to social justice education." Griffin's work is useful for understanding both student and collegial resistance to diversity and social justice education. She notes, "when we raise social justice issues, we unsettle both unconscious and deeply held beliefs about society, self, and social relations. This disequilibrium can create resistance, as familiar ground shifts and students encounter uncertainty, doubt, and self-questioning as they attempt to regain their balance" (p. 292). She pointed out several different forms of student resistance that I have encountered often over the year in working with students and colleagues in pursuit of social justice outcomes including individuals' tendency to believe that the status quo is the natural order, to invalidate minorities' experiences with oppression, to assert the need to have their own pain and hurt recognized, to invalidate the course, and even to invalidate the instructor. "Sometimes students will claim that the teacher is biased, especially if she is a member of a target (minority) group ... for being too personally involved to be objective. On the other hand, facilitators who are members of the agent (dominant-culture) group are sometimes invalidated by both agent and target group participants because students do not understand how an agent can understand oppression without personal experience" (p. 293). Colleagues, as well, may accuse diverse faculty members of caring too much about diversity and always using diversity as a filter in the lenses through which we view work and relationships.

While dominant-culture individuals may choose to share their feelings experienced as they navigate processes involved in learning about oppression and accompanying white privilege, minority individuals do not have those options for joining with dominant-culture students and colleagues as they explore threatening facets of oppression theory. Dominant-culture individuals are able to model their employment of coping mechanisms that facilitated their acceptance and integration of the emotionally challenging subject matter, all the while aligning with other dominant-culture individuals in citing the difficulty of the journey throughout the process—not only reminding those to whom they present diversity education that the journey of social justice education works to create opportunities for minorities but also explaining how they as members of dominant culture have also benefited from social justice education. On the other hand, minority educators must find alternate ways to create comfortable learning and working environments for dominant-culture colleagues and students and minority students and colleagues—finding novel ways to join with predominantly white, middle-class, nondisabled, heterosexual individuals and minority students and colleagues around an issue that can be divisive. I continue to use this insight and information to challenge me to design diversity curricula that is inviting and yet historically accurate, comprehensive, relevant, inclusive, progressive, and significant in its ability to affect positive change for diverse groups of educators and students. This challenge led to the approach presented in this text.

I employ experiential, student-centered strategies that are mostly constructivist in nature. I provide my students (and colleagues in professional development work) with abundant opportunities to learn firsthand (if possible) or from reading the experiences (stories) of diverse peoples as they are told by the diverse peoples themselves through personal narratives; involve them in critical analysis of information and information sources, including theories, practices, and historical accounts; and then ask them to question previously assimilated concepts (their knowledge) and utilize self-reflection and communication skills to take actions that help them further understand and apply what they have encountered. I have found that when people hear minority voices and perspectives; critically analyze diversity content and constructs; share their feelings, thoughts, and perspectives with others; and then create products that apply and extend their knowledge of oppression theory, they become advocates who want to share what they have learned about minority group members and their treatment in society. Along with the understandings they integrate, they often express outrage they feel toward institutional discrimination—a learning outcome that prepares them to maintain their resolve to act on the knowledge they have acquired as teachers, counselors, administrators, family members, and citizens. I have found that it is vital to provide students with opportunities to reflect on and express their feelings and beliefs that are triggered as they integrate information that is often different from their previous understandings about relations, power, society, schools, family, and self.

In addition to supporting learners and providing outlets to allow them to reflect on their reactions to their encounters with new diversity constructs, it's important to help students take stock of what they know and think they know about diversity over the course of study. The instructor's manual for this text provided multiple-choice and short-answer questions for each chapter to allow for effective assessment of students' knowledge of diversity. Also, I have modified existing educator diversity competencies and a diversity knowledge survey to measure students' pre- and post-perceived knowledge of diversity and performance of diversity competencies required for educators (see Table 1 and 2).

As an educator of color, I realize the many assets I bring to this endeavor as well as maintain an awareness of individuals' potential reactions to me and

**Table 1** Educator Diversity Competencies

**Educator Diversity Competencies**

1. Recognizes and articulates oppression and diversity theories, issues, and variables in instruction.
2. Makes learning relevant for diverse learners' through the incorporation of diverse cultural content in curricula.
3. Demonstrates the belief that all students can learn by differentiating instruction to meet the needs of all learners.
4. Demonstrates collaboration and cooperation with resource personnel to increase the learning for all students.
5. Respects diverse families' cultures and languages and uses knowledge of these factors to facilitate students' achievement.
6. Identifies students' learning styles and uses this information to differentiate instruction.
7. Values all students' contributions and efforts and provides appropriate constructive feedback.
8. Utilizes recognized methods for facilitating the learning of ELL students.
9. Displays a knowledge of stratification effects on achievement and adjustment of historically marginalized groups based on gender, race, class, ethnicity, religion, disability, and sexual orientation in schools and society.
10. Displays a knowledge of and ability to analyze structural inequities in society and schools.
11. Displays an informed and reasoned openness to and understanding of human differences in perspective and behavior.
12. Displays a commitment to creating a just and equitable society.
13. Submits a facilitative bibliography that evidences the preparation to effectively teach social justice curricula.

**Table 2** Diversity Knowledge Survey

**INSTRUCTIONS:** Circle the number which best assesses the extent of your knowledge of each topic:
None = complete unfamiliarity
Minimal = some familiarity
Average = ability to discuss the topic
Extensive = ability to debate/explain/lead a discussion on the topic

| MY KNOWLEDGE ABOUT ... IS | None | Minimal | Average | Extensive |
|---|---|---|---|---|
| 1. Multicultural teaching philosophy and practices | 1.  1 | 2  3 | 4  5 | 6  7 |
| 2. African American culture, history, and text in the United States | 2.  1 | 2  3 | 4  5 | 6  7 |
| 3. Special education issues and services | 3.  1 | 2  3 | 4  5 | 6  7 |
| 4. Latino culture, history, and text in the United States | 4.  1 | 2  3 | 4  5 | 6  7 |
| 5. Civil rights legislation | 5.  1 | 2  3 | 4  5 | 6  7 |

(continued)

**Table 2** Continued

| MY KNOWLEDGE ABOUT ... IS | None | Minimal | Average | Extensive |
|---|---|---|---|---|
| 6. Standardized test bias | 6. 1 | 2 3 | 4 5 | 6 7 |
| 7. Systemic racism in public schools | 7. 1 | 2 3 | 4 5 | 6 7 |
| 8. Asian American culture, history, and text in the United States | 8. 1 | 2 3 | 4 5 | 6 7 |
| 9. Native American culture, history, and text in the United States | 9. 1 | 2 3 | 4 5 | 6 7 |
| 10. Educational tracking policy and practice | 10. 1 | 2 3 | 4 5 | 6 7 |
| 11. History of multicultural education reform in the United States | 11. 1 | 2 3 | 4 5 | 6 7 |
| 12. PL 94-142 | 12. 1 | 2 3 | 4 5 | 6 7 |
| 13. ESL programs and ELL | 13. 1 | 2 3 | 4 5 | 6 7 |
| 14. Religious histories, doctrines, and practices other than your own | 14. 1 | 2 3 | 4 5 | 6 7 |
| 15. Prominent people of color | 15. 1 | 2 3 | 4 5 | 6 7 |
| 16. Bilingual education | 16. 1 | 2 3 | 4 5 | 6 7 |
| 17. Low-income life circumstances | 17. 1 | 2 3 | 4 5 | 6 7 |
| 18. Social-class educational barriers | 18. 1 | 2 3 | 4 5 | 6 7 |
| 19. Racial identity development | 19. 1 | 2 3 | 4 5 | 6 7 |
| 20. Multicultural education resources in your community | 20. 1 | 2 3 | 4 5 | 6 7 |
| 21. LGBTQ culture, history, and text in the United States | 21. 1 | 2 3 | 4 5 | 6 7 |
| 22. Intercultural communication | 22. 1 | 2 3 | 4 5 | 6 7 |
| 23. Oppression theory | 23. 1 | 2 3 | 4 5 | 6 7 |
| 24. School funding practices related to SES | 24. 1 | 2 3 | 4 5 | 6 7 |
| 25. Multicultural curricula and curriculum transformation | 25. 1 | 2 3 | 4 5 | 6 7 |
| 26. Women's history, culture, and text in the United States | 26. 1 | 2 3 | 4 5 | 6 7 |
| 27. IDEA and ADA | 27. 1 | 2 3 | 4 5 | 6 7 |
| 28. Affirmative action purpose and implementation | 28. 1 | 2 3 | 4 5 | 6 7 |
| 29. Gender bias in education | 29. 1 | 2 3 | 4 5 | 6 7 |
| 30. Title IX education guidelines | 30. 1 | 2 3 | 4 5 | 6 7 |
| 31. Second language acquisition | 31. 1 | 2 3 | 4 5 | 6 7 |
| 32. Effects of oppression on achievement and career | 32. 1 | 2 3 | 4 5 | 6 7 |
| 33. Heterosexism | 33. 1 | 2 3 | 4 5 | 6 7 |
| 34. Effects of privilege on equity | 34. 1 | 2 3 | 4 5 | 6 7 |
| 35. Disability culture | 35. 1 | 2 3 | 4 5 | 6 7 |
| 36. Teaching diverse student populations | 36. 1 | 2 3 | 4 5 | 6 7 |
| 37. Conducting effective advocacy for educational equity | 37. 1 | 2 3 | 4 5 | 6 7 |

my course content, and I know that my support, enthusiasm, knowledge, and skills are all significant. This text supplies ingredients that have been successful and enriching for me. I am excited to share them with you and to hear how you experience this approach. Please email me to share your views at LKSpradlin@ insightbb.com.

Lynn Kell Spradlin
2010

PART 1

# Social Context of U.S. Schooling

Minority Experience

*We all carry worlds in our heads, and those worlds are decidedly different. Educators set out to teach, but how can we reach the worlds of others when we don't even know they exist? Indeed, many of us don't even realize that our own worlds exist only in our heads and in the cultural institutions we have built to support them. It is as if we are in the middle of a great computer-generated virtual reality game, but the "realities" displayed in various participants' minds are entirely different terrains. When one player moves right and up a hill, the other player perceives him as moving left and into a river ... What should we be doing? The answers lie not in a proliferation of new (education) reform programs but in some basic understandings of who we are and how we are connected to and disconnected from one another.*

**Delphit, 1995, pp. xiv–xv.**

CHAPTER

# Minority Status and Marginalization

## Defining Terminology

One way to end an argument that stirs up conflict and emotion is to say, "You're just arguing semantics." It is true, especially in terms of diversity, that there are many concepts (like race, racism, equality, equity, culture, and so on) whose definitions are not fully understood or commonly shared among individuals. And while you may effectively end an argument by identifying that there is a lack of common understanding of terms discussed, you may also effectively end possibilities for significant growth and change that can result from encountering different perspectives and learning from the experiences of others. A better strategy for engaging in discussions on the topic of diversity is to agree, in the beginning, on some clearly defined definitions of terms under discussion so that participants can be clear about what they are communicating as they work to build understandings and connections. "By engaging in this type of dialogue, those who possess the knowledge get the opportunity to share it, and those who do not have the knowledge yet learn and grow from the experience. In building mutual understanding, educators discover what they need to collectively foster equity..." (Singleton & Linton, 2006, p. 53).

Diversity discussions (or *courageous conversations*—as Singleton and Linton [2006] call them) are highly challenging because they require participants to risk speaking their truths while being open to experience the truths of others. Such discussions must go beyond merely presenting different views; they must, more significantly, deal directly with issues of differential power, disparity, privilege, and marginalization. Because marginalization functions not only through overt conscious prejudice and discrimination but also through unconscious attitudes and behaviors, effective diversity discussions must help participants to explore their strongly held beliefs in order to unearth underlying assumptions and biases. Most individuals resist confronting unpleasant aspects of their existence. As such, diversity discussions are often avoided or glossed over, creating the illusion that diversity work is either unnecessary or complete, when nothing could be farther from the truth. Some of the most vile and pernicious attacks against minority group members come from well-meaning individuals who consider themselves to be open-minded and fair because the lack of awareness of the ways their practices and perspectives perpetuate injustice is never revealed and examined. In fact, schools, in their long history of existence, have not been able to effectively eliminate achievement gap disparities and have yet to systematically affirm racial, gender, social class, ability status, and sexual orientation diversity. These disparities are built on age-old inequities that continue to discriminate against and restrict the opportunities of marginalized students at every point in their education. Resistance to discussing the taboo subjects of racism, classism, sexism, ableism, and heterosexism exists and serves, whether consciously or not, to protect individuals who have benefitted from these societal ills from acknowledging privilege and gains that have resulted. Privilege that is gained from the lack of opportunity available to others is often difficult for dominant-culture individuals to see and believe and therefore discuss. It is essential, however, that diversity discussions include a shared understanding of these fundamental aspects of diversity in order to address the continuing problems of achievement gap disparity and inequity in schooling.

All students have the right to experience fair and empowering conditions in schools and to be taught by effective and quality educators. Anyone who has a child engaged in schooling knows that one of the main fears one experiences as a parent is how one's child will be treated in schools. The concern any parent has about the treatment of her or his children in U.S. schools is magnified for members of minority communities who have experienced a history of diminished status and opportunity, denied access and cultural affirmation, and widespread overt and unacknowledged discrimination in schools. To produce the fair and just schooling conditions that the United States is expected to provide given its democratic ideals will require widespread implementation, keen examination, and effective monitoring of systematic diversity education practices enacted on a daily basis by educators in schools.

The United States is and will continue to become an increasingly diverse nation. According to census projections, the number of Latinos in the United States will grow to 98 million in the year 2050, African Americans will number 59 million, and the number of Asians and Pacific Islanders will increase to approximately 38 million (Henderson, 2000; U.S. Department of Education, 2004). Given these projections, we can expect that teachers will undoubtedly teach students from a wide range of language, social class, gender, ethnic, ability status, sexual orientation, and cultural backgrounds. A culturally diverse classroom is the rule, not the exception, and such diversity has important implications for educators (Alba, Rumbaut, & Marotz, 2005; Alba, 2000).

## EXERCISE 1-1

Let's begin by seeing what concepts you already know. Use the following word bank to select the correct concept for each of the six definitions that appear after the word bank provided here:

Privilege                           Prejudice                           Racism

Stereotype                          Discrimination                      Oppression

1. _____ The placement of all members of a group into a category that may only reflect a selected few.
2. _____ Judgments about an individual(s) that are based on information obtained prior to interacting with the individual(s).
3. _____ A right that only some individuals have access to because of their social group membership.
4. _____ Treatment or distinction in favor of or against a person or thing based on the group, class, or category to which that person or thing belongs rather than on individual merit.
5. _____ The systematic subjugation of one relatively less powerful social group by another relatively more powerful group which is sanctioned by cultural beliefs and institutional practices, the results of which benefit one group at the expense of the other.
6. _____ A system of advantage based on race based on the belief that members of the dominant racial group are inherently superior to members of a subordinate racial group(s).

Answers: 1. Stereotype, 2. Prejudice, 3. Privilege, 4. Discrimination, 5. Oppression, 6. Racism

Consider the differences between these terms. After reading this chapter, review these definitions and think about why understanding each is important for identifying the ways marginalization in society operates and affects all aspects of individuals' lives.

Teachers will need to acquire new knowledge and keen awareness in order to meet the needs of diverse classrooms. They will need to increase their knowledge of diversity, their cultural sensitivity, and their intercultural communication skills and competence in order to meet the needs of a culturally diverse student population. In addition, teachers, as professional educators and advocates for all children, will need to develop the skills necessary to become allies and to work for changes in institutional policies, practices, and legislation in order to address discrimination that targets marginalized groups.

This book is intended to facilitate the professional development of educators who meet these standards. As the first step, this chapter will introduce you to the fundamental concepts of culture, race, ethnicity, social class, gender, sexual orientation, ability status, oppression, discrimination, inequity, privilege, and marginalization (see Exercise 1-1).

## CHAPTER OBJECTIVES

1. Define culture, cultural lens, race, ethnicity, social class, gender, sexual orientation, and disability.
2. Define *privilege, inequity, oppression,* and *discrimination* and how individuals may experience privilege in one aspect of their life and marginalization in another.

3. Describe different stages of minority and White *racial identity development*.
4. Describe different types and effects of racism.
5. Explain the terms dominant culture, minority, assimilation, and acculturation.
6. Define racism, sexism, classism, heterosexism, and ableism.
7. Describe different approaches to *affirmative action*.

## CULTURE

The cumulative effect of our life experiences creates in each of us a lens through which we observe our environment. This cultural lens focuses our attention on particular aspects of what we see. Society defines principles and values for present and future generations through customs, traditions, and rituals that focus the lens through which we view our lives and form our opinions. Throughout history, cultures have passed their family values to future generations by these means. Think about an important family value, custom, tradition, or ritual that you have experienced. Discover how you came to learn the value, custom, tradition, or ritual and how it relates to the identity of your family. Consider what would happen if the value, custom, tradition, or ritual was not upheld by you. What does all this information tell you about the ways your culture influences your perspectives and actions?

Cultural heritage and background influence our lives in many ways. In fact, all aspects of human life are touched and altered by culture. Our personalities, the way we think, and the ways we solve problems, as well as methods we use to organize ourselves, are all given shape, in large part, by cultural experiences. However, we frequently take the great influence of culture on our lives for granted and fail to identify the significant and sometimes subtle ways culture affects our behavior and thinking.

If teachers are to be effective, they must understand cultural diversity and its many elements and be skilled intercultural communicators. They will need to understand and appreciate the power of cultural values reflected in their students' behavior (Sleeter & Grant, 2002). Because "students who feel their culture is valued and understood by the school and the larger community tend to perform better in school than those who feel it is rejected," it is important that educators understand and respect diverse cultural perspectives and ways of being in the world (Ashworth, 1992, p. 14).

## Defining Culture

Culture is defined in various ways. This concept may be broadly described as encompassing a group's common beliefs, including shared traditions, language, styles, values, and agreement about norms for living. Culture, however, always intersects individuals' race, social class, gender, age, ability status, sexual orientation, and family traditions (Laird, 2000). In this text, the definition of *culture* includes values, beliefs, notions about acceptable and unacceptable behavior, and other socially constructed ideas that members of the culture are taught (Garcia, 1994, p. 51). As such, culture, in effect, defines and actively guides one's thinking and behavior. If, for you, proper student behavior includes not only making decisions independent of others, speaking up about them, and feeling proud about such an accomplishment, you are not alone among your colleagues in the United States. However, there are many cultural groups, whose values are explored in this text, that embrace

## EXERCISE 1-2    Point of Reflection: Stereotypes Restrict Knowledge

As noted earlier in the chapter, it is important to add human experience to the sometimes sterile world of theory and research. Therefore, a number of exercises and opportunities for reflection and observation are included within each chapter of the text. To think about the ways *stereotypes* restrict useful knowledge, do the following activity in small groups.

1. Each member of the small group should have a red apple that she or he brings to class.
2. Place all of the apples on a table in front of the group and ask if they all look pretty much the same to everyone.
3. Discuss the ways the apples look similar. Then ask each person to take a careful look at his or her own apple by spending a few minutes examining it carefully.
4. Then put all the apples on the table in front of the class again.
5. Ask each person to come and retrieve his or her own apple from the table.
6. Take turns letting each person tell how she or he found her or his own apple describing what is unique about it.
7. Finally, each student should write a **reflection** that uses what each learned about stereotyping apples that can be used to better understand the way stereotyping people or groups of people have reduce one's knowledge. Adapted from *Rainbow Activities*. (1977). Creative Teaching Press, Inc. South El Monte, CA.

interdependence as opposed to independent decision-making, that restrict communication and expression of feelings, and that take pride in group rather than individual accomplishments. Consider how cultural stereotypes limit and restrict the ability to truly know. Exercise 1-2 will help you explore the effects of stereotyping.

## Variation within Culture

It is not uncommon to find references to "the" African American experience or Latino culture or to "the" culture of the Europeans. While those within a culture by definition share much in terms of commonly shared values and behavior, such broad categorization fails to do justice to the wide variation within each cultural group. Thus, a more functional approach for defining culture is one that recognizes intergroup differences in culture as well as the plethora of subcultures that exist.

It is extremely important to note that not all people from one cultural group can be grouped together and assumed to be alike. You can assume that members of a group may share certain cultural characteristics, but you must also recognize subcultural, intracultural, and individual differences. Within a culture, subgroupings around a more specific shared history of experience, social values, and role expectations exist. These subcultures can be formed along racial, ethnic, regional, economic, or social community lines. A subculture provides its members with values and expectations that may not be demonstrated by the larger cultural group or found elsewhere. In addition, these subcultural differences found between groups within a culture may result in the development of communication patterns and barriers, both for members within the same culture and for individuals across many different cultures.

To further complicate matters and to more accurately explain this idea, we must also remember that within a culture or subculture, a person can be different from others of the same reference grouping as a function of her or his specific educational background, socioeconomic status, and regional particulars. These intracultural differences clearly depict the reality that, while we are all *a part* of a culture, our individual, regional, educational, socioeconomic, and other contextual identities will always keep us somewhat *apart* from any one culture.

## RACE

Probably no one term elicits more visceral, emotive reactions than the term **race**. For many, the mere mention of this term results in huge discomfort. Because the issue of race has sociopolitical and even moral ramifications, it is an important element of diversity that needs to be thoroughly understood and addressed by classroom teachers. Race is, in actuality, an anthropological concept used to classify people according to physical characteristics, such as skin and eye pigmentation, facial features, shape of head, and texture of body hair (Hernandez, 1989). However, because there is no pure set of physical characteristics that exist among any group of people, race is more significantly a socially constructed concept that is given power by the way it is used to differentiate and assign privilege within society.

## Race: Not a Physically but a Socially Defined Construct

While the definition of race was historically founded on unique physical characteristics of a group of people, the ever-increasing mobility and migration of people from one geographic region to another, and the resulting interracial pairings, make valid and reliable identification of individuals along racial lines impossible. Yet even with this reality, the concept of race continues to play a role in distinguishing people. This is, in large part, because race has become a social rather than a physical construct. As a social construct, race is often used as an unjust, invalid standard upon which to generalize and draw conclusions about any one person or group of people. Because such racial bias has been identified and recognized as a damaging process, many educators ignore racial differences for fear of being perceived as racist.

Teachers are, frankly, pretty unsure about how to approach the issue of racial differences within their classrooms. Valli (1995), for example, noted that educators vacillate from believing that "teachers should be colorblind" to being color sensitive, from saying "I treat all students the same and pay no attention to the color of their skin" to claiming "If you don't see the color, you don't see the whole child—and her/his unique contributions" (p. 121). "The 'good' (= nonracist) White person was supposed to treat everyone equally, which was taken to mean not noticing a person's race at all … This perspective denies the possible existence of formidable obstacles and strong resistance to the conscious recognition of racism" (Sullivan, 2006, p. 5). Understandably, many teachers wish to treat all students equally. But equitable treatment does not mean approaching and working with all students in the same way. Equitable treatment of students does not require homogenization and a flattening of all individual differences, including racial differences, even though, based on teachers' actions, many educators still believe this is the case. In fact, Ladson-Billings (2004) noted, "the notion of equity as sameness only makes sense when all students *are* exactly the same" (p. 33). Failing to recognize and adequately address real differences may be one way to ensure *inequity*. Differences in achievement between racial groups, and potential reasons for such differences, need to be understood if they are to be corrected. And this will not and cannot happen as long as teachers attempt to wear "color-blinders."

Even with the limitations of classification by race, it is important not to dismiss the concept of race when recognizing and describing human differences in perspective. Considered as a single identity, racial identification does not provide much information about a person. However, race as a construct is highly significant when used to identify cultural characteristics that subordinate and elevate groups based on societal laws, policies, and practices. In this sense, racial classifications can provide great insight into subordinated individuals' worldviews, dispositions, and behaviors. To put it simply, *racism* is first and foremost a system of advantage for dominant culture based on race (Tatum, 1992). It is important to note that despite the fact that most people can identify individuals who are disadvantaged in U.S. society (based on gender, sexual orientation, ability status, social class, or other group membership), they may yet have trouble acknowledging that other (dominant-culture) individuals are advantaged by the same system that systematically disadvantages minority group members. The net effect of prejudice (experienced by oppressed groups) places the object of prejudice at some disadvantage not merited by her or his misconduct (Allport, 1954). As such, discontinuing the use of the concept of race to describe differences in group perspective may sufficiently ignore the treatment differences that various groups receive in society (Johnson, 1990). Such ignorance would also deny any exposure of racism, a process essential to affecting societal change and social justice for all minority groups.

## Race Is Not Ethnicity

Because **ethnicity**, when used in the broadest sense, includes references to physical characteristics of a group of people, it is sometimes equated with and used interchangeably with *race* (Glazer, 1971). However, a more narrow and fruitful definition of *ethnicity* is taken from the Greek root word *ethos*, meaning nation (Feagin, 1989). Using this ideology, ethnicity distinguishes groups based on nationality and cultural, rather than physical, characteristics. As such, an *ethnic group* is defined as a group in which the members share a unique social, cultural, and sometimes geographic and language heritage that is passed down from one generation to the next (Schaefer, 1988).

## Racial Identity Development of Dominant Culture and Minority Group Members

Helms (1990) defined **racial identity development** as "a sense of group or collective identity based on one's perception that she or he shares a common racial heritage with a particular racial group" (p. 3) (see Table 1-1). Cross (1971) identified five stages in African American racial identity development that were later used to describe the racial identity development of minority group members in general (see Table 1-2).

Although the stages of racial identity development do not necessarily occur chronologically in a linear process, they are believed to include most racial

**Table 1-1** Helms' (1990) White Racial Identity Development Model

1. **Contact Stage:** In this stage, a person lacks an awareness of racism and her or his own White privilege. The person internalizes negative stereotypes about persons of color.
2. **Disintegration Stage:** During this stage, a person's lack of awareness of racism is replaced by discomfort, shame, and/or guilt. The person may at first deny that racism exists and near the end of this stage try to help other Whites see that racism does exist.
3. **Reintegration Stage:** In this stage, a person's desire to be accepted by her or his own group leads to a reshaping of her or his belief system that has become more accepting of racism. A person may become stuck at this stage if she or he can avoid direct contact with people of color.
4. **Pseudo-Independent Stage:** In this stage, a person abandons beliefs of White superiority but may unintentionally perpetuate the status quo. The person may feel alienated from Whites (as a group) and rejected by people of color (as a group). During this stage, a person begins to seek out White antiracist allies and models and may attempt to disavow her or his own Whiteness through active affiliation with persons of color.
5. **Immersion/Emersion Stage:** During this stage, a person searches for a new, more comfortable way to be White. The person seeks to replace racially related myths and stereotypes with accurate information about what it means and has meant to be White in the United States. An important part of racial identity development at this point is learning about Whites who have been antiracist allies to people of color.
6. **Autonomy Stage:** In this stage, a newly defined sense of oneself as White energizes one's efforts to confront racism in one's daily life. A person in this stage is continually open to new information and ways of thinking about race. Alliances with people of color are more easily forged because antiracist attitudes and behaviors are more consistently expressed.

*Source:* Helms, J. E. (1990). *Black and white racial identity: Theory, research and practice.* Westport, CT: Greenwood.

**Table 1-2** Cross's (1971) Minority Group Member Racial Identity Development Model

1. **Pre-Encounter Stage:** At this stage, a person internalizes negative racial stereotypes. A person in this stage may not be aware of racism.
2. **Encounter Stage:** This stage of racial identity development is typically precipitated by an event. A person in this stage is forced to acknowledge racism. At this point, the person begins to identify with her or his own race.
3. **Immersion/Emersion Stage:** During this stage, a person may avoid symbols of Whiteness. A person in this stage tends to surround herself or himself with visible symbols of her or his own race.
4. **Internalization Stage:** During this stage, a person is secure with her or his own sense of self as a racial being. There is less need during this stage to assert extreme pro–same-race attitudes and actions. A person in this stage is more open to joining with other racial groups.
5. **Internalization/Commitment Stage:** A person in this stage has found ways to translate her or his personal sense of self as a racial being into a plan of action or general sense of commitment to the concerns of people of color and to the concerns of social justice in general.

*Source:* Cross, W. E. (1971). The Negro to black conversion experience: Toward a psychology of black liberation. *Black World,* 20, 13–27.

interaction patterns involving minority group members and dominant culture in the United States (Cross, 1991). Racial identity development is, therefore, another factor that affects differences in students' choices to cross racial boundaries in schools, that identifies social dynamics within minority community social structures, and that understandably influences the sometimes oppositional nature of individual minority students toward dominant-culture institutions and their teachers.

## SOCIAL CLASS

A number of successful television shows take viewers behind the scenes and into the lived experiences of the rich in the United States—people who have money, power, and social status. MTV and other pop culture forums show viewers the lifestyles (reality shows), homes (cribs), parties (Sweet 16), and cars (rides) of the wealthy. It seems that to some degree many people in the United States dream of living lifestyles of the rich and famous depicted in TV shows in hopes of someday becoming members of the upper social class.

Social class or *socioeconomic status* (SES) is the term used to distinguish a person's position in society relative to others within that society. Parental occupation, education level, political power, and income serve as the bases for a student's social class or socioeconomic status. For educators, several questions arise: Other than perhaps the obvious material benefits, are there any important benefits or effects of SES? Is student SES associated with academic achievement? Is a student's social class something a teacher should be sensitive to and address somehow in teaching? The answer to all of these questions, as you will discover, is "yes!"

Social class differences do exist in the United States, and social class affects the lives of individuals in many significant ways. As with other ways of categorizing individuals, it is a serious mistake to stereotype people based solely on their SES because intragroup social class differences in attitudes, values, and beliefs may be sharply pronounced. But given this caveat, it is still vital for educators to be aware of the impact of SES on students and the effects of social class on schooling and society.

Class distinctions determine the quality of the schooling we receive; the location, safety, comfort, and convenience of homes and neighborhoods in which we live; the health and development of our loved ones; the worldviews we hold; and how we relate to others in society. In identifying the significant influence of social class on every aspect of life, it is important to note that social class status may be difficult to recognize and identify on a day-to-day basis.

In the United States, a great deal of effort is put into to mystifying and hiding social class differences. Students and adults alike routinely wear clothes and buy cars, homes, and other material possessions that are more expensive than they can afford in order to be perceived as being wealthier than they are. The media takes part in these deceptions by presenting the illusion that the United States is an egalitarian society in which everyone has an equal chance to succeed and attempts to either downplay the existence of the poor by failing to feature images and perspectives that present the needs and issues of the poor (Manstios, 1995b) or by portraying the poor as undeserving and as having only themselves to blame for their position in life. When it comes to SES, myths abound. For example, many believe that the United States is mostly a middle-class country, with the wealth distributed mainly within the middle class. Contrary to this belief, U.S. Census Bureau reports reveal that less than 20 percent of the population in the United States own more than 80 percent of the wealth. That means 80 percent of the wealth may never change hands; leaving only 20 percent of the total wealth in the United States for all other individuals to work to attain. It is true that myths about SES abound. However, there are certain social class "truths" that are crucial for teachers to understand.

The lack or reduction of opportunities for working class and poor students can be one of the most oppressive forces encountered. People do not choose to be working class or poor. Instead, they are confined by opportunities afforded or denied them by society based on their birth into a particular social class family. The lower one's class standing, the more difficult it is to secure safe housing, the more time is spent on everyday routine tasks in life, the greater the percentage of income that goes to pay for basic necessities, and the less likelihood one has to participate in enrichment and growth-related activities (Manstios, 1995a). Class standing, therefore, has a significant impact on educational attainment and economic opportunity.

It is clear that the lack of power and privilege associated with poverty negatively affects students' achievement in school. *Classism,* the institutionalized system in society that operates to disadvantage working-class and poor people, greatly influences students' motivation to achieve, opportunities afforded, as well as their levels of career ambition (Dodge, Pettit, & Bates, 1994). SES affects students' performance in school (Reed & Sautter, 1990), discipline problems (Dodge et al., 1994), feelings of low self-esteem and learned helplessness (Rice, 1993).

Schools are part of the societal social-class stratification system because they operate as social microcosms that embody and implement prejudice, oppression, and discrimination evident in larger society. Specifically, according to Greer (1972), schools do the job today that they have always done. Schools select individuals for opportunities according to a hierarchical schema that runs closely parallel to existing social-class patterns. The resultant social structure disadvantages working-class students, weakening their academic achievement levels (Gans, 1995; Sennett & Cobb, 1972). Educational researchers have documented a statistically significant relationship between working-class student status and academic achievement. According to Wolf (1977), a poor child is roughly twice as likely to be a low academic achiever as a child who is not poor.

While teachers cannot remedy all social inequities and problems of the world, they can take steps to ensure that they do not negatively affect the achievement of working-class and poor students within their classrooms. It is important that teachers examine their beliefs about social class and identify the subtle, yet profound, effects these beliefs may have on their curriculum choices and classroom interactions. Exercise 1-3 provides a structure for investigating your beliefs about SES and considering the potential impact these beliefs may have on your teaching and your students.

## EXERCISE 1-3    Classroom Applications: True or False SES Myths

**Part I**

**Directions:** Identify which of the following statements are true and which are false.

| Statement | True | False |
| --- | --- | --- |
| 1. The largest number of poor people live in urban settings. | | |
| 2. The majority of poor children in the United States are African American. | | |
| 3. Families are impoverished because the household heads are unemployed. | | |
| 4. Almost 80 percent of all poor children who attend school live in single-parent households. | | |
| 5. There is little real difference in self-esteem levels and achievement-test scores across SES. | | |

**Part II**

**Directions:** Each of the previous statements is false. With a classmate or your instructor, discuss the potential impact that belief in these statements may have on a teacher's interactions with students in her or his classroom.

## SEX AND GENDER DISTINCTIONS

When it comes to gender expectations, what teacher behaviors communicate patterns of gender socialization present in society? For example, if a sixth grade boy expresses vulnerability when confronted with a feared environment in the same way that a sixth grade girl might express the same feeling of vulnerability, will his teacher respond to his behavior in the same way that she or he responds to vulnerability expressed by the sixth grade girl? We now understand that girls lose their voices as they enter adolescence—becoming lost to themselves and society, mostly as a result of gender socialization and the effects of sexism which render them less likely to choose and excel in math and science curriculum (Gilligan, 1982). And we are starting to understand that:

> … by contrast, boys may exhibit bravado and braggadocio even as they find it more difficult to express their genuine selves even in private with friends and family … and while significant gaps in girls' science and math achievement are improving, boys' scores in reading are lagging behind significantly and continue to show little improvement. Recent studies also show that not only is boys' self-esteem more fragile than that of girls and that boys' confidence as learners at a young age is impaired but also that boys are substantially more likely to endure disciplinary problems, be suspended from classes, or actually drop out from school entirely. (Pollack, 1998, p. xxi–xxiv)

Schools have worked to disadvantage boys in the early grades and girls in middle and high school leaving both groups worse off than they were before they entered schools.

Classrooms, curricula, and teachers' behaviors and comments within the classroom can teach much more than is identified in course objectives. Phrases such as "Okay, guys, settle down," "I need a strong boy to come up here and help me move this table," and "Would one of the girls mind straightening up these art materials?" can be heard in almost any classroom on any given day. Each of these phrases appears innocuous enough. However, when the phrases reflect an oversimplification of gender-based characteristics and expectations, there is a problem. Gender typing and bias can and have pigeonholed students into curriculum paths and career options (for example, entry into science and math careers for boys and into the helping professions and language and arts careers for girls), restricted social and recreational choices (for example, boys on the debate team, girls in sewing classes), and even affected the quality and quantity of teacher–student interactions experienced within classrooms (Merret & Wheldall, 1992). Such conditions prohibit free expression and individual growth of both male and female students in various areas of their development. Gender socialization and sexism are constructs that teachers must recognize and understand so as to avoid the subtle and sometimes not-so-subtle biasing effects that all too often occur.

## Are There Differences between Boys and Girls?

Boys and girls are different. This we know to be true. The question is not whether boys and girls are different, but rather: In what ways are boys and girls different? Why do these differences occur? How do these differences affect learning in the classroom?

*Gender schema theory* suggests that genetic predispositions may account for some behaviors, personality traits, and interests. This same theory, however, notes that differential treatment remains the major source of differences in attitude, behavior, and achievement found between males and females (Bern, 1981). Differential treatment is pervasive in our society and clearly evident within our schools. Society's gender-based norms and expectations create role definitions for boys and girls and later for men and women that ultimately lead to the systematic marginalization of women as a group (Gilbert, 1992). This condition, which disadvantages women while advantaging men, is referred to as *sexism*. Sexism acts to deprive women of equal access to opportunities, equal pay for equal work, and allows for discrimination in school admission and hiring. Such conditions not only restrict development but also weaken their access to economic success.

## Sex versus Gender

*Sex* refers to biological conditions of maleness or femaleness: the possession of the XY chromosomal configuration for males and the possession of the XX pattern for females, along with corresponding anatomical, hormonal, and physiological structures. As such, sex is assigned at birth (Richardson, 1981). **Gender** is a learned psychological, social, and cultural aspect of a person that describes expected and sanctioned male and female behavior that results from socialization in the United States.

Recent attempts to describe brain-based differences in types of intelligence, psychological disorders, classroom behavior, and academic performance identify ways male and female students are disadvantaged in U.S. schools. Gurian and Henley (2001) described ways in which brain structures, hormonal differences, and functional and processing differences influence male and female student behavior. Nonetheless, most differences assumed to exist between the sexes are gender-related rather than sex-related—that is, learned rather than innate. Men are typically seen as masculine and are rewarded when they act in culturally approved, "gender-appropriate" ways, and likewise, women are applauded for acting in ways that are labeled feminine and that are considered appropriate for women in this culture. Because many of the so-called gender-appropriate feminine characteristics and behaviors are devalued in the United States, women *and* men who adhere to them (exhibiting emotionality, nurturance, and delicacy) are devalued and systematically disadvantaged in society (Schaffer, 1981).

The American Association of University Women (1992) conducted a comprehensive examination of gender studies in education and found that U.S. schools shortchange girls. According to this report, "Girls and boys enter school roughly equal in mental ability. Twelve years later, girls have fallen behind their male classmates in key areas such as higher-level mathematics and measures of self-esteem" (p. 1). Sadker, Sadker, and Long (1993) also found that male students in elementary and middle school called out answers eight times more often than female students did and that when males called out, teachers listened. But when females called out, they were told to raise their hands if they wanted to speak. In addition, the researchers concluded that school authorities choose classroom activities that appeal to male students' interests and in formats in which males generally excel. Moreover, teaching methods that foster competition are standard, even though a preponderance of research has demonstrated that female students learn better when they undertake projects and activities cooperatively rather than competitively (Belenky, Clinchy, Goldberger, & Tarule, 1986; Brown, 1991; Gilligan, 1982; Radil, 1992).

According to Ostling and Urquhart (1992), girls face pervasive barriers to academic achievement and are systematically discouraged from pursuing studies that would enhance their prospects for well-paying jobs, even though the U.S. school classroom is in many ways technically a feminine domain. More than three-quarters of teachers are women. However, these mostly female teachers routinely hold male students in higher esteem, believing they are intellectually superior to female students, and implement curricula and instructional strategies that advantage boys. Although during childhood both sexes do equally well in math and science, girls outperform boys overall in the early grades. In verbal skills, girls move into the lead around fifth or sixth grade and thereafter do better than boys in writing and, by most measures, reading. Females constitute less than a third of students identified as emotionally disturbed or learning disabled. Despite teen pregnancy, girls are less likely to drop out of high school and are more likely to attend college (Ostling, 1992, p. 62).

However, Sadker et al. (1993) noted that "males outperform females substantially on all subsections of the Scholastic Aptitude Test (SAT) and girls attain only 36 percent of the more than 6,000 National Merit Scholarships awarded each year. These awards are based on the higher Preliminary Scholastic Aptitude Test (PSAT) scores attained by boys" (p. 119). Moreover, while women dominate the teaching profession and young female students generally succeed in the early grades and even outperform male students in some academic areas, the culture of the school is in fact masculine because schools are controlled by a male-dominated society (Noddings, 1992). And even successful female students have less confidence in their abilities, higher expectations of failure, habits of dependency, negative attribution styles, weakened leadership skills, and more modest occupational aspirations than boys do. Girls are less likely, therefore, to reach their potential than boys (Keating, 1990).

It is important to understand the social construction of gender and the often subtle ways in which schools, and specifically teachers, support, maintain, and even encourage differential treatment based on gender and thus disadvantage individual students in their classrooms. Exercise 1-4 will help you begin to identify the ways gender typing and gender bias manifest within the classroom.

## Sexual Identity

Human sexuality is complex. *Sexual identity* is the degree to which we identify with the social and biological aspects of being a man or a woman. Some perceive sexual orientation and sexual identity to be simple, straightforward products of biology. Such a position, often termed "an Essentialist position," argues that sexual orientation is part of an individual's core being. This stance often leads to the conclusion that heterosexuality is the "right and correct" form of sexuality and thus homosexuality is "improper." It is important to note that not all people who exhibit so-called gender nonconformity are gay or lesbian; people, having various sexual identities and orientations, actually engage in a whole range of sexual behaviors. Sexual orientation is an integral part of sexual identity and is defined by who we are emotionally and/or to whom we are physically attracted. One's sexual orientation may be lesbian, gay, bisexual, transgender, or heterosexual.

## Sexual Orientation

An aspect of humanness that serves as another basis for discrimination and various forms of differential treatment within society and within school classrooms is **sexual orientation**. For many, attraction (physical and emotional) to a person of the opposite sex (heterosexual orientation) is assumed to be the norm. Often, heterosexuality is presented as the only acceptable sexual orientation. From this *heterosexist* position, those who partner with members of the same sex (homosexual orientation) are perceived to be sexually deviant and pathologic. While the term *homosexual* is often applied to individuals whose partners are persons of the same sex, the use of term is seen as limiting because it places primary emphasis on an individual's sexual orientation, which is only one aspect of members of this cultural group. As with other marginalized groups, the nomenclature used for referring to gay people reveals evidence of their oppressed status in the United States. Clark (1977) explained that the term *gay* is a preferred label assigned by members of the group "as a way of reminding ourselves and others that awareness of our sexuality facilitates a capacity rather than creating a restriction. It means that we are capable of fully loving a person of the same gender by involving ourselves emotionally, sexually, spiritually, and intellectually" (p. 73). This terminology affirms gay culture (Rofes, 1989). While the terminology is becoming more widely used, members of

# EXERCISE 1-4    Field Experience: Gender Socialization Observation

***Directions:*** The following exercise involves a classroom observation. As you observe the class, look for obvious and subtle forms of gender typing.

1. Seating: Are there discernable seating arrangements for boys and girls? If so, what is one potential impact of this arrangement?
2. Interaction: In a five-minute period, record how many times the teacher calls upon or verbally responds to boys and girls. Place a check mark in the box for each interaction.

| | Boys | Girls |
|---|---|---|
| 1. Calls upon a student who is raising hand. | | |
| 2. Selects a student to perform a task. | | |
| 3. Praises a student. | | |
| 4. Reprimands a student. | | |
| 5. A student volunteers to participate. | | |
| 6. A student is removed from participation. | | |

3. Language and References: Record any use of stereotypical language (for example, "Okay, guys …" or "Ladies!") or gender-based curricula and/or instructional illustrations (for example, "Alice bought three dresses….").
4. Activities: If during the observation the teacher directs students to engage in an activity, list the activity and the gender and age of the student(s) performing it. In addition, identify whether students *actively* participate in the activities assigned.

Examples:

| | | |
|---|---|---|
| Competitive activities | ____ girls | ____ boys |
| Individual tasks | ____ girls | ____ boys |
| Group work | ____ girls | ____ boys |
| Notetaking during group work | ____ girls | ____ boys |
| Leading during group work | ____ girls | ____ boys |
| Speaking for the group when reporting | ____ girls | ____ boys |
| Helping other students understand the assignment | ____ girls | ____ boys |

Remember: Research predicts that you will find that elementary and middle-school girls will reveal characteristics that might be defined as "gender-appropriate" for males. That is to say, they may exhibit the qualities of independence, assertiveness, and outspokenness. However, during high school, female students are said to display more "gender-appropriate" female behaviors.

Share your observations with your classmates, your colleagues, or your instructor, and discuss the implications of your observations.

this cultural group continue to face widespread discrimination in society. Heterosexism is a system of advantage based on sexual orientation in which gay, lesbian, bisexual, and transsexual individuals are denied rights and opportunities enjoyed by those who identify themselves as heterosexual.

Kinsey, Pomeroy, and Martin's (1948) report on sexual behavior in the human male is credited with bringing homosexuality and bisexuality into U.S. consciousness. In it, Kinsey et al. found wide variations in sex concepts and behavior. They explained that the hetero/homo division of sexuality could not be divided neatly into two polar categories explaining, "only the human mind invents categories and tries to force facts into separate pigeonholes. The living world is a continuum" (Kinsey et al., 1948, p. 637). This report raised questions about what is considered "normal" and "abnormal" sexual behavior in males and females (Kinsey, 1941; Kinsey, Pomeroy, & Martin, 1953). However, the medical model that described homosexuality as a sickness prevailed until the late 1960s. It was not until New York City police conducted one of their many raids of the time of gay bars in Greenwich Village touching off three days of rioting, that gay men and lesbian women began to forge a more unified public fight for their rights and survival. This incident, dubbed the Stonewall Riots, marked the birth of the modern gay and lesbian rights movement (Griffin, 1997). Still today, heterosexism is seen as the only "normal" and acceptable sexual orientation by many members of dominant culture, leaving gay and lesbian individuals to face pervasive physical, psychological, legal, political, social, and economic threats, dangers, hardships, and losses. Statistics indicate that lesbian, gay, and bisexual people are among the most frequent targets of hate crimes (Marecek, Finn, & Cardell, 1992). And educators have been overwhelmingly resistant to acknowledging and addressing heterosexism in schools (Sears, 2005).

## DEFINING DISABILITY

Just as institutional discrimination targets lesbian, gay, bisexual, and transgender (LGBT) persons in the process of *questioning* their sexual identities (LGBTQ), students with disabilities also experience pervasive marginalization in schooling and society. *Disability* has been defined as an observable, measurable characteristic of an individual which interferes with the individual's functioning—a functional limitation within the individual caused by physical, mental, or sensory impairment. While defining *disability* continues to be a matter of social debate and construction, recently the term has come to refer to a restriction or lack of ability to perform an activity in the manner or within the range considered "normal" for humans. *Impairment,* on the other hand, is defined as the loss or abnormality of psychological, physiological, or anatomical structure or functioning, and *handicaps* involve the loss or limitation of opportunities to take part in the "normal" life of the community on an equal level with others due to physical or social barriers. As such, handicaps may be considered barriers, demands, and environmental presses placed on persons by various aspects of their environments, including other people.

The medical model of disability focuses on individuals' functional limitations (impairments) and identifies impairments as the cause of disadvantages experienced by persons with disabilities. The social model, in contrast, shifts the focus from impairment to disability. In this case, *disability* refers to the disabling social, environmental, and attitudinal barriers rather than solely to individuals' "lack of ability." Thus, the only way to rectify disabling conditions using the medical model is through treatments and cures of individuals, while social change and the removal of disabling barriers are solutions for those who support the social model.

Even if the definition of *disability* was restricted to those having health problems or disabilities that prevent them from working or that limit the kind or amount of work one can do, in 2004 there would still have been an estimated 7.9 percent (plus or minus 0.2 percentage points) of civilian, noninstitutionalized men and women aged 18 to 64 in the United States categorized as disabled. This would amount to about 1 in 13 U.S. citizens (Houtenville, 2005).

But even with advances in technology, education, and laws attempting to remove barriers that exclude persons with disabilities, individuals with disabilities continue to encounter discrimination ranging from outright intentional exclusion to a lack of access to substandard services, programs, activities, benefits, jobs, or other opportunities.

## MARGINALIZATION: WHAT IT IS AND HOW IT OPERATES

Historically, the United States has prided itself on being a cultural melting pot in which all cultures are blended or melted into one common culture. Immigrant groups, to this day, understand that living in the United States requires them to acculturate—to become "Americanized."

**Acculturation** refers to the acquisition of the cultural patterns of **dominant culture** while simultaneously relinquishing traditions and customs associated with one's own culture of origin. Here and throughout the text, *dominant culture* refers to groups in society that benefit from the power and prestige of their membership in the race, social-class, gender, ability status, and sexual-orientation groups that control society through policies, legislation, and practices that advantage them over marginalized groups. These groups experience **privilege**, or "unearned assets" that create and provide a constant stream of opportunities denied to others in society (Lucal, 1996, p. 247). This system for relegating power to dominant culture is so entrenched that it perpetuates itself, while seeming to be so natural that it goes largely unrecognized by dominant-culture members (Vera, Feagin, & Gordon, 1995). Sullivan (2006) described White privilege as embodying sets of often unconscious habits whereby "human beings enact them without thinking as manners of being and acting that constitute an organism's ongoing character"—explaining that habits are simultaneously limiting and enabling as they provide the means by which one is able to act in the world, and in doing so they exclude other possible styles of acting (at least until a change of habit occurs.) White unconscious resistance to understanding racism as a problem must be tackled if inroads are to be made against specific problems of racism. Not only can White people not help challenge racism if they do not see it, but also non-White people's attempts to combat racism cannot be maximally successful if White people's unconscious commitments thwart such work (p. 22–24). Decades earlier, DuBois (1986) concurred, "I now realize that in the fight against race prejudice, we were not facing simply a rational, conscious determination of white folk to oppress us; we were facing age-long complexes sunk now largely to unconscious habit and irrational urge" (p. 296).

In her seminal work, McIntosh (1988) also described White privilege as "an invisible package of unearned assets" that members of dominant culture can cash in on a daily basis (p. 76). As a White person, she notes:

If she has low credibility as a leader, she can be sure that her race is not the problem; she can choose public service accommodations (like hotel stays, apartment rentals, and so on) without fearing that people of her race cannot get in or will be mistreated in the places she has chosen; she can easily find academic courses and institutions that give extensive attention to people of her race; she can, if she wishes, arrange to be in the company of people of her race most of the time; she can turn on the television or open the front page of the newspaper and see people of her race widely and positively represented; she can arrange to protect her young children in school and society most of the time from those who might not like them based on their race; and she did not have to educate her children to be aware of systemic racism for their own daily physical protection" (pp. 79–81). In addition, many U.S. citizens, like McIntosh, are members of groups that are marginalized (for example, women or persons with disabilities) and are also members of groups who experience privilege (for example, middle-class or White). Privilege confers dominance and permission to control by virtue of one's race, social class, ability, sex, ability status, and/or sexual orientation. The privilege enjoyed by members of dominant culture allows them to decide which groups are accepted and therefore permitted to assimilate in society. Therefore, the opportunity for minority group members to be assimilated and, hence, more able to reap rewards as fully recognized members of society is to a large extent dependent upon the wishes of dominant culture and is within their power to determine. Whereby acculturation is required for all minority groups coming to the United States and involves the relinquishing of cultural traditions while acquiring dominant-culture customs, **assimilation** involves dominant-culture acceptance of a minority group as respected members of society. And while acculturation may be a desired goal for some minority individuals, many find the idea of acculturation objectionable because it calls for relinquishing their traditional cultural values and norms in favor of those of dominant culture. Consider holidays that are set aside so that citizens are able to celebrate without missing work. Consider clothing, foods, and other goods that are readily available in stores so that citizens may conveniently purchase them, and languages that are respected and approved for use in businesses and schools. Do these traditions, characteristics, and cultural artifacts represent dominant or various different minority cultures and values? And, even though some minorities and their descendants may desire to become acculturated and may make every effort to adopt the culture of dominant society, total assimilation into dominant culture may actually be unattainable for most minorities because assimilation requires that they be fully accepted as equals by dominant-culture members of society. Under these conditions, many minority group members often live, in a sense, on the fringe of societal opportunity, contributing to the resources and productivity of dominant culture while not completely assimilated or accepted and suffering the experience of **marginalization** through the processes of ethnocentrism, racism, classism, sexism, heterosexism, and ableism.

Because many teachers in today's classroom enjoy unearned privilege in one form or another (that is by virtue of their race, social class, sexual orientation, gender, and/or ability status), it is extremely important that they become self-reflective in seeking to identify their stereotypes and biases. The development of self-criticism and reflection skills along with a willingness and an openness to hear feedback that may reveal prejudices requires courage and fortitude. In fact, these practices are among the most challenging aspects of social justice education. Having the ability to take in, digest, analyze, and address feedback on one's shortcomings and then monitor one's behavior to ensure that lessons learned are performed in everyday life is the ultimate demonstration of learning (Adams, 1997). Teachers must work to model these qualities to facilitate their own development and encourage their students to learn from their example.

## ETHNOCENTRISM

Listen to the language of those speaking about people who are different from themselves. Phrases such as, "Why can't they be like us?" "They've been in this country long enough—why do they have to dress like that?" "Speak like that?" "Act that way?" reflect ethnocentrism. Individuals or societies who expect different cultural groups to acculturate are in essence saying that the existing dominant culture is superior to any other culture. Such sentiments are ethnocentric.

**Ethnocentrism** is the view that one's own group is the center of everything, and all others are scaled and rated with reference to it (Sumner, 1960). Ethnocentrism results in *prejudice,* which includes all negative attitudes, thoughts, and beliefs toward entire categories of people who are different from the accepted norm (Schaefer, 1988). People, for the most part, prejudge other persons or groups based on whatever information they have encountered about the persons or groups. But, prejudice frequently goes overlooked because it is not always evident in behavior. Instead, it may manifest in any number of subtle and covert teacher attitudes and beliefs and in ways they may unconsciously treat students differently based on their racial, ethnic, gender, SES backgrounds, ability status, and sexual orientation.

## RACISM, CLASSISM, SEXISM, HETEROSEXISM, AND ABLEISM

Jones (1972) identified three types of *racism:* individual, institutional, and cultural. Individual racism involves the personal attitudes, beliefs, and behaviors that assert the superiority of one's own race. Institutional racism is the pervasive social policies and laws that purposefully maintain the economic and social advantage of the dominant racial group in society. Finally, cultural racism involves societal customs and beliefs that promote the assumption that products are designed to address the needs and wishes of members of dominant culture and are superior to those of all other cultures determining which holidays are recognized, the race of dolls manufactured and sold in stores, the racial tone of flesh-colored bandages that line the shelves of pharmacies, and so on. In addition, effects of **aversive racism** in past and current hiring and admissions procedures and decisions continue to exist (Alba & Nee, 2003; Rumbaut & Portes, 2001). *Aversive racism* refers to the adapted attitudes that result when individuals have internalized racist beliefs about minorities and these strongly held beliefs (conscious or not) influence their judgments in decision making in all aspects of human life (Dovidio, Mann, & Gaertner, 1989).

Racism in the United States reflects attitudes and behaviors that denote the superiority of the dominant White racial group. However, racism is not the only institutional norm that involves the assignment of the superiority of one group over another. *Classism,* for example, is the beliefs and actions that decry the superiority of middle and capitalist social-class status; *sexism* involves all attitudes and actions that support the belief that males are superior to females; *heterosexism* denotes the belief system that heterosexuality is superior to homosexuality and other forms of sexuality; and *ableism* refers to the notion that persons with no identified physical or mental disabilities are superior to persons labeled disabled. These institutional "isms" result in a host of discriminatory policies, legislation, and practices that systematically oppress groups whose status is marginalized in the United States.

## OPPRESSION AND MINORITY STATUS

Oppression is the state of being deprived of human rights and dignity while lacking the power to do anything about it (Goldenberg, 1978). Frye (1983) used the metaphor of the birdcage to explain the systematically related barriers that serve to confine groups of people such that their options are reduced to only a very few and all of which expose them to penalty, censure, or deprivation. Frye noted that a myopic scrutiny of one wire of a bird's cage would not explain why the bird does not escape the cage of oppression. Even a careful study of each wire separately would not explain the state of absolute confinement. It is not until one step back and instead of looking at the wires of the cage one by one, looks at the whole cage constructed to securely and permanently confine the bird that one can easily understand why and how the bird is kept—motion and mobility restricted. It becomes obvious at that point that the bird is surrounded by a network of systematically related barriers, no one of which would hinder flight, but which, by their relations to each other, are as confining as the solid walls of a dungeon. This metaphor helps us see why oppression can be hard to recognize. Several terms are used in the fields of diversity and multicultural education to refer to oppressed groups in society. Each has drawbacks: The use of the term *disadvantaged,* for example, calls forth the idea of so-called cultural deficiency that members of minority groups are said to have. The term *minority* is often too narrowly equated with populations whose numbers make up less than 50 percent of the population.

In this text, oppressed groups are identified as "marginalized" or "minority" groups. This means these groups have a marginalized status in society. The groups themselves are not marginal. The use of the term *minority group* may seem misleading because many scholars mean it to refer only to the numerical size and proportion of a group in relation to others in society. Wirth (1945), however, described minority status based on the concept of oppression. It is in this sense of minority as oppressed that is reflected in the term *minority* used in this text. In this case, the term **minority** refers to those who, because of their cultural characteristics, are singled out from others in the society for differential and unequal treatment, and who therefore are objects of systematic collective discrimination.

## AFFIRMATIVE ACTION

Members of minority groups and their allies continue to strive to achieve equity in schooling and access to economic success. The Civil Rights Act, passed over 45 years ago in 1964, declared basic human rights to fair housing, job opportunities, and the like for marginalized groups in society. It was 14 years later still when the Supreme Court ruled that race could be a factor in making college admissions decisions that the start of **affirmative action** policy in the United States began (Orfield & Kurlaender, 2001).

Tatum (1997) outlined the evolution of affirmative action in the United States noting that the term *affirmative action* was introduced in an Executive Order signed by President Lyndon Johnson in 1965. The order required federal contractors to take affirmative action to ensure that all applicants, without regard to their race, color, religion, sex, or national origin, were hired and treated fairly in their employment. Employers were required to use every effort necessary to implement strategies that would result in equal employment opportunities for historically disadvantaged groups. The order did not, however, specify *how* affirmative action programs would be designed. To this day, there is great debate and variety in the ways these programs have been developed and implemented throughout the United States. Nevertheless, affirmative action policies that outline institutions' attempts to make progress toward equality of opportunity for groups, currently underrepresented in significant positions in society, typically take either a process-oriented or a goal-oriented approach.

**Process-oriented affirmative action** programs seek to create a fair application process in hopes that such a process will result in fair outcomes. These types of programs are often preferred by dominant culture because this approach supports the ideology of the United States as a meritocracy in which anyone can succeed if his or her work merits it. Unfortunately, the process-oriented approach, along with the meritocracy myth, does not account for the aversive racism and discrimination that are sure to interfere with decisions made during application processes.

**Goal-oriented affirmative action** programs, on the other hand, attempt to employ open and fair processes as well, but they go a step further. With this approach, once a pool of qualified applicants has been identified, those among the pool of equally qualified applicants who move the organization closer to its diversity goals are then favored for hiring or admittance over other equally qualified applicants. So when all candidates are equally qualified, if a certain candidate provides the organization with something extra that is valued by the organization (in this case, diversity), that candidate is favored for acceptance. Acting in this manner is not dissimilar to the way decisions are made when diversity is not the consideration. In other words, if an organization were attempting to hire an employee, and two White males applied for the same position, both applicants equally qualified, the organization would attempt to identify other qualities and characteristics of each candidate that would make one more desirable for employment. They would consider what each would bring to the position and what the organization most valued among employment criteria. Goal-oriented affirmative action seeks to place diversity high on the list of employers' and organizations' lists of values. Even with the continued assaults on affirmative action policies and practices, affirmative action is a necessary step in the journey toward equality for minority groups who continue to be systematically disadvantaged in the United States by racism, sexism, heterosexism, and ableism (Beauchamp, 1998; Orfield & Kurlaender, 2001; Leach, 2004).

# FROM CONCEPTS TO LIVED EXPERIENCE

Too often texts on diversity get lost in abstract definitions, research, theories, and statistics, at the expense of lived experiences behind those definitions, theories, and statistics. Throughout this text, you will find theory and research, but also lived experiences encountered by members of minority groups.

Students in classrooms care little if the discrimination they encounter is a form of racism, sexism, or any other "ism" or whether they are considered members of minority or marginalized groups; what they know is what they have experienced. They know the constraints, the harm, the humiliation, and other elements of their oppression that impair their ability to thrive and grow in the directions they desire. It matters little to them what these ideas are called, and it matters greatly to all members of a society that these ills cease to continue.

So while it is important that we as educators understand the concepts presented within this chapter so that we may talk effectively with each other and think critically about these issues as a path to work toward the creation of equity, remember that facts, findings, and definitions do not tell the whole story. We must not diffuse our awareness and valuing of the human condition reflected in that information. Knowing of oppression and seeing that oppression can result in very different attitudes about and actions to eliminate oppression. As such, this chapter ends with a student's reflection on a school experience shaped by "isms," and an exercise designed to provoke thought about the injustices of a racist classroom (see Exercise 1-5).

## ANNIE'S STORY

When I walked into the school in first grade holding my mother's hand, I knew I was going to have to prove something. They looked at us like we were so inadequate and foreign to them. I assume that because I'm black, they promptly placed me in the lowest (remedial) reading group. Never mind that my mother told them I had been reading since I was 4 years old. She was a single parent who cleaned houses, so what did she know? I was eventually moved to the highest reading group by the end of the school year. But I boiled and churned through the whole process of proving to them that I was somebody, that I knew something, that I was even a better student than most of the white students in the school. I still remember feeling so embarrassed by the hostility and resentment that was heaped on me throughout the process. I didn't want the other kids see them treat me that way. I would ask my mom what I had done to deserve this treatment. It was as though they actually worked to refute the fact that I was an excellent student to prove to themselves something about them. I was only a scrawny little six year old black girl and they resented me for being well-educated and poised. This reality was so far from what they imagined could possibly be true that I guess they could never see it or admit it—even with all the evidence I provided. When I graduated from that school with high honors, they were sure that they had "made me who I am." I knew who really made me: my mom who taught me to bear up in the face of veiled hatred and to endure the constant taunts and slaps at my ability. "Be strong," she'd say when I came home from school crying. It was my mom who kept me going through it all—in every way, my mom.

## EXERCISE 1-5    Point of Reflection: Designing a Racist Classroom

*Directions:* After reading Annie's story, think about the injustices she endured. So that you can get a good sense of what it takes to maintain such an oppressive school environment, this exercise asks you to work with a small group of your classmates to design a racist school.

1. Think about a group of students that will be oppressed in the make-believe school you will construct with your group members, then design specific policies, rules, attitudes, beliefs, strategies, and structures that oppress the group you have chosen and will keep them oppressed for generations to come. For example, you may want to create school rules and practices that let that group of students and all others in the school know that the group is inferior. Find specific ways to curtail their opportunities and squelch their hopes and beliefs in their abilities.

Imagine all that you can add to the environment to ensure that the group is and stays oppressed.

PLEASE DO *NOT* READ BENEATH THE LINE UNTIL YOU HAVE CREATED (IN WRITING) YOUR RACIST SCHOOL WITH YOUR CLASSMATES. IT IS VERY IMPORTANT THAT YOU STOP READING BEFORE THE LINE UNTIL AFTER YOU HAVE FINISHED THIS PART OF THE ASSIGNMENT.

---

2. After you and your group members create your racist school, share your design with other groups of students in your class and discuss ways your newly created school is like schools that actually exist today. Explain what this means in terms of the experience of minority students in U.S. schools today.

Modified from an activity by Katz, J. H. (1989). *White awareness: Handbook for antiracism training.* Norman: University of Oklahoma Press.

## SUMMARY

**Culture**    *Culture* includes values, beliefs, notions about acceptable and unacceptable behavior, and other socially constructed ideas that members of the culture are taught are "true." It is important to remember that even within the same culture, intergroup and intragroup differences exist.

**Race**    *Race* is most importantly a socially constructed construct with social relevance that is used to elevate a dominant group while oppressing others.

**Ethnicity**    *Ethnicity* is defined as one's membership in a group in which the members share a unique social, cultural, and sometimes geographic and language heritage that is passed down from one generation to the next.

**Social Class**    *Social class* or *socioeconomic status* (SES) is a term used to distinguish people's relative

position to others in society. Research has shown a relationship between SES and achievement.

**Sexual Orientation**    *Sexual orientation* determines the sex of the person to whom persons are attracted. LGBTQ individuals are lesbian, gay, bisexual, transgender and individuals who are in the process of questioning their sexual orientation. Statistics indicate that LGBT individuals are among the most frequent targets of hate crimes and educators have been overwhelmingly resistant to acknowledging and addressing heterosexism in schools.

**Disability**    A *disability* is an observable, measurable characteristic of an individual that interferes with the individual's functioning—a functional limitation within the individual caused by physical, mental, or sensory impairment. The medical model of disability focuses on individuals' functional limitations (impairments) and identifies impairments as the cause of disadvantages experienced by persons with disabilities. The social model, in contrast, shifts the focus from impairment to disability. In this case, *disability* refers to the disabling social, environmental, and attitudinal barriers rather than solely to individuals' "lack of ability."

**Privilege**   *Privilege* involves the receipt unearned assets" that create and provide a constant stream of opportunities denied others in society. It embodies sets of often unconscious habits whereby "human beings enact them without thinking as manners of being and acting and acts as an invisible package of unearned assets that members of dominant culture can cash in on a daily basis.

**Inequity**   *Inequity* involves unfairness and injustice in treatment, status, and opportunity.

**Ethnocentrism**   *Ethnocentrism* is the view that one's own group is the center of everything, and all others are scaled and rated with reference to it.

**Oppression**   *Oppression* is the state of being deprived of human rights and dignity while lacking the power to do anything about it. Oppression acts through a network of systematically related barriers like the wires that construct a birdcage, no one of which would hinder flight, but which, by their relations to each other, are as confining as the solid walls of a dungeon.

**Discrimination**   *Discrimination* is treatment or distinction in favor of or against, a person or thing based on the group, class, or category to which that person or thing belongs rather than on individual merit.

**Dominant culture**   *Dominant culture* refers to groups in society that benefit from the power and prestige of their membership in the race, social-class, gender, ability status, and sexual-orientation groups that control society through policies, legislation, and practices that advantage them over marginalized groups.

**Acculturation**   *Acculturation* refers to the acquisition of the cultural patterns of dominant culture while simultaneously relinquishing traditions and customs associated with one's own culture of origin. And while acculturation may be a desired goal for some minority individuals, many find the idea of acculturation objectionable because it calls for relinquishing their traditional cultural values and norms in favor of those of dominant culture.

**Assimilation**   *Assimilation* involves dominant-culture acceptance of a minority group as fully respected members of society.

**Racial Identity Development**   *Racial identity development* is a sense of group or collective identity based on one's perception that she or he shares a common racial heritage with a particular racial group and is factor that affects differences in students' choices to cross racial boundaries in schools and that identifies social dynamics within minority community social structures, and which also understandably influence the sometimes oppositional nature of individual minority students toward dominant-culture institutions and their teachers.

**Marginalization**   *Marginalization* results when groups in society are oppressed often living, in a sense, on the fringe of societal opportunity, contributing to the resources and productivity of dominant culture while not completely assimilated or accepted and suffering the experience of marginalization through the processes of ethnocentrism, racism, classism, sexism, heterosexism, and ableism. Marginalization functions not only through overt conscious prejudice and discrimination but also through unconscious attitudes and behaviors. Marginalized groups have a marginalized status in society. The groups themselves are not marginal.

**Racism, Classism, Sexism, Heterosexism, and Ableism**   *Racism* is a system of advantage based on race that denotes the superiority of the White racial group in the United States; *classism* is beliefs and actions that provide privileges for and decry the superiority of middle and capitalist social-class status; *sexism* involves all attitudes and actions that support the belief that males are superior to females; and *sexual orientation bias* denotes the belief system that heterosexuality is superior to homosexuality and other forms of sexuality. *Ableism* refers to the notion that persons with no identified physical or mental disabilities are superior to persons labeled disabled. Each "ism" works to advantage the dominant group while disadvantaging minority group members.

**Minority**   *Minority* refers to those who, because of their cultural characteristics, are singled out from others in the society for differential and unequal treatment, and who therefore are objects of systematic collective discrimination. The term *minority group* may seem misleading because

many mean it to refer only to the numerical size and proportion of a group in relation to others in society. However, minority status when defined based on the concept of oppression results as the net effect of prejudice (experienced by oppressed groups) that places the object of prejudice at disadvantage not merited by her or his misconduct.

**Affirmative Action**   *Affirmative action* was introduced in an Executive Order signed by President Lyndon Johnson in 1965. The order required federal contractors to take affirmative action to ensure that all applicants, without regard to their race, color, religion, sex, or national origin, were hired and treated fairly in their employment. Employers were required to use every effort necessary to implement strategies that would result in equal employment opportunities for historically disadvantaged groups.

## Questions for Review

1. How does culture operate to shape individuals' views, attitudes, choices, and actions?

2. It has been said that terms like *oppression* have been used loosely to describe all injuries

individuals confront. What makes oppression different from discrimination and prejudice?

3. How does power affect the "isms"? What role does it play?

## Important Terms

| | | | |
|---|---|---|---|
| acculturation | culture | marginalization | racial identity |
| affirmative action | dominant culture | minority | sexual orientation |
| assimilation | ethnicity | oppression | social class |
| aversive racism | ethnocentrism | privilege | |
| cultural lens | gender | race | |

## Enrichment

Adams, M. (1997). Pedagogical frameworks for social justice education. In M. Adams, L. A. Bell, & P. Griffin (Eds.), *Teaching for diversity and social justice: A sourcebook*. New York: Routledge.

Apple, M. W. (2004). *Ideology and curriculum* (3rd ed.). New York: Routledge Falmer.

Davis, B. M. (2007). *How to teach students who don't look like you: Culturally relevant teaching strategies*. Thousand Oaks, CA: Corwin Press.

Dyson, M. E. (1997). *Race rules: Navigating the color line*. NY: Vintage Books, a division of Random House.

Goodlad, J. I., & Keating, P. (Eds.). (1990). *Access to knowledge: An agenda for our nation's schools.* New York: College Entrance Examination Board.

Helms, J. E. (1995). An update of Helms' white and people of color racial identity development. In J. G. Ponterotto, J. M. Casas, L. A. Suzuki, & C. M. Alexander (Eds.), *Handbook of multicultural counseling* (pp. 181–198). Thousand Oaks, CA: Sage.

Johnson, R. S. (2002). *Using data to close the achievement gap: How to measure equity in our schools.* Thousand Oaks, CA: Corwin Press.

Ladson-Billings, G. (1995). Multicultural teacher education: Research, practice, and policy. In J. Banks, & C. A. McGee Banks (Eds.), *Handbook of research on multicultural education* (pp. 747–759). New York: Macmillan.

Ladson-Billings, G. (2004). New directions in multicultural education: Complexities, boundaries, and critical race theory. In J. A. Banks, & C. A. M. Banks (Eds.), *Handbook of research on multicultural education* (2nd ed., pp. 50–65). San Francisco: Jossey Bass.

Lewis, D. L. (1993). *W. E. B. Du Bois: Biography of a race 1868–1919.* NY: Henry Holt and Company, Inc.

Patton, J. M. (1991). The Black male's struggle for education. In L. E. Gary (Ed.), *Black men* (pp. 199–214).

Sears, J. T. (1992). *Sexuality and the curriculum. The policies and practices of secondary education: Critical crisis in the curriculum.* New York: Teachers College.

Singleton, G. E., & Linton, C. (2006). *Courageous conversations about race: A field guide for achieving equity in schools.* Thousand Oaks, CA: Corwin Press.

Rothenberg, P. S. (Ed.). (1997). *Race, class, and gender in the United States: An integrated study* (4th ed.). New York: St. Martin's Press.

Rumbaut, R. G., & Portes, A. (2001). *Ethnicities: Children of immigrants in America.* Berkeley: University of California Press.

Sullivan, S. (2006). *Revealing whiteness: The unconscious habits of racial privilege.* Bloomington, IN: Indiana University Press.

West, C. (1999). *The Cornel West reader.* NY: Civitas Books.

## Connections on the Web

https://implicit.harvard.edu/implicit/demo/

Project Implicit features demonstrations that involve bias to help the view identify whether she or he is truly in touch with the way she or he feels about diversity. This website presents a method that demonstrates the conscious–unconscious divergences. This new method is called the Implicit Association Test, or IAT for short.

http://www.crashfilm.com/

Lions Gate 2005 film, *Crash* takes a provocative unflinching look at the complexities of racial tolerance in post 911 LA. This site features an emotional experience that allows to view three video clips and document emotional responses geared to heighten viewers' awareness of their own racial attitudes.

The following three links feature clips from the 1993 film *The Color of Fear* by Lee Mun Wah. The film explores different issues of race in the United States through a dialogue between eight men of different ethnic backgrounds. You may use the film clips to prompt a discussion of issues of racism and White privilege in U.S. society.

http://www.youtube.com/watch?v=0Rbfh5oM3EQ
http://www.youtube.com/watch?v=-vAbpJW_xEc
http://www.youtube.com/watch?v=eOzO340IJYw

Lee Mun Wah's production company, Stirfry Seminar.com provides an excellent selection of materials on consulting and diversity training.

http://www.diversityweb.org/

Diversity Web is an interactive resource hub for higher education. At this site you will find information about conferences, diversity research, and publications.

# References

Adams, M. (1997). Pedagogical frameworks for social justice education. In M. Adams, L. A. Bell, & P. Griffin (Eds.), Teaching for diversity and social justice: A sourcebook. New York: Routledge.

Alba, R. (2000). Beyond the melting pot: 35 years later. *International Migration Review*, 34(1), 123.

Alba, R., & Nee, V. (2003). Remaking the American mainstream: Assimilation and contemporary immigration. Cambridge, MA: Harvard University Press.

Alba, R., Rumbaut, R. G., & Marotz, K. (2005). A distorted nation: Perceptions of racial/ethnic group sizes and attitudes towards immigrants and other minorities. *Social Forces*, 84 (2), 901–909.

Allport, G. W. (1954). *The nature of prejudice*. Cambridge, MA: Addison Wesley.

American Association of University Women. (1992). *Shortchanging girls: Shortchanging America*. Washington, DC: Author.

Ashworth, M. (1992). *The first step on the longer path: Becoming an ESL teacher*. Markham, ON: Pippin Publishing Limited.

Beauchamp, T. L. (1998). In defense of affirmative action. *Journal of Ethics*, 2(2), 143–158.

Belenky, M. F., Clinchy, B. M., Goldberger, N. R., & Tarule, J. M. (1986). *Women's ways of knowing*. New York: Basic Books.

Bern, S. (1981). Gender schematic theory: A cognitive account of sex typing. *Psychological Review*, 88, 354–364.

Brown, L. M. (1991). Telling a girl's life. Self-authorization as a form of resistance. In C. Gilligan, A. G. Rogers, & D. C. Tolman (Eds.), *Women, girls, and psychotherapy:*

*Reframing resistance* (pp. 71–86). New York: Harrington Park.

Clark, D. (1977). *Loving someone gay*. Millbrae, CA: Celestial Arts.

Cross, W. E. (1971). The Negro to black conversion experience: Toward a psychology of black liberation. *Black World*, 20, 13–27.

Cross, W. E. (1991). *Shades of black: Diversity in African American identity*. Philadelphia: Temple University.

Delphit, L. (1995). *Other people's children: Cultural conflict in the classroom*. NY: The New Press.

Dodge, K. A., Pettit, G. S., & Bates, J. E. (1994). Socialization mediators of the relation between socio-economic status and child conduct problems. *Child Development*, 65, 649–665.

Dovidio, J. F., Mann, J., & Gaertner, S. L. (1989). Resistance to affirmative action: The implication of aversive racism. In F. A. Blanchard & F. J. Crosby (Eds.), *Affirmative action in perspective*. New York: Springer-Verlog.

Du Bois, W. E. B. (1986). Writings. New York: Viking.

Feagin, J. R. (1989). *Racial & ethnic relations*. Englewood Cliffs, NJ: Prentice Hall.

Frye, M. (1983). *The politics of reality*. Trumansburg, NY: The Crossing Press.

Gans, H. (1995). Deconstructing the underclass. In P. S. Rothenberg (Ed.), *Race, class, and gender in the United States: An integrated study* (pp. 51–56). New York: St. Martin's.

Garcia, E. (1994). *Understanding and meeting the challenge of student cultural diversity*. Boston: Houghton Mifflin.

Gilbert, L. A. (1992). Gender and counseling psychology: Current knowledge and directions for research and social action. In S. D. Brown, & R. W. Lent (Eds.), *Handbook of counseling psychology* (2nd ed., pp. 383–416). New York: Wiley.

Gilligan, C. (1982). *In a different voice: Psychological theory and women's development.* Cambridge, MA: Harvard University.

Glazer, N. (1971). Blacks and ethnic groups: The difference, and the political difference it makes. *Social Problems*, 18, 447.

Goldenberg, I. I. (1978). *Oppression and social intervention.* Chicago: Nelson Hall.

Greer, C. (1972). *The great school legend: A revisionist interpretation of American public education.* New York: Basic Books.

Griffin, P. (1997). Facilitating social justice education courses. In M. Adams, L. A. Bell, & P. Griffin (Eds.), *Teaching for diversity: A sourcebook* (pp. 279–298). New York: Routledge.

Gurian, M., & Henley, P. (2001). Boys and girls learn differently: A guide for teachers and parents. San Francisco: Jossey Bass.

Helms, J. E. (1990). Black and white racial identity: Theory, research and practice. Westport, CT: Greenwood.

Henderson, G. (2000). Race in America. *National Forum*, 80(2), 12–15.

Hernandez, H. (1989). *Multicultural education: A teacher's guide to content and practice.* Upper Saddle River, NJ: Merrill/Prentice Hall.

Houtenville, A. J. (2005). *Disability statistics in the United States.* Ithaca, NY: Cornell University Rehabilitation Research and Training Center on Disability.

Johnson, S. D., Jr. (1990). Toward clarifying culture, race, and ethnicity in the context of multicultural counseling. *Journal of Multicultural Counseling and Development*, 18, 41–50.

Jones, J. M. (1972). *Prejudice and racism.* Reading, MA: Addison Wesley.

Keating, P. (1990). Striving for sex equity in schools. In J. I. Goodlad & P. Keating (Eds.), *Access to knowledge* (pp. 91–106). New York: College Board Publications.

Kinsey, A. C. (1941). Homosexuality: Criteria for a hormonal explanation of the homosexual. *Journal of Clinical Endocrinology*, 1, 424–428.

Kinsey, A. C., Pomeroy, W. B., & Martin, C. E. (1948). *Sexual behavior in the human male.* Oxford, UK: Saunders.

Kinsey, A. C., Pomeroy, W. B., & Martin, C. E. (1953). *Sexual behavior in the human female.* Oxford, UK: Saunders.

Ladson-Billings, G. (1994). The dreamkeepers: Successful teachers of African American children. San Francisco: Jossey Bass.

Laird, J. (2000). Gender in lesbian relationships: Cultural, feminist, and constructionist reflections. *Journal of Marital and Family Therapy*, 26(4), 455–467.

Leach, B. W. (2004). Race as mission critical: The occupational need rationale in military affirmative action and beyond. *Yale Law Review*, 113(3), 1093–1143.

Lucal, B. (1996). Oppression and privilege: Toward a relational conceptualization of race. *Teaching Sociology*, 24, 245–255.

Manstios, G. (1995a). Class in America: Myths and realities. In P. Rothenberg (Ed.), *Race, class, and gender in the United States: An integrated study* (3rd ed., pp. 131–143). New York: St. Martin's Press.

Manstios, G. (1995b). Media magic: Making class invisible. In P. Rothenberg (Ed.), *Race, class, and gender in the United States: An integrated study* (3rd ed., pp. 409–417). New York: St. Martin's Press.

McIntosh, P. (1988). White privilege and male privilege: A personal account of coming to see correspondences through work in women's studies.

Merrett, F., & Wheldall, K. (1992). Teachers' use of praise and reprimands to boys and girls. *Educational Review*, 44(1), 73–79.

Marecek, J., Finn, S., & Cardell, M. (1982). *Gender roles in the relationships of lesbians and gay men*, 8(2), 45–49. (AN 11783047).

Noddings, N. (1992). The gender issue. *Education Leadership*, 65–70.

Orfield, G., & Kurlaender, M. (Eds.). (2001). *Diversity challenged: Evidence on the impact of affirmative action*. Cambridge, MA: Harvard Education.

Ostling, R. N., & Urquhart, S. (1992). Is school unfair to girls? *Time*, 139(8), 62.

Pollack, W. (1998). Real boys: Rescuing our sons from the myths of boyhood. NY: Random House, Inc.

Radil, A. (1992). Can single-sex schools make a difference for girls? *Kids, Kids, Kids*, 4, 9–10.

Rumbaut, R. G., & Portes, A. (2001). *Ethnicities: Children of immigrants in America*. Berkeley: University of California.

Reed, S., & Sautter, C. S. (1990). Children of poverty: The status of 12 million young Americans. *Phi Delta Kappan*, 71(10), K1–K12.

Rice, P. F. (1993). *The adolescent: Development, relationships, and culture*. Boston: Allyn & Bacon.

Richardson, L. W. (1981). *The dynamics of sex and gender: A sociological perspective* (2nd ed.). Boston: Houghton Mifflin.

Rofes, E. (1989). Opening up the classroom closet: Responding to the educational needs of gay and lesbian youth. *Harvard Educational Review*, 59(4), 444–453.

Sadker, M., Sadker, D., & Long, L. (1993). Gender and educational equality. In J. A. Banks, & C. A. Banks (Eds.), *Multicultural education* (pp. 111–126). Needham Heights, MA: Allyn & Bacon.

Schaefer, R. T. (1988). *Racial and ethnic groups* (3rd ed.). Glenview, IL: Scott, Foresman.

Schaffer, K. F. (1981). *Sex roles and human behavior*. Cambridge, MA: Winthrop.

Sears, J. T. (2005). Sexual minorities: Discrimination, challenges, and development in America, *journal of Gay and Lesbian Issues in education*, 3(1), 107. (AN 19565589).

Sennett, R., & Cobb, J. (1972). *The hidden injuries of class*. New York: Vintage.

Singleton, G. E., & Linton, C. (2006). *Courageous conversations about race: A field guide for achieving equity in schools*. Thousand Oaks, CA: Corwin Press.

Sleeter, C. E., & Grant, C. A. (2002). *Making choices in multicultural education: Five approaches to race, class, and gender* (4th ed.). New York: John Wiley & Sons.

Sullivan, S. (2006). *Revealing whiteness: The unconscious habits of racial privilege*. Bloomington, IN: Indiana University Press.

Sumner, W. G. (1960). *Folkways*. New York: Mentor.

Tatum, B. D. (1997). *"Why are all the black kids sitting together in the cafeteria?" and other conversations about race. A psychologist explains the development of racial identity*. New York: Basic Books.

Tatum, B. D. (1992). Talking about race, learning about racism: The application of racial identity development theory in the classroom. *Harvard Educational Review*, 62, 1–24.

U.S. Department of Education, National Center for Education Statistics. (2004). *The condition of education 2004*. Washington, DC: U.S. Government Printing Office.

Valli, L. (1995). The dilemma of race: Learning to be colorblind and color conscious. *Journal of Teacher Education*, 46(2), 120–129.

Vera, H., Feagin, J. R., & Gordon, A. (1995). Superior intellect? Sincere fictions of the White self. *Journal of Negro Education*, 64 (3), 295–306.

Wirth, L. (1945). The problem of minority groups. In R. Linton (Ed.), *The science of man in the world crisis*. New York: Columbia University.

Wolf, A. (1977). *Poverty and achievement* (1991, No. 3). Washington, DC: National Institute of Education.

*I came to the meeting worried ... but also hopeful. Maybe this time we could figure out what we can do to help Raul. I love him ... he does so struggle in school ... always has. But like other times ... I've tried to work with the teachers ... this time was just the same. I feel worse now than before I went to the meeting. They say they want to meet with me to come up with strategies to help Raul, but when I try to say something, the principal and the teachers just keep talking over me. They don't respect me. They don't understand Raul. When I bring up something that I think might work or try to tell them how I feel about their suggestions, they say we can think about that and talk about it at the next meeting ... but they never do. They are putting me off and don't think I know it. It's the same old thing ... I'm his mom ... but I have no say. We only meet or talk when they feel it is important ... not when I ask for a meeting or for information about his grades. They are all too busy when the problems are building. Then when he's failed, they want to meet and talk to me. If you ask me, you can't teach a child you don't respect. You can't teach a child you don't understand. Raul and I ... we're left out—It's like we're nothing.*

**Ms. Esposito, Raul's mother**

CHAPTER

2

# Power, Disparity, and Expectations Collide

## Minority Family Attitudes, Academic Expectations, and Treatment in Schools

Much of the research on minority family interaction with schools focuses on parent involvement. Many school officials hold the view that minority parents with low educational attainment attach little value to or interest in their children's schooling often citing this as the reason for low levels of minority parent involvement. School administrators and teachers may suggest that minority parents are irresponsible and disinterested. Some even believe that parents of minority students are too lazy to come to the school to participate. However, upon closer inspection, we find that many parents of minority students, like Raul's mother, are not lazy, irresponsible, or disinterested. They are more likely beaten down and out by years (perhaps even generations) of frustrations and experiences of being devalued in their interactions in schools.

Clearly the ways parents perceive their role in their children's schooling is, in part, a function of how school officials treat them. On the surface, invitations from school administrators to parents may appear to be a search for collaboration—working together as coequals in the education of their children. The reality, however, is more often than not, these communications are requests from those who see themselves as providers, overseers, and experts in their fields to parents who they perceive to be unknowing, uncaring, or uneducated. The goal implied in this type of correspondence (which is more of an insult than an invitation) is to transmit the "absolute knowledge and expertise" from school personnel to the families about what is best for students. School personnel seek to have parents fulfill their roles in the so-called partnership with schools, which, as school officials see it, is to simply agree and do whatever is being asked of them. This approach is a one-way model of *provider–receiver* service that actually decreases communication between families and schools, even when the goal is to increase parent involvement. Such patterns of communication place parents in a subordinate *consumer/responder* role as merely receptors of information and not in genuine participant roles in the schooling of their children (Smrekar & Cohen-Vogel, 2001).

For many minority parents who seek and anticipate a collaborative relationship with schools in which they are encouraged to offer ideas that will have an effect on school practices, policies, and curricula, the reality of being relegated to the role of passive recipient is disheartening and ultimately disempowering—a condition that is clearly evident in the words of Mrs. Esposito, Raul's mom, which began this chapter.

Further, when this experience is repeated and widespread, the impact is parent/family/caregiver alienation and the loss of valuable allies and resources in the mission of educating students. The current chapter explores prevalent minority family attitudes and expectations and communication barriers in schools, along with the impact these variables have on minority student achievement.

## CHAPTER OBJECTIVES

1. Describe common school-related attitudes and expectations found among minority families.
2. Describe ways in which schools may alienate minority families and restrict their involvement.
3. Identify reasons for minority family confusion and ambiguity about the intentions of schools and teachers.
4. Identify barriers that separate families of minority students from schools.

## STACKING THE DECK: OPPOSITION AND ALIENATION

In contrast to the perception that minority parents do not care about their children's education, the truth is that all too often minority parents are not provided with avenues or opportunities to participate meaningfully in schools. Smrekar and Cohen-Vogel (2001) examined sources of minority parent participation in school-based activities and found that despite high verbal support for parent involvement among educators, school norms that reflect hierarchy over reciprocity, limited resources, and a lack of knowledge about how to involve parents in schools were key barriers (Intrator & Kunzman, 2006; Marzano, Waters, & McNulty, 2005;

## Personal Narrative 2-1     An Invitation to Parents

The following is a copy of the "invitation" to parents to take part in a New York Learns Parent Night Program on PBS (February 28, 2002), entitled *Real Parents—Real Schools.*

Dear Parents and Families:
All parents want their children to do well in school and grow up to lead healthy, productive lives. When parents and families help children learn, students of all ages achieve more. Throughout New York State, we have many good examples of partnerships created by parents and schools working together on behalf of children. But gaps exist. Too many students do not have the knowledge and skills they need to be successful in school. We need to do better, and together, we can.

The education of our children is a shared responsibility. Schools need to be partners with parents, families, and the community to help students achieve high academic standards. Our New York Learns Parent Night Program, *Real Parents—Real Schools,* broadcast on PBS February 28, 2002, provided an invitation to all parents to take a journey with us, and help us all to work together for our children. This guide, created for that program, is a starting point to help us all understand how we can help our children succeed in school. Thank you for joining us to make parent and family involvement a reality in all of our New York State schools.

Sincerely,
Richard P. Mills Commissioner of Education

Sparks, 2005). The researchers found that elements coming from both inside and outside schools hinder the quality of minority family–school interactions. Factors such as time, distance, and childcare restraints also served to lessen minority family involvement in schools. But sometimes the barriers exceed the obvious. Consider Personal Narrative 2-1. This invitation "to all parents to take a journey with us and help us all to work together for our children" appears to be a useful way to involve parents, or is it?

While the invitation appears "inviting," a more insightful examination of the subtleties connoted reveals the existence of barriers that could exclude many parents from responding enthusiastically. Does the invitation provide the welcome, space, and opportunity for parents to help shape the strategies involved and the focus of the planned activities? Consider the parent who works third shift—are there provisions made for providing the information at another time, in other formats? Do all families have access to PBS or other required resources? Can all parents read and understand the language of the letter? If you believe these to be good questions that you had not considered, you are not alone. Schools, classroom teachers, and entire school districts routinely send out "invitations" such as these to families. If schools want full parental participation, they must be sensitive to and capable of removing communication barriers that interfere with that participation.

## BARRIERS TO EDUCATIONAL OPPORTUNITY AND ACHIEVEMENT

The illustration of the invitation to parents presented in Personal Narrative 2-1 makes it clear that frequently (whether consciously or not) parents are kept at a distance when it comes to the education of their children. And although this may not be the intent, such distancing is magnified for minority parents, who are even further estranged due to the powerful barriers of difference (communication, customs, language, perspectives, representation, and so on) that may serve to restrict and inhibit their school involvement (York-Barr, Sommers, Ghere, & Montie, 2006; Zander & Zander, 2000).

## Potential School Barriers

Poor and minority students may encounter a number of school-related roadblocks. For example, it is common to find minority students attending schools that offer limited educational resources, deteriorating buildings, **restricted curricula, lowered expectations**, and harsh and unwelcoming school climates. These are but a few school barriers to their academic success.

U.S. legislators and educators often talk about the democratic right of all students to receive an education (Tyack, 2003). Yet, when applied to many minority students, this policy has been meant the democratic right of all students to have access to *some* education. Ask any educator for her or his wish list for improving her or his school, and you are likely to hear the same from everyone: more resources, more time to pursue professional development, and more funding. Clearly, schools operate on tight budgets and limited resources.

When limits exist, decisions must be made to determine the best use of resources. Because dominant-culture students have strong political representation at the local, state, and national levels, as compared to low-income and minority students, schools and school officials have consistently chosen to place resources where they are believed to be capable of doing the most good. Such actions perpetuate the privilege of dominant-culture students who are most represented in educational, political, and legislative arenas. Federal school funding formulas continue to advantage these students. Research shows that gaps between opportunities to learn and students' appropriation of those opportunities are produced and maintained by the amount of resources and quality of instruction students receive. This same research demonstrates that working-class and poor students are often denied access to essential resources and quality instruction and thus knowledge in schools (Bourdieu, 1977; Gayle-Evans, 1993; Rose, 2000; Yair, 2000).

> Schools transmit dominant culture's socio-cultural values while excluding cultural features coming from other groups while educational practices maintain and legitimize social inequities for some by not recognizing and valuing their cultural practices. Hence, many students are denied the possibility of achieving the same educational results as their peers from the majority culture. (Aguado, Ballesteros, & Malik, 2003, p. 50)

Inner city, rural, low-income, and minority students are thus shortchanged.

Schools go unchecked as they recreate a dual school system year after year, decade after decade, separate and unequal whereby a widening and unacceptable chasm exists between good schools and bad, between students who achieve an empowering education and those who emerge from school having experienced *mis*-education—exiting the schooling process barely able to read and write. The *A Nation Still at Risk* report (1999) pointed out in the last decade that the economically fortunate continue to thrive within and around the education system, while millions of economically disadvantaged Americans live without basic rights to a quality education. The report noted, the poor are "stuck with what 'the system' dishes out to them, and all too often they are stuck with the least qualified teachers, the most rigid bureaucratic structures, the fewest choices and the shoddiest quality." It is interesting to note that students who attend public schools with few resources tend to be completely unaware that there are schools across town that provide their students with swimming pools, gleaming gymnasiums and auditoriums, first-class classrooms, technological innovations, accommodations, and abundant extracurricular options. Similarly, students who attend public schools in wealthy neighborhoods are often unaware of the sparse conditions that students in public schools located in poor neighborhoods endure. Part of the logic of confidence that maintains social class stratification is this lack of awareness of conditions of great wealth and great poverty that other groups experience. Performing observations in both wealthy and poor public schools will acquaint you with these educational disparities (see Exercise 2-1) and encourage you to consider the effect of the disparate environments on the educational ease and related attainment of students attending each school.

**Restricted Curricula and Tracking**  Restricted curriculum, tracking, and other ability-grouping practices have a negative influence on schools' intergroup relations because these practices tend to separate students along cultural, socioeconomic status (SES), and racial lines and thereby perpetuate segregation and unequal educational conditions and benefits. Schools determine how and when advanced classes are offered, what is taught in those courses of study compared to courses of study provided for so called average and vocational students, how students' abilities are measured, and how students are placed into classes that offer specific curricula. These determinations work together to influence students' access to knowledge and thus varying degrees of economic opportunity based on the jobs that leave school prepared to pursue. The so-called ability-grouping policies and practices

---

| EXERCISE 2-1 | **Field Experience: A Visit to the Schools That Have and Those That Have Not** |

*Directions:* Visit two schools: One that enrolls wealthy or high SES students and one that enrolls poor or low SES students. As you visit the schools, observe the following:

1. The look and maintenance of the school building, facilities—including the lobby, auditorium, cafeteria, gymnasium, pool, track, tennis courts, and so on; Examine the school furniture and technology. Do they reflect materials that are outdated or modern? Do they support or hinder the teaching–learning process?

2. Identify the climate of the school: Is the environment warm and inviting or sterile and cold? Are staff members friendly or distant? Would you want to spend the day in that environment? Why or why not?

3. Immediately after leaving each school, record your observations (take pictures, if it is permitted) and then imagine yourself a student in that school. Describe your feelings and thoughts about being a student in each school? Identify the differences and disparities between each school environment.

dictate student placement in tracks and therefore define what knowledge and learning experiences are deemed suitable for particular students. The resulting differences in learning opportunities present significant schooling inequities. Depending on students' academic track placement, they have access to significantly different types of knowledge and skills. Students in "high-ability" (advanced) classes are more likely to be exposed to topics and skills that assist them in preparing for college and careers that require a college degree, while students in "low-ability" (average and remedial) classes are taught basic skills, often using mostly workbooks and tasks that require memorization rather than critical thinking (Oakes & Lipton, 1990).

Ability grouping has the effect of segregating low-income and minority students into vocational and low-ability academic tracks within the school that alienates them, denying them access to the rich resources that are provided for "average" and "above-average" ability students, and, therefore, leads them blindly down a path that results in feelings of futility, degradation, low levels of academic self-confidence, underachievement, and economic failure (Garcia, 1994). Students and their families are not told that their placement in remedial classes will most likely leave them ill-prepared to compete for high-paying jobs in their future. And, the curricula they are offered often lacks relevance and fails to provide significant empowering and fruitful relationships with school personnel which could lead to support for their continued academic success. Even if this effect occurs unintentionally when teachers or other school officials track students into basic, average, or advanced reading and math curricula levels in elementary schools, practices that at first look like an effort to facilitate the students' learning are, in fact, actions that restrict learning and alienate students who are in the greatest need of help while also restricting their job and career options and ultimately their earning power and future socioeconomic success. Further, for many students, the placement in "low-ability" tracks results in the development of a less than adequate perception of self, thus producing an insidious cycle of lowered expectations, leading to less effort and motivation that results in poor performance, which in turn reinforces educators' initial low expectations for their academic achievement. As such, poor and minority students may receive differential and "watered-down" instruction in which they are academically socialized to be passive consumers of purportedly static knowledge that works to hinder rather than benefit their achievement.

**School Climate**   It is not only access to curricula and educational resources that can inhibit the development of poor and minority students, but also quite often the very psychosocial climate of the school—of the classroom and school itself—can act to hinder their achievement (Barth, 2006; Mastropieri & Scruggs, 2004). Poor and minority students and their families may be confronted with subtle and sometimes not-so-subtle messages that they are neither valued nor welcomed as full participants in the educational system. Consider the feelings expressed by Raul's mother in the opening of this chapter. While on the surface it appeared that she had been invited to participate in the education of her son, she, however, experienced instead, devaluation, exclusion, and alienation. The effects of school climate on student achievement are discussed further in Chapter 3.

## otential Minority Community Barriers

Forces within minority communities may also negatively affect poor and minority students' academic motivation, levels of involvement in school, and eventual academic achievement.

**Cultural Inversion**    Ogbu (1990) found that a frequent response of minority students and their families to the discrimination they face in schools is **cultural inversion**. *Cultural inversion* is the process of regarding certain forms of behavior, symbols, and meanings as inappropriate for a minority-group member to exhibit because they are seen as characteristic of White America. In a scene from the movie *Stand and Deliver* (Warner Brothers, 1988), the true-life story of Jaime Escalante, a successful teacher working with students in a poor Los Angeles high school, a student in Mr. Escalante's class asks him for two copies of the textbook so that he can keep one at home to study and one in his desk. The student explains, "I can't let my 'homies' see me hauling books around." Mr. Escalante gives the student three books—one for his desk, one for home, and one for his locker. Such behavior on the part of the student is reflective of cultural inversion. In order to save face and to fit in with his cultural group, he must not be seen as compliant and conforming to school rules (therefore aligning with the oppressor). Sometimes seemingly oppositional behavior and resistance to participation in schools are actually examples of cultural inversion, as with the case of Jaime Escalante in *Stand and Deliver* where he shows a sensitivity and willingness to understand the posturing of his student and provide an effective interpersonal communication to encourage the student who may be in the process of trying to decide whether or not to find ways to work with rather than against a school system that oppresses his effort to achieve his academic goals.

Cultural inversion may exist as part of a minority group's collective opposition to widespread intergenerational discrimination faced in school and society. Forms of opposition displayed by students can be subtle or not-so-subtle ways to express their displeasure and opposition toward a social structure that limits their attainment of highly valued social goals, including obtaining educational and economic viability (Fordham, 1982). For these students, academic success is weakened when curricula used are missing reflections of their lives and culture (relevance), limited and insufficient supplies prevail, inexperienced or uninformed teachers lack expertise in their fields (relationships), and chances of continuing in their academic development and being employed to use associated skills are restricted (rights). It is important to note that this type of opposition among poor and minority group students creates the need for the display of subtle and creative forms of school opposition so that these students do not cross the lines of "bad" behavior for which they will be formally disciplined. As such, this type of opposition is an ingenious response and coping strategy utilized to maintain cultural integrity in the face of institutional discrimination experienced throughout the learning process. Coping skills such as these help group members fight for pride within a system that denies them and their cultural group.

**Educational Salience in Minority Communities**    A mistake many educators make is to assume that minority students and their families do not care about education.

The truth is that while minority students generally voice high educational and occupational aspirations for themselves, these expressions are not often heard by school officials and members of dominant culture, especially when the forces of cultural inversion and cultural group stereotyping are at work. Further, even when the minority students aspire to high occupational goals tied to educational attainment, they often fail to translate their expectations into successful school behaviors. As noted by Valentine and Lloyd (1989), too often minority students, in an attempt to defend against oppressive dominant-cultural policies and practices promulgated in schools, develop strategies that are generally incompatible with their academic achievement. Thus, while their actions may seem to connote "We are too cool for school" or "We don't need to learn this stuff," underlying that behavior is the feeling that "We don't trust you or your system to be fair with us. We can't get a fair shake. We want to progress, but we won't learn from you."

**Minority Student School and Cultural Group Orientation**    Tatum (1987) explained that for some African American students to succeed, a renunciation of their Black cultural frame of reference is required. Forced to relinquish their own culture or to reject the dominant White culture, many African American students consciously or unconsciously tailor their academic performance to the scaled-down expectations of school officials in an effort to maintain cultural integrity while enduring devaluing and alienating conditions in school. And those who attempt to achieve by crossing cultural boundaries and seeming to align with school officials may become alienated from their own cultural communities (Smith & Andrews, 1988). Fordham (1996) explained that minority students who are perceived by their peers to be aligned with school authorities, as evidenced by their compliance with school rules and efforts to study, may be labeled "sell-outs," meaning, at least in the eyes of some minority students, that "to achieve is to be White."

## Potential Generational Barriers

Minority parents—as do their counterparts in the dominant culture—view schooling as a vehicle for financial success, the acquisition of effective interpersonal skills, and the obtainment of technological and academic knowledge and skills. Parents who hold such beliefs are likely to encourage and support their children in their educational endeavors. For many poor and minority students, however, the trust and belief that schooling is a door through which their children can enter to begin to reap the rewards of the "American Dream" of economic prosperity is questioned, given their own personal experiences in school. Some minority parents express a belief in the value of formal education for success in life, while ever cognizant of their experiences with oppression and discrimination in schools—a situation that results in their distrust of educational institutions and resistance to support the school when conflict between their children's actions and attitudes and school expectations arises. These feelings of distrust often lead to ambiguity on the part of minority parents. When that ambiguity is communicated (consciously or not) to their children, minority students respond through cultural inversion and other forms of resistance that embody their parents' lack of confidence that they will be treated fairly in schools. Parents communicate their awareness that the deck is stacked against them. Feeling the need to resist their mistreatment and exclusion, utilizing behaviors that deflect oppression in schooling cannot help but to promote poor and minority student's weakened motivation, achievement, and affiliation in school.

## FROM CONCEPTS TO LIVED EXPERIENCE

The first day of school is an event that is known to stimulate many feelings for students and their families. Children entering schools for the first time may be torn between the anxiety of leaving home and the excitement of facing new challenges and growing up. Parents may have mixed feelings as well—joy for all that the day may bring and yet anxiety about whether the day will go as they hope, wondering if their children will find the support, encouragement, and stimulation they need to maximize their growth and development.

It is clear that first-day expectations, aspirations, hopes, dreams, and experiences vary dramatically, given the opportunities afforded students, **school climates**, cultures in which children spend many years of learning, and the subtle and not-so-subtle messages conveyed to them by school staff, administrators, teachers, their family members, and peers. Poor and minority students' parents not only face the anxieties that are associated with the start of their children's highly significant (life-changing) new experience but they also confront these realities with the awareness that their children will meet with the same devaluation, stereotyping, discrimination, and exclusion they experience in wider society. Such conditions may lead to the discouragement and fear of their children—a substantial impediment and barrier that are not experienced by dominant-culture families—and may also lead to the underachievement of their children. Other minority students may develop their resilience to adapt in the face of the oppression they confront. However, success for these students may come at an undeniable price—affecting their cultural group membership and status. Consider the following story of Lawrence who graduated from elementary school at the top of his class.

### LAWRENCE D.

Lawrence has big plans for repeating this feat in high school, earning a college scholarship, and becoming a doctor. He has a strong mother, Cynthia, who runs a tight ship. She is a single parent; divorced when he was five years old; Lawrence sees his father maybe once a year. Cynthia is an accountant, and has been taking courses over the last three years in hopes of becoming a Certified Public Accountant. She states, when asked what allowed Lawrence's school success, "Nothing but the Lord. I pray constantly because the streets are so dangerous. Lawrence calls me at work when he gets home from school. He knows to do his homework first; if he does not have any, or not enough for an hour, I bought him workbooks to supplement. He can watch television, but only for two hours each day. We also have one hour for reading a library book of his choice each day. He writes a paper about the book that is due before he goes out to play on Saturday. We read the Bible daily, and attend church regularly." Lawrence who is very quiet, responded, when asked how he felt about his school success, "My friends sometimes call me a sissy because I don't play as long as they do and because I get good grades. I try to get my mom to let me play more basketball and learn martial arts. I think she is becoming more understanding. She is tough, but what can I say? She runs it." (Kunjufu, 1986, p.22)

# SUMMARY

**Inviting Parent Participation?** On the surface, invitations from school administrators to parents may appear to be a search for collaboration—seeking to work together as coequals in the education of their children. Often these communications are requests from those who see themselves as providers, overseers, and experts in their fields to parents who they perceive to be unknowing, uncaring, or uneducated. This approach is a one-way model of *provider–receiver* service that actually decreases communication between families and schools, even when the goal is to increase parent involvement. Such patterns of communication place parents in a subordinate *consumer/responder* role as merely receptors of information and not in genuine participant roles in the schooling of their children.

**School Barriers** Poor and minority students may encounter a number of school-related roadblocks including attending schools that offer limited educational resources, deteriorating buildings, restricted curricula, lowered expectations, and harsh and unwelcoming school climates.

**Restricted Resources and Funding** Research demonstrates that, all too often, working-class and poor students are denied meaningful access to needed resources, quality instruction, and thus knowledge in schools.

**Restricted Curricula** Often, students are "tracked" according to their so-called ability level. The so-called ability-grouping policies and practices dictate student placement in tracks and therefore define what knowledge and learning experiences are deemed suitable for particular students. The resulting differences in learning opportunities present significant schooling inequities. Depending on students' academic track placement, they have access to significantly different types of knowledge and skills.

**School Climate** Poor and minority students and their families may be confronted by subtle and not-so-subtle messages that they are neither valued nor welcomed as full participants in the system. The effects of school climate on student achievement are discussed further in Chapter 3.

**Minority Community Barriers** Forces such as cultural inversion, parental ambiguity stemming from generational experiences with discrimination in schools, and refusal to align with an oppressive dominant-culture system that exist within minority communities may also negatively affect poor and minority students' academic motivation, levels of involvement in school, and eventually their academic achievement.

## Questions for Review

1. How are one-way forms of school communications harmful to family/school relationships?

2. How is "ability grouping"/tracking in schools a barrier for minority students?

3. Why might minority families exhibit distrust of schools?

## Important Terms

ability grouping
cultural inversion

low or lowered
   expectations

restricted curricula
school climate

tracking

## Activities

A search through the literature will reveal numerous articles, research studies, position papers, and books describing the poor and minority student achievement gap and the often separate and equal treatment of poor and minority students in U.S. schools. This literature highlights statistics on money allocated to various school districts, standardized test scores, and student attitudes and behaviors that influence academic achievement. What is often missing from these reports is the experience—the frustration of the damning experience that can result from attending a school that alienates you and your family through its overt and covert policies and practices on a daily basis.

Answer the following field experience questions related to the topics covered within this chapter to help acquaint you with sometimes overlooked differences and disparities.

1. Visit two different public schools (one located in an upper-middle or upper SES community and one in a poor or lower-middle to lower SES setting) and spend a day shadowing a single student in each school, or follow two students in the same setting but in different curriculum tracks. Then answer the following questions:

   a. Were the same or similar teaching techniques employed? If not, what differences did you note, and what impact did the different teaching approaches have on the students' attitudes and achievement?

   b. Were texts, supplemental teaching materials, technology, and facilities in the schools and classrooms of the same quality and effectiveness?

   c. How would you evaluate the classroom climates? Supportive? Encouraging? Open? Welcoming? Or were they harsh, sterile, combative, tense, or flat? If you noted a difference in the teaching style, quality of materials, and/or climate of the school and classroom in these two observations, come up with some hypotheses about the potential impact on the students who experience these two different sets of conditions.

2. Schedule an appointment with a school, an administrator, or perhaps a school counselor and ask about the following:

   a. The method for assigning students in academic "ability" tracks, the likelihood and frequency of students' movement to higher tracks throughout the school year, and statistics that identify the representation of poor and minority students in each track

   b. The manner in which parents are invited to participate in the education of their children (for example, open houses, parent nights, parent/teacher meetings, Internet homework support, e-mail)

   c. The steps that the school administration, staff, and teachers take to provide alternative means for parental involvement when specific parents or groups of parents cannot access the mainstream methods (that is, work in the evening or have no one to watch the younger child, no home computer, difficulty with speaking/reading English, and so on)

Share your observations with your instructor and your classmates in small groups to develop a list of strategies geared to increase the level of responsiveness to students and their families as well as increase the active engagement of all members of the school community in the education of the students.

## Enrichment

Andersen, M. L., & Collins, P. H. (2004). *Race, class, and gender: An anthology* (5th ed.). Belmont, CA: Wadsworth/Thomson.

Carter, R. T., & Goodwin, A. L. (1994). Racial identity and education. In L. Darling-Hammond (Ed.), *Review of research in education: Vol. 20* (pp. 291–336). Washington, DC: American Educational Research Association.

Delpit, L. (1995). *Other people's children: Cultural conflict in the classroom*. New York: W. W. Norton &; Co.

Fordham, S. (1982, December). *Cultural inversion and black children's school performance*. Paper presented at the annual meeting of the American Anthropological Association, Washington, DC.

Fordham, S. (1996). *Blacked out: Dilemmas of race, identity, and success at Capital High*. Chicago: University of Chicago.

Kohl, H. (1994). *"'I won't learn from you': And other thoughts on creative maladjustment."* NY: The New Press.

Ladson-Billings, G. (1994). *The dreamkeepers: Successful teachers of African American children*. San Francisco, CA: Jossey-Bass, Inc.

Merton, R. K. (1968). *Social theory and social structure*. New York: The Free Press.

Ogbu, J. U. (1992). Understanding cultural diversity and learning. *Educational Researcher, 21,* 5–24.

Tatum, B. D. (1987). *Assimilation blues: Black families in a White community*. Northampton, MA: Greenwood Press.

Williams, D. (2005). Caroline is a boy. *Teaching Tolerance, 27,* 1.

## Connections on the Web

http://www.ericfacility.net/databases/ERIC_Digests/ed358198.html

This site offers strategies for building successful parent centers in schools.

http://www.ed.gov/PressReleases/02-1994/parent.html

This U.S. Department of Education site provides strategies for connecting parents and schools.

## References

Aguado, T., Ballesteros, B., & Malik, B. (2003). Cultural diversity and school equity: A model to evaluate and develop educational practices in multicultural education contexts. *Equity and Excellence in Education, 36*(1), 50–63.

Barth, R. (2006). Improving relationships within the schoolhouse. *Educational Leadership, 63*(6), 813.

Bourdieu, P. (1977). Cultural reproduction and social reproduction. In J. Karabel & A. H. Halsey (Eds.), *Bower and ideology in education* (pp. 487–510). New York: Oxford University.

Garcia, E. (1994). *Understanding and meeting the challenge of student cultural diversity*. Boston: Houghton Mifflin.

Gayle-Evans, G. (1993). *Making cultural connections for African American children under six: Affirming culture through literature and the arts*. Paper presented at the Annual Conference of the Southern Association on Children under Six, Biloxi, MS, March 25–27.

Intrator, S. M., & Kunzman, R. (2006). Starting with the soul. *Educational Leadership*, 63(6), 38–42.

Kunjufu, J. (1986). *Countering the conspiracy to destroy Black boys, Volume II*. Chicago: African American Images.

Marzano, R. J., Waters, T., & McNulty, B. A. (2005). *School leadership that works: From research to results*. Alexandria, VA: Association for Supervision and Curriculum Development.

Mastropieri, M. A., & Scruggs, T. E. (2004). *The inclusive classroom: Strategies for effective instruction* (2nd ed.). Upper Saddle River, NJ: Merrill/Prentice Hall.

Oakes, J., & Lipton, M. (1990). Tracking and ability grouping: A structural barrier to access and achievement. In J. I. Goodlad & P. Keating (Eds.), *Access to knowledge: An agenda for our nation's schools*. New York: College Entrance Examination Board.

Ogbu, J. U. (1990). Minority education in comparative perspective. *Journal of Negro Education*, 59, 45–55.

Rose, S. J. (2000). *Social stratification in the United States*. New York: New Press.

Smith, K. L., & Andrews, L. D. (1988, April). *An explanation of the beliefs, values, and attitudes of black students in Fairfax County*. Paper presented at the annual meeting of the American Educational Research Association, New Orleans.

Smrekar, C., & Cohen-Vogel, L. (2001). The voices of parents: Rethinking the intersection of family and school. *Peabody Journal of Education*, 76(2), 75–101.

Sparks, D. (2005). *Leading for results*. Thousand Oaks, CA: Corwin Press.

Tatum, B. D. (1987). *Assimilation blues: Black families in a White community*. Northampton, MA: Greenwood.

Tyack, D. (2003). *Seeking common ground: Public schools in a diverse society*. Cambridge, MA: Harvard University.

Valentine, P., & Lloyd, A. (1989, March). *Living in Franklin Square: An exploration of black culture*. Paper presented at the annual meeting of the American Educational Research Association, San Francisco.

Yair, G. (2000). Educational battlefields in America: The tug-of-war over students' engagement with instruction. *Sociology of Education*, 73(4), 247–269.

York-Barr, J., Sommers, W., Ghere, G., & Montie, J. (2006). *Reflective practice to improve schools* (2nd ed.). Thousand Oaks, CA: Corwin Press.

Zander, B., & Zander, R. (2000). *The art of possibility*. Boston: Harvard Business School Press.

*This is the first time I felt welcome—truly welcome in a school. When I walk down the halls, I feel connected. I feel like the teachers and principals like me. They know who I am and they appreciate me. They're glad I attend this school. I can tell. We have these classes called Affective Skills that the school counselors teach. They are fun, and they help me understand myself, learn to express my feelings—get things off my chest. We also get to know each other in these classes. We have sleepover school retreats where we get to bring our own music and lyrics and share them with our classmates while sitting around a bonfire. We tell why the music has meaning for us and stay up late sharing our lives and experiences with the group of teachers, parents, and counselors who come. At this school, we have assignments where we have to interview a family member to find out what they think is important for us to learn in school and ways the school could do better. It's neat that they listen to my grandma like this—she's really smart.*

**Katherine, 10th-grade Cuban student attending a private high school**

CHAPTER

# School Climate

## Effects on Minority Student Achievement and Socioemotional Adjustment

Walking down the hall and feeling connected, liked, and valued is what all students, and their families, should feel as they enter schools. However, many students and their families feel unwelcome, unsafe, alienated, targeted, devalued, and alone in schools. Such conditions are anything but supportive and facilitative for academic achievement. And while the stated mission for most schools is to provide structures and processes necessary to facilitate students' educational development, many are failing minority students (Aguado, Ballesteros, & Malik, 2003; Rubin, 2006). It is clear that more than a traditional approach to and delivery of academic curricula is required to fulfill this mission. Fostering student academic achievement and development necessitates the establishment and maintenance of a school climate that meets the needs of a diverse population of students and their families, who have highly diverse values, languages, and social norms (Sugai & Horner, 2002; Patrikakou, Weissberg, Redding, & Walberg, 2005).

According to Abraham Maslow (1954) each of us is motivated by our needs. Our most basic needs are inborn, having evolved over generations. Maslow's Hierarchy of Needs (originally developed in 1954 and adapted in the 1970s, 1980s, and

| Lower Order/Basic/Deficiency Needs | Higher Order/Growth Needs |
|---|---|
| 1. **Biological and physiological needs**—air, food, drink, shelter, warmth, sex, sleep | 4. **Esteem needs**—self-esteem, achievement, mastery, independence, status, dominance, prestige, responsibility |
| 2. **Safety needs**—protection from elements, security, order, law, limits, stability | 5. **Cognitive needs**—knowledge, meaning |
| 3. **Belongingness and love needs**—work group, school, family, friends, affection, relationships | 6. **Aesthetic needs**—appreciation and search for beauty, balance, form |
| | 7. **Self-actualization needs**—realizing personal potential, self-fulfillment, seeking personal growth and peak experiences |
| | 8. **Transcendence needs**—helping others to achieve self actualization |

1990s) has been used to explain how these needs motivate all of us. Maslow states that we must satisfy each need in turn, starting with the first, which deals with the most obvious needs for survival itself. Only when the lower order needs of physical and emotional well-being are satisfied are we concerned with the higher order needs of influence and personal development. Conversely, if our lower order needs are successfully met, we are no longer concerned about them. However, higher order needs are continually addressed as these needs are felt insatiably.

In applying what we understand from Maslow about the effects of our needs on motivation, we recognize that, at a minimum, students must feel safe in schools (Devine & Cohen, 2007). Students and their families must be able to trust that they will be acknowledged, valued, attended, respected, and included. In order to be able to focus on learning, they must not worry about whether or not they will be the objects of neglect, prejudice, and rejection in their schools. Yet, for many minority students, the school day is a day of total immersion in a hostile environment. It is a day where basic survival, not growth, takes center stage. Students in such settings experience a school climate that fails to nurture the academic, social, and emotional growth that every student deserves.

What type of school climate is effective for promoting diversity and student development? How is such a school climate created and maintained? While the first question may be answered by critical analysis, planning, and visionary thinking, addressing the second question requires expert leadership and proactive advocacy on the part of educators (Adelman & Taylor, 2005; Hord & Sommers, 2008). Further, it must be understood that the weight of producing a school climate which meets the needs of all members of the school community is the responsibility of school leadership. However, to create and maintain a truly liberating, growth-oriented, student-centered school climate, all school officials, including teachers, school counselors, and staff members must also take responsibility for providing and promoting the most favorable learning conditions for all students. Because school climates tend to evolve without much attention paid to how and why they develop, it is often difficult for teachers and school leadership to identify all school climate influences and clear differences in views about how members of the school community should treat each other. Open forums and meetings of site-based decision-making councils that bring together representatives of all members of the school community are needed to be conducted often to not only identify differences in philosophy and approach but also to create opportunities for all members of the school community to have a voice and buy in as school climate improvement efforts are generated. Many schools conduct formal cultural audits to identify their weaknesses associated with including diverse members of their school community in their foundational decision making. A **cultural audit** is the study and examination of an organization's cultural characteristics (such as its assumptions, **norms**, philosophy, and values) to determine whether it hinders or supports its vision and mission. It is easy to forget that students are connected to families and broader communities of potential school partners who are significant in the lives of each student. But it is important to remember that if a school's actions alienate and otherwise turn off the families of students, they alienate and turn off the very people and main supports for students schools seek to educate and empower. It is clear that schools devise authentic strategies to embrace and display respect for all of their partners in order to facilitate the achievement of all students.

This chapter will describe school climate variables and the impact these elements have on student achievement. Further, the chapter will explore some minority family attitudes, expectations, and communication barriers that are experienced in schools.

## CHAPTER OBJECTIVES

1. Identify significant dimensions of school climate.
2. Describe the effects of school climate on the academic success of students.
3. Describe various elements of positive school climate.
4. Identify aspects of incivility that interfere with positive school climate.
5. Explain possible areas of conflict between minority family attitudes and expectations and some elements of school climate.
6. Identify barriers to effective, facilitative home–school communication.

## THE SCHOOL AS A SOCIAL SETTING

Schools are more than buildings made of bricks and stone. They are more than curricula. Schools are active, living compilations of individuals interacting around a common purpose—education. As such, schools are truly settings that embody human ecology. **Human ecology** involves not only the influence of humans on their environment but also the influence of the environment on human behavior, as well as their adaptive strategies as they come to understand those influences. Schools are settings with unique interactions, relationships, and interdependencies among all those operating within the environment. They also are environments shaped by and reflective of many societal forces and pressures, including institutional racism, sexism, classism, ableism, and heterosexism.

The degree to which the school setting supports healthy, stimulating, and growth-oriented interactions and relationships strongly influences the degree to which academic achievement occurs.

## Effects of Incivility

Incivility is an aspect of school climate that has a huge effect on school function, yet is not often explored. Incivility is the quality of being uncivil, lacking courtesy, and conveying rudeness and disrespect. Ferriss (2002) described civility as involving manners, decorum, deportment, and politeness while Sennett (1976) said civility is "the activity which protects people from each other and yet allows them to enjoy each other's company" (p. 264). In schools and in broader society, people have, indeed, become less civil to each other. Staff and students routinely experience instances of incivility, bullying, or mobbing by peers, students, parents/guardians, or school officials that negatively affect individuals' feelings of safety, acceptance, inclusion, and productivity in schools. Bullying involves the act of intimidating or dominating a weaker person to derive some result and may involve humiliation, degradation, gossip, and verbal and physical abuse. Mobbing encompasses various forms of bully behavior including the starting of rumors and slander, and discipline, demotion, or loss of rights or position performed by groups of individuals in a system. Victims of incivility are thereby ostracized, shunned, or marginalized by a group of bullies as a part of the daily operation of the school (Twale & De Luca, 2008). Because of the covert nature of many of the uncivil acts of bullying and mobbing and the fear of reprisal, victims often suppress their emotions and do not fully reveal to others what has happened to them (Lewis, 2004; White, 2004). Any human ecology that involves competition and power differentials has the potential for the development of incivility. Because incivility is so detrimental to positive school climate, it is imperative that school officials identify and deal directly with it in all its many forms. Incivility is a part of the school climate that can be effectively managed through policy design and implementation and training. However, schools must be aware of the existence and inculcation of incivility within their environment and take ongoing steps to prevent and eliminate it. Beyond putting policies, grievance procedures, and sanctions in place, schools must conduct a cultural audit in order to identify and specifically address all dimensions of existent incivility.

As is true with any other societal institution, to be effective, schools must have common goals and articulated roles that are embraced and enacted by its members. They must also establish social norms, values, and operational assumptions that support the performance of these roles and the achievement of goals formed (McLaughlin & Talbert, 2006). It is these social norms, values, and operating assumptions that give form to the culture and climate of schools that can either facilitate or hinder student development. Consider the case of the two schools described in Personal Narrative 3-1. Think about how you would feel working or learning in each of these schools. Consider the effects of each school environment on your attitude and potential productivity.

## Personal Narrative 3-1    Two Schools: Focusing on Product or Person?

### J. R. Anderson Elementary School

Established in 1950, J. R. Anderson Elementary School is in pretty good shape for its 50-plus years in existence. Clearly, some fresh paint and a few new windows here and there would certainly help. But for all outward appearances, it is much like any other elementary school.

Entering the lobby, you immediately become aware that, contrary to your initial impression, this school is *not* like any other elementary school. It is deadly quiet—in the middle of the day! As you walk through the lobby toward the main office, you realize that not only are the lobby and the building clean but they are almost septic—sterile. The walls are bare; no student work is displayed and there is no evidence of class projects, activities, or coming events. Upon entering the school office, you are met by a person who seems a bit tired and perhaps overworked. She addresses your requests as if she were simply completing one more of her hundreds of tasks that she completes in a day with the routine stiffness of a worker who has learned to process requests without becoming moved or getting involved. At that point, you say to yourself, "Thank goodness I don't have to stay too long in this school on this day." As you look up and down the halls, signs of life are hard to find. Classroom doors are closed; students are at their desks (which are typically straight and orderly); and teachers, in almost lock-step fashion, standing at the front of the classroom, present their lectures to unaffected students who seem to endure their environment without much emotion. The "business" of the classes—the lesson plans—appears to be being delivered, but the sense of excitement, the joy of learning, and the energy of childhood seem to have taken leave.

### Ashland Elementary School

Cloaked in the yellowish brick of its day, Ashland Elementary School attests to its years of service. The doors to the school are huge, old metal doors that, while clean, could certainly use some paint. Ashland Elementary School was also built in the early 1950s and clearly begs for a new life, but only on the outside.

On entering the lobby, you are struck by the color and the vibrancy of the building. Children's work fills the hallways. A banner congratulating the chess club for a victory and a poster announcing the Halloween dance are posted outside the main office. When entering the school office, you are greeted by the smile of a staff member who looks happy to be in this environment. She speaks to you as if she were meeting you at a party—with a friendly delivery and person-centered focus on addressing your requests. You think to yourself, "I wouldn't mind spending the day here, observing and even wishing I could interact in the ongoing activities of the school." Through open doors, you can hear teachers providing instruction and children engaging in activities that take them all over their classrooms. Students and teachers alike laugh, approach, and question each other in workshop-like groups engulfed by a purposeful urgency to apply concepts learned and problem solve together. Teachers and students seem to like and respect each other as well as enjoy spending time together. You arrived on a day when some students are playing chess in groups on the floor of the gymnasium while others are joined around several computers writing newspaper articles or working backstage of the theatre learning new dance steps for the spring theatrical production in which every student in the school performs. It is clear that there is life and love—a sense of family even—at Ashland Elementary. The spirit of the school appears alive and well.

## SCHOOL CLIMATE DIMENSIONS

What do we mean when we talk about school climate? A simple definition of school climate is "the way we do things around here." **School climate** is a general term that refers to the feel, atmosphere, tone, ideology, or milieu of a school. Just as individuals have personalities, so too do schools; a school climate may be thought of as the personality of a school. The climate of a school is central to its educational mission. Four essential dimensions of school climate have been identified (Center for Social and Emotional Education, 2007). Table 3-1 lists school climate variables associated with each dimension.

**Table 3-1**  Four Essential Dimensions of School Climate

| Dimension | Major Indicators and *Sample Questions* |
|---|---|
| **Safety** | |
| **1. Rules and norms** | Clearly communicated rules about physical violence and verbal abuse and clear and consistent enforcement. <br><br> • *In my school, there are clearly stated rules against insults, teasing, harassment, and other verbal abuse.* <br> • *Adults in the school will stop students if they see them physically hurting each other (for example, pushing, slapping, or punching).* |
| **2. Physical safety** | Sense that students and adults feel safe from physical harm in the school. <br><br> • *I feel physically safe in all areas of the school building.* <br> • *I have seen other students being physically hurt at school more than once (for example, pushed, slapped, punched, or beaten up).* |
| **3. Social and emotional security** | Sense that students feel safe from verbal abuse, teasing, and exclusion. <br><br> • *I have been insulted, teased, harassed, or otherwise verbally abused more than once in this school.* <br> • *There are groups of students in the school who exclude others and make them feel bad for not being a part of the group.* |
| **Teaching and Learning** | |
| **1. Support for learning** | Supportive teaching practices, such as constructive feedback and encouragement for positive risk taking, academic challenge, individual attention, and opportunities to demonstrate knowledge and skills in a variety of ways. <br><br> • *My teachers show me how to learn from my mistakes.* <br> • *My teachers encourage me to try out new ideas (think independently).* <br> • *My teachers help me figure out how I learn best.* |
| **2. Social and civic learning** | Support for the development of social and civic knowledge and skills, including effective listening, conflict resolution, reflection and responsibility, and ethical decision making. <br><br> • *In my school, we have learned ways to resolve disagreements so that everyone can be satisfied with the outcome.* <br> • *In my school, we talk about the way our actions will affect others.* |

*(continued)*

**Table 3-1**  Continued

| Dimension | Major Indicators and *Sample Questions* |
|---|---|
| **Interpersonal Relationships** | |
| 1. Respect for diversity | Mutual respect for individual differences at all levels of the school—student–student, adult–student, adult–adult. <br>• *Students in this school respect one another's differences (for example, gender, race, culture).* <br>• *Adults in this school respect one another's differences (for example, gender, race, culture).* |
| 2. Social support—adults | Collaborative and trusting relationships among adults and adult support for students in terms of high expectations for success, willingness to listen, and personal concern. <br>• *Adults in my school seem to work well with one another.* <br>• *If students need to talk to an adult in school about a problem, there is someone they trust who they could talk to.* |
| 3. Social support—students | Network of peer relationships for academic and personal support. <br>• *Students have friends at school they can turn to if they have questions about homework.* <br>• *Students have friends at school they can trust and talk to if they have problems.* |
| **Institutional Environment** | |
| 1. School connectedness/ engagement | Positive identification with school, sense of belonging, and norms for broad participation in school life for students and families. <br>• *I feel good about what I accomplish in school.* <br>• *I think my parents/guardians feel welcome at my school. My school encourages students to get involved in other things than schoolwork (for example, sports, music/drama clubs).* |
| 2. Physical surroundings | Cleanliness, order, and appeal of facilities and adequate resources and materials. <br>• *My school is physically attractive (pleasing architecture, nicely decorated, etc.).* <br>• *My school building is kept in good condition.* <br>• *My school has up-to-date computers and other electronic equipment available to students.* |

*Source:* Adapted from *The 12 Dimensions of School Climate Measured* by Center for Social and Emotional Education, 2007, New York: Author. Copyright by Center for Social and Emotional Education. Available: www.csee.net/climate/pdfNew/dimensions_chart_pagebars.pdf. Used with permission.

Research has confirmed the importance of school climate dimensions in identifying that a positive and sustained school climate promotes students' socioemotional development and academic achievement (Harris & Lowery, 2002). Not surprisingly, a positive school climate also promotes teacher retention, which itself enhances student success (Center for Social and Emotional Education, 2007). However, the effects of school climate on learning have not been incorporated in contemporary school reform strategies including No Child Left Behind, which notes the importance of character education and supportive learning environments, but requires accountability systems to measure only reading, math, physical violence, and (recently) science scores. These are all meaningful indicators of education quality, but education policy makers have become increasingly aware that NCLB-type accountability may be too narrowly focused (Cohen, 2006).

## ASSESSING SCHOOL CLIMATE

States and school districts have always been interested in measuring school climate—not only to identify effects of school climate on learning but also to find ways to support and improve learning. Schools can also use school climate data to promote meaningful staff, family, and student engagement—and to enhance the social, emotional, ethical, civic, and intellectual skills and dispositions that contribute to students' success in school and in life (Cohen, 2006). Schools can assess school climate in a variety of ways—for example, using focus groups; observational methods; interviews; town hall discussions; study circles; participatory action research; and student, staff, and family surveys. However, school climate is best evaluated with surveys that have been developed in a scientifically sound manner and are comprehensive in two ways: (1) recognizing student, parent, and school personnel voice; and (2) assessing all the dimensions that color and shape the process of teaching and learning and educators' and students' experiences in the school building (Cohen, 2006). Exercise 3-1 provides

| **EXERCISE 3-1** | **Point of Reflection: School Climate Survey** |
| --- | --- |

*Directions:* Think about the elementary, middle, or high school in which you were previously enrolled. (If you were homeschooled, interview someone who attended school in order to answer the following questions.)

1. Forget the grades you received in this school. How good do you think your own work in school was?

| | |
| --- | --- |
| Excellent | 1 |
| Good | 2 |
| Same as most other students | 3 |
| Below most other students | 4 |
| Poor | 5 |

2. How good a student did the teacher you liked the most expect you to be in school?

| | |
| --- | --- |
| One of the best | 1 |
| Better than most other students | 2 |
| Same as most other students | 3 |
| Not as good as most other students | 4 |
| One of the worst students | 5 |

3. How many students did not do as well as they could do in school because they were afraid that other students would not like them as much if they did well?

| | |
| --- | --- |
| Almost all of the students | 1 |
| Most of the students | 2 |
| About half of the students | 3 |
| Some of the students | 4 |
| None of the students | 5 |

4. When you attended the school, did you believe that people like you did not do well in school?

| | |
|---|---|
| Strongly agree | 1 |
| Agree | 2 |
| Not sure | 3 |
| Disagree | 4 |
| Strongly disagree | 5 |

5. How many teachers in the school tried to help students get better grades when they were struggling?

| | |
|---|---|
| Almost all of the teachers | 1 |
| Most of the teachers | 2 |
| About half of the teachers | 3 |
| Some of the teachers | 4 |
| Almost none of the teachers | 5 |

6. How good a student did your family members expect you to be in that school?

| | |
|---|---|
| One of the best | 1 |
| Better than most other students | 2 |
| Same as most other students | 3 |
| Not as good as most other students | 4 |
| One of the worst students | 5 |

7. How did you feel when you were in the school?

| | |
|---|---|
| Very comfortable | 1 |
| Pretty comfortable | 2 |
| Somewhat comfortable | 3 |
| Uncomfortable | 4 |
| Very uncomfortable | 5 |

8. How did teachers and school staff treat you?

| | |
|---|---|
| Very warmly with lots of respect | 1 |
| Respectfully | 2 |
| With some kindness and respect | 3 |
| With little respect and kindness | 4 |
| Very coldly with no respect | 5 |

9. How involved were you with extracurricular activities in the school?

| | |
|---|---|
| Very involved in lots of clubs/teams | 1 |
| Pretty involved in some clubs/teams | 2 |
| Involved in a couple of clubs/teams | 3 |
| Not very involved | 4 |
| Not at all involved | 5 |

10. Would you recommend the school to a member of your family?

| | |
|---|---|
| I would strongly recommend it | 1 |
| I would not recommend it | 2 |

Go back and look at your responses to the questionnaire items. What do they tell you about the school's psychological climate and the effect on your motivation and learning? Write a reflection discussing the elements of school climate (explored in this chapter) that you feel are the most important for creating a positive learning environment.

a measure of school climate that can be used to provide some insight into the effects of school climate on student motivation and achievement from a student's perspective.

# EFFECTS OF SCHOOL CLIMATE ON MINORITY STUDENTS

When assessing school climate as a factor that affects minority student performance, teachers must initially consider the degree to which the environment affords students' physical and psychological safety. Research shows that schools that provide safety (including safety from public ridicule and excessive criticism) facilitate student learning (Alexander & Murphy, 1998; Murphy, Weil, & McGreal, 1986), whereas students who are educated in climates in which they encounter ridicule and devaluation, especially when they attempt to participate and share their own perspectives, are unlikely to continue to take risks, which decreases their involvement and results in the loss of necessary opportunities to achieve.

The climate of a school sets the stage for encouraging or discouraging student motivation and achievement (Raviv, Raviv, & Reisel, 1993). But the impact of a school's climate affects much more than a student's level of motivation and achievement; school climate also directly affects students' self-concepts, life chances, and opportunities.

What happens when minority students encounter a school climate that is psychologically unsafe, rejecting, and/or alienating? What happens to the student who experiences a school climate that offers low expectations and limited opportunities for academic success? Such circumstances have an impact that engulfs one's entire educational experience and spreads well beyond the walls of the classroom and the hours of a school day.

Research (for example, Brookover, Beady, Flood, Schweitzer, & Wisenbaker, 1979) demonstrates that students' views of the importance of schooling, their academic self-concept, the presence or absence of feeling academic futility in their school environments, and the extent to which students feel alienated and/or oppositional toward school curricula and officials affect their academic achievement and socioemotional adjustment. Further, minority students who experience environments that fail to support and reinforce their diverse worldviews, experiences, and values may end up believing that in order to achieve they must reject aspects of their culture—that is, they must act more like members of the dominant culture in order to be perceived as good students and be provided with opportunities to achieve in school. As Ogbu (1990) pointed out in reference to African American students, achievement for some requires them to become more like Whites. The result of denying one's culture, in essence what is often seen as "selling out," can be devastating in terms of the students' loss of cultural identity, psychosocial well-being, and community connections (Fordham, 1996; Smith & Andrew, 1988; Spradlin, Welsh, & Hinson, 1999; Valentine & Lloyd, 1989). Consider Exercise 3-2.

## EXERCISE 3-2    Identifying The Impact of School Climate

### Part I: School Elements

Interview four people in your life by asking them to respond to the following questions. After you review their answers, what conclusions can you draw about the effect of school climate on student learning?

1. Remember a time when you felt devalued or humiliated in school. How did it affect your ability to function that day? How did it affect your view of the class (or activity or school)?
2. Describe a classroom, teacher, or particular experience you had in school where you felt extremely safe and able to risk sharing your opinion, your perspectives, and your answers. What made that environment feel safe?
3. If you were to suggest to school administrators one thing they could do to make a school warm, supportive, and facilitative, what would you suggest?

After reviewing the responses, share your observations and conclusions with your instructor, your colleagues, or your classmates. Identify the degree to which the shared lived experiences reflect the concepts and research presented within this chapter.

### Part II: Parent/Guardian Perspectives

Interview three parents and ask them the following questions.

1. To what degree do you feel heard by your children's school administration, staff, and teachers?
2. What things can you identify as factors that reduce your active participation in school affairs?
3. If you were asked by faculty and administration how they might improve parental involvement in their school, what recommendations would you make?

Share your observations with your instructor, your colleagues, or your classmates, and identify the degree to which the shared lived experiences reflect the concepts and research presented within this chapter.

## INVOLVING MINORITY FAMILIES AND COMMUNITIES

A crucial feature for creating a positive school climate that empowers minority students and their families is the presence of effective parent and community involvement. As was noted in Chapter 2, minority students often feel alienated from schools when their families are not involved in the school's mission and execution of that mission to educate their children.

Despite the expected verbal support for parent involvement from educators and parents alike, "parents continue to be kept at a distance in most schools" (Swap, 1993, p. 13). And when communication does occur, it is typically formal and one-way, that is, from the school to home and most often as a result of a problem or crisis described by the school (Henderson, Marburger, & Ooms, 1986).

Instituting and maintaining parental involvement are not easy. Multiple barriers restrict the formation of collaborative relationships between students' homes and the school. Factors such as changing demographics that restrict the time and availability of teachers and parents alike, school norms that reflect hierarchy over reciprocity, limited resources, and a lack of knowledge about how to effectively involve and motivate parents must be addressed if parental involvement is to be actualized. Exercise 3-1 invites you to identify ways how a school may overcome barriers to include parents and communities in the education of children.

In order to engage parents and communities, school personnel ask: "What can students' families tell us that will help us understand their needs and wishes so that we will know which actions increase and decrease their genuine involvement in the school's mission?" Asking this question and truly listening to the responses may help identify and address factors that currently alienate parents from schools (Goodson, 1991; Swartz, 2003). Further, such a step may begin the process needed to empower students' families and include them as essential partners in the creation of a positive learning environment. Table 3-2 provides a few guidelines for facilitating this process of empowering and including families.

## SOCIAL CLASS AND SCHOOL CLIMATE

Only about 1 in 10 low-income parents belong to parent–teacher organizations nationwide (Educational Testing Service, 1992). Statistics like this may mislead educators to believe that working-class, poor, and minority parents do not care about their children's education. Although class-related childrearing practices and occupational socialization (see Bronfenbrenner, 1966; Heath, 1982; Kohn, 1969, 1971; Wright & Wright, 1976) may negatively affect some families' involvement, schools are often unaware of the reasons why working-class and poor families may have attitudes and utilize childrearing and communication strategies that negatively affect their children's achievement. With increased understanding of low-income families' educational values, ideas, and attitudes and their relation to these families' school participation, schools will be better able to determine ways to improve school climates.

Quite often, working-class lifestyles and values are not represented in school curricula. For many working-class families, practical and applicable skills and knowledge are highly valued. School curricula primarily reflect theoretical constructs and instructional activities that may not seem relevant to actual life and

**Table 3-2**  Empowering and Including Parents

1. Provide for multiple levels of family participation, making sure all contact with students' families is positive, warm, respectful, and genuine. A good rule of thumb is, Never ask a question to a family to which you think you already know the answer. Go into communications with families with openness to learning from them and hearing new information that will be helpful to you.

2. Implement different modes of warm, inviting contact. It is helpful to develop a relationship *before* beginning any problem solving. Use various modes of communication with the families of students (for example, home visits, phone calls, e-mails, written letters) to convey your sincere interest in and positive feelings about their children.

3. Create networks that make it easy for families to be involved with the school (for example, involving families in the writing of school and classroom newsletters, asking for family input directly by phone or note before decisions are made for which parents' support is needed). When working in committee formats, be sure to share names and contact information.

4. Communicate appreciation and respect for diverse cultural values, language differences, and resources presented by students' families.

5. Be flexible and responsive to families' needs and wishes when scheduling times and locations for meetings.

6. Create ways to involve parents as equals in social arenas in which friendship and trust can form (for example, arrange bowling nights, movie weekends, school picnics) and also involve parents' communities to construct and reinforce the presentation of their perspectives in programming, curricula, policies, and practices (Coleman, 1991).

work circumstances. In addition, due to family income limitations, enrichment programs, college preparation courses, and afterschool activities may be inaccessible to poor and working-class students. Further, when teachers request parental help in their children's classrooms or if school meetings and parent services offered by the school can be accessed only at times during which parents are working in jobs from which they cannot get release time, or can be accessed only by means that may not be readily available to working-class and poor students and their families (for example, e-mail, websites), a clear, disenfranchising message is conveyed. Finally, biased testing and school accountability standards that ignore the advantage enjoyed by middle- and upper-class students have been found to further contribute to the disaffection of marginalized students and their families (Rustique-Forrester & Riley, 2001).

Schools must be charged with helping to create human capital in schools that include working-class and poor students by working collaboratively with them.

## FROM CONCEPTS TO LIVED EXPERIENCE

The experience of a hostile, nonsupportive, devaluing school environment cannot be understated. The impact of such an environment on a student's sense of self, level of aspiration, and actual achievement can be devastating. Consider Lyla's memories of school as a child living in homeless shelters and the effects of those memories on her education.

**MEMORIES OF SCHOOL**

I can remember every teacher I ever had. Some are memorable for their competence and courtesy. Others I remember for their indifference and bottled up hostility towards me. If I could talk to one of those teachers today, I'd tell them how being ignored when I was standing right in front of them felt. I'd call their attention to the fact that I could see and hear their pleasant conversations with other students that turned to business-only, cold responses to my questions or requests for help. I soon learned to keep quiet and to myself—that was the best way through school. I was a good student who learned to teach myself when needed. There were some good teachers along the way but because of my experiences I always braced for the coldness, the psychological exclusion from the group, the stony indifference to me, the stifled and tempered conversations, and the stoic obligatory postures. Those interactions with teachers had quite an effect on my young soul. I remember that I began to shut down my needs and expectations that I'd feel a sense of belonging and care in school—so much so that when I encountered it, it took me by surprise and I could never tell if it was real or not. I'd say the damage has been long lasting. I still look for the hidden biases in my interactions with my college professors and peers and find myself pulling away from the possibility of closeness to others in every course I take.

# SUMMARY

**The School as a Social Setting**  Schools are settings in which there are unique interactions, relationships, and interdependencies among all persons operating within the environment. The degree to which the school setting supports healthy, stimulating, and growth-oriented interactions and relationships strongly influences the degree to which academic achievement will occur. Maslow explained that humans must have each need satisfied in turn, starting with the first, which deals with the most obvious needs for survival itself. Only when the lower order needs of physical and emotional well-being are satisfied are we concerned with the higher order needs of influence and personal development. In applying what we understand from Maslow about the effects of our needs on motivation, we recognize that, at a minimum, students must feel safe in schools. Students and their families must be able to trust that they will be acknowledged, valued, attended, respected, and included.

**Effects of Incivility**  Staff and students routinely experience instances of incivility, bullying, or mobbing by peers, students, parents/guardians, or school officials that negatively affect individuals'

feelings of safety, acceptance, inclusion, and productivity in schools. Any human ecology that involves competition and power differentials has the potential for the development of incivility. Because incivility is so detrimental to positive school climate, it is imperative that school officials identify and deal directly with it in all its many forms. Beyond putting policies, grievance procedures, and sanctions in place, schools must conduct a cultural audit in order to identify and specifically address all dimensions of existent incivility.

**School Climate Dimensions**  The following four key dimensions make up school climate: safety, teaching and learning, interpersonal relationships, and institutional environment. Each dimension has associated factors that must be addressed in the development of positive school learning environments. Research has confirmed the importance of a school climate dimension in identifying that a positive and sustained school climate promotes students' socioemotional development and academic achievement.

**Assessing School Climate**  Schools can also use climate data to promote meaningful staff, family, and student engagement—and to enhance the social, emotional, ethical, civic, and intellectual skills and dispositions that contribute to academic success. School climate is best evaluated with surveys that have been developed in a scientifically sound manner and are comprehensive in two ways: (1) recognizing student, parent, and school personnel voice; and (2) assessing all the dimensions that color and shape the process of teaching and learning and educators' and students' experiences in the school building.

**School Climate Effects on Minority Students**
Students' views of the importance of schooling, their academic self-concept, the presence or absence of academic futility in their school environments, and the extent to which they feel alienated and/or oppositional toward school officials affect their academic achievement and socioemotional adjustment.

**Involving Family and Community** A crucial feature in creating a positive school climate for minority students and their families is the presence of effective, collaborative family and community involvement. Teacher attitudes toward parents and their skill in developing parent-involvement strategies are significant in creating a positive school climate. Quite often, working-class lifestyles and values are not represented in school curricula, which contribute to the fact that only about 1 in 10 low-income parents belong to parent–teacher organizations nationwide.

## Questions for Review

1. How is Maslow's Hierarchy of Needs applicable for analyzing school climate elements?

2. How might teacher incivility toward one or more other teachers affect student learning?

3. How are the elements for each of the four dimensions of school climate particularly significant for minority students and families?

## Important Terms

bullying
human ecology

incivility
mobbing

norms
school climate

## Enrichment

Alvine, L., & Cullum, L. (Eds.). (1999). *Breaking the cycle: Gender, literacy, and learning* (pp. 7–12). Peterborough, NH: Heineman Boynton-Cook.

Anderson, D. C. (1998). Curriculum, culture, and community: The challenge of school violence. In M. Tonry & M. Moore (Eds.), *Youth violence* (pp. 317–363). Chicago: University of Chicago.

Banks, J. A. (1995). Multicultural education: Its effects on students' racial and gender attitudes. In J. Banks & C. A. McGeeBanks (Eds.), *Handbook of research on multicultural education* (pp. 617–627). New York: Macmillan.

Brookover, W. R., Beady, C., Flood, P., Schweitzer, J., & Wisenbaker, J. (1979). *School social systems and student achievement: Schools can make a difference*. Brooklyn, NY: Praeger.

Epstein, J. L. (1985). Parents' reactions to teacher practices of parent involvement. *Elementary School Journal, 86,* 277–294.

Epstein, J. L. (1995). School/family/community partnerships: Caring for the children we share. *Phi Delta Kappan, 76,* 701–712.

Epstein, J. L., & Becker, H. (1982). Teachers' reported practices of parent involvement: Problems and possibilities. *Elementary School Journal, 83,* 103–114.

Epstein, J. L., & Dauber, S. L. (1991). School programs and teacher practices of parent involvement in inner-city elementary and middle schools. *Elementary School Journal, 91,* 291–305.

Hernandez, T. J. (2004). A safe school climate: A systemic approach and the school counselor. *Professional School Counselor, 7*(4), 256–263.

Hord, S. M., & Sommers, W. A. (2008). *Leading professional learning communities: Voices from research and practice.* Thousand Oaks, CA: Corwin Press.

Jenkins, P. (1997). School delinquency and the school social bond. *Journal of Research in Crime and Delinquency, 34,* 31–35.

Ladson-Billings, G. (1989, May). *A tale of two teachers: Exemplars of successful pedagogy for black students.* Paper presented at the Educational Equality Project Colloquium, New York, NY.

McLaughlin, M. W., & Talbert, J. E. (2006). *Building school-based teacher learning communities: Professional strategies to improve student achievement.* New York: Teachers College Press.

Nieto, S. (1996). *Affirming diversity: The sociopolitical context of multicultural education* (2nd ed.). (Adapted from *The 12 Dimensions of School*) White Plains, NY: Longman.

Ogbu, J. U. (1974). *The next generation: An ethnography of education in an urban neighborhood.* New York: Academic.

Spradlin, L. K. (1999). Taking black girls seriously: Addressing discrimination's double bind. In L. Alvine & L. Cullum (Eds.), *Breaking the cycle: Gender, literacy, and learning, 7-12.* Peterborough, NH: Heineman Boynton-Cook.

Stockard, J., & Mayberry, M. (1992). *Effective educational environments.* Newbury Park, CA: Corwin Press.

Tatum, B. D. (1997). *"Why are all the black kids sitting together in the cafeteria?" and other conversations about race: A psychologist explains the development of racial identity.* New York: Basic Books.

Thompson, A. (1998). Not the color purple: Black feminist lessons for educational caring. *Harvard Educational Review, 68,* 522–554.

Welsh, W. (2000). The effects of school climate on school disorder. *Annals of the American Academy of Political and Social Science, 567,* 88–107.

## Connections on the Web

www.csee.net/climate/pdfNew/dimensions_chart_pagebars.pdf

This site explicates in detail the 12 dimensions of school climate discussed in this chapter.

http://csee.net/climate/aboutcsee/school_climate_challenge.pdf

This site provides school climate data and strategies for narrowing the gap between school climate research and school climate policy, practice guidelines, and teacher education policy.

www.wholechildeducation.org/resources.dyn/Learningcompact7-07.pdf

This site offers information that is helpful for gearing up educators in their actions to improve learning environments.

http://www.projectappleseed.org/

The website for Project Appleseed, the national campaign for improving public education, is an excellent resource on improving school–community and school–parent relationships.

http://www.eyeoneducation.com/

This site is an excellent resource for books and materials on improving school and community relationships, creating positive school climates, and involving parents within the school.

## References

Adelman, H., & Taylor, L. (2005). *The school leader's guide to student learning supports: New directions for addressing barriers to learning.* Thousand Oaks, CA: Corwin Press.

Aguado, T., Ballesteros, B., & Malik, B. (2003). Cultural diversity and school equity. A model to evaluate and develop educational practices in multicultural education contexts. *Equity and Excellence in Education, 36*(1), 50–63.

Alexander, P., & Murphy, P. (1998). The research base for APA's learner-centered psychological principles. In N. Lambert & B. McCombs (Eds.), *How students learn: Reforming schools through learner-centered education* (pp. 25–60). Washington, DC: American Psychological Association.

Bronfenbrenner, U. (1966). Socialization and social class through time and space. In R. Bendix & S. M. Lipset (Eds.), *Class, status, and power* (pp. 239–270). New York: Free Press.

Brookover, W. R., Beady, C., Flood, P., Schweitzer, J., & Wisenbaker, J. (1979). *School social systems and student achievement: Schools can make a difference.* Brooklyn, NY: Praeger.

Center for Social and Emotional Education. (2007). New York: Author. www.csee.net/climate/pdfNew/dimensions_chart_pagebars.pdf

Cohen, J. (2006). Social, emotional, ethical, and academic education: Creating a climate for learning, participation in democracy, and well-being. *Harvard Educational Review, 76*(2), 201–237.

Coleman, J. (1991). *Parental involvement in education.* Washington, DC: U.S. Department of Education, Office of Educational Research and Improvement (ERIC Document Reproduction Service No. ED334028).

Devine, J., & Cohen, J. (2007). *Making your school safe: Strategies to protect children and promote learning.* New York: Teachers College Press.

Dorsey, J. (2000). Institute to end violence [Online version]. In *End School Violence.* Retrieved May 2002, from http://www.endschoolviolence.com/strategy/

Educational Testing Service. (1992). *America's smallest school: The family.* Princeton, NJ: Author.

Ferriss, A. (2002). Studying and measuring civility: A framework, trends, and scale. *Sociological Inquiry, 72,* 376–392.

Fordham, S. (1996). *Blacked out: Dilemmas of race, identity, and success at Capital High.* Chicago: University of Chicago.

Goodson, I. (1991). Sponsoring the teacher's voice: Teachers lives and teachers. *Cambridge Journal of Education, 21*(1), 35–46.

Harris, S. L., & Lowery, S. (2002). A view from the classroom. *Educational Leadership, 59*(8), 64–65.

Heath, S. B. (1982). Questioning at home and at school: A comparative study. In G. Spindler (Ed.), *Doing the ethnography of schooling* (pp. 102–131). New York: Holt, Rinehart, & Winston.

Henderson, A., Marburger, C., & Ooms, T. (1986). *Beyond the bake sale: An educator's guide to working with parents.* Columbia, MD: National Committee for Citizens in Education (ERIC Document Reproduction Service No. ED270508).

Hord, S. M., & Sommers, W. A. (2008). *Leading professional learning communities: Voices from research and practice.* Thousand Oaks, CA: Corwin Press.

Kohn, M. (1969). *Class and conformity*. Homewood, IL: Dorsey.

Kohn, M. (1971). Social class and parent–child relationships. In M. Anderson (Ed.), *Sociology of the family* (pp. 323–338). Middlesex, UK: Penguin.

Lewis, D. (2004). Bullying at work: The impact of shame among university and college lecturers. *British Journal of Guidance and Counseling, 32*, 281–299.

Lewis, T., & Sugai, G. (1999). Effective behavior support: A systems approach to proactive school-wide management. *Focus on Exceptional Children, 31*(6), 1–24.

Maslow, A. H. (1954). *Motivation and personality*. New York: Harper & Row.

McLaughlin, M. W., & Talbert, J. E. (2006). *Building school-based teacher learning communities: Professional strategies to improve student achievement*. New York: Teachers College Press.

Murphy, J., Weil, M., & McGreal, T. (1986). The basic practice model of instruction. *Elementary School Journal, 87*, 83–95.

Ogbu, J. U. (1990). Minority education in comparative perspective. *Journal of Negro Education, 59*, 45–55.

Raviv, A., Raviv, A., & Reisel, E. (1993). Environmental approach used for evaluating an educational innovation. *Journal of Educational Research, 86*(6), 317–325.

Rubin, B. (2006). Tracking and detracking: Debates, evidence, and best practices for a heterogeneous world. *Theory into Practice, 45*(1), 6–14.

Rustique-Forrester, E., & Riley, K. (2001). *Bringing disenfranchised young Black people back into the frame: A UK perspective on disaffection from school and the curriculum*. Paper presented at the Annual meeting of the American Educational Research Association, Seattle, WA, April 10–14.

Sennett, R. (1976). *The fall of public man: On the social psychology of capitalism*. New York: Vintage Books.

Smith, K. L., & Andrew, L. D. (1988, April). *An explanation of the beliefs, values, and attitudes of black students in Fairfax County*. Paper presented at the annual meeting of the American Educational Research Association, New Orleans.

Spradlin, L. K., Welsh, L. A., & Hinson, S. L. (1999). Exploring African American Academic Achievement: Ogbu and Brookover Perspectives. *Journal of African American Men, 12*, 17–32.

Sugai, G., & Horner, R. (2002). Introduction to the special services support in schools on positive behavior. *Journal of Emotional and Behavioral Disorders, 10*(3), 130–136.

Swap, S. M. (1993). *Developing home–school partnerships: From concepts to practice*. New York: Teachers College.

Swartz, E. (2003). Teaching white preservice teachers: Pedagogy for change. *Urban Education, 38*(3), 255–278.

Twale, D. J., & De Luca, B. M. (2008). *Faculty incivility: The rise of the academic bully culture and what to do about it*. San Francisco, CA: Jossey-Bass.

Valentine, P., & Lloyd, A. (1989, March). *Living in Franklin Square: An exploration of black culture*. Paper presented at the annual meeting of the American Educational Research Association, San Francisco.

White, S. (2004). A psychodynamic perspective of workplace bulling: Containment, boundaries and a futile search for recognition. *British Journal of Guidance and Counseling, 32*, 269–280.

Wright, J. D., & Wright, S. R. (1976, June). Social class and parental values for children: A partial replication and extension of the Kohn thesis. *American Sociological Review, 41*, 527–537.

*Good teachers affect eternity; they can never tell where their influence stops.*

**Henry Brooks Adams, American Historian**

# CHAPTER

# 4 Teaching
## Power to Influence

"Real learning does not happen until students are brought into relationship with the teacher, with each other, and with the subject" (Palmer, 1993, p. xvi). As such, teaching is a social influence process. Teachers influence students to learn not only content but also worldviews and approaches for integrating incoming stimuli from the environment. To influence students to learn, teachers are required to understand and then develop students' existing attitudes, beliefs, and behaviors. As such, teachers have the power to inspire and ignite as well as squelch and deplete students' knowledge of self and the surrounding world.

While all teachers in training are taught about the necessity to become masters of their content, it is important to remember that teachers are more than transmitters of information (Cochran-Smith, 2004; Delpit, 1995). They are responsible for helping students learn effective ways to perceive and interpret their observations; to effectively problem solve; and to collaborate with others in working toward significant goals beyond their individual reach.

Teachers influence their students through the depth of content they teach and the quality of contact they make with their students. Teachers must fully realize their influence in their positions of authority as they lead and persuade their students. They affect the lives of their students through all the ways in which they communicate their values and beliefs, not only about their subject matter but also about students, themselves, and the whole enterprise of teaching (Allen, 2002; Carey, 2004). The ways in which teachers communicate content as well as their approaches to living are often consumed by their students without question, ignoring teachers' biases, blind spots, and inadequacies. Because teachers have such great powers of influence, they must examine their dispositions and fundamental expectations for students, thereby identifying deficiencies and biases that could result, not only in misuse of teacher power but also in potential harm to student understanding, motivation, empowerment, and learning (Tschannen-Moran, 2004).

This chapter explores teacher qualities and behaviors that affect student achievement and social adjustment in the classroom.

## CHAPTER OBJECTIVES

1. Identify the effects of teacher expectations on achievement.
2. Describe teacher qualities that affect student achievement.
3. Describe teacher qualities that encourage student psychosocial adjustment.
4. Describe teacher qualities needed to effectively facilitate empowerment and learning of minority students.

## BEYOND CONTENT KNOWLEDGE

Expert teachers most certainly have a command over their subject area, but, in addition to being a storehouse of knowledge, expert teachers have effective systems for understanding the process of and problems encountered in teaching and learning (Blankenstein, 2004; Brown, 2002). For example, effective teachers are adaptable and flexible in their approaches. They can adjust lesson plans, knowing they are but one road map to desired learning outcomes. The expert teacher understands there is more than one way to approach a topic, develop a test, and engage students in the learning process (Rice, 2003; Rockoff, 2004).

In addition to having pedagogical content knowledge, expert teachers have specific personal qualities and interpersonal skills that contribute to their effectiveness (see Entwistle & Tait, 1990; Lowman & Mathie, 1993; Ramsden, 1992; Swartz, White, & Stuck, 1990). **Pedagogical content knowledge** involves the blending of subject content knowledge and pedagogy into an understanding of how particular topics, problems, or issues are organized, represented, and adapted to the diverse interests and abilities of learners and are presented for instruction. Successful teachers exhibit pedagogical content knowledge; establish interpersonal rapport; exhibit enthusiasm; and demonstrate respect for their students as well as a comprehensive knowledge of learner development, student diversity, and intercultural competence.

## EFFECTS OF TEACHER EXPECTATIONS

Most teachers claim to hold high expectations for all students. In reality, however, that is often not the case. While some teachers maintain uniformly high expectations for all students, others have "great expectations" for some students but low expectations for others—particularly low-income and minority students. For these students the current ceiling "is really much closer to where the floor ought to be" (Hilliard, 1991). As such, there is great disparity between what youngsters are capable of learning and what they actually learn (Bishop, 1989). Bamburg (1994) noted that the expectations teachers have for their students and the assumptions teachers make about potentials have tangible effects on student achievement—playing a significant role in determining how well and how much students learn. Students tend to internalize the beliefs teachers have about their ability and they rise and fall in achieving the level of expectation of their teachers (Raffini, 1993).

When students are viewed as lacking in ability or motivation and are not expected to make significant progress, they tend to adopt this perception of themselves. In particular, when low-income and minority students discover that their teachers consider them incapable of handling demanding work, they match those expectations with their school performance (Gonder, 1991). Teachers' expectations for students— whether high or low—can become a **self-fulfilling prophecy**. That is, students tend to give to teachers as much or as little as teachers expect of them. Pohan (1996) noted, "Differential expectations lead to differential treatment, which results in differential student outcomes" (p. 5). Teacher beliefs influence the type of activities in which students are engaged, the feedback students receive, and the degree of interaction that takes place between teachers and students. It is, therefore, important to examine teachers' beliefs and the effects of these beliefs on classroom practices and most importantly, the academic achievement of their students (Jones, 2004).

## TEACHER QUALITY AND DIVERSITY

Effective teachers must not only have knowledge of cultural diversity but also a knowledge of their own cultural backgrounds and embedded preconceived assumptions and biases. **Cultural Consciousness** is the condition of being conscious of *culture,* the lens through which we view and interpret the world, as a human construct subject to human choice. Teachers must become conscious and self-aware of their cultural underpinnings, worldviews, and preconceived notions about groups of people, and be vigilant in their pursuit of knowledge about diverse cultural groups in society in order to develop cultural consciousness.

Teachers' self-reflection and development of cultural consciousness are imperative for improving the educational opportunities and outcomes for minority students (Gay & Kirkland, 2003; Wayne & Young, 2003). To be effective in multicultural classrooms, teachers must be committed to becoming more aware of who they are as people and what they believe, and be willing to identify and question their cultural assumptions (Gay, 2002; Ladson-Billings, 2001). Without reflecting on one's own perspectives, biases, and relative position in society, little more than good intentions to value diversity can be delivered.

A number of researchers have suggested the importance of personal reflection and self-assessment for working effectively with culturally diverse students. Gorski (1997), for example, called for teachers to reflect on their experiences and assess their attitudes, prejudices, and values as they relate to dealing with people from different ethnic groups. Banks et al. (2001) noted that in order for teachers to respond sensitively to the cultural diversity in their classrooms, they must look first at their own cultural backgrounds and understand how their biases affect their interactions with students. It is clear that to be effective teachers need to develop a personal and professional code of ethics and cultural consciousness that reflects respect and appreciation for racial, gender, social class, sexual orientation, and ethnic diversity. Only through the development of such a code of ethics and heightened consciousness will they be able to develop intercultural competence and enact culturally responsive teaching (Exposito & Favela, 2003; Gay & Kirkland, 2003).

An excellent example of this type of reflection has been offered by Frank (2002), a White, middle-class female in U.S. society. Frank noted that her attitudes, behaviors, and words needed to reflect and embody humanity, not just those who "looked" like her. She described how she opened herself to the challenges offered by others who were not like her. Challenges not only to her thinking and her assumptions but also to her behavior were addressed to provide her with cultural insight. She highlighted the importance of understanding who she is, not just in terms of labels but also in terms of her relative place in society and the privileges it affords. Exercise 4-1 will help you begin this process of self-reflection.

## RACIAL IDENTITY DEVELOPMENT

Frank's (2002) reflections are poignant. They are also prescriptive in that they remind us that teachers must reflect on their own racial identities and how they are affected by racism in society (see Chapter 1, Tables 1-1 and 1-2) in order to enrich their interactions with diverse others. And, while the stages of racial identity development do not necessarily occur chronologically or in a strict linear fashion, as noted in Chapter 1, they are believed to include most racial interaction patterns involving minority group members and dominant culture in the United States. Racial identity development is, therefore, another factor that affects differences in teachers' comfort levels and abilities to interact effectively with students from different racial groups (Adams, 1997). As such, it is recommended that teachers reflect on their own evolution through the racial identity development models (be they members of dominant or minority groups) as they seek to discover their own intercultural strengths and limitations. The value of reflection on one's racial attitudes and racial consciousness is immense. It provides teachers with increasingly more awareness of what they feel and believe about student diversity, where these thoughts and feelings might come from, what realities of humanity are not seen, and what privileges are given to some individuals yet denied to others (Frank, 2002). This value of self-reflection is reinforced in Exercise 4-2.

## MEANS OF INFLUENCE

### Maintaining High Expectations and Enthusiasm

Research has shown that teachers' expectations for students tend to be self-fulfilling. Brophy (1986) found that effective teachers routinely project attitudes, beliefs, expectations, and attributions that imply that your students share your own enthusiasm for learning. He noted that when teachers treat their students as if they already are eager learners, they will be more likely to become eager learners. Clearly having high expectations does not magically equalize students' innate abilities and learning rates. To accommodate differences among students and help all students achieve mastery without resorting to watering down standards and expectations, teachers should expertly manage three variables: time spent with diverse students, grouping of diverse students, and the utilization of various methodologies for teaching diverse students (Omatani & Omatani, 1996). Teachers must be sensitized to their possible unconscious biases and heighten their awareness of the detrimental effects of holding differential expectations for students. Teachers who view intelligence as dynamic and fluid rather than static and unchanging are less likely

## EXERCISE 4-1    Classroom Applications: Roundtable Feedback

**Directions:** In groups of eight students or less, sit in a circle with your group members. Review the following guidelines before you begin the discussion.

### Discussion Guidelines

1. A group member volunteers to share an issue of concern for her or him related to diversity (for example, "I don't know much about people from different groups. I fear I will not be an effective teacher of diverse students because of this," or "I am not patient when I hear accents that are different from my own. I find myself tuning out and even thinking negatively about people who speak with an accent.").

2. That same group member shares his or her concern and then asks the group for specific feedback related to the concern (for example, "I would like to know what you would think of a teacher who does not have much experience with diversity," or "Please give me suggestions to help me change this behavior.").

3. Before other members of the group provide the feedback requested, they may each ask one question to clarify the request and make sure they will provide the feedback requested. During this go-round at which members seek clarification about the request for feedback, the group member with the concern answers the questions posed as succinctly as possible and does not add additional information that is not queried.

4. After the clarification round is complete, each group member provides the feedback requested in as honest and yet constructive manner as possible. It is helpful to begin by saying, "If I were experiencing this concern, I would ..." or "If I encountered this behavior, I'd feel distanced from that person because ...," and so on.

5. It is very important that the person who is seeking the feedback NOT be allowed to comment when each group member provides her/his feedback. No questions may be asked at this point, and no responses to the feedback may be given. The only activity that should go on at this point is each member sharing honestly and sensitively while the person who is seeking feedback silently listens and writes down what is communicated.

6. After all group members have provided feedback, the person seeking feedback should respond to all the feedback provided. Using the notes he or she took when each group member provided feedback, the person seeking feedback should first thank the group for taking time and energy to think about and respond honestly to his or her concern and then tell each member how he or she intends to use the feedback provided.

This activity will take at least 40 minutes to complete. In order for each person in the group to have an opportunity to experience this wonderful opportunity to gain self-reflection and feedback utilization skills, this activity should be repeated enough number of times throughout the semester that every group member has an opportunity to share a concern.

---

to have rigid preconceived notions about what students will or will not be able to achieve. In addition, teachers and administrators who maintain high expectations, encourage in students a desire to aim high rather than to slide by. To expect less is to create conditions for weakened self-concept among their students and student underachievement.

The maintenance of high expectations is enhanced by teacher enthusiasm. Brophy and Evertson (1976) found that successful teachers see teaching as an interesting and worthwhile challenge and display enthusiasm for their job, students, and the possibilities of learning. They embrace problems as they arise and believe that solutions can be found, whereas teachers with low self-efficacy see teaching as a chore to be endured—a dull and often unpleasant job requiring patience (waiting for students to finally catch on) rather than enthusiastically seeking new ways to

## EXERCISE 4-2    Classroom Application: The Value of Reflection

**Directions:** As noted, it is important to understand who you are, not just in terms of labels but in terms of your relative position in U.S. society and the privileges and advantages that you experience based on that position. The goal of this exercise is to help you become more aware and sensitive to what is given freely to you and denied to others who are different from you.

1. In the chart you will find a listing of identity categories. Identify how you fit within each category and then identify one of the social benefits that may accompany each characteristic. Share your reflections with someone who is culturally different from you.

| Category | Your Personal Identification | What Benefits Are Afforded? | What Challenges or Disadvantages Are Encountered? |
|---|---|---|---|
| Gender | | | |
| Social class | | | |
| Profession | | | |
| Cultural group | | | |
| Physicality (height/weight) | | | |
| Ethnicity | | | |
| Educational background | | | |
| Couple status | | | |
| Sexual orientation | | | |
| Age | | | |

## EXERCISE 4-2    Continued

| Category | Your Personal Identification | What Benefits Are Afforded? | What Challenges or Disadvantages Are Encountered? |
|---|---|---|---|
| Disability status | | | |
| Language(s) spoken | | | |

2. After completing the first two columns, go back and identify challenges or disadvantages that you experience and feelings you have that are associated with these disadvantages. Consider what you would want teachers to know and do to address the disadvantages you have identified.

reach students. When confronted with difficulties, these teachers often give up, shedding the responsibility for student learning and blaming their students for not learning. These teachers do not believe that they can make a difference, have generally low expectations (particularly for low-achieving students), and as a result exhibit little enthusiasm for engaging in the process of teaching and reaching students. The idea that enthusiasm can be "catching" certainly applies to classroom dynamics. Research suggests that teachers who are enthusiastic about their subjects not only increase student achievement but also facilitate their students' enthusiasm in the learning process, sense of self-confidence, and self-efficacy (Perry, 1985; Perry, Magnusson, Parsonson, & Dickens, 1986).

The value of teacher self-efficacy and enthusiasm as it relates to student motivation and academic self-concept is highlighted in Personal Narrative 4-1, which explains the story of Annesah, an Indian writer working in northern California.

## MAKING CONNECTIONS WITH STUDENTS: EMPATHY AND CARE

As highlighted in Chapter 3, research has demonstrated that students tend to be motivated and to achieve at higher levels when they are educated in safe, trustworthy, and supportive environments—school climates created by teachers who exhibit care and empathy for their students individually (Brown & Atkins, 1993; McCombs, 1998). Effective teachers realize and value the fact that they do not teach mathematics or literature or social studies; instead, they teach *students*. These teachers value the uniqueness of each student and are committed to their students' growth and development. They are teachers who (1) show respect, (2) value individuality, (3) understand students' learning styles and barriers, (4) extend themselves to find ways to engage students in learning, and (5) extend themselves to let students know that they want to authentically join with the students as partners in

## Personal Narrative 4-1    Annesah: Enthusiasm and Efficacy

I was never really a star student. I did okay. I was one of the kids that went through school doing the minimum, never a problem or a concern … just not investing much of myself in the process of learning. School wasn't my thing.

Well, at least not for the first eight years! Now with my master's in English and working for a large newspaper on the West Coast as a freelance writer, I guess writing and education *is* my thing, and I owe it all to Mr. Peter Duncan, my ninth-grade English teacher.

Mr. Duncan was hard—real hard. He gave us lots of vocabulary words to master every evening, he made us produce essays weekly, and each marking period he assigned extensive research papers. Mr. Duncan was very hard, and he would accept nothing but our best. Hand in something that was done at the last minute? He would smile, thank you for the "draft," and assign a new deadline for the finished product. We all became familiar with the "draft," and while we moaned and groaned, I would bet there is not one of his students who doesn't think he was the greatest.

Mr. Duncan had excellent credentials. He also had 15 years of teaching experience when I first met him. But, truthfully, it wasn't his knowledge or his competence in presenting lessons that opened my heart and mind to the joy of writing. It was his enthusiasm.

Mr. Duncan would light up whenever he read a well-written passage. He would become really excited when a student would incorporate word play or skillfully employ a fitting metaphor. It was impossible not to be excited in his class. It wasn't an act. He was so genuine and into it. It was a privilege to attend his classes, although I didn't realize that then. You could tell that he loved literature; he loved poetry and well-written prose. But, most importantly, he loved to watch us grow! He loved to challenge us to greater achievement and would encourage and support us along the way, using a myriad of creative projects, including field trips, plays, and music.

Mr. Duncan's enthusiasm inspired us. He would celebrate our rewrites, he would extol our accomplishments, and he would publicly affirm our efforts. But for me, the most important thing he did was to simply believe in me. He saw in me the ability to express myself and my view of the world in words well before I knew who I was or what my worldview entailed. He saw me before I saw myself, and his excitement in my discoveries made me want to discover that much more.

Mr. Duncan was more than a competent teacher—he was a man who loved his profession, loved his subject area, and loved sharing it. I benefited, to say the very least!

---

the students' own education (Tileston, 2004; Bosworth, 1995). Effective teachers maintain and continually develop these personal characteristics in efforts to help their students connect with them, other students, and the subject matter taught (Black & Howard-Jones, 2000; Davis, 2007). Exercise 4-3 operationalizes these qualities and invites you to reflect on your own experience with caring teachers.

McDermott and Rothenberg (2000), in studying the characteristics of exemplary teachers in low-income urban schools, found that effective urban teachers are those who construct empathic, caring, respectful, and trusting relationships with students and their families. In their study, effective teachers valued students' ideas. This valuing was demonstrated in the way they accommodated students' input in the teaching process. In order to build trusting, respectful relationships, teachers must understand the individuality of each student and vital teacher–learner relationship dynamics (McDiarmid, 1991). One interesting approach to developing this understanding was described by Giroux (1993). Giroux suggested that teachers must listen critically to the voices of their students. He noted that "teachers become border-crossers through their ability to not only make different narratives available

## EXERCISE 4-3    Point of Reflection: A Caring Teacher

*Directions:* The purpose of this brief exercise is to help you connect your personal experience to the concept and value of caring as a teacher trait. The exercise is best performed with a partner or classmate.

1. As quickly as possible, attempt to identify, by name and grade, five teachers you had in your K-12 education.
2. Using a scale of 1 to 10, with 1 indicating "least effective" and 10 indicating "most effective," assess each of the teachers listed on a scale of teacher effectiveness.
3. For each of the following, identify a teacher who best represents the statement.
    a. This teacher would spend time outside of class getting to know students.
    b. This teacher would make time to ask how students were.
    c. This teacher would praise students for their efforts.
    d. This teacher would make sure students knew that their contributions were valuable, even when their responses to academic questions were incorrect.
    e. This teacher would use soft reprimands (private) rather than publicly reprimanding students for misbehavior.
    f. This teacher seemed to know what students were saying even when they struggled to "get it out" when they participated in class.
    g. In class discussion, this teacher tried to encourage all ideas and perspectives on issues discussed.
    h. This teacher showed little favoritism based on gender, class, race, disability, sexual orientation, or ethnicity,
    i. Even when correcting students, this teacher made them feel that it was their behavior, not the students as people, that was being corrected.

4. Did you notice that one or two teachers' names kept appearing on your list? Were the names that appeared most often also of teachers with higher effectiveness scores? The items listed in #3 are characteristics of a caring teacher. Share your observations with your instructor and classmates in small-group discussion and see if their "caring teachers" were also those identified as most effective. Then list qualities you have already that will lead to your becoming a caring teacher.

### For Further Reflection

Obtain and view the movie *Stand and Deliver.* Write a reflection about what you learned regarding caring and effective teacher attitudes and actions from Jaime Escalante as his true-life story is depicted in the movie.

to themselves and other students but also by legitimating difference as a basic condition for understanding the limits of one's own voice" (p. 170). Both teachers and students benefit from this process of "border-crossing" by encountering different perspectives and therefore expanding their knowledge of others and their worldviews.

## FROM CONCEPTS TO LIVED EXPERIENCE

With knowledge and skill, the classroom teacher can positively influence the lives of those in his or her charge. Research has shown that not only content expertise but also teacher quality variables and the values teachers embody reach and teach students. We may never be sure of the full impact teachers have, but when teachers are committed to developing their self-awareness and cultural consciousness, they will enliven, empower, and educate their students to achieve at higher levels. Read the following "best teacher" descriptions to get an idea of the power and influence teachers can exercise.

- *My best teacher ever was my Geography teacher in 8th grade. Why? Because we did projects! And I wrote about India and I have never forgotten what I learned … Maybe that is why I embrace the subject today. He brought to life the culture by letting me become part of it. He also listened to us and was always ready with a kind word. So in my opinion the best teacher is the teacher who listens to his/her pupils. I mean really listens!!!*
- *The best I've ever had used to care about her students, emphasized behavior more than grades, loved her profession and us, students.*
- *My favorite teacher was my freshman math teacher. He was one of the goofiest people I ever knew, but incredibly nice and you could really tell he cared about the subject and all of his students. His class was always the best—I felt most comfortable in the environment he set up and it was fun every day. I had hated math up until that point, but he taught me to love it! He was always so clear in his explanations and I could always understand what he was trying to get at. He always came into the classroom bring a positive attitude that set us all going.*

## SUMMARY

**Teaching: The Power to Influence** Teachers influence students to learn not only content but also worldviews and approaches for integrating incoming stimuli from the environment. To influence students to learn, teachers are required to understand and then develop students' existing attitudes, beliefs, and behaviors. As such, teachers have the power to inspire and ignite and to squelch and deplete knowledge of self and the surrounding world.

**More than Content** Successful teachers exhibit pedagogical content knowledge; establish interpersonal rapport; exhibit enthusiasm; and demonstrate respect for their students as well as a comprehensive knowledge of learner development, student diversity, and intercultural competence.

**Effects of Teacher Expectations** The expectations teachers have for their students and the assumptions they make about their potential have tangible effects on student achievement—playing a significant role in determining how well and how much students learn. Students tend to

internalize the beliefs teachers have about their ability and they rise and fall in achieving the level of expectation of their teachers.

**Teacher Quality and Diversity** Effective teachers must not only have knowledge of cultural diversity but also a knowledge of their own cultural backgrounds and embedded preconceived assumptions and biases. Teachers must become aware of their cultural underpinnings, worldviews, preconceived notions about groups of people, and be vigilant in their pursuit of knowledge about diverse cultural groups in society in order to develop cultural consciousness. Teachers' self-reflection and development of cultural consciousness are imperative for improving the educational opportunities and outcomes for minority students.

**Valuing Self-Awareness and Reflection** To be effective, teachers must know and be interested in becoming more aware of who they are as people and what they believe, including the identification and questioning of their biases and assumptions. Otherwise, their differential expectations for students will lead to differential treatment, which results in differential student outcomes. In order for teachers to respond sensitively to the cultural diversity in their classrooms, they must first look at their own cultural backgrounds and understand how their biases affect their interactions with students.

### Maintaining High Expectations and Enthusiasm

Research has shown that teachers' expectations for students tend to be self-fulfilling. Brophy (1986) found that effective teachers routinely project attitudes, beliefs, expectations, and attributions that imply that their students share their own enthusiasm for learning. He noted that the extent that teachers treat their students as if they already are eager learners, they will be more likely to become eager learners. In addition, successful teachers see teaching as an interesting and worthwhile challenge displaying enthusiasm for their job, students, and the possibilities of learning.

### Modeling Enthusiasm

**Teacher Racial Identity Development** Teachers' racial identity development is another factor that affects differences in their comfort levels and abilities to interact effectively with students from different racial groups.

**Making Connections through Empathy and Care** Research has demonstrated that students tend to be more motivated and as a result more achieving when they are educated in safe, trustworthy, and supportive environments, with teachers who exhibit care and concern for each student individually. Effective teachers value students as coequal human beings sharing in the process of education. Such valuing requires a teacher to demonstrate a deep nonjudgmental respect for the thoughts, feelings, and potentials that each student brings to the classroom.

## Questions for Review

1. It's often said that teachers have very little power in society. In what ways do teachers have significant (often unrecognized) power?

2. What are important components of cultural consciousness for educators?

3. What are teacher qualities that have direct effects on student achievement?

## Important Terms

cultural consciousness       pedagogical content             self-fulfilling prophecy
                             knowledge

## Activities

Teachers are a powerful force in students' academic development and the formation of a child's sense of personal efficacy and worth. They select and employ strategies and behaviors that give shape to students' academic achievement and sense of self. Sometimes, these influences are less clear or intentional to the teacher who manifests them. The following are a series of field-experience questions related to the topics addressed in this chapter. Use them to guide a classroom observation. Share your experience with your instructor and classmates in small-group discussion.

1. In observing a classroom, imagine yourself in the place of various students in the class. How do you feel as the smart student? The student failing to know the answers to

questions? The talkative student? The minority student?

2. What are the teacher's expectations for dominant-culture and diverse students? Are there differential expectations? Do you see evidence of self-fulfilling prophecy?

3. How are warmth and caring demonstrated or not demonstrated in the classroom? Is teacher warmth and caring dependent on performance or given freely to all students?

4. How does the teacher respond to challenges coming from students? How does the teacher handle difference of opinions in the classroom?

5. How is teacher enthusiasm expressed or not expressed? Is enthusiasm tied to material? Content? Teaching activity? What effect does the teacher's level of enthusiasm have on the students? Is it "catching"?

## Enrichment

Bucher, R. D. (2000). *Diversity consciousness: Opening our minds to people, cultures, and opportunities*. Upper Saddle River, NJ: Prentice Hall.

Davis, B. M. (2007). *How to teach students who don't look like you: Culturally relevant teaching strategies*. Thousand Oaks, CA: Corwin Press.

Howard, G. R. (1999). *We can't teach what we don't know: White teachers, multiracial schools*. New York: Teachers College.

Sarason, S. (1990). *The predictable failure of educational reform: Can we change course before it's too late?* San Francisco: Jossey Bass.

Schunk, D. H. (1995). Self-efficacy and education and instruction. In J. E. Maddus (Ed.), *Self-efficacy, adaptation and adjustment* (pp. 213–278). New York: Plenum.

Sheets, R. H. (2000). Advancing the field or taking centre stage: The White movement in multicultural education. *Educational Researcher*, 29, 15–21.

Singham, M. (1998). The canary in the mine: The achievement gap between black and white students. *Phi Delta Kappan*, 80, 9–15.

Tatum, B. D. (1997). *"Why are all the black kids sitting together in the cafeteria?" and other conversations about race. A psychologist explains the development of racial identity*. New York: Basic Books.

Wentzel, K. R. (2002). Are effective teachers like good parents? Teaching styles and student adjustment in early adolescence. *Child Development*, 73(1), 287–302.

Weinstein, R. S. (1998). Promoting positive expectations in schooling. In N. M. Lambert & B. L. McComb (Eds.), *How students learn: Reforming schools through learner-centered education* (pp. 81–111). Washington, DC: American Psychological Association.

Young, B. N., Whitley, M. E., & Helton, C. (1998). *Students' perceptions of characteristics of effective teachers* (ERIC Document Reproduction Service No. ED426962).

## Connections on the Web

http://www2.ed.gov/admins/lead/account/saa.html

This No Child Left Behind website features standards, laws, policies, and resources that can be used to address school and teaching deficiencies and to identify improvement guidelines for effective instruction of diverse learners.

http://ncee.education.ucsb.edu/discussionareas .htm

> The National Coalition for Equity in Education provides information on classroom practice, curricula, and climate as they impact equity in education.

http://www.nwrel.org/request/octOO/textonly .html

> This booklet from the Northwest Regional Educational Laboratory provides insight into the role of teacher and factors in teaching that influence student achievement.

## References

Adams, M. (1997). Pedagogical frameworks for social justice education. In M. Adams, L. A. Bell, & P. Griffin (Eds.), *Teaching for diversity and social justice: A sourcebook*. New York: Routledge.

Allen, R. (2002). *Impact teaching*. New York: Allyn & Bacon.

Bamburg, J. (1994). *Raising expectations to improve student learning*. Oak Brook, IL: North Central Regional Educational Laboratory. ED 378 290.

Banks, J. A., Cookson, P., Gay, G., Hawley, W. D., Irvine, J. J., Nieto, S., et al. (2001). Diversity within unity: Essential principles for teaching and learning in a multicultural society. *Phi Delta Kappan*, 83(3), 196–203.

Blankenstein, A. M. (2004). *Failure is NOT an option: Six principles that guide student achievement in high-performing schools*. Thousand Oaks, CA: Corwin Press.

Bishop, J. (1989). Motivating students to study: Expectations, rewards, achievement. *NASSP Bulletin*, 27–38. EJ 398 995.

Black, R. S., & Howard-Jones, A. (2000). Reflections on best and worst teachers: An experiential perspective of teaching. *Journal of Research and Development in Education*, 34(1), 1–13.

Bosworth, K. (1995). Caring for others and being cared for: Students talk about caring in school. *Phi Delta Kappan*, 76, 686–693.

Brophy, J. (1986). *On motivating students*. East Lansing, MI: Institute for Research on Teaching, Michigan State University. ED 276 724.

Brophy, J., & Evertson, C. (1976). *Learning from teaching: A developmental perspective*. Boston: Allyn & Bacon.

Brown, D. F. (2002). *Becoming a successful urban teacher*. Portsmouth, NH: Heinemann.

Brown, G., & Atkins, M. (1993). *Effective teaching in higher education*. London: Routledge.

Bruning, R., Schraw, G., & Ronning, R. (1995). *Cognitive psychology and instruction* (2nd ed.). Upper Saddle River, NJ: Prentice Hall.

Carey, K. (2004). *The real value of teachers: Using new information about teacher effectiveness to close the achievement gap*. Washington, DC: The Education Trust.

Cochran-Smith, M. (2004). *Walking the road: Race, diversity, and social justice in teacher education*. New York: Teachers College.

Davis, B. M. (2007). *How to teach students who don't look like you: Culturally relevant teaching strategies*. Thousand Oaks, CA: Corwin Press.

Delpit, L. (1995). *Other people's children: Cultural conflict in the classroom*. New York: New Press.

Entwistle, N. J., & Tait, H. (1990). Approaches to learning, evaluations of teaching, and preferences for contrasting academic environments. *Higher Education*, 19, 169–194.

Exposito, S., & Favela, A. (2003). Reflective voices: Valuing immigrant students and teaching with ideological clarity. *Urban Review*, 35(1), 73–91.

Frank, J. L. H. (2002). My voice is changing. *Multicultural Perspectives*, 4(1), 41–44.

Gay, G. (2002). Preparing for culturally responsive teaching. *Journal of Teacher Education*, 53(2), 106–116.

Gay, G., & Kirkland, K. (2003). Developing cultural critical consciousness and self-reflection in pre-service teacher education. *Theory into Practice*, 42(3), 109–135.

Giroux, H. (1993). *Border crossings*. New York: Routledge.

Giroux, H. (1999). Rewriting the discourse of racial identity: Toward a pedagogy and politics of whiteness. In C. Clark & J. O'Donnell (Eds.), *Becoming and unbecoming white* (pp. 224–252). Westport, CT: Bergin & Garvey.

Gonder, P. O. (1991). *Caught in the middle: How to unleash the potential of average students*. Arlington, VA: American Association of School Administrators. ED 358 554.

Gorski, P. (1997). *Initial thoughts on multicultural education-multicultural pavilion*. New York: Macmillan.

Helms, J. E. (1995). An update of Helm's White and people of color racial identity development. In J. G. Ponterotto, J. M. Casas, L. A. Suzuki, & C. M. Alexander (Eds.), *Handbook of multicultural counseling* (pp. 181–198). Thousand Oaks, CA: Sage.

Hilliard III, A. (1991). Do we have the will to educate all children? *Educational Leadership*, 49(1), 31–36. EJ 432 688.

Jones, H. (2004, March). A research-based approach to teaching to diversity. *Instructional Psychology*, 31(1), 18–25.

Kagan, D. (1992). Professional growth among pre-service and beginning teachers. *Review of Educational Research*, 62, 129–169.

Ladson-Billings, G. (2001). *Crossing over to Canaan: The journey of new teachers in diverse classrooms*. San Francisco: Jossey Bass.

Lowman, J., & Mathie, V. A. (1993). What should graduate teaching assistants know about teaching? *Teaching of Psychology*, 20, 84–88.

McAvin, M. W., & Gordon, L. V. (1981, October). Attributions of interpersonal values and teaching effectiveness. *Psychological Reports*, 49(2), 539–542.

McCombs, R. (1998). Integrating metacognition, affect, and motivation in improving teacher education. In N. Lambert & B. McCombs (Eds.), *How students learn: Reforming school through learner-centered education* (pp. 379–408). Washington, DC: American Psychological Association.

McDermott, P., & Rothenberg, J. (2000). *The characteristics of effective teachers in high poverty schools—triangulating our data* (ERIC Document Reproduction Service No. ED442887)

McDiarmid, G. W. (1991). What teachers need to know about cultural diversity: Restoring subject matter to the picture. In M. M. Kennedy (Ed.), *Teaching academic subjects to diverse learners* (pp. 257–269). New York: Teachers College.

McIntosh, P. (1998). White privilege: Unpacking the invisible knapsack. In P. S. Rothenberg (Ed.), *Race, class, and gender in the United States: An integrated study* (4th ed., pp. 87–143). New York: St. Martin's.

Omotani, B. J., & Omotani, L. (1996). Expect the best: How your teachers can help all children learn. *The Executive Educator*, 18, 8, 27–31. EJ 519 766.

Palmer, P. J. (1993). *To know as we are known: Education as a spiritual journey*. San Francisco: Harper & Row.

Perry, R. (1985). Instructor expressive: Implications for improving teaching. In J. Donald & A. Sullivan (Eds.), *Using research to improve teaching* (pp. 35–49). San Francisco: Jossey Bass.

Perry, R., Magnusson, J., Parsonson, K., & Dickens, W. (1986). Perceived control in college classroom: Limitations in instructor expressiveness due to noncontingent feedback and lecture content. *Journal of Educational Psychology*, 78, 96–107.

Pohan, C. A. (1996). Preservice teachers' beliefs about diversity. Uncovering factors leading to multicultural responsiveness. *Equity and Excellence in Education*, 29(3), 62–69.

Raffini, J. (1993). *Winners without losers: Structures and strategies for increasing student motivation to learn*. Needham Heights, MA: Allyn and Bacon. ED 362 952.

Ramsden, P. (1992). *Learning to teach in higher education*. London: Routledge.

Rice, J. K. (2003). *Teacher quality: Understanding the effectiveness of teacher attributes*. Washington, DC: Economic Policy Institute.

Rockoff, J. (2004). The impact of individual teachers on student achievement: Evidence from panel data. *American Economic Review*, 94(2), 247–252.

Swartz, C. W., White, K. P., & Stuck, G. B. (1990). The factorial structure of the North Carolina Teacher Performance Appraisal Instrument. *Educational and Psychological Measurement*, 50, 175–185.

Tileston, D. W. (2004). *What every teacher should know about diverse learners*. Thousand Oaks, CA: Corwin Press.

Tschannen-Moran, M. (2004). *Trust matters: Leadership for successful schools*. San Francisco, CA: Jossey-Bass.

Wayne, A. M., & Young, P. (2003). Teacher characteristics and student achievement gains: A review. *Review of Educational Leadership*, 73(1), 89–122.

# Minority Voices

Personal Narratives for Gaining Cultural Insight

*I am an Indian; and while I have learned much from civilization, I have never lost my Indian sense of right and justice. When I reduce civilization to its most basic terms, it becomes a system based on trade. Each man stakes his powers, the product of his labor, his social, political, and religious standing against his neighbor. To gain what? To gain control over his fellow workers and the results of their labor. Is there not something worthy of perpetuation in our Indian spirit of democracy, where Earth, our mother, was free to all, and no one sought to impoverish or enslave his neighbor? Where the good things of Earth were not ours to hold against our brothers and sisters, but were ours to use and enjoy together with them, and with whom it was our privilege to share?*

**Ohiyesa, quoted in The Wisdom of the Native Americans, pp. 132–133.**

CHAPTER

# Learning from Native American Stories

U.S. society and schools emphasize individualism, competition, and consumption. The traditional Native American value for humans to live as companions with all other living things and serve as stewards rather than owners of the earth signifies a fundamental difference in approach to life and education between Native Americans and dominant-culture individuals in the United States.

The values underlying Ohiyesa's words and the impact such values have on the perspectives and experiences of people who share similar values are the focus of this chapter. This chapter features views, barriers, strengths, and lived experiences of Native Americans. It highlights values, traditions, and worldviews of Native peoples as they come to bear on their orientation to and relationship with U.S. schools and society.

As explained in the Preface of this book, this chapter and the seven chapters that follow are organized around six cultural factors that identify different aspects of culture that are used in this text to structure categories of information about each of the marginalized groups presented. These factors include (1) the historical and current treatment of the cultural group in the United States; (2) initial terms of incorporation of the group into the United States; (3) commonly shared values and traditions of the cultural group; (4) the group's view of spirituality (including the group's view of humans' relation to nature and temporal focus of life); (5) group acculturation patterns and experiences with exclusion and alienation; and (6) language differences, strengths, and challenges of the group. In the personal narratives that present the voices of members of this group, you will be able to identify cultural values that have helped to shape individuals' views and decisions as well as barriers experienced in learning–teaching relationships encountered by group members in their interactions with dominant-culture teachers and schools and associated cultural group members' coping strategies for addressing oppression.

## CHAPTER OBJECTIVES

1. Describe the early experiences of Native Americans in the United States.
2. Describe salient values commonly held by traditional Native Americans.
3. Identify how the people, profiled in the personal narratives, experienced and addressed the six cultural factors explored in this text.
4. Explain academic and intercultural interaction implications related to the six cultural factors for members in this ethnic group.
5. Describe coping strategies commonly utilized by members of this group.
6. Identify classroom strategies for cultivating the resources provided when traditional Native American worldviews are integrated into the curriculum.

## CULTURAL FACTOR 1: HISTORICAL AND CURRENT TREATMENT IN THE UNITED STATES

Historically, dominant culture in the United States, including federal laws, policies, and institutions (e.g., schools, churches, agencies), has deliberately attempted to destroy and eliminate Native American culture and cultural institutions (Lame Deer & Erodes, 1972; Metcalf, 1979). Chief Seattle's famous speech given in December 1853 on the shores of what is now the state of Washington is one of the most widely quoted and revered speeches ever given. His words have been preserved in many documents (some later reworked by a playwright leading to claims that Chief Seattle did not actually originate the words and ideas present in the speech) as he responded to the words of the newly appointed governor of the Washington territory, Isaac Stevens' endeavoring to facilitate the settling of the area and to remove Native inhabitants so they would not impede the progress of the White settlers. Chief Seattle was a thoughtful man who chose his words carefully—speaking clearly and from the heart—as is the Indian way. A small portion of Chief Seattle's speech, as transcribed by Dr. Henry Smith who was present when the speech was delivered, is reproduced here.

> … Every part of the soil is sacred in the estimation of my people. Every hillside, every valley, every plain and grove, has been hallowed by some sad or happy event in days long vanished. Even the rocks, which seem to be dumb and dead as they swelter in the sun along the silent shore, thrill with memories of stirring events connected with the lives of my people. And the very dust upon which you now stand responds more lovingly to their footsteps than to yours, because it is rich with the blood of our ancestors and our bare feet are conscious of the sympathetic touch … (Chief Seattle of the Suquamish people, quoted in Nerburn, 1999, p. 198).

It is estimated that 3 to 5 million indigenous people lived in North America prior to 1492. Precipitated by deadly contact with Europeans, the indigenous population in America was reduced to 250,000 by 1850 (U.S. Bureau of the Census, 2003).

Ford (1983) identified five stages of U.S. government policy actions toward Native Americans. The first stage involved the removal of Native Americans. Because Native Americans did not make "good" slaves and were from the onset at odds with European individualistic and capitalist orientations, White settlers in North America, from the 17th century to the 1840s, sought to remove Native Americans from North America. Whites immigrating from Europe began to acquire Native-controlled lands by killing Native Americans in large numbers (Tatum, 1997). The next stage involved the relocation of Native Americans to reservations. From 1860 to the late 1920s, White settlers drove Native Americans from their expansive lands in North America and forced them to live on small plots of land (reservations) defined by the U.S. government. Forced to leave their homes, they were denied their ways of living in harmony with nature and their environment. In addition, the U.S. government attempted to civilize Native Americans in order to save the person beneath what they believed was "savage." In concert with the establishment of reservations, the creation of off-reservation boarding schools was one of the major strategies used to facilitate the remaking and acculturation of Native Americans. For over 50 years, schools like the Carlisle Indian School in Carlisle, Pennsylvania, established in 1879, schooled thousands of Native American children who were forcibly removed from their families. With their families too far away to protect and nurture them, Native American children were forced into hard labor and physically, emotionally, and sexually abused by their White holders. They were also forced to deny their cultural heritage. It was not until the 1930s that the U.S. practice of removing Native American children from their families was reversed (Tatum, 1997). The third stage of U.S. government's treatment of Native Americans was that of reorganization. From the 1930s to the 1950s, when the U.S. government permitted schools on reservations, systematic cultural repression was the focus as these schools were used to indoctrinate Native American children to endorse dominant-culture values. The fourth stage, termination, occurred during the 1950s and 1960s. During this period, the U.S. government sought to terminate relations with Native American nations, to end Native Americans' so-called dependence on the federal government, and to integrate acculturated Native Americans into mainstream dominant culture. In the wake of the lack of opportunities to make a living on reservations after having been removed from their land and supports, many Native Americans realized they had to work and live in urban areas in order to make money to survive. Traditional Native American cultural values could not be practiced under these conditions. The upheaval, cultural conflict, isolation from family and support, language barriers, and institutional discrimination they encountered (for which they were vastly unprepared) led to widespread alcoholism, suicide, and death for many (Tatum, 1997). In addition, at this time, large tracts of Native American lands were illegally sold, which further increased their poverty. From the mid-1970s up until the present, the U.S. government has emphasized Native Americans' self-determination. This meant that after the U.S. government denied Native Americans the right to act independently throughout their relations with them, they are now encouraging Native Americans to "fend for themselves" without any government-instituted resources after oppressing them throughout history and depleting all their resources. Native Americans resisted the termination policy that ended in the 1960s which forced the pan-Indian movement that required the federal government to condemn its legalized destructive policies toward Native Americans. In the 1980s and 1990s, legislation that promoted Native American-controlled schools, protected Native American religious freedom, and preserved traditional Native American languages, was passed (Tatum, 1997).

While this phase of self-determination was welcomed by many traditional Native Americans, overwhelming struggles created by generations of oppression and marginalization remain. In fact throughout history, lands, customs, lifestyles, successes and innovations of Native American culture have been either denigrated or denied (Vogel, 1987; Deloria, 2003) to such an extent that even today, the greatest struggles Native Americans face are those of survival and identity. Pulitzer prize-winning author N. Scott Momaday, speaking at a 1992 celebration of the 500th anniversary of Columbus's arrival in the Western Hemisphere, described what life is like for him living in the United States:

> ... how to live in the modern world, how to remain Indian, how to assimilate without ceasing to be Indian, with our languages being lost, at a tremendous rate, poverty is rampant, as is alcoholism. It's a matter of identity. It's thinking about who I am. I grew up on Indian reservations, and then I went away from the Indian world and entered a different context.
>
> But I continue to think of myself as Indian. I write out of that conviction. I think this is what most Indian people are doing today. They go off the Reservation, but they keep an idea of themselves as Indians. That's the trick. (quoted in Tatum, 1997, pp. 148–149)

Attempting to keep alive a sense of one's culture is an enormous task for minority groups who are oppressed and alienated in the United States. And while many works highlight this struggle and evidence the destruction of Native cultures, it must also be noted that there is a tremendous cost to all members of society of lost knowledge and resources when oppression reins. Not only do Native Americans suffer incredibly but opportunities for dominant culture to benefit from Native American and other minority groups' cultural values are also lost. Because Native American tradition encompasses a broad "culture that offers valuable lessons for the contemporary industrial generation in danger of being crushed by the sheer weight of 'civilization,' and [that] therefore often sacrifices the deepest and most meaningful values of life by identifying with an endless series of distracting and often destructive gadgets" (Brown, 1964, p. 9), dominant culture could greatly benefit from its teachings.

The estimated population of American Indians and Alaska Natives is 4.9 million. Members of this ethnic group make up 1.6 percent of the total population. By 2050, it is projected that the population of American Indians and Alaska Natives will number 8.6 million comprising 2 percent of the total population. Only about 20 percent of Native Americans live on reservations. More than half of the population lives in urban areas, and most large cities in the United States have at least 10,000 Native American residents with approximately 50 percent of the Native American population residing west of the Mississippi River. American Indians and Alaska Natives are the largest race or ethnic minority group in five states including Alaska, Montana, North Dakota, Oklahoma, and South Dakota

**Table 5-1**  Largest Native American Reservations in the United States

| Rank | Name | Population |
|------|------|-----------|
| 1. | Navajo Nation (Ariz.–N.M.–Utah) | 175,228 |
| 2. | Cherokee (Okla.) | 104,482 |
| 3. | Creek (Okla.) | 77,253 |
| 4. | Lumbee (N.C.) | 62,327 |
| 5. | Choctaw (Okla.) | 39,984 |
| 6. | Cook Inlet (Alaska) | 35,972 |
| 7. | Chickasaw (Okla.) | 32,372 |
| 8. | Calista (Alaska) | 20,353 |
| 9. | United Houma Nation (La.) | 15,305 |
| 10. | Sealaska (Alaska) | 15,059 |

*Note:* Population listed includes only the American Indian and Alaska Native population, alone or in combination with one or more races. Total population of reservation, which includes non-Indians, is not given. A reservation's total population is sometimes significantly larger than Indian population.

*Source:* U.S. Bureau of the Census, 2000. *Census of Population and Housing: Profiles of General Demographic Characteristics.*

while eleven states have more than 100,000 American Indian and Alaska Native residents. These states are California, Oklahoma, Arizona, Texas, New Mexico, New York, Washington, Florida, North Carolina, Michigan, and Alaska. Combined, these states are home to 61 percent of the nation's American Indian and Alaska Native residents (U.S. Bureau of the Census, 2008).

There are 505 federally recognized tribal entities and an additional 365 state-recognized tribes and bands. Native Americans represent more than 500 different cultural communities defined as *sovereign entities* by the U.S. government. It is conservatively estimated that there are 250 Native groups not recognized by the U.S. government. Table 5-1 lists the 10 largest Native American reservations in the United States.

There are currently about 545,400 American Indian and Alaska Native families living in the United States. The average number of people in an American Indian and Alaska Native family is 3.64. This is larger than the average size of all families (3.2 people) in the United States. Fifty-five percent of American Indian and Alaska Native households have their own homes. The median values of homes owned by American Indians and Alaska Natives is $129,000 and median income of households is $37,815—more than 50 percent of that for Whites in the United States (U.S. Bureau of the Census, 2008).

It is clear that many Native Americans continue to face enormous economic, social, and psychological challenges. The Native American unemployment rate is currently 24.2 percent—a rate that soars above the rates for the total U.S. population at large. High school dropout rates reach 60 percent for Native American schoolchildren (Gade, Hurlburt, & Fuqua, 1986), and Native American adolescent suicides increased 1,000 percent over the past 20 years (Berlin, 1984); Native Americans also show high rates of drug use (Beauvais, 1980) and an alcoholism rate that is double the national average (Bock et al., 1972). Twenty-nine percent of American Indians and Alaska Natives speak a language other than English at home and seventy-six percent of American Indians and Alaska Natives age 25 and older have at least a high school diploma, while only thirteen percent have at least a bachelor's degree.

# CULTURAL FACTOR 2: INITIAL TERMS OF INCORPORATION INTO U.S. SOCIETY

The initial terms of minority group members' incorporation into U.S. society (be it voluntary or involuntary) and the patterns of adaptive responses minority group members exhibit in response to the discriminatory treatment they receive may account for many of the differences in their social adjustment and academic success (Ogbu, 1992). **Voluntary minorities** are those groups of people whose ancestors came to the United States in search of greater economic opportunities. Voluntary minority group members are said to believe that they will succeed in mainstream society through hard work and compliance with authority. These individuals' parents, grandparents, and great-grandparents chose to enter the United States, often favorably comparing the treatment received in the United States with that in their countries of origin. In contrast, **involuntary minorities** are groups whose ancestors suffered slavery or colonization in the United States and who historically have been denied true assimilation into U.S. society. Involuntary minorities are keenly aware of the intergenerational oppression received.

When Europeans arrived in North America in the 1400s, they attempted to make Native Americans their slaves. However, Native Americans' knowledge of the terrain and defiant refusals to be held in bondage resulted in frequent

## Intercultural Communication Strategies for Teachers 5-1

### Classroom Applications: Informing and Inviting

A review of the history of Native Americans highlights their struggle for personal and cultural survival. Their shared cultural history would lead to mistrust of the dominant culture and the anticipated pressure to acculturate at the cost of losing cultural identity. Knowing this can help you create effective learning communities for these students. Specifically, you should do the following:

- Keep in mind that these students and their families bring with them a history of experience with discrimination in schools and in larger society. With these experiences often come caution and mistrust.
- Do not assume that your policies, procedures, and instructional strategies are understood and valued opportunities. Send frequent communications home that invite questions, reactions, and suggestions.
- From the beginning of the school year and throughout the year, remind the students about the importance of bringing their perspective and worldviews into the classroom. Invite them to share their perspectives on the topics discussed and the approaches taken within the classroom.
- Reread the Native American accounts in this chapter. Using this worldview as a cultural lens through which to view relationships and education, how do you envision altering lesson plans you create? Classroom rules and procedures? Style of interacting? Through ongoing reflection such as this, you may find an increased awareness and with it an increased sensitivity to the diversity of your students.

attempted and successful escapes, making Native Americans difficult slaves for Europeans to own (Kolchin, 1993).

The extreme oppression and colonization experienced at the hands of dominant culture in North America led Ogbu (1990) to categorize Native Americans as involuntary minorities. Going a step further, it is not hard to understand that students who are members of involuntary minority groups are more likely than students who are members of voluntary minority groups to reject dominant-culture paths to success and equate compliant behaviors with denying their cultures, in essence, "selling out" their families, culture, and cultural values (Ogbu, 1990). For insight into this phenomenon, consider the experience of Mary Crow Dog. As you read her story, identify the impact school officials' treatment of her had on her academic achievement.

## MARY CROW DOG

And that priest they sent here from Holy Rosary in Pine Ridge because he molested a little girl. You [dominant culture] couldn't think of anything better than dump him on us. All he does is watch young women and girls with that funny smile on his face. Why don't you point him out for an example?

Charlene and I worked on the school newspaper. After all, we had some practice. Every day we went down to Publications. One of the priests acted as the photographer, doing the enlarging and developing. He smelled of chemicals, which has strained his hands yellow. One day he invited Charlene into the darkroom. He was going to teach her developing. She was developed already. She was a big girl compared to him, taller too. Charlene was nicely built, not fat, just rounded. No sharp edges anywhere. All of [a] sudden she rushed out of the darkroom, yelling to me, "Let's get out of here! He's trying to feel me up. That priest is nasty." So there was this too to contend with—sexual harassment. We complained to the student body. The nuns said we just had a dirty mind.

We got a new priest in English. During one of his first classes, he asked one of the boys a certain question. The boy was shy. He spoke poor English, but he had the right answer. The priest told him, "You did not say it right. Correct yourself. Say it over again." The boy got flustered and stammered. He could hardly get out a word. But the priest kept after him: "Didn't you hear? I told you to do the whole thing over. Get it right this time." He kept on and on.

I stood up and said, "Father, don't be doing that. If you go into an Indian's home and try to talk Indian, they might laugh at you and say, 'Do it over correctly. Get it right this time!'" He shouted at me, "Mary, you stay after class. Sit down right now!" I stayed after class, until after the bell. He told me, "Get over here!" He grabbed me by the arm, pushing me against the blackboard, shouting, "Why are you always mocking us? You have no reason to do this." I said, "Sure I do. You were making fun of him. You embarrassed him. He needs strengthening, not weakening. You hurt him. I did not hurt you." He twisted my arm and pushed real hard. I turned around and hit him in the face, giving him a bloody nose. After that, I ran out of the room, slamming the door behind me. He and I went to Sister Bernard's office. I told her, "Today, I quit school. I'm not taking this anymore. None of this treatment. Better give me my diploma. I can't waste any more time on you people."

Sister Bernard looked at me for a long, long time. She said, "All right, Mary Ellen, go home today. Come back in a few days and get your diploma." And that was that. Oddly enough, that priest turned out okay. He taught a class in grammar, orthography,

## EXERCISE 5-1   Point of Reflection: A Young Student's Diary Entry

**Directions:** The following will require you to use your imagination and to let go of your current sense of who and where you are at the present time.

1. Imagine that you are a young Native American between the ages of 8 and 11, and you have just been placed, against your parents' wishes, in a faraway desolate boarding school.

2. Picture a school that has only White teachers, administrators, and staff and mostly White children from Anglo-Saxon, Protestant backgrounds. The school requires a strict dress code requiring the wearing of uniforms and Oxford shoes, along with specified hair lengths and styles and prohibition of makeup or jewelry. Meals are provided on a rigid schedule and consist primarily of dishes and styles of cooking that are unfamiliar to you. Families are permitted to write and call regularly, but visitations are allowed only on designated parent-family days.

3. As you finish your first day in this school, you come to your room and begin to write in your journal. Write a diary entry that describes what it feels like to be a young Native American student living in these conditions who has been taken from family (isolated far from home), had hair and clothes dramatically altered, and been forced to speak only English (a language you don't know). Imagine the extreme living circumstances you encounter and, as you write, describe the feelings you believe might be present in the absence of care and support from your family while coping within a hostile environment.

4. Generate a list of words describing the feelings you, or anyone who is an involuntary minority, might have toward dominant-culture teachers in U.S. schools. How might these feelings affect your achievement?

composition, things like that. I think he wanted more respect in class. He was still young and unsure of himself. But I was there too long. I didn't feel like hearing it. Later he became a good friend to the Indians, a personal friend of myself and my husband. He stood up for us during Wounded Knee and after. He stood up to his superiors, stuck his neck way out, became a real people's priest. He even learned our language. He died prematurely of cancer. It is not only the good Indians who die young, but the good [W]hites, too. It is the timid ones who know how to take care of themselves who grow old. I am still grateful to that priest for what he did for us later and for the quarrel he picked with me—or did I pick it with him?—because it ended a situation which had become unendurable for me. The day of my fight with him was my last day in school. (Crow Dog & Erodes, 1990, pp. 39–41)

Exercise 5-1 will provide you with the opportunity to imagine yourself in the place of a young Native American student as she experiences the harsh reality of Native American relocation in the United States.

## CULTURAL FACTOR 3: SHARED VALUES AND TRADITIONS

Because of the large number of tribes and languages spoken, it is important to realize the tremendous diversity among Native Americans (Attneave, 1982; Manson, 1986). Even with this caveat, it is possible to identify similarities in values that exist across tribes and regions (Blanchard & Mackey, 1971; Lazarus, 1982; National Indian Child Abuse and Neglect Resource Center, 1980; Richardson, 1981; Trimble, 1981).

The values of traditional Native American culture arose primarily (but not exclusively) within the context of a nomadic hunting and gathering economy that has been almost completely destroyed. As with African Americans, Asian Americans, and Latinos, extended-family and kinship obligations are considered very important for Native Americans. Therefore, group needs are commonly seen as more significant than individual needs. Communal sharing with those who have less is generally expected and rewarded in Native American culture (Sutton & Broken Nose, 1996). But it must be noted that while tribes may share these values with traditional Native American culture, individuals within this group may vary in the degree to which they hold and manifest these values.

As is true for all minority peoples, the degree to which the Native American cultural values are embodied is determined by the degree to which individuals embrace traditionalism in contrast to the degree of acculturation in mainstream society that they have experienced (Attneave, 1982).

Native American women are typically seen as equal to Native American men, but that does not mean they assume the same roles and functions. Gender roles among different tribes and ancestry are specific to tribes. For example, among Pueblo Indians, men worked in cornfields controlled by female members of their tribe yet men dominated religion and politics. Pueblo women built and owned the family home, and it is through women that many Native American peoples trace descent (Deloria, 2000).

Native American gender roles prescribe male bravery and strength. Males are expected to protect and be loyal to the tribe. Typically, hunting and survival skills were passed down from one generation to the next, with the bravest and strongest but also wisest becoming leaders of the tribes. Tribal leaders played significant roles in maintaining cultural continuity, and Native American women were equally important to the survival of the tribe and were treated accordingly. Besides child-rearing, women were responsible for direct care of the elderly and the daily operations of the tribe. Cooking, tailoring, and washing were also traditional tasks assigned to women in Native American culture.

As you reflect on what you have read, it is quite possible that the history of your family, your incorporation into dominant U.S. culture, the values you hold, and the gender roles you assume may be quite different from or in some ways like those described here for Native Americans. Before proceeding, stop and reflect on what has been presented, especially as it relates to conflicts in values, traditions, and expectations found in a typical dominant-culture classroom (see Exercise 5-2).

## CULTURAL FACTOR 4: VIEW OF SPIRITUALITY AND HUMANS' RELATION TO NATURE

Traditional Native American values include an orientation that reveres harmony with nature versus dominant culture's view of nature as subjugated to man. Native Americans believe that all creation is equal—that all living things are interdependent and that humans must value the sanctity of the wholeness of the universe in its purity. These beliefs contradict dominant-culture beliefs of human superiority over nature and the need for humans to own, control, change, and otherwise dominate all aspects of it.

# EXERCISE 5-2    Classroom Applications: The Confluence of Values

**Directions:** In the first column of the table are descriptions of characteristics that have been associated with Native American peoples. In the middle column are descriptions of typical processes or procedures found within dominant-culture schools. Your task is to describe the effect experienced when these two value systems meet. Describe how you think students placed in this situation, in which both are important, may react. Share your hypotheses with your instructor and classmates in small-group discussion in order to develop strategies geared to reduce any negative impact.

| Native American Characteristic | School Orientation, Process, or Procedure | Anticipated Impact |
|---|---|---|
| Value community above the individual | • Academic competitions including math bowls and spelling bees<br>• Acknowledging most talented students<br>• Awards assemblies | |
| Emphasize cooperation and sharing | • Homework assignments<br>• Seatwork assignments<br>• Board work<br>• Participation in debates | |
| Respect for nature | • Communicated value of living things (including domesticated animals/classroom pets and dissection animals)<br>• Emphasis on environmental issues/greening<br>• Existent capitalist values system | |
| Spirituality over materialism | • Use of extrinsic motivation (prizes, stickers, awards)<br>• Homecoming queen contests<br>• Providing incentives for students to sell products in fundraisers | |
| Present versus future focus | • Curriculum mapping for future college and career<br>• Essay assignment titled "What I Want to Be When I Grow Up"<br>• Use of portfolio as a means of assessing student progress | |
| Valuing of fate and destiny versus self-determination | • Goal-setting in the process of problem solving | |

Mind, body, spirit, and nature are perceived as one process, with little separation existing between religion, medicine, and all activities of daily life (Kaplan & Johnson, 1964; Richardson, 1981), just as there is no separation of life in nature. In Native American culture, reverence for nature and for all forms of life is central.

Qualities of the Creator are said to be reflected in all forms of nature, so each aspect of nature is seen as a link to the Creator (Brown, 1964).

A key concept of Native American philosophy is holism, and one of the most important symbols is the circle, or hoop of life. Consider the importance of the circle as evidenced in the words of Black Elk, a Sioux medicine man:

> Everything an Indian does is in a circle, and that is because the Power of the World always works in circles, and everything tries to be round. In the old days when we were a strong and happy people, all our power came to us from the sacred hoop of the nation, and so long as the hoop was unbroken, the people flourished. (Brown, 1964, pp. 13–24)

When traditional Native Americans come together as a group, they meet in a circle formation depicting the importance of all present, the equality distributed among all, and the belief in loyalty to the group that keeps the circle whole.

Traditional Native Americans see themselves as extensions of the tribe. The individual is a part of a whole, and the wholeness of the tribe provides strength and gives meaning to life. For example, one petal of a flower has little beauty by itself, but together the petals make up the experience, beauty, and wholeness of the flower. Similarly, in traditional Native American culture a person is judged primarily in terms of whether his or her behavior contributes to the harmonious functioning of the tribe. Native American philosophy does not oppose individual accomplishment but sees the individual as an extension of the tribe. Therefore, artistry and sport accomplishment reflect positively on the group, its teachings, and the wholeness of Native American culture.

The strong valuing of spirituality can be seen in the practice of the Native American transforming rituals of the vision quest and sweat lodge, which still serve as rites of passage or processes for religious renewal. These ceremonies often include fasting to allow one's mental capacities to be more attentive to the natural world. The vision quest, in which a youth is taken to a remote and isolated area for four days and nights without food and water, offers time for reflection and prayer and examination of one's goals and plans. This ritual directs individuals toward a focus on their relationship with the universe and the role they are to play in it. Individuals marshal their abilities, skills, fears, experiences, goals, and hopes to further their quest for spiritual knowledge.

Similarly symbolic of important cultural tenets, the circular shape of the sweat lodge (tepee) represents the Universe itself, and the pit at the lodge's center is the navel of the Universe wherein dwells the Great Spirit, with the fire representing the power of the Creator. The willow branches that form the frame of the lodge represent all growing things, whose annual cycles of defoliation and refoliation symbolize the death and rebirth of the spirit. The rocks in the firepit represent the earth and the indestructible nature of the Creator. The water sprinkled on the rocks is the Creator's ever-flowing life-giving spirit. The steam is both the holy breath of the Universe and the visible prayers of the people. The opening of the flap of the sweat lodge that lets cool air and light in symbolizes liberation from the darkness of ignorance and entering the world of light and truth and goodness (Brown, 1964; Halifax, 1979).

Traditional Native American rituals and values like these are oriented to help group members fully experience the present and to follow old ways versus a dominant-culture orientation to the future and toward progress and change at the expense of attending to needs and life goals in the present. Native Americans are sometimes mistakenly judged as lazy or undependable if they do not arrive on time for scheduled commitments. Such behavior reflects not a lack of commitment or irresponsibility but instead a respect for and focus on the here and now. A traditional Native American might ask, "Why would someone miss or hurry something solely for the sake of finishing at a certain point in time?"

In addition, Native American culture emphasizes a belief in destiny in contrast to dominant-culture attitudes that espouse the idea that if one wants something to happen, it is up to the individual to make it happen. One consequence of this cultural belief is that Native Americans place less emphasis on planning and scheduling. As a culture, Native Americans place more emphasis on seeing how situations develop and on valuing the present and what it brings as it unfolds, and less value on planning for the future.

## CULTURAL FACTOR 5: ACCULTURATION AND EXPERIENCE WITH EXCLUSION AND ALIENATION

More than 75 percent of the total Native American population lives off-reservation (U.S. Bureau of the Census, 1981). Many leave the reservation in search of work in order to care for their families. The transition is difficult, especially when Native Americans move to high-density urban areas. It is not uncommon for transitioning Native Americans to feel lonely, insecure, and alienated (Carlson, 1975).

The dominant culture has exerted enormous force and pressure on Native Americans to adopt its values. As a result, a great deal of cultural heritage was lost as generations of Native American children were raised in the boarding schools and foster homes of dominant culture—environments in which the mission was to make the Native American children more "White." The degree to which acculturation has occurred, along with the decline of interest in traditional Native American culture, varies considerably among Native Americans (Heinnch, Corbine, & Thomas, 1990). Some fight to hold on to their Native American traditions while functioning within the dominant culture. These individuals may dream of making enough money in U.S. cities to move back to reservations when they retire. They may make long commutes to the reservation for feasts, powwows, religious ceremonies, and visits with relatives. They may fear that the traditions will be lost because of the exodus of so many Native Americans to cities (Mulhern, 1988).

Such a response to acculturation has been described as **traditionalism** (Valle, 1986). **Biculturalism** is another response to the pressures of acculturation. Bicultural individuals are said to have a dual perspective. They are a part of two systems: the larger system of the dominant society and the smaller system of the individual's immediate cultural environment. To survive in both systems, individuals consciously perceive, understand, and compare simultaneously the values, attitudes, and behavior of the larger societal system with those of individuals' immediate family and community systems, often finding conflict that leads them to choose to express themselves most freely in whichever environment feels most comfortable and beneficial to them

## Intercultural Communication Strategies for Teachers 5-2

### Classroom Applications: Pressure and Pressured

As noted in the text, the loss of one's native culture and total cultural assimilation into that of the dominant culture may not be a problem for some Native Americans, but for others it is viewed as cultural genocide. Where any one Native American student may exist along the continuum of acculturation is hard to know, but all require teacher support in addressing discrimination and other psychosocial concerns experienced in schools. The following points will help you to provide that support.

- Provide students with the freedom to make choices in the classroom. Allow for choices between written and oral and between group and individual assignments when possible. In addition, provide various and diverse resources from which students can learn.
- Ask families and other community members of your students to help you create book lists, field-trip destinations, and guest-speaker possibilities.
- Use journal-writing assignments frequently to give your students outlets for expression and the opportunity for regular individualized communication with you.
- Be sensitive to the fact that not all Native American students are at the same point along the acculturation continuum. While some may want to give voice to their traditions, rituals, and values, others may be attempting to more closely fulfill dominant-culture expectations.

in various situations, including schools (Hanson & Eisenbise, 1981). A third position on the continuum of acculturation would be **total cultural assimilation**. While the complete loss of one's native culture and the total cultural assimilation into that of the dominant culture may not be a problem for some Native Americans, for others it is viewed as cultural genocide (Ford, 1983).

## CULTURAL FACTOR 6: LANGUAGE DIFFERENCES, STRENGTHS, AND CHALLENGES

There are 304 federal Native American reservations, and over 150 tribal languages are still spoken today (Bureau of Indian Affairs, 1988). Even so, the elimination of Native American language is almost complete.

Native Americans have been forced to replace Native languages with English in order to survive in dominant-culture-controlled boarding schools, reservations, and institutional policies and practices. As such, Native American languages have been systematically discounted and erased.

Traditional Native American speech patterns are often slower and softer than dominant-culture speech patterns, with few interjections into the conversation of others. Intense eye contact is avoided, as it may be considered a sign of rudeness. Native Americans may exhibit limited facial expression and may appear guarded, aloof, or cold. In addition, Native American responses may seem delayed, if they occur at all. Silence is seen as a sign of equilibrium. The fruits of silence are self-control, courage, patience, dignity, and reverence. Nonverbal communication through rituals, signing, drumming, and dancing are highly prized, as they are perceived to be more in concert with nature and others, than are solitary verbal monologues.

Traditional Native Americans emphasize learning through observation, listening, and practice. As such, children are often taught through demonstration rather than verbal communication alone. While these descriptors of Native American communication styles seem small or insignificant, consider the effect when this style encounters the expectations, demands, and models of communication reinforced within dominant-culture schools, as seen in Chief Luther Standing Bear's explanation of differences in educational approach and content.

> In talking to children, the old Lakota would place a hand on the ground and explain: "We sit in the lap of our Mother. From her we, and all other living things, come. We shall soon pass, but the place where we now rest will last forever." So we, too, learned to sit or lie on the ground and become conscious of life about us in its multitude of forms.
>
> Sometimes we boys would sit motionless and watch the swallows, the tiny ants, or perhaps some small animal at its work and ponder its industry and ingenuity; or we lay on our backs and looked long at the sky, and when the stars came out made shapes from the various groups.
>
> Everything was possessed of personality, only differing from us in form. Knowledge was inherent in all things. The world was a library and its books were the stones, leaves, grass, brooks, and the birds and animals that shared, alike with us, the storms and blessings of earth. We learned to do what only the student of nature ever learns, and that was to feel beauty. We never railed at the storms, the furious winds, and the biting frosts and snows. To do so intensified human futility, so whatever came we adjusted ourselves, by more effort and energy if necessary, but without complaint.
>
> Even the lightning did us no harm, for whenever it came too close, mothers and grandmothers in every tipi put cedar leaves on the coals and their magic kept danger away. Bright days and dark days were both expressions of the Great Mystery, and the Indian reveled in being close to the Great Holiness.
>
> Observation was certain to have its rewards. Interest, wonder, admiration grew, and the fact was appreciated that life was more than mere human manifestation; it was expressed in a multitude of forms.
>
> This appreciation enriched Lakota existence. Life was vivid and pulsing; nothing was casual and commonplace. The Indian lived—lived in every sense of the word—from his first to his last breath.
>
> Chief Luther Standing Bear
> Teton Sioux

## POTENTIAL BARRIERS IN LEARNING–TEACHING RELATIONSHIPS WITH DOMINANT-CULTURE TEACHERS AND SCHOOLS

In addition to conflicts in values, communication patterns, and learning-style preferences discussed in this chapter, Native Americans exist largely unrecognized in U.S. schools. Because many Native Americans in the United States today have last names that originated in Europe and there are wide variations in the physical appearance of Native Americans, it is quite possible that students with Native American backgrounds may provide teachers with no visible signs of their ancestry. Due to the high proportion of mixed-heritage individuals, it may be difficult for teachers to determine whether there are Native Americans students in their classrooms (Little Soldier, 1997). This potential for invisibility in the dominant culture can prove to be a major obstacle for Native Americans as they seek to retain their cultural heritage and identity and to have their perspectives included in U.S. schools.

## AN UNRECOGNIZED HISTORY

Not only is it difficult for members of this group to be recognized as Native Americans, but they also face a major lack of recognition of their existence in North American, in particular U.S., history. Native American writings, worldviews, and contributions are typically not included in texts and curricula, and Native American leaders and philosophies are not embraced in the media or dominant-culture consciousness. In many ways, it is as if Native Americans do not exist in U.S. schools and culture.

---

**EXERCISE 5-3**   **Point of Reflection: Redskins, Tomahawk Chants, and Other Cultural Icons**

*Directions:* Gather data from the following sources in order to develop a profile of Native Americans as they are currently depicted in dominant culture.

| Source of Data | Image Projected |
| --- | --- |
| Identify two sports teams that use a logo or symbol associated with Native Americans (for example, Atlanta Braves, Washington Redskins). | |
| Review the art of Frederic Remington or Charles Russell. | |
| Use a U.S. history textbook and identify:<br><br>1. The context (or circumstances) in which Native Americans are discussed<br>2. The image employed to depict Native Americans | |
| Locate advertisements and commercials with a Native American theme (for example, "It's Barbie as an American Indian caring for her cousin, Baby Blue Feather™. This Collector Edition Barbie wears a tan buckskin-like dress with matching boots. The tiny papoose she carries has a 'buckskin' headband and diaper and comes with a matching backpack. Children will love the magical story Barbie tells. From the American Stories Series™, this very special Barbie doll comes with her own historical storybook, so she's educational as well as fun"). | |

1. Reflect on what you have read about Native American culture in this chapter. Describe how the information you have learned from your research for this exercise would affect the lives of Native Americans living in the United States. Do the characterizations accurately reflect their values and help them feel connected to dominant culture? Discuss your views in writing or with classmates.

2. Consider the significant cultural principles presented in this chapter and determine if there is evidence that Native American values and culture are understood in dominant culture.

The absence of contemporary images of Native Americans in popular culture is widespread. Even in places with a large and visible Native American population, they are presented as people of the past rather than people of the present. Consider the messages conveyed in the profiles of Native Americans depicted in the artifacts that dominant culture has reinforced (see Exercise 5-3).

## WHEN VALUES AND DEMANDS CLASH

As previously noted, traditional Native American values embrace cooperation and conscious submission of the self for the welfare of the group versus the dominant-culture value that stresses competition, with each individual maximizing her or his own welfare in order to succeed in life, often at the expense of others. This may not seem, at first glance, to be an obstacle for Native Americans within dominant-culture schools. However, consider a simple and typical situation in which an individual student is asked to answer a question in class, a process repeated throughout every classroom in the United States on any given day. For a traditional Native American student who answers the question correctly it is an act of individual superiority, while answering it incorrectly or standing mute would bring humiliation to the individual and the group. This is a classic no-win situation brought on by cultural value differences and conflicts. In another example, consider the practice of an academic competition, honors ceremony, or any activity that attempts to highlight the superiority of one student over another. When contrasted with traditional Native American values, which are grounded in a holistic approach to life and living where all aspects of life are seen as connected and cherished for the roles they play as a part of the whole, is there conflict? Traditional Native American values and approaches to life and education are, indeed, lost or at least ignored within a dominant school and societal culture that emphasizes individual achievement above all else—even at the expense of loss achievement opportunities for others.

---

### Intercultural Communication Strategies for Teachers 5-3

**Classroom Applications: Making Classrooms and Curricula Reflective of Student Experience**

- Teachers need to become more aware of Native American cultural values. Classroom activities need to be shaped to reinforce values and strategies employed in the home.
- Use demonstration, modeling, and coaching during "hands-on" instructional activities. Native American students may prefer global/holistic approaches that offer visual and tactile stimuli.
- Move beyond commercial curriculum materials; tailor readings, activities, and illustrations to students' experiential backgrounds.

- Become aware of alternative curriculum materials appropriate to your students' backgrounds (for example, oral and written Native American literature suitable for classroom use and integration of Native American history and governance into the social studies curriculum).
- Employ more cooperative group work as opposed to heavy reliance on individual classroom activities or competition within the classroom.

# FROM CONCEPTS TO LIVED EXPERIENCE

In the following narrative from Mary Crow Dog, she describes her Native American history in her own voice. As you read, look for the values manifested as they reflect traditional Native American values and approaches to living presented in this chapter. Also consider the extent to which this account has been featured in typical U.S. history and social studies texts.

### WOUNDED KNEE

When I heard the words "Wounded Knee," I became very, very serious. Wounded Knee—*Cankpe Opt* in our language—has a special meaning for our people. There is the long ditch into which the frozen bodies of almost 300 of our people, mostly women and children, were thrown like so much cordwood. And the bodies are still there in their mass grave, unmarked except for a cement border. Next to the ditch, on a hill, stands the white-painted Catholic church, gleaming in the sunlight, the monument of an alien faith imposed upon the landscape. And below it flows *Cankpe Opt Wakpala,* the creek along which the women and children were hunted down like animals by Custer's old Seventh, out to avenge themselves for their defeat by butchering the helpless ones. That happened long ago, but no Sioux ever forgot it.

Wounded Knee is a part of our family's history. Leonard's great-grandfather, the first Crow Dog, had been one of the leaders of the Ghost Dancers. He and his group had held out in the icy ravines of the Badlands all winter, but when the soldiers came in force to kill all the Ghost Dancers, he had surrendered his band to avoid having his people killed. Old accounts describe how Crow Dog simply sat down between the rows of soldiers on one side, and the Indians on the other, all ready and eager to start shooting. He had covered himself with a blanket and was just sitting there. Nobody knew what to make of it. The leaders on both sides were so puzzled that they just did not get around to opening fire. They went to Crow Dog, lifted the blanket, and asked him what he meant to do. He told them that sitting there with the blanket over him was the only thing he could think of to make all the hotheads, white and red, curious enough to forget fighting. Then he persuaded his people to lay down their arms. Thus he saved his people just a few miles away from where Big Foot and his band were massacred. (Crow Dog & Erodes, 1990, pp. 124–125)

# SUMMARY

**Cultural Factor 1: Historical and Current Treatment in the United States** Historically, dominant culture in the United States, including federal laws, policies, and institutions (e.g., schools, churches, agencies), has deliberately attempted to destroy Native American culture and cultural institutions, through five stages:

- Stage One: Removal (killing Native Americans)
- Stage Two: Reservations (isolation)
- Stage Three: Reorganization (systematic cultural repression)
- Stage Four: Termination (integration of acculturated Native Americans)

- Stage Five: Self-determination (encouragement to make their own way)

**Cultural Factor 2: Initial Terms of Incorporation into U.S. Society** Native Americans are an involuntary minority group, having been colonized and denied assimilation into U.S. society.

**Cultural Factor 3: Shared Values and Traditions** Because of the large number of tribes and languages spoken, it is important to realize the tremendous diversity among Native Americans. The values of traditional Native American culture arose primarily (but not exclusively) within the context of a nomadic hunting and gathering economy that has been almost completely destroyed. Extended-family and kinship obligations are considered very important for Native Americans. As such, group needs are more significant than individual needs.

**Cultural Factor 4: View of Spirituality and Humans' Relation to Nature** Traditional Native American values include an orientation of harmony with nature versus dominant culture's view of nature as subjugated to man. A key concept of Native American philosophy is holism, and one of the most important symbols is the circle, or hoop of life. Mind, body, spirit, and nature are perceived as one process, and little separation exists between religion, medicine, and the activities of daily life. Traditional Native Americans see themselves as extensions of the tribe. The individual is a part of a whole, and that wholeness of the tribe gives meaning to life.

Traditional Native American values are oriented to the present and to following old ways versus a dominant-culture orientation to the future and toward progress and change. Native American culture emphasizes a belief in destiny in contrast to dominant-culture attitudes that if you want something to happen, it is up to you to make it happen. Native American women are seen as equal to Native American men. Gender roles among different tribes and ancestry, however, are group specific.

**Cultural Factor 5: Acculturation and Experience with Exclusion and Alienation** Some Native Americans fight to hold on to their traditions while functioning within the dominant culture; this is a

traditional response to acculturation. A bicultural response is one in which the person attempts to be part of two systems: the larger system of the dominant society and the smaller system of the individual's immediate social environment. The final position on the continuum of acculturation would be total cultural assimilation.

**Cultural Factor 6: Language Differences, Strengths, and Challenges** Through dominant culture-controlled boarding schools, reservations, and institutional policies and practices, Native American languages have been systematically discounted and erased. Native American speech patterns are often slower and softer than dominant-culture speech patterns. Native Americans may exhibit limited facial expression and may appear guarded, aloof, or cold.

Silence is seen as a sign of equilibrium. The fruits of silence are self-control, courage, patience, dignity, and reverence. Nonverbal communication, however, through rituals, signing, drumming, and dancing, is highly prized as it is perceived to be more in concert with nature and others, than are solitary verbal monologues.

**Potential Barriers in Learning–Teaching Relationships with Dominant-Culture Teachers and Schools** Native Americans go largely unrecognized in U.S. schools. There is a lack of recognition of their existence in North American history. Native American writings and contributions typically are not included in curricula, and Native American leaders and philosophies are not embraced in the media or dominant-culture consciousness. In many ways, it is as if Native Americans do not exist in U.S. schools and culture.

## Questions for Review

1. What are the significant traditional values commonly shared by Native Americans that would be in conflict with dominant-culture perspectives and practices?

2. How would the Native American emphasis on seeing individuals as part of a greater

whole provide strength and give meaning to life?

3. How is it that this cultural group is said to go unrecognized in U.S. schools?

## Important Terms

biculturalism  
involuntary minorities  
relocation  
removal  

reorganization  
self-determination  
termination  

total cultural  
  assimilation  
traditionalism  

traditional Native  
  American values  
voluntary minorities  

## Enrichment

Crow Dog, M., & Erodes, R. (1990). *Lakota woman*. New York: Harper Perennial.

Gilliland, H. (1995). *Teaching the Native American* (3rd ed.). Dubuque, IA: Kendall/Hunt.

Lame Deer, J., & Erodes, R. (1972). *Lame Deer: Seeker of visions*. New York: Simon & Schuster.

Nabokov, P. (Ed.). (1991). *Native American testimony: A chronicle of Indian–White relations from prophecy to the present, 1492–1992*. New York: Viking.

Nerburn, K. (1999). *The wisdom of Native Americans*. Novato, CA: New World Library.

U.S. Bureau of the Census. (1993). *We, the first Americans*. Washington, DC: U.S. Government Printing Office.

U.S. Department of Health and Human Services. (1977). *Health of the disadvantaged chart book*. Washington, DC: U.S. Government Printing Office.

## Connections on the Web

http://www.greatdreams.com/native.htm

This site contains a wealth of cultural information, values, and resources about many Native American tribes, and educational activities for students.

http://www.ewebtribe.com/NACulture/stories.htm

This site compiles a wide variety of Native American stories and legends.

http://www.gatheringofnations.com/videos/index.htm

This website features extensive photo galleries and current Native American events calendars; showcases information, history, and issues; and provides cultural resources and references.

## References

Attneave, C. L. (1982). American Indians and Alaska native families: Emigrants in their own homeland. In M. McGoldrick, J. Pearce, & J. Giorando (Eds.), *Ethnicity & family therapy* (pp. 55–83). New York: Guilford.

Beauvais, F. (1980). *Preventing drug abuse among American Indian young people*. Ft Collins, CO: Colorado State University (ERIC Document Reproduction Service No. ED196630).

Berlin, I. N. (1984). *Suicide among American Indian adolescents*. National Indian Court Judges Association (ERIC Document Reproduction Service No. ED245847).

Blanchard, E., & Mackey, J. (1971). *The American Indian* (SRS Training Grant 755 770). Washington, DC: National Rehabilitation Association.

Bock, G., Fortuine, R., Bergman, R., Bopp, J., Exendine, J., Lafromboise, R., et al. (1972). *Alcoholism—A high priority health problem*. Rockville, MD: Indian Health Service Task Force on Alcoholism (ERIC Document Reproduction Service No. ED148536).

Brown, J. (1964). *The spiritual legacy of the American Indian*. Wallingford, PA: Pendle Hill.

Bureau of Indian Affairs. (1988). *American Indians today*. Washington, DC: Author.

Carlson, E. (1975). Counseling in native context. *Canada's Mental Health, 23*, 7–9.

Crow Dog, M., & Erodes, R. (1990). *Lakota woman*. New York: Harper Perennial.

Deloria, P. J. (2003). American Indians, American studies, and the ASA. *American Quarterly, 55*(4), 669–680.

Deloria, Jr., V. (2000). The "vanishing" Americans. *Indian Life, 21*(1), 12–14.

Ford, R. (1983). *Counseling strategies for ethnic minority students*. Tacoma, WA: University of Puget Sound (ERIC Document Reproduction Service No. ED247504).

Gade, E., Hurlburt, G., & Fuqua, D. (1986). Study habits and attitudes of American Indians: Implications for counselors. *School Counselor, 34*, 135–139.

Halifax, J. (1979). *Shamanic voices: A survey of visionary narratives*. New York: Dutton.

Hanson, W. D., & Eisenbise, M. D. (1981). *Human behavior and American Indians*. San Francisco: San Francisco State University (ERIC Document Reproduction Service No. ED231589).

Heinnch, R. K., Corbine, J. L., & Thomas, K. R. (1990). Counseling Native Americans. *Journal of Counseling & Development, 69*, 128–133.

Kaplan, B., & Johnson, D. (1964). The social meaning of Navaho psychopathology and psychotherapy. In A. Kiev (Ed.), *Magic, faith, and healing* (pp. 203–229). New York: MacMillan.

Kolchin, P. (1993). *American slavery, 1619–1877*. New York: Hill & Wang.

Lame Deer, J., & Erodes, R. (1972). *Lame Deer: Seeker of visions*. New York: Simon & Schuster.

Lazarus, P. (1982). Counseling the Native American child: A question of values. *Elementary School Guidance and Counseling, 17*, 83–88.

Little Soldier, L. (1997, April). Is there an Indian in your classroom? Working successfully with urban Native American students. *Phi Delta Kappan*, 650–653.

Manson, S. M. (1986). Recent advances in American Indian mental health research: Implications for clinical research and training. In M. R. Miranda, & H. H. L. Kitano (Eds.), *Mental health research and practice in minority communities: Development of culturally sensitive training programs* (pp. 51–89). Rockville, MD: National Institute of Mental Health (ERIC Document Reproduction Service No. ED278754).

Metcalf, A. (1979). Family reunion: Networks and treatment in a Native American community. *Group Psychotherapy, Psychodrama & Sociometry, 32*, 179–189.

Momaday, N. S. (1992). Confronting Columbus again. In P. Nabokov (Ed.), *Native American testimony: A chronicle of Indian–White relations from prophecy to the present*, 1492–1992 (p. 438). New York: Viking.

Mulhern, B. (1988). Wisconsin's Indians: Their progress, their plight. *The Capital Times*, p. 1.

National Indian Child Abuse and Neglect Resource Center. (1980). *The social worker and the Indian client*. Tulsa, OK: Anton.

Nerburn, K. (1999). The wisdom of Native Americans. Novato, CA: New World Library.

Office for Governmental Affairs and the Rural Condition. (1985). *American Indian unemployment: Confronting a distressing reality*. Washington, DC: Full Employment Action Council (ERIC Document Reproduction Service No. ED275472).

Ogbu, J. U. (1990). Minority education in comparative perspective. *Journal of Negro Education, 59*, 45–55.

Ogbu, J. U. (1992). Understanding cultural diversity and learning. *Educational Researcher, 21*(8), 5–24.

Richardson, E. H. (1981). Cultural and historical perspectives in counseling American Indians.

In D. N. Sue (Ed.), *Counseling the culturally different*. New York: Wiley.

Sutton, C. T., & Broken Nose, M. A. (1996). American Indian families: An overview. In M. McGoldrick, J. Pearce, & J. Giorando (Eds.), *Ethnicity and family therapy* (pp. 31–44). New York: Guilford.

Tatum, B. D. (1997). *"Why are all the Black kids sitting together in the cafeteria?" and other conversations about race*. New York: Basic Books.

Trimble, J. E. (1981). Value differentials and their importance in counseling American Indians. In P. Pedersen, J. Draguns, W. Lonner, & J. Trimble (Eds.), *Counseling across cultures* (pp. 203–226). Honolulu: University Press of Hawaii.

U.S. Bureau of the Census. (1981). *Census of the population: 1980*. Washington, DC: U.S. Government Printing Office.

U.S. Bureau of the Census. (2003). *Statistical Abstract of the United States: 2003* (123rd ed.). Washington, DC: U.S. Government Printing Office.

U.S. Bureau of the Census (2008). *Population Census*. Washington, DC: U.S. Government Printing Office.

Valle, R. (1986). Cross-cultural competence in minority communities: A curriculum implementation strategy. In M. R. Miranda, & H. H. L. Kitano (Eds.), *Mental health research and practice in minority communities: Development of culturally sensitive training programs* (pp. 51–89). Rockville, MD: National Institute of Mental Health (ERIC Document Reproduction Service No. ED278754).

Vogel, V. J. (1987). The blackout of Native American cultural achievements. *American Indian Quarterly*, 11, 11–35.

*Racism was probably the hardest challenge and most difficult obstacle that I've encountered in the United States. ... One day on the way home from school, a group of white boys riding in a pickup truck tried to intimidate me. They yelled and cursed at me. They gave me the finger and screamed a four-letter word repeatedly. I heard them say, "Go back home! This is our country!" Then they spat at me and laughed. One of them pointed his finger at me as if he were shooting me. I could hear him laugh and say, "Bang! Bang! You're dead, you f_____ Hmong." I had witnessed similar violent actions toward other Asians before, so I knew they were just trying to intimidate me. Instead of reacting angrily, I took a turn and disappeared. Of course I was shocked and angry, and wanted to get back at them, but I held my temper. I knew that if I tried to get revenge, I would be as inhumane as they were.*

**Tcha Vu in Chan, 1994, p. 202.**

CHAPTER

# Learning from Asian American Stories

Racism, violence, bullying, and intimidation—all acts we realize are perpetrated daily in the United States. Vu's silence, restraint, and deference were not signs of weakness or fear but rather a way of coping in an environment that he knew from experience was fraught with uncertainty, harm, degradation, and various other forms of discrimination. Asian immigrants have historically faced discrimination throughout the process of acculturation in the United States—many enduring such conditions because they had no other choice (as is the case for refugees, like Vu) or because they believe the United States offers great opportunity and therefore facing discrimination is but a part of the bargain.

The term *Asian Americans* is a collective reference to Asian and Pacific Islander populations who live in the United States. Tatum (1997) identified various cultural groups included among the collective: including people from East Asia (for example, persons with Chinese, Japanese, and Korean cultural backgrounds), Southeast Asia (persons with Vietnamese, Laotian, and Burmese cultural backgrounds), the Pacific Islands (persons with Samoan, Guamanian, and Fijian cultural backgrounds), South Asia (persons with Indian, Pakistani, and Nepali cultural backgrounds), West Asia (persons with Iranian, Afghani, and Turkish cultural backgrounds), and the Middle East (persons with Iraqi, Jordanian, and Palestinian cultural backgrounds). Asian Americans encompass at least 43 ethnic groups from the Pacific Islands and the continent of Asia. Not surprisingly, language, cultural values, and religious beliefs vary greatly among these groups (Lee, 1996; Yashima & Tanaka, 2001).

This chapter explores traditional ethnic group values, traditions, conflicts, and coping strategies common to many of the various populations of Asian Americans.

## CHAPTER OBJECTIVES

1. Describe common values and worldviews of Asian American ethnic group members.
2. Identify ways by which persons profiled in the case narratives experienced and addressed the six cultural factors explored in this text.
3. Explain academic and intercultural interaction implications related to the six cultural factors for members in this ethnic group.
4. Describe coping strategies often utilized by members of this group.
5. Identify classroom strategies for cultivating the resources provided when traditional Asian American worldviews are integrated into your curriculum.

## CULTURAL FACTOR 1: HISTORICAL AND CURRENT TREATMENT IN U.S. SOCIETY

Like other immigrant groups, Asian Americans have experienced a history of discrimination in the United States (Daniels, 1971; Jones, 1972; Nishi, 1982; Sue & Sue, 1993). Knowledge of institutional racism experienced by Asian Americans is often unspoken and a barely visible part of U.S. history.

Because it is important to understand your own cultural influences of your actions if you are to move beyond simply knowing about other cultures to understanding the feelings and experiences of others, take some time to reflect and critically examine your own values and beliefs about handling conflict and alienation before identifying the interaction behaviors that are common to members of this group. Exercise 6-1 is provided to help you with this reflection.

### Historical Beginnings in the United States

Some of the first Chinese immigrants came to the United States in response to social and economic instability occurring in China in the mid 1840s (DeVos & Abbot, 1966). At that time, Chinese men were often hired as cheap labor to help build the transcontinental railroad (Daniels, 1971). This required them to leave their families behind in China. However, White American hostilities toward the Chinese grew when labor jobs in the United States became scarce in the late 1870s. At that time, numerous laws (denying citizenship, home ownership, and the right to marry), like the Page Law, which prohibited the immigration of Chinese contract laborers, were passed. Such laws culminated in the Federal Chinese Exclusion Act of 1882, which was not repealed until 1943 when the United States sought to form an alliance with China during World War II.

Japanese people experienced similar severe discrimination when they began immigrating to the United States. While many Japanese people initially served as cheap agricultural laborers, the more the Japanese experienced success in the fishing and farming industries, the more Americans responded with prohibitive legislation,

## EXERCISE 6-1    Point of Reflection: A Reflection and an Awareness

*Directions:* Respond to the series of questions following with the first thoughts that come to mind. Write these down and share your responses with a classmate, a colleague, and/or your instructor in small-group discussion. Take note of the differences you observe when you compare your responses to the responses of others.

By examining your own preferences, you may better appreciate the idea that some traditional Asian American cultural beliefs that may have previously seemed exotic or alien to you are actually in some ways quite similar to your own values and preferences. All are values, behaviors, and attitudes learned in context that serve as ways to navigate life and function within the context of one's unique cultural experiences.

*After* reading the chapter, return to your responses and compare your responses to the questions with what you imagine may be the responses of traditional Asian American students to these same questions.

1. You have been wronged and publically humiliated because you are a member of your ethnic group. How do you respond?
2. Assume you are sitting at the table during a family dinner. Perhaps you have a grandparent or an elderly family member in attendance. If the discussion around the table focuses on something about which you strongly disagree or that makes you feel uncomfortable, what do you do?
3. You are currently in a classroom in which all of the class members are sharing their ideas about an important school concept. Do you initiate your participation to share your ideas, wait to be asked, wait for silence, or hold your thoughts to yourself? Explain your reasoning for responses.

much like the Chinese experienced (Kitano, 1969). Hostility toward Japanese men, women, and children living in the United States escalated in 1942 when more than 111,000 Japanese were "relocated" by the U.S. government into **internment camps** in several different locations in the United States. In doing so, the government interned its own citizens, thus violating the fifth and fourteenth amendments to the Constitution providing for "due process" and "equal protection under the law for all citizens." This forced eviction and complete disruption of the lives, homes, relationships, jobs, belongings, and privacy of Japanese American men, women, and children and was rationalized as a "military necessity" after bombs fell on Pearl Harbor in 1941. It is interesting to note that although the United States was also at war with Germany and Italy at that time, Americans with ancestors from those countries were not placed in internment camps (Uchida, 1982).

More than 250,000 Southeast Asian refugees were admitted to the United States between 1975 and 1979 (U.S. Department of Health and Welfare, 1979). During the evacuation of Saigon in 1975, many of the first immigrants were educated Vietnamese government employees and their families (Chan, 1981). Between 1980 and 1984, an additional 450,000 refugees arrived in the United States from the same area (U.S. Bureau of the Census, 1985, 1986). Some from Cambodia and Laos among this group were also educated and spoke some English. However, subsequently, many immigrant refugees from these areas came from rural and farming communities and were less well-prepared to cope with the rigors of acculturation. Many of these immigrants suffered long stays in refugee camps in Thailand and Malaysia. They were often separated from their families and experienced great uncertainty about their futures. Family reunification legislation currently permits an ongoing stream of refugee immigrants into the United States (U.S. Committee for Refugees, 1987). Not surprisingly, Southeast Asian immigrants face similar discrimination confronted by Chinese and Japanese Americans in the United States. However, many may be much less prepared to acculturate (Nicassio, 1985). The provision of refuge in the United States has saved the lives of many refugees while simultaneously leading to the erosion of traditional Asian values, traditions, and intergenerational relations.

## Current Conditions

In 1980, more than 2.5 million Asian immigrants entered the United States, up from under 500,000 in 1960. The Immigration Act of 1990 increased the number of Asians coming to the United States by raising the total quota and reorganizing the system of preferences to favor certain professional groups. This allowed Asians with training in medicine, high technology, and other specialties to enter the United States more easily. In 1990, nearly 5 million Asian immigrants were reported, second only to those coming from Latin America. Currently, there is an estimated 15.2 Asian American residents in the United States, comprising about 5 percent of the total population. California has the largest Asian population in the United States (5 million residents). There are 1.4 million Asian American residents in New York and 915,000 in Texas. In Hawaii, Asians make up the highest proportion of the total population (55 percent), followed by California (14 percent) and New Jersey and Washington (8 percent each). Asian Americans are the largest minority group in Hawaii and Vermont. There are reportedly 3.5 million Asian Americans of Chinese descent, 3 million Filipinos, 2.8 million Asian Indians, 1.8 million Vietnamese, 1.6 million Koreans, and 1.2 million Japanese American residents in the United Sates. Approximately 50 percent of Asian Americans hold a bachelor's degree or higher level of education, compared with 28 percent for all Americans. Eighty-six percent have at least a high school diploma and 20 percent have a graduate (e.g., master's or doctorate) or professional degree, compared with 10 percent for all Americans. The Asian American population comprises many groups who differ in language and culture, which is reflected in the demographic characteristics of these groups. For instance, 68 percent of Asian Indians hold a bachelor's degree or more education, while only 27 percent of Vietnamese Americans have a bachelor's degree or higher. The poverty rate for Asian Americans is 10 percent; the median household income for Asian Americans is currently $66,000, the highest among all racial groups and statistically unchanged from 2006. However, median household income differs greatly by Asian group. For Asian Indians, for example, the median income is $84,000 while for Vietnamese Americans, it is $54,000 (U.S. Bureau of the Census, 2008).

Such statistics, on first review, might appear to suggest that Asian Americans are the highest wage earners and achievers compared to any other group in the United States—making members of this cultural group what has been called the **model minority**. Yet, although supported by these census data, the concept of a "model minority" is, in fact, a myth. These references to higher median income do not take into account the widely varying educational levels and wage earning reported for the many different Asian American ethnic groups comprising all Asian

American citizens, a higher percentage of more than one wage-earner in families, immigration policies' targeting of Asian professionals for entry into the United States, and the fact that although Chinatowns and similar clustering of Asian American residence and work areas within large cities of the United States are popular tourist attractions, they are, in fact, low-income areas in which the population is very dense and poor. Unemployment, health problems, poverty, and violence pervade these communities.

## A "Model Minority" Group

The fact that Asian Americans are largely perceived to be a model minority group works to limit financial and social support for this group. Asian American students are routinely depicted in the media as star students (especially in the math and science fields) who are supported by their industrious parents dedicated to their education and upward mobility. And while such a stereotype might appear to be beneficial and is certainly helpful in many ways to Asian Americans in terms of opportunity, it also disguises institutional racism and systematic discrimination that Asian Americans continue to confront in the United States. In terms of intergroup relations, such overly favorable depictions of Asian Americans pit them against other minority groups who have not received such good press from the media and who are, instead, accused of being lazy or stupid and incapable of accomplishing the perceived academic success of Asian Americans in the United States. A close examination of educational attainment statistics reveals wide variations among Asian Americans. For example, high school completion rates are 35 percent for Cambodians, 36 percent for Laotians, and 58 percent for Vietnamese students, well below the 82 percent average for Asian Americans as a group (Tatum, 1997).

Therefore, the view that Asian Americans are all successful and functioning well is a popular and widespread belief that does not tell the whole story of this marginalized group who have in the past experienced and continue to experience insidious institutionalized acts of discrimination. The model minority myth discounts and even dismisses the disadvantage and discrimination that Asian Americans still face. Anti-Asian activities, including violence and intimidation, continue to occur.

## CULTURAL FACTOR 2: INITIAL TERMS OF INCORPORATION INTO U.S. SOCIETY

Many Asian American immigrants fit into the category of **voluntary minorities** in that their ancestors came to the United States voluntarily in search of greater economic opportunities. Those who came to the United States with this hope and orientation generally believed that they would succeed in mainstream society through hard work and compliance with authority. There were, however, members of this cultural group, such as the Southeast Asian refugees, who experienced little or no choice in their immigration. These **involuntary minorities** may display opposition to society and its institutions due to the oppression received from being forcibly incorporated into U.S. society. As such, they are less likely to adopt the same compliant behaviors that may be used by voluntary minorities in efforts to achieve (Ogbu, 1990). Their lack of trust that dominant culture and its systems will treat

## Intercultural Communication Strategies for Teachers 6-1

### Sensitivity to History, Current Treatment, and Initial Terms of Incorporation

Knowledge of the histories, current treatment, and initial terms of incorporation into the society of Asian American students will help you prepare to create effective learning communities for them. Specifically, you should do the following:

- Keep in mind that students and their families bring with them a history of experiences with discrimination brought about in schools and in larger society. With these experiences may come caution and mistrust.
- Address trust issues proactively through the utilization of cohesion-building activities in the classroom and such activities that spread to the families of students through newsletters, telephone calls, and interactions in students' homes and communities. For example, you can spend time at the beginning of the year and throughout the learning process facilitating structured activities to help learners feel connected to you and their classmates.
- Begin the school year by sending information home on a regular basis that informs individual student's families about the student's strengths, successes, and school interactions. Such strategies seek to actively form relationships with students and their families around positive aspects of the student. Gradually, as trust builds, you will be able to use the strong relationship bonds you have built with students and their families to effectively address challenges and difficulties, if any, encountered by these students throughout the learning process.

them fairly and their acute awareness that the "deck" is stacked against them may keep them from aligning with dominant culture in any of its institutions, including schools.

Therefore, it is important not to lump all minority group members who share a common ethnic background together in one category. The terms of their incorporation into society alone may account for extreme differences in attitude and adjustment.

## CULTURAL FACTOR 3: SHARED VALUES AND TRADITIONS

Much of the information contained in this chapter is based on generalizations that may or may not account for cultural differences you may encounter with Asian American students and their families. Like all bodies of knowledge, what we know about different ethnic and cultural group values must be considered as information that must be further refined through one's specific knowledge of specific circumstances for individuals in the group. That is to say, no tenet or principle may be applied absolutely to all members of this group or any other.

This is especially important to remember given that the term *Asian American* refers to at least 40 distinct subgroups that differ from each other in language, religion, and cultural values (Yoshika et al., 1981). Within the broader ethnic group of Asian Americans, many differing and often conflict-filled worldviews exist. For instance, among Chinese Americans, cultural differences exist between persons who have immigrated from Hong Kong, Taiwan, and mainland China.

However, even with the great variability within the Asian American population, some values, traditions, and beliefs are commonly shared among members of

## Intercultural Communication Strategies for Teachers 6-2

### Sensitivity to Variations and Uniqueness

Given the levels of acculturation, minority racial identity development, diverse ethnic backgrounds, and individual experiences, Asian American students vary greatly in terms of identity.

- Because one's identity is very important for self-confidence and direction, categorizing members of this group as "Asian" or "Asian American" denies significant aspects of each individual student and may negatively affect her or his academic work. Create times in the school day for individual conferences with your students to offer each student an opportunity to share information with you about his/ her or his family heritage.
- Some Asian American families have immigrated to the United States in hopes of finding opportunities, while others have been forced from their homeland. It is important to be sensitive to differences in initial incorporation into society that may dramatically affect the ways students and their families feel about school. Work to create a climate in your classroom that does not force students to regurgitate what you teach them. Instead, strive to create an environment in which all of your students discover and construct their own knowledge using engaging activities that you facilitate.
- Students of Asian descent are not spokespersons for their ethnic groups or examples of Asian culture. First, educate yourself (through reading and listening to others) about members of ethnic groups enrolled in your classes. Second, do not put minority students on the spot by placing them in the position of educating their peers and you about their culture unless you ask each student (dominant-culture and minority students alike) to share cultural values and traditions with the class.
- In forming work groups, do not assume that students of Asian descent prefer and can work well together. Remember—there is no one "Asian" culture—and concerns can stem from differences within and between their histories, languages, religions, and so on.
- Not all students share similar learning-style preferences; this is true for those of Asian descent as well. Therefore, employing a variety of instructional approaches is best.
- With the value and respect many Asian Americans afford to those who are older and in positions of prestige (for example, teachers), Asian American students may find it difficult to approach you outside of class, even if they require help. Be sensitive to the subtle signs that a student may wish to talk with you and be proactive in requesting to speak individually with your students about topics that go beyond their academic performance to include their social and emotional adjustment in school.

this group. Having a basic knowledge of cultural elements that are exhibited as shared values, traditions, and characteristics is an important foundation on which to begin one's understanding of issues and conflicts experienced.

One of the most important shared values of traditional Asian culture is the strongly held belief in **filial piety** (a supreme respect and devotion to one's family). This value takes formal root in the form of Confucianism, which holds filial piety as a major principle and defines specific rules of conduct in family relationships. Several key concepts follow from the principle of filial piety:

- Family roles are highly structured, hierarchical, male-dominated, and paternally oriented.
- The welfare and integrity of the family are of great importance. An individual is expected to repress his or her emotions, desires, behaviors, and individual

goals to further the family welfare and to maintain its reputation. The individual is obligated to achieve so as not to bring shame on the family. There is pressure, therefore, to keep problems within the family.

- Interdependency is highly valued in traditional Asian culture and stems from the strong sense of obligation to the family. This concept influences relationships among and beyond nuclear family members. The family provides support and assistance for each individual member; in turn, individual members provide support and assistance for the entire family. Further, modesty, discipline, and restraint are qualities that are generally valued among many Asian Americans. Such qualities, relationships, interactions, and obligations are important standards of behavior and are considered lifelong commitments. Goals for members of the group include the development of community and support for other members as opposed to the dominant-culture values emphasizing autonomy and independence. These concepts are critical for understanding Asian American students and their families. Therefore, teachers and school officials, when they observe behaviors consistent with traditional Asian cultural values and beliefs, should avoid seeing members of this group as incapable of assertiveness, codependent, or enmeshed.

Traditional Asian relations and family structures tend to be patriarchal. Fathers may present themselves as aloof and remote and tend to be authoritarian. Communication flows from the top down, and therefore family conflicts are minimized. Mothers are primarily charged with caring for and guiding the education and development of their children. Traditionally, male children may be favored

## Intercultural Communication Strategies for Teachers 6-3

### Infusing Curriculum

Knowledge of commonly shared Asian values, beliefs, and traditions provides teachers with a resource bank of information and ideas to infuse their curricula with diverse worldviews.

- Seek out and include lost and intentionally omitted information from Asian history as curricular content essential to your field.
- Examine your procedures and routines to see if they reflect a dominant-culture bias. That is to say, ask yourself, "Do I value impulsivity (getting one's hand up as quickly as possible to answer a question in the classroom) versus reflection (taking one's time to think deeply about the connections between variables presented in the classroom and then thoughtfully formulate a thorough response)?"

- After using knowledge of the commonly shared values of Asian culture to examine your own practices in the classroom, design ways to make use of cultural elements from Asian culture that would improve the learning environment for all students. For example, an emphasis on cooperation and cooperative learning could be implemented in the classroom to reinforce the interdependence stressed in Asian culture. Specifically, you could utilize base groups (small, cooperative peer-learning communities in the classroom) that are formed at the beginning of the year and to which students return frequently throughout the school year in order to work together in analysis, problem-solving, and task-oriented activities and assignments.

over female children and provided with more benefits and educational opportunities. Asian girls are expected to obey their fathers, carry out domestic duties, marry, and become obedient helpers to their husbands. When children achieve in school, it is a source of pride and accomplishment for their mothers as well as for the students themselves. Similarly, dishonor brought to the family by any one member reflects on all family members. The power of one's name and the maintenance of the family's reputation are clearly noted in the words of Pang-Mei from Chang's *Bound Feet & Western Dress: A Memoir* (1966):

> Now, as you know, we Changs are very proud people. We believe firmly in the Chinese saying, "Your reputation is your second life." This means that to lose your good reputation, your family name, is almost as bad as it is to lose life itself. We Changs lost everything when we were young, but we never lost the Chang name, and this is important. We stayed together as a family and held on to our dignity, our *zhiqi*. Watch people when they win, and you will learn something. But watch people when they lose, and you will learn even more. Our misfortune made us strong, helped us become who we are today. Understand that and you will understand your bloodline.

## CULTURAL FACTOR 4: VIEW OF SPIRITUALITY AND HUMANS' RELATION TO NATURE

Traditional Asian values also place great emphasis on understanding and respecting nature. In poetry, art, and all aspects of life, symbols from nature and legends that provide meaning and can be interpreted for guidance are abundant. Adherence to a framework of disciplined reflection and purposeful action are all hallmarks in this belief system.

While Asian Americans embrace varying theologies and institutional religious practices, three of them have often been most associated with Asian culture: Buddhism, Confucianism, and Taoism. For those that embrace the spiritual concept of reincarnation (for example, Buddhism), pain and suffering in this life may be accepted as one's fate. A major principle of Confucianism is filial piety. From a Taoist perspective, maintaining harmony and balance with nature is important for one's spiritual well-being. The concept of maintaining harmony extends to social relationships, and as such Asian family members may seek to avoid conflict and confrontation with others; may appear passive, indifferent, or indecisive; and may be overtly compliant and agreeable when, in fact, they may disagree with others.

In general, Asian Americans as a group tend to be more formal, structured, cautious, reserved, and conservative than members of dominant culture. There is a concerted emphasis on learning from the past in Asian culture that provides a temporal focus of life on the past. In addition, Asian Americans tend to maintain a focus on the future in their attempts to strive for better lives for themselves and their children.

For Asians who embrace Buddhism as a spiritual structure, time is viewed as circular rather than linear. Many Asians believe in the concepts of reincarnation and karma. Simply stated, *karma* refers to the notion that what happens to you in this life is due to your behaviors and actions in your past life, and your behaviors and actions in this life will influence what will happen to you in the next life.

# CULTURAL FACTOR 5: ACCULTURATION AND EXPERIENCE WITH EXCLUSION AND ALIENATION

Acculturation, the process of adopting dominant-culture attitudes, values, and behavior, is quite often a double-edged sword for Asian and Asian American students. You will see in Yoshiko Uchida's story how her cultural values emphasizing restraint and modesty become components of her protective coping strategies to address discrimination she faces as she attempts to acculturate (Burleson & Mortenson, 2003). She exhibits the tendency of stifling her own feelings and wishes in efforts to escape from the intercultural interaction without rejection. However, to fully acculturate, stifling behaviors proved insufficient. In her story, Yoshiko explained how she was forced to relinquish her value of restraint and modesty in favor of dominant-culture values endorsing assertiveness, directness, and a kind of marketing of oneself that is often interpreted in dominant culture as confidence.

## YOSHIKO'S STORY: JAPANESE IN THE UNITED STATES

I think the first time I became acutely aware of the duality of my person and the fact that a choice in loyalties might be made was when I went with my cousins in Los Angeles to an event at the Olympic Games. Dressed in my red, white, and blue outfit, I was cheering enthusiastically for the American team when I became aware that my cousins were cheering for the men from Japan. It wasn't that they were any less loyal to America than I, but simply that their upbringing in the tightly knit Japanese American community of Los Angeles and their attendance at Japanese Language School has caused them to identify with the men who resembled them in appearance. But I was startled and puzzled by their action. As Japanese as I was in many ways, my feelings were those of an American and my loyalty was definitely to the United States.

As I approached adolescence, I wanted more than anything to be accepted as any other white American. Imbued with the melting-pot mentality, I saw integration into white American society as the only way to overcome the sense of rejection I had experienced in so many areas of my life. The insolence of a clerk or a waiter, the petty arrogance of a bureaucrat, discrimination and denial at many establishments, exclusion from the social activities of my white classmates—all of these affected my sense of personal worth. They reinforced my feelings of inferiority and self-effacement I had absorbed from the Japanese ways of my parents and made me reticent and cautious.

For many years I never spoke to a white person unless he or she spoke to me first. At one of my freshman classes at the university, I found myself sitting next to a white student I had known slightly at high school. I sat silent and tense, not even turning to look at her because I didn't want to speak first and be rebuffed. Finally, she turned to me and said, "Yoshi, aren't you going to speak to me?"

Only then did I dare smile, acknowledge her presence, and become the friendly self I wanted to be. Now, my closest friend for the past 20 years has been a white person, but if I had met him in college, I might never have spoken to him, and probably would not have gone out with him.

When I was in junior high school, I was the only Japanese American to join the Girl Reserve Unit at our school and was accepted within the group as equal. On one occasion, however, we were to be photographed by the local newspaper, and I was among the girls to be included. The photographer casually tried to ease me out of the picture, but one of my white friends just as stubbornly insisted on keeping me in. I think I was finally included, but the realization of what the photographer was trying to do hurt me more than I ever admitted to anyone.

In high school, being different was an even greater hardship than in my younger years. In elementary school one of my teachers had singled out the Japanese American children in class to point to our uniformly high scholastic achievement. (I always worked hard to get A's.) But in high school, we were singled out by our white peers, not for praise, but for total exclusion from their social functions. There was nothing I could do about being left out, but I could take precautions to prevent being hurt in other ways. When I had outgrown my father's home haircuts and wanted to go to a beauty parlor, I telephoned first to ask if they would take me.

"Do you cut Japanese hair?" "Can we come swim in the pool? We're Japanese." "Will you rent us a house? Will the neighbors object?" These were the kinds of questions we asked in order to avoid embarrassment and humiliation. We avoided the better shops and restaurants where we knew we would not be welcome. Once during my college years, when friends from Los Angeles came to visit, we decided to go dancing, as we occasionally did at the Los Angeles Palladium. But when we went to a ballroom in Oakland, we were turned away by a woman at the box office who simply said, "We don't think you people would like the kind of dancing we do here." That put enough of a damper on our spirits to make us head straight for home, too humiliated to go anywhere else to try to salvage the evening.

Society caused us to feel ashamed of something that should have made us feel proud. Instead of directing anger at society that excluded and diminished us, such was the climate of the times and so low our self-esteem that many of us *Nisei* tried to reject our own Japaneseness and the Japanese ways of our parents. We were sometimes ashamed of the *Isseim* their shabby clothes, their rundown trucks and cars, the skin darkened from years of laboring in sun-parched fields, their inability to speak English, their habits, and the food they ate.

I would be embarrassed when my mother behaved in what seemed to me a non-American way. I would cringe when I was with her as she met a Japanese friend on the street and began a series of bows, speaking all the while in Japanese.

"Come on, Mama," I would interrupt, tugging at her sleeve. "Let's go," I would urge, trying to terminate the long exchange of amenities. I felt disgraced in public.

Once a friend from Livingston sent my parents some pickled *daikon*. It had arrived at the post office on Sunday, but the odor it exuded was so pungent and repugnant to the postal workers that they called us to come immediately to pick it up. When the clerk handed the package to me at arm's length with a look of disgust, I was mortified beyond words. (Uchida, 1982, pp. 40–42)

The narrative related by Yoshiko calls our attention to the cultural conflicts encountered in the process of her acculturation. It is clear that her acquisition of dominant-cultural standards of behavior required a true loss of self that was not easily or perhaps even willingly sought and acknowledged (Adkinson, Morten, & Sue, 1992). Use Exercise 6-2 to connect Yoshiko's story with associated feelings.

We know that minority groups respond in numerous and distinct ways to cultural conflict they experience when dominant-culture norms violate their cultural

## EXERCISE 6-2    Point of Reflection: Reflecting on Yoshiko

*Directions:* Review Bich's and Yoshiko's stories. Write down the feelings, attitudes, and opinions you feel toward them. Identify which of these feelings, attitudes, and opinions could influence your relationship with them as their teacher. How might teacher responses affect their achievement and peer interactions?

1. Write a reflection that describes what you would like to remember from these stories for your work with members of Asian minority groups. Consider how you might be perceived by Asian students, what you do that may be helpful or harmful as you interact, and what you would want your students to experience in their interactions with you.

2. Share your reflections with a classmate, colleague, and/or teacher in small-group discussion.

standards of behavior and ways of thinking. Their responses can vary from the rejection of their own cultural backgrounds entirely to a retrenchment and adherence to traditional cultural values in an attempt to resist acculturation. Still others' behaviors and attitudes fall somewhere in between these two patterns of coping. According to Park (1950), the **marginal man** (a person caught between two cultures) lives in "a permanent state of crisis due to an internalized cultural conflict—manifesting in intensified self-consciousness, restlessness, and malaise" (p. 356). The acculturation process that occurs as minority group members interact in and seek to incorporate into U.S. society is linked directly or indirectly to several psychological problems, including feelings of inferiority and depression (DeVos, 1980; Kitano, 1969, 1989; Nidorf, 1985). Further, the requirements associated with acculturation for students in U.S. schools may negatively affect relationships, effective communication, and ultimately academic achievement. Bich Minh Nguyen's experience with acculturation in school shed more light on alienation and dual existences.

### BICH'S STORY: NAME CALLING

Almost all these kids were way ahead of me and Anh. Their parents were anxious for them to fit into Grand Rapids and found the three quickest avenues: food, money, and names. Food meant American burgers and fries. Money meant Jordache jeans and Izod shirts. Names meant a whole new self. Overnight, Thanh's children, Truoc and Doan, became Tiffany and David, and other families followed. Huong to Heather, Quoc to Kevin, Lien to Lynette. Most of the kids chose their names and I listened while they debated the merits of Jennifer versus Michelle, Stephanie versus Crystal. They created two lives for themselves: the American one and the Vietnamese one—Oriental, as we all said back then. Out in the world they were Tiffany and David; at home they were Truoc and Doan. The mothers cooked two meals—pho and sautés for the elders, Campbell's soup and Chef Boyardee for the kids … My sister tried out Ann for a little while, until laziness prevailed and she went back to Anh. It was an easy name anyway, and caused her little stress. Not like my name: Bich. In Vietnamese it meant jade, which was all well and fine in Vietnam but meant nothing in Michigan. It was pronounced with an accent tilting up, the tone leading almost toward a question, with a silent h. Bic! I hated the sound—too harsh, too hard, and the c so slight that it evaporated in air. I preferred to hear it as Bit. The sound seemed tidier, quieter. So that's what I made my name to be, and it was fine until my classmates learned to read and swear. By second grade I was being regularly informed that I was a bitch. I started fantasizing about being a Beth, or maybe a Vanessa or Polly. I long to be Jenny Adams with the perfect simple name to match her perfect honeyed curls. But I knew I could never make it stick. Who would listen to me? Who would allow me to change? Not my family or anyone at school. I could not tell my stepmother, my father, my sister—I could tell no one—what I suffered each day during roll call. The shame layered upon embarrassment equaled silence. I felt I could judge the nature and compassion of teachers by the way they read my name. The good ones hesitated and gently spelled it, avoiding a phonetic pronunciation. The evil ones called out, Bitch? Bitch Nu-guy-in? (Nguyen, 2008, pp. 48–49)

As experienced by Bich Nguyen, Yoshiko Uchida's account is a story of the gradual loss of cultural identity that may occur during the acculturation process and what is often referred to as *self-hatred* or hatred of one's own culture. While such behavior is typically perceived by theorists and school officials, including teachers and counselors, as being unhealthy, deprived, uninformed, irreverent, and just plain wrong-headed, few members of acculturated groups in U.S. society cannot identify with the conflicted feelings Yoshiko expressed—people whose own stories echo these fears, insecurities, and seemingly disloyal sentiments as well. The complexity of these feelings makes them difficult to understand and communicate to others who have not experienced them, thus further complicating and impairing intercultural relations.

As described, Yoshiko is one who was seeking entrance into society while operating with less power. From this powerless position, she was required to defer to the wishes and standards of the dominant system while disguising and suppressing her own thoughts, needs, feelings, and wishes out of necessity for survival. The questions Yoshiko learned to ask to spare additional hurt and humiliation (for example, "Do you cut Japanese hair?" "Can we come swim in the pool? We're Japanese." "Will you rent us a house? Will the neighbors object?") are further examples of not only the extent to which she had to go to attempt to reduce the discrimination and exclusion that she battled in the process of acculturation but also the psychological toll and resulting cultural alienation that is clearly understood in the asking of these questions.

When considered in this light, it is no wonder members of this group may be hesitant to initiate communication with members of dominant culture or to confront conflict in ways members of dominant culture may address conflict (as was seen in the story presented at the beginning of this chapter), due to the risks and potential loss of opportunity entailed for self and family. It is also no wonder that many feel torn by their yearning to be a part of, while at the same time apart from, the dominant culture. This process of aligning with one's oppressor, while objectionable to the oppressed, is often seen as the only available means of survival and will enable eventual progress within the context of a stratified society. This aspect of acculturation—feeling torn between remaining apart from while needing to be a part of the dominant culture—is commonly experienced by minority students and their families. It is a point highlighted at the end of this chapter in the story of Pang-Mei.

## CULTURAL FACTOR 6: LANGUAGE DIFFERENCES, STRENGTHS, AND CHALLENGES

Approximately 2.5 million U.S. residents speak Chinese at home. After Spanish, Chinese is the most widely spoken non-English language in the country. In addition, Tagalog, Vietnamese, and Korean are each spoken at home by more than 1 million people. As is true for many other minority group members, languages used by members of this diverse cultural group provide great richness and means of personal expression that cannot be accomplished using the English language. However, language challenges and interpersonal communication with dominant-culture individuals are of particular concern for Asian Americans. English language and grammar are extraordinarily different from Chinese, Japanese, Korean, and other Asian languages. The English language is incredibly difficult to learn and use effectively for Asian Americans.

> The American language is very difficult because a lot of different words have the same meaning. One problem I have had in learning English is that after I learned what one word means, I got all confused when I found out that another word had the same meaning. For example, good, nice, beautiful, perfect have similar meanings. In Hmong, different words have different meanings." (Xiong in Chan, 1994, p. 102)

To greatly compound the problem, the English as a Second Language (ESL) programs in schools, which are charged with the insurmountable task of teaching all students whose first language is not English to speak fluent English, are underfunded and ill-equipped with persons who speak the huge variety of world languages to effectively teach minority ESL students the language of dominant culture in the United States.

## POTENTIAL BARRIERS IN LEARNING–TEACHING RELATIONSHIPS WITH DOMINANT-CULTURE TEACHERS AND SCHOOLS

Cultural emphasis on restraint, respect for authority, and discretion may lead Asian American students to refrain from asking questions during class when needed. They may also be unlikely to challenge viewpoints or openly disagree with peers in group discussion. Displaying respect for others and keeping the peace are cherished qualities for traditional members of this ethnic group. Depending on students' levels of acculturation, their orientations to dominant culture (be they voluntary or involuntary), and their stages of racial identity development (see Chapter 1 for information on racial identity development), Asian American students may or may not appear compliant and deferential in the classroom. In addition, it may appear that Asian American students agree with adults when they nod their heads out of respect for authority. Teachers need to be careful to identify the actual thoughts and feelings of Asian American students that may not be consistent with their nonverbal behavior and facial expressions. In addition to working to understand how these students actually feel in the classroom, teachers must also work to improve the school climate and teachers' individual relationships with each of their students and their families in efforts to create positive collaborative learning environments.

Language is a huge hurdle for many schools. Asian students may miss out on a considerable part of each school day when their English language deficits are ignored or dealt with ineffectively due to the lack of expertise, training, and resources to help them translate content material into their languages of origin or learn English well enough to understand and communicate in each of the subjects taught.

# FROM CONCEPTS TO LIVED EXPERIENCE

Similar to Yoshiko Uchida's story, in Pang-Mei's story we find that not only must adaptation be a prime consideration for Asian and Asian American students but also issues of personal and psychological survival must be faced. The impact of discrimination and rejection on those who attempt to retain their cultural identities while functioning within the dominant society is great.

Pang-Mei gives voice to suspicions borne from her experience of discrimination in U.S. society. As you read her story, you will see how this discrimination and the resulting suspicions chafe at the very core of her identity and, therefore, her relationships with members of dominant culture as well as with her own cultural group.

## PANG-MEI'S STORY: AN IDENTITY IN FLUX

How exotic, quixotic Hsu Chih-mo must have seemed to his Western friends: an intelligent, extravagantly romantic Chinese discovering kindred spirits and traditions in the West. Hsu Chih-mo had the best of both worlds, I thought. I envied his being able to mix in the western world so well—better than I, and I was brought up here. How did he do it, become friends with Westerners and not have them call him "Chink," not have them call him names? It seemed that he had everything: the admiration of the Chinese and the admiration of the westerners. Or was it that he accepted Englishmen, treated them with a blindness he did not have toward his fellow countrymen? Toward his own wife? Most of my friends were non-Chinese also. Did that mean that I was like Hsu Chih-mo, a sucker for white faces?

When I was in college I envied those Chinese who associated primarily among themselves, speaking Chinese to one another and hanging around in a large group. They always looked so comfortable. Whereas, whenever I was with other Chinese, I could not help but feel self-conscious, concerned as we walked around campus that others might think we were foreigners, outsiders.

At the same time I could not be with my Western friends and walk by a group of Chinese without wondering what they thought of me. Did they think I had disdain for my own heritage? I had trouble with everyone. For example, if I walked into a Chinese restaurant and the waiter began speaking in Chinese to me immediately, I felt put upon. But, if he did not speak Chinese with me, I was equally disturbed.

I wanted to go out with Chinese men. However, I also wanted to go out with Western men, but only on the condition that they knew something about China. Yet, Western men who dated mainly Chinese women aroused my suspicion. Did such men consider us Chinese women more subservient or exotic than our American counterparts? To my even greater distaste were those Westerners who claimed so great an affinity with China that they thought they knew the Chinese better than we knew ourselves. And most of all, I hated anyone, man or woman, who dared attempt to explain me to myself. (Chang, 1996, pp. 110–111)

# SUMMARY

**Cultural Factor 1: Historical and Current Treatment in the United States** The first Chinese immigrants came to the United States in response to the social and economic instability occurring in China in the mid-1840s. At that time, numerous laws (denying citizenship, home ownership, and the right to marry) were passed to discriminate against Chinese people. While initially serving as cheap agricultural laborers, the more the Japanese experienced success in the fishing and farming industries, the more Americans responded with prohibitive legislation.

Many of the first Vietnamese, Cambodian, and Laos immigrants were educated government employees and their families were educated too. Subsequently, many immigrant refugees from this area came from rural and farming communities and were less well-prepared to cope with the rigors of acculturation in the United States.

**Cultural Factor 2: Initial Terms of Incorporation into U.S. Society** Many Asian American immigrants fit into the category of "voluntary minorities." There, were, however, other individuals in the cultural group, such as Southeast Asian refugees, who experienced little or no choice in their immigration. These "involuntary minorities" are more likely to experience greater discord with and discomfort in their interactions with the dominant culture.

**Cultural Factor 3: Shared Values and Traditions** One of the important shared elements of traditional Asian culture is the strongly held beliefs in filial piety (a supreme respect and devotion to one's family). Interdependence, respecting nature, and adhering to a framework of disciplined reflection and purposeful action are also valued among traditional members of the group.

**Cultural Factor 4: View of Spirituality and Human's Relation to Nature** While Asians embrace varying theologies and institutional religious practices, three of them have often been most associated with Asian culture: Buddhism, Confucianism, and Taoism. For those that embrace the spiritual concept of reincarnation (for example, Buddhism), pain and suffering in this life may be accepted as one's fate. A major principle of Confucianism is filial piety; and from a Taoist perspective, maintaining harmony and balance with nature is important to one's spiritual well-being.

**Cultural Factor 5: Acculturation and Experience with Exclusion and Alienation** Responses to acculturation can vary, from the rejection of one's own cultural background entirely to a retrenchment and adherence to traditional cultural values in an attempt to resist assimilation. The acculturation process has been linked directly or indirectly to several psychological problems, including feelings of inferiority, depression, and weakened academic achievement.

**Cultural Factor 6: Language Differences, Strengths, and Challenges** Languages used by members of this cultural group provide great richness and means of expression that cannot be accomplished using the English language. However, language challenges and interpersonal communication with dominant culture are particular concerns for Asian Americans. English language and grammar are extraordinarily different from Asian languages. It is often difficult for Asian Americans to learn and use it effectively. To greatly compound the problem, the English as a Second Language (ESL) programs in schools, which are charged with the insurmountable task of teaching all students whose first language is not English to speak fluent English, are under-funded and ill-equipped.

**Potential Barriers in Learning–Teaching Relationships with Dominant-Culture Teachers and Schools**  Cultural emphasis on restraint, respect for authority, and discretion may lead Asian American students to refrain from asking questions during class when needed. They may also be unlikely to challenge viewpoints or openly disagree with peers in group discussion. Displaying respect for others and keeping the peace are cherished qualities for traditional members of this ethnic group.

Language is a huge hurdle for many schools. Asian students may miss out on a considerable part of each school subject and interaction when their English language deficits are not adequately addressed.

## Questions for Review

1. What are significant traditional values commonly shared by Asian Americans that would be in conflict with dominant-culture perspectives and practices?

2. How is the "model minority" myth a problem for Asian Americans? Are there any benefits?

3. How would the Asian American emphasis on filial piety provide strength and give meaning to life?

## Important Terms

filial piety
internment camps

involuntary minorities
marginal man

voluntary minorities

## Enrichment

Chang, P. M. (1996). *Bound feet & Western dress: A memoir*. New York: Doubleday.

Daniels, R. (1971). *Concentration camps USA: Japanese Americans and WWII*. New York: Holt, Rinehart, & Winston.

Ford, R. (1983). *Counseling strategies for ethnic minority students*. Tacoma, WA: University of Puget Sound. (ERIC Document Reproduction Service No. ED247504)

Houston, J. W., & Houston, J. (1973). *Farewell to Manzanar*. New York: Bantam Books.

Kingston, M. H. (1976). *The woman warrior: Memoirs of a girlhood among ghosts*. NY: Vintage Books.

Kitano, H. H. L. (1969). *Japanese Americans: The evolution of a subculture*. Englewood Cliffs, NJ: Prentice Hall.

Sunee, K. (2008). *Trail of crumbs: Hunger, love, and the search for home: A memoir*. NY: Hachette Book Group.

Uchida, Y. (1982). *Desert exile: The uprooting of a Japanese-American family*. Seattle: University of Washington.

## Connections on the Web

http://www.asian-nation.org/
  This site provides comprehensive information on Asian cultures including resources, statistics, and perspectives on issues relevant to the population.

http://www.lib.berkeley.edu/MRC/AsianAmvid.html

This site offers a rich array of Asian American video resources with detailed descriptions of each resource.

http://en.allexperts.com/q/Asian-American-Culture-2723/

This website is a question and answer site on which experts address questions posed about Asian American culture.

## References

Adkinson, D. R., Morten, G., & Sue, D. W. (Eds.). (1992). *Counseling American minorities: A cross-cultural perspective* (4th ed.). Dubuque, IA: Brown & Benchmark.

Burleson, B. R., & Mortenson, S. R. (2003). Explaining cultural differences in the evaluation of emotional support behaviors: Exploring the mediating influences of value systems and interaction goals. *Communication Research*, 30(2), 113–146.

Chan, K. (1981). Education for Chinese and Indochinese. *Theory into Practice*, 20(1), 35–44.

Chan, S. (1994). *Hmong means free: Life in Laos and America*. Philadelphia: Temple University Press.

Chang, P. M. (1996). *Bound feet & western dress: A memoir*. New York: Doubleday.

Daniels, R. (1971). *Concentration camps USA: Japanese Americans and WWII*. New York: Holt, Rinehart, & Winston.

DeVos, G. (1980). Acculturation: Psychological problems. In I. Rossi (Ed.), *People in culture*. New York: Praeger.

DeVos, G., & Abbot, K. (1966). *The Chinese family in San Francisco*. Unpublished master's thesis, University of California, Berkeley.

Jones, J. M. (1972). *Prejudice and racism*. Reading, MA: Addison Wesley.

Kitano, H. H. L. (1969). *Japanese Americans: The evolution of a subculture*. Englewood Cliffs, NJ: Prentice Hall.

Kitano, H. H. L. (1989). A model for counseling Asian Americans. In P. B. Pedersen, J. G. Draguns, W. J. Lonner, & J. E. Trimble (Eds.), *Counseling across cultures* (pp. 139–152). Honolulu: University of Hawaii.

Lee, E. (1996). Asian American families: An overview. In M. McGoldnck, J. G. Giordano, & J. K. Pearce (Eds.), *Ethnicity and family therapy* (2nd ed., pp. 227–248). New York: Guilford.

Nguyen, B. M. (2008). *Stealing Buddha's dinner: A memoir*. NY: Penguin Books.

Nicassio, P. M. (1985). The psychological adjustment of the Southeast Asian refugee. *Journal of Cross-Cultural Psychology*, 16(2), 153–173.

Nidorf, J. F. (1985). Mental health and refugee youths: A model for diagnostic training. In T.C. Owan (Ed.), *Southeast Asian mental health* (pp. 391–430). Rockville, MD: National Institute of Mental Health.

Nishi, S. M. (1982). The educational disadvantage of Asian Pacific Americans. *AHRC Research Review*, 1, 4–6.

Ogbu, J. U. (1990). Minority education in comparative perspective. *Journal of Negro Education*, 59, 45–55.

Park, R. E. (1950). *Race and culture*. Glencoe, IL: Free Press.

Sue, D., & Sue, D. (1993). *Counseling the culturally different: Theory and practice*. New York: Wiley.

Tatum, B. D. (1997). *"Why are all the Black kids sitting together in the cafeteria?" and other conversations about race*. New York: Basic Books.

Uchida, Y. (1982). *Desert exile: The uprooting of a Japanese-American family*. Seattle: University of Washington.

U.S. Bureau of the Census. (1985). *Statistical abstract of the United States*. Washington, DC: U.S. Department of Commerce.

U.S. Bureau of the Census (1986). *Statistical abstract of the United States*. Washington, DC: U.S. Department of Commerce.

U.S. Bureau of the Census. (2008). *Statistical abstract of the United States*. Washington, DC: U.S. Government Printing Office.

U.S. Committee for Refugees. (1987). *World refuge survey: 1986 in review*. Washington, DC: American Council for Nationality Service.

U.S. Department of Health and Welfare. (1979). *The congress Indochinese refugee assistance program*. Washington, DC: Social Security Administration Office of Refugee Affairs.

Yashima, T., & Tanaka, T. (2001). Roles of social support and social skills in the intercultural adaptation of Japanese adolescents. *Psychological Reports Part 2*, 88(3), 1201–1211.

*...you scale the seven flights to an oasis on the roof, high above the city noise, where you can think to the rhythms of your own land. Discordant notes rise with the traffic at five, mellow to a bolero at sundown. Keeping company with the pigeons, you watch the people below, flowing in currents on the street where you live, each one alone in a crowd, each one an island like you.*
**Judith Ortiz Cofer (1996, p. ix)**

CHAPTER

7

# Learning from Latino/a Stories

Cofer describes her experiences living among strangers through the images of her poetry. Her description is of her flight to a rooftop in an effort to find an oasis within a city, where she can reconnect with her culture.

The current chapter explores stories of Latino/as. As with Chapters 5 and 6, the focus of this chapter is on the rich traditions, shared values, experiences with institutional discrimination, and coping strategies of this cultural group. Autobiographical case narratives are presented to illuminate the six major cultural factors presented in this text. As you fully understand the cultural values, perspectives, and lived experiences of Latino/as living in the United States, you will be better able to create learning environments that effectively engage, enrich, and empower Latino/a students.

## CHAPTER OBJECTIVES

1. Describe common traditional values and worldviews shared by Latino/as.
2. Identify ways in which the individuals profiled in the case narratives experienced and addressed the six cultural factors explored in this text.
3. Explain academic and intercultural interaction implications related to the six cultural factors for members in this ethnic group.
4. Describe coping strategies utilized by members of this group.
5. Identify classroom strategies for cultivating the resources provided when traditional Latino/as' worldviews are integrated in your curriculum.

# CULTURAL FACTOR 1: HISTORICAL AND CURRENT TREATMENT IN THE UNITED STATES

The Latino population, like the Asian American population, is an ethnically diverse group comprised of Mexican Americans, Puerto Ricans, Cubans, and Central and South Americans, each coming from a distinct land of origin, yet linked by a common language and cultural heritage. Some Latino groups have recently immigrated, while others have been in the United States since long before the arrival of the Pilgrims (Barrett et al., 2005). The terms **Latino** and **Hispanic** have both been used to identify members of this minority group. *Hispanic*—stemming from and related to the word *Hispano* which means a native or resident of Spanish descent living in the southwest United States—is a term used by the U.S. Bureau of the Census to include persons of Spanish origin or descent and those who designate themselves as Mexican, Mexican American, Chicano, Puerto Rican, or Cuban. It has also been used by the government as an ethnic label to denote ethnically mixed combinations of White, Black, indigenous Indian, and Latin American ancestry. In contrast, *Latino + Latina—Latino/as,* a preferred term for many members of this minority group, emphasizes a Latin American background as opposed to reflecting a label placed by dominant culture that unites a group of Spanish-speaking people.

Latinos are the largest and fastest-growing minority group in the United States. More than 60 percent of Latinos in the United States have Mexican ancestry, a population that includes recent Mexican immigrants and U.S.-born Mexican Americans (also called Chicanos) whose ancestors lived in the Southwest generations before Europeans landed in North America.

The history of Chicanos resembles that of other involuntary minority groups in the United States. Following the U.S. conquest and annexation of Mexican territory in 1848 and with the resulting domination of these Mexican residents of the United States came their involuntary incorporation into dominant culture. It seems these Mexican residents did not cross the border, instead the border crossed them. And, as was the case for other minority groups, their involuntary incorporation was *incorporation* in name only. Mexican residents were then forcibly segregated into a few states (for example, Texas and California) that passed laws to oppress them, including outlawing the use of the Spanish language in schools.

Like the conquered Mexicans, Puerto Ricans did not choose to become U.S. citizens. Puerto Rico became an unincorporated territory of the United States in 1898, ceded by Spain at the conclusion of the Spanish–American War. Puerto Rico struggled to become independent from Spain while fighting subjugation by the United States. When U.S. policy attempted to replace the Spanish language with English as the dominant language for school instruction in Puerto Rico, residents resisted, culminating in a student strike at Central High School in San Juan. The U.S. government responded by passing the Jones Act of 1917 that imposed citizenship on Puerto Ricans but simultaneously denied these new citizens the right to vote.

In 1951, Puerto Ricans were permitted to vote on whether to remain an independent territory or to become a commonwealth of the United States. Puerto Ricans chose to become a commonwealth, which gave them greater control of their schools, including the restoration of the Spanish language as the primary language of instruction. However, economic conditions in Puerto Rico persuaded many of its residents to move to Northeastern cities in the United States, especially during the 1940s and 1950s. The difficulty of finding stable work in Puerto Rico and in the United States forced many Puerto Ricans to move back and forth in order to earn a living. As a result, Puerto Ricans tend to be among the poorest of the Latino groups in the United States, with a poverty rate at nearly 60 percent (U.S. Bureau of the Census, 2000).

A third Latino group, Cuban Americans, tends to be, in general, older and more affluent than other Latino groups in the United States. Cubans have lived in Florida and New York since the 1870s, but experienced their largest immigration to the United States in 1959, following the revolution led by Fidel Castro. The first wave of immigrants was considered to be, for the most part, upper-class individuals. During this early phase of immigration, many Cubans were able to leave Cuba with much of their personal wealth, and many quickly established businesses in the United States. The next immigrants to leave Castro's Cuba were mainly middle-class professionals and skilled workers. Unlike their predecessors, most were unable to bring their possessions with them but received support from the U.S. government. The last major group of Cubans who immigrated to the United States arrived in 1980, having lived under a socialist government for much of their lives. These Cubans were, as a group, much poorer and less educated than earlier refugees from Cuba (Leslie & Leitch, 1989). It is clear that depending on the disparate conditions under which different groups of Latinos came to the United States and the varying treatment experienced based on their social status and characteristics, there are many varying conditions, experiences, and worldviews shared by various members of the Latino group. Exercise 7-1 will help you to widen your awareness of the extensive variation among members in this cultural group.

It is widely known that Latinos are the fastest-growing ethnic minority groups in the United States, growing five times as fast as any other group (U.S. Bureau of the Census, 2003). Not only are Latinos unique in terms of their high growth rate in the United States but they are also unique as a group, because they have tended to settle in fewer areas of the United States than other ethnic groups.

## EXERCISE 7-1    Field Experience: Not One But Many

**Directions:**

1. Select any two Latino ethnic groups. Find articles that describe the cultural values and traditions of each of these two groups. Alternatively, interview two people from each of the selected groups, gathering information about their values and practices, including their perspectives on family, church, and community. Identify what values and traditions do they uphold and pass on?

2. Compare and contrast the data reflecting the cultural values and traditions of each of the two groups you studied. What similarities and differences do you find between the groups you researched? With which values and traditions do you identify? Consider the advantages that stem from the cultural values and traditions that Latino students may share. List these characteristics. Finally, identify ways by which teachers may be able to build on the characteristics you have listed to positively affect the academic achievement of students in their classrooms who possess these qualities.

Nearly 90 percent of the Latino population is located in nine states: California, Texas, New York, Florida, Illinois, New Jersey, Arizona, New Mexico, and Colorado. In addition, the vast majority of the population is concentrated in urban centers of U.S. cities. These two factors, close clustering and rapid growth, have provided both strengths and challenges for members of the group (Suarez-Orozco & Suarez-Orozco, 1995).

On the one hand, the densely populated Latino community has served to help preserve traditional culture by providing opportunities to hand down values, knowledge, beliefs, and customs from one generation to the next. Further, such demography has provided the group with a degree of political power in states heavily populated by Latino/as. On the other hand, their minority status (which contributes to low-paying jobs and high unemployment), a high growth rate, and close clustering of the Latino population in major urban centers in the United States has led to problems as well, such as poverty, enrollment in poorly funded schools, underachievement in U.S. schools, overcrowded housing, and neighborhood violence. The poverty rate for Latino/as in the United States is astounding. According to the U.S. Bureau of the Census (2003), approximately 28 percent of Latino families live in poverty, compared to 9.2 percent of non-Latino families (See Table 7-1).

**Table 7-1**  U.S. Latino Population

| National origin | Population | Percent |
|---|---|---|
| Total | 35,305,818 | 100.0 |
| Mexican | 20,640,711 | 58.5 |
| Puerto Rican | 3,406,178 | 9.6 |
| Cuban | 1,241,685 | 3.5 |
| Dominican (Dominican Republic) | 764,945 | 2.2 |
| Central American (excludes Mexican) | 1,686,937 | 4.8 |
| Costa Rican | 68,588 | 0.2 |
| Guatemalan | 372,487 | 1.1 |
| Honduran | 217,569 | 0.6 |
| Nicaraguan | 177,684 | 0.5 |
| Panamanian | 91,723 | 0.3 |
| Salvadoran | 655,165 | 1.9 |
| Other Central American | 103,721 | 0.3 |
| South American | 1,353,562 | 3.8 |
| Argentinean | 100,864 | 0.3 |
| Bolivian | 42,068 | 0.1 |
| Chilean | 68,849 | 0.2 |
| Colombian | 470,684 | 1.3 |
| Ecuadorian | 260,559 | 0.7 |
| Paraguayan | 8,769 | (1) |
| Peruvian | 233,926 | 0.7 |
| Uruguayan | 18,804 | 0.1 |
| Venezuelan | 91,507 | 0.3 |
| Other South American | 57,532 | 0.2 |
| All other Latino | 6,211,800 | 17.6 |

*Source:* U.S. Census Bureau, Census 2000.

# CULTURAL FACTOR 2: INITIAL TERMS OF INCORPORATION INTO U.S. SOCIETY

Many of the early Latino immigrants came to the United States from nonindustrial, agrarian-based countries. Most were monolingual, speaking only Spanish, and were unskilled for working industrial jobs in cities. As such, the majority of the Latino population was forced to join the millions of other minority groups in competition for low-paying jobs in the United States. One exception to these economic conditions was the immigration pattern of the initial group of Cuban immigrants. The first of the immigrants from Cuba were mostly highly educated, middle-class, skilled workers. Skilled or unskilled, incorporation was not easy for Cuban immigrants. Their traditions, customs, and language separated and, in many cases, isolated many of them from dominant culture. Further, the conditions under which some groups of Latinos left their homelands and immigrated to the United States often hindered the process of their incorporation into U.S. society. For example, refugees arriving from El Salvador and Nicaragua faced and continue to face additional challenges stemming from the civil wars in which they and/or their family members have been embattled. Whereas other politically exiled refugees like Cubans and many Chileans may have anticipated their immigration and made arrangements to establish support before coming to the United States, many displaced persons, like those coming from Central America, who experienced a history of oppression and exploitation in their country of origin, became members of the poor and working class in the United States. These individuals often left their countries without preparation or support and were suddenly relocated to the United States with few resources (Leslie & Leitch, 1989).

Coming from such upheaval and violence, this group of Latinos, having lived life as refugees fearing deportation, may be reluctant to trust governmental institutions. In addition, parents of children in this cultural group may closely monitor and try to protect their children from institutional discrimination and harm out of anxiety learned in their pervasive exposure to war (Petuchowski, 1988). Institutional discrimination leading to reluctance to forge relationships with different others as well as group members' traditional patterns of keeping close to home, close to family, and close to cultural group members understandably may interfere with many Latinos' transition and establishment of intercultural relationships in the United States.

# CULTURAL FACTOR 3: SHARED VALUES AND TRADITIONS

Many Latino/as are united by customs, language, religion, and values. There is, however, extensive diversity among members of this group. One characteristic of particular importance for most Latino/as is commitment to family, which involves loyalty, a strong support system, a belief that a child's behavior reflects the honor of the family, and a duty to care for immediate and extended family members.

Traditionally, Latino families are patriarchal. Fathers are authoritarian, and wives do not publicly question their husbands' decisions. However, the appearance of power distribution between Latinos can be deceiving. It is important to be aware that **Latinas** hold a special position of respect in the household. They are revered by their husbands and children for their protection, strength, and work.

Males are expected to have **machismo**. But machismo, which in dominant culture may seem akin to male chauvinism, in Latino culture is actually a form of chivalry that includes gallantry, courtesy, charity, and courage (Baron, 1991). Machismo requires Latinos to protect their wives and family and at the same time display sexual prowess, masculinity, and strength by remaining emotionally withdrawn and sometimes having extramarital affairs.

Latinos are expected to be rational, brave, independent, and virile, while Latinas are expected to be submissive, dependent, and pure (Semour, 1977). **Marianismo**, which is a traditional Latina's socialized code of behavior, dictates that Latinas remember their docile and subjugated place in society, put their own needs below those of their husbands and families, refrain from criticizing their husbands, keep personal problems to themselves, and remain faithful to the marriage and family at all costs (Gil & Vazquez, 1990).

The importance of fathers and family of origin can be seen in Spanish tradition, in which patrilineal descent is traced via naming through wives' second-to-last name. A mother's maiden name (her father's) may also become her child's last name.

In traditional Latino culture, extended family members are considered integral. **Familismo** (familism), which extends kinship beyond nuclear-family boundaries, is also highly valued. Familismo emphasizes interdependence over independence, affiliation over confrontation, and cooperation over competition (Bernal & Gutierrez, 1988; Falicov, 1982, 2005). How might these gender roles and expectations conflict with dominant culture gender prescriptions in the United States? Consider Exercise 7-2 "Uncovering Media Messages."

As an extension of familismo, Latinos tend to be a cohesive cultural group. Personal security is gained through a strong family bond rather than from solitary actions and self-reliance. One manifestation of familismo that is unlike the

---

**EXERCISE 7-2**    **Point of Reflection: Uncovering Media Messages**

***Directions:***

1. Many of the values held as part of the Latino/a culture are in direct contrast to dominant-culture values. As you view movies, watch television, and read magazines and newspapers, identify five different views of what makes the so called good life. Record the images and essential messages and values you observe in viewing these media.

2. Describe the values implied or conveyed. Contrast these values endorsed by dominant culture with those promulgated within Latino culture. For example, perhaps a movie plot involves disbelief that a grown man lives at home with his parents, as in the movie *Failure to Launch* (Paramount Pictures, 2006). Would such a belief system conflict with Latino/as' cultural values?

3. Review your data and discuss with a colleague, classmate, and or instructor the possible impact that these messages may have on young Latino/as and the resulting potential for family community conflict.

dominant-culture's view of using school and work as tools for gaming independence from their families is the Latino tendency to value school and work because success in both arenas creates possibilities for supporting and remaining in close contact with their families (Suarez-Orozco & Suarez-Orozco, 1995). In general, Latinos value **collectivism**—a collective community and willingness to sacrifice for the welfare of the group, where trust among group members and interdependence are emphasized.

Other values extending from this cultural group's value of interdependence are **simpatia**—the promotion of pleasant, nonconflicting social relationships—and displaying **respeto** (respect). For members of the group, *simpatia* and *respeto* are manifested in appropriate deferential behavior toward others on the basis of age, socioeconomic status, gender, and authority. In addition, members of the group may strongly believe that one's behavior outside the family reflects directly on the family. As such, each individual is responsible for the reputation of the entire family.

While history is valued and often kept alive through family stories, the primary orientation of traditional Latino/as is to the present. Unlike many people in dominant culture who may find their days and their lives driven by appointment books, calendars, and to-do lists, Latino cultural values do not emphasize rigid adherence to schedules. Whereas dominant-culture members may interpret a guest coming late to a dinner party as disrespectful, tardiness would not necessarily be interpreted that way by Latinos. Instead, in keeping with a focus on the resent, when a guest is twenty minutes late to arrive for a meal, traditional Latinos are more likely to believe that the guest is giving the hosts more time to prepare the meal without needing to hurry. Consider Exercise 7-3.

---

## EXERCISE 7-3   Classroom Applications: Discovering Cultural Insight

### Directions:

1. Cut about 100 phrases or words and images from various magazines to develop a collage box of your clippings. Make sure you use magazines that reflect different gender, cultural, age, and social-class interests and preferences. As you cut out words and images, do not think too much about which phrases or words and pictures you clip. Instead, cut out anything that catches your eye and interest.

2. Using your collage box, find about 10 phrases, words, and or pictures that depict significant values endorsed by Latinos. Construct a collage from these materials.

3. Construct a second collage that depicts dominant-culture values.

4. Review both collages with a colleague, classmate, and/or teacher and identify the primary messages conveyed in each collage.

5. After reflection, develop three strategies for ensuring that the values endorsed by Latinos are present in the materials, resources, and curricula you intend to employ as a teacher.

6. Keep your collage box of clippings to use to enhance additional reflections suggested in this text. When you utilize images as well as words in your reflections, you engage additional creative energies that will sharpen your thinking and analysis.

## Personal Narrative 7-1   Aria

My story discloses the essential myth of childhood—inevitable pain. If I rehearse here the changes in my private life after my Americanization, it is finally to emphasize the public gain. The loss implies the gain: the house I returned to each afternoon was quiet. Intimate sounds no longer rushed to the door to greet me. There were other noises inside. The telephone rang. Neighborhood kids ran past the door of the bedroom where I was reading my schoolbooks—covered with shopping-bag paper.

Once I learned public language, it would never again be easy for me to hear intimate family voices. More and more of my days were spent hearing words. But that was only by a way of saying that the day I raised my hand in class and spoke loudly to an entire roomful of faces, my childhood started to end.

I grew up a victim to disabling confusion. As I grew fluent in English, I no longer could speak Spanish with confidence. I continued to understand spoken Spanish. And in high school, I learned how to read and write Spanish. But for many years I could not pronounce it. A powerful guilt blocked my spoken words; an essential glue was missing whenever I'd try to connect words to form sentences. I would be unable to break a barrier of sound, to speak freely. I would speak, or try to speak, Spanish, and I would manage to utter halting, hiccupping sounds that betrayed my unease.

When relatives and Spanish-speaking friends of my parents came to the house, my brother and sisters seemed reticent to use Spanish, but at least they managed to say a few necessary words before being excused. I never managed so gracefully. I was cursed with guilt. Each time I'd hear myself addressed in Spanish, I would be unable to respond with any success. I'd know the words that I wanted to say, but I couldn't manage to say them. I would try to speak, but everything I said seemed to me horribly anglicized. My mouth would not form the words right. My jaw would tremble. After a phrase or two, I'd cough up a warm, silvery sound. And stop.

*Source: Hunger of Memory: The Education of Richard Rodriguez.* Richard Rodriquez. Copyright 2004. Reprinted by permission of David R. Godine, Publishers.

# CULTURAL FACTOR 4: VIEW OF SPIRITUALITY AND HUMANS' RELATION TO NATURE

Latino/as also tend to extend the value of interdependence to include nature. However, nature is not conceptualized as something to be controlled or mastered. With a strong, agrarian background, Latino culture values nature, seeing in it a partner for life.

Richly colored by Catholicism, Latino spirituality reflects a strong belief in **cultural fatalism**. The belief often takes the form of a resolution to the way things are and as the way they are meant to be. The belief simply reflects the position that things that happen are *meant* to happen and are beyond individuals' control; this belief is embodied in the phrase: "It was God's will."

In contrast to the Catholicism of Catholic School, the Mexican Catholicism of home was less concerned with man the sinner than with man the supplicant. God the Father was not so much a stern judge as One with the power to change our lives. My family turned to God not in guilt so much as in need. We prayed for favors and at desperate times. I prayed for help in finding a quarter I had lost on my way home. I prayed with my family at times of illness and when my father was temporarily out of a job. And when there was death in the family, we prayed.

I remember my family's religion, and I hear the whispering voices of women. For although men in my family went to church, women prayed most audibly. Whether by man or woman, however, God the Father was rarely addressed directly. There were intermediaries to carry one's petition to Him. My mother had her group of Mexican and South American saints and near-saints (persons moving toward canonization). She favored a Black Brazilian priest, who, she claimed, was especially efficacious. Above all mediators there was Mary, Santa Maria, the Mother. Whereas at school the primary mediator was Christ, at home the role was assumed by the Mexican Virgin, Nuestra Senora de Guadalupe, the focus of devotion and pride for Mexican Catholics. The Mexican Mary "honored our people," my mother would say. "She could have appeared to anyone in the whole world, but she appeared to a Mexican." Someone like us. And she appeared, I could see from her picture, as a young Indian maiden—dark just like me.

*Source:* Richard Rodriguez, *Hunger of Memory: The Education of Richard Rodriguez* (2004), p. 90.

Research has identified the importance of religion in Latino culture. In fact, Latino adolescents are more inclined than dominant-culture adolescents to adopt their parents' commitment to religion (Black, Paz, & DeBlassie, 1991).

## CULTURAL FACTOR 5: ACCULTURATION AND EXPERIENCE WITH EXCLUSION AND ALIENATION

I was six years old when my family moved from México to the US. My older siblings were eight and ten and even though they didn't know how to speak English, they were familiar with how school worked as they had attended private school in México and seemed to make the cultural and linguistic adjustments. I couldn't. It took me a while to catch on. We were the only Latinos in the school, and back then there weren't any ESL or Bilingual programs to help students learn English, or acculturate. It was total immersion and pretty much sink or swim. I felt lost most of the time and not knowing how to speak English or how school worked made me very anxious. I was afraid I would say or do the wrong thing—and usually did. I was invisible to my teachers and my classmates and ended-up repeating first grade. Eventually I caught on. I graduated from high school as the first Latino student body president from an all-white high school. Yet to this day, I still feel that elementary school anxiety, when I step into a graduate school classroom. I get to the classroom early—so I can sit in the back of the room.

*Source:* William Salazar, *personal communication,* March 2010.

Unique stresses created by the process of immigration to another country and discrimination faced in the new country can create psychological distress for many immigrants. The process of acculturation and adaptation is believed to proceed through a series of stages. These stages, while not rigidly linear might include: (1) initial joy and relief, (2) disillusionment with the new country, and (3) acceptance of the good and the bad in the host country (Arrendondo-Dowd, 1981). Evidence of movement through stages of acculturation and adaptation can be seen in both internal processes and external conflicts.

Addressing the conflict between valuing one's family, history, and cultural legacy while finding a place within the dominant society, can be particularly stressful. Adolescent Latinos are especially challenged as they try to balance their cultural values, including strong family loyalty, language differences, and their need to find a place among their school peers, whose dominant-cultural values of self-expression and individuality may conflict with their family values and beliefs.

> No learning experience was more painful or damaging than the silence imposed on our Mexican culture, history, and beautiful Spanish language. To speak Spanish was not only illegal but also a sin in Catholic School: "Bless me Father, for I have sinned. I spoke Spanish in class and during recess..." Mea culpa, mea culpa, mea maxima culpa! I gently rapped my closed fist on my chest. I knew I would sin again but that was all right because there was always confession, now called "reconciliation".
>
> The silence of our language, culture, and history was broken at home by our mother, a former school teacher in Mexico. She taught her six children to know, love, and respect our language, our customs and our history.
>
> This is one reason why I write—to express those beliefs and to teach what was once a silent sin. These words etched in black ink are made not from individual letters bur scars that perforate the paper like open wounds to the soul of a young Chicano who sought the truth in his own refection.
>
> Blessed be the teachings of many cultures in the classrooms! Blessed be the truth in her many fashions and forms! Blessed be God in her Glory and wisdom!
>
> *Source:* Jose Antonio Burciaga, *Drink Cultura: Chicanismo,* 1993, p. 40.

## CULTURAL FACTOR 6: LANGUAGE DIFFERENCES, STRENGTHS, AND CHALLENGES

Sociolinguistic studies in the Latino community have shown the important ways in which language usage relates to issues of identity, racial stigma, and social power relations (Garcia, Monn, & Rivera, 2001; Torres, 1997). Language for traditional Latinos is inextricably linked to cultural identity. It is not only an instrumental tool for communication but also an expression of cultural values. Research suggests that feelings of racial, ethnolinguistic, and economic subordination play key roles in one's willingness to adopt dominant-culture language (see Zentella, 1997; Urciuoli, 1997). How Latino/as reflect and relate to their language and how language contributes to their ethnic identity will largely be affected by the degree of their racial identity development and the degree of stigma experienced. The Spanish language continues to be devalued in U.S. society. Such discrimination facilitates a loss of cultural identity that weakens Latino connections with others in the Latino community once the English language is acquired. Consider the stifling of expression described in Personal Narrative 7-1 and the reactions of a young Puerto Rican girl who experienced discrimination in her interactions with dominant-culture school which is described in Personal Narrative 7-2. Even though proficiency in one's native language positively correlates with proficiency in a second language, English as a Second Language (ESL) programs, in which only the English language is taught, continue to be the main method for accommodating students' needs to acquire the language of dominant

## Personal Narrative 7-2    The Importance of Language

The school building was not a welcoming sight for someone used to the bright colors and airiness of tropical architecture. The building looked functional. It could have been a prison, an asylum, or just what it was: an urban school for the children of immigrants built to withstand waves of change, generation by generation. Its red brick sides rose to four solid stories. The black steel fire escapes snaked up its back like an exposed vertebra. A chain-link fence surrounded its concrete playground. Members of the elite safety patrol, older kids, sixth graders mainly, stood at each of its entrances, wearing their fluorescent white belts that criss-crossed their chests and their metal badges. No one was allowed in the building until the bell rang, not even on rainy or bitter-cold days. Only the safety-patrol stayed warm.

My mother stood in front of the main entrance with me and a growing crowd of noisy children. She looked like one of us, being no taller than the sixth-grade girls. She held my hand so tightly that my fingers cramped. When the bell rang, she walked me into the building and kissed my cheek. Apparently my father had done all the paperwork for my enrollment, because the next thing I remember was being led to my third-grade classroom by a [B]lack girl who had emerged from the principal's office.

Though I had learned some English at home during my first years in Paterson, I had let it recede deep into my memory while learning Spanish in Puerto Rico. Once again I was the child in the cloud of silence, the one who had to be spoken to in sign language as if she were a deaf-mute. Some of the children even raised their voices when they spoke to me, as if I had trouble hearing. Since it was a large troublesome class composed mainly of [B]lack and Puerto Rican children, with a few working-class Italian children interspersed, the teacher paid little attention to me. I relearned the language quickly by the immersion method. I remember one day soon after I joined the rowdy class when our regular teacher was absent and Mrs. D., the sixth-grade teacher from across the hall, attempted to monitor both classes. She scribbled something on the chalkboard and went to her own room. I felt a pressing need to use the bathroom and asked Julio, the Puerto Rican boy who sat behind me, what I had to do to be excused. He said that Mrs. D. had written on the board that we could be excused by simply writing our names under the sign. I got up from my desk and started for the front of the room when I was struck on the head hard with a book. Startled and hurt, I turned around expecting to find one of the bad boys in my class, but it was Mrs. D I faced. I remember her angry face, her fingers on my arms pulling me back to my desk, and her voice saying incomprehensible things to me in a hissing tone. Someone finally explained to her that I was new, that I did not speak English. I also remember how suddenly her face changed from anger to anxiety. But I did not forgive her for hitting me with that hard-cover spelling book. Yes, I would recognize that book even now. It was not until years later that I stopped hating that teacher for not understanding that I had been betrayed by a classmate, and by my inability to read her warning on the board. I instinctively understood then that language is the only weapon a child has against the absolute power of adults.

Source: Cofer, J. O. (1990). Silent Dancing: A Partial Remembrance of a Puerto Rican Childhood (pp. 65–66). Houston: Arte Publico.

culture in U.S. schools. There is abundant research demonstrating the superiority of bicultural language programs for teaching non-English-speaking students to become fluent in the English language while retaining their native language. Still, English-only ESL programs are widely utilized because they do not require the utilization of Spanish-speaking teachers as bicultural language programs do. ESL programs are now called *English Language Learners* (ELL) programs because

## Intercultural Communication Strategies for Teachers 7-1

### Classroom Applications: Learning to Include

Some Latino students have little or no association with Latino culture. For others, being Latino is an all-encompassing aspect of their daily lives. Teachers should not assume that each student whose surname suggests a Latino background can present the Latino perspective or is fluent in Spanish. In order to facilitate positive interactions, teachers should do the following:

- Avoid generalizations about Latino/as. This will provide opportunities for all students to display their cultural characteristics within an open, nonjudgmental learning environment.

- Because of various levels of interest, family exposure, and competency, not all students share the same knowledge of Spanish language. Invite the students to use and make reference to words, metaphors, and stories from their culture, but do not assume they can or wish to do so.

- Acknowledge and celebrate cultural diversity through the use of varied learning curricula and resources, including Latino poetry, stories, and perspectives.

English is usually not the second language for immigrants coming to the United States, who often speak more than two languages. Latino students who do not speak English when they enter U.S. schools have little chance of being able to learn math, language arts, science, and social studies concepts in academic subjects when they are provided with three or less years of access to English-only ESL programs for English instruction dispersed in segments throughout their school day—especially if these students come to U.S. schools enrolled at older grade levels where course content involves the understanding of complex terms and concepts explored in English. The truth is, these students have a slim chance of becoming fluent and proficient in English in academic subjects, and their achievement drops accordingly (Moran & Hakuta, 1995). In fact, special-education classrooms have become a dumping ground for students whose first language is not English—mistaking their lack of English-language proficiency for learning disabilities. Such occurrences greatly stigmatize and disadvantage these students.

Teachers of Spanish-speaking students who are aware of Spanish-language devaluation in the United States can improve the learning environment in their classrooms by speaking in English and Spanish during class. If teachers do not speak Spanish, they may arrange for Spanish-speaking members of the community to act as interpreters in the classroom and to teach Spanish lessons for all students in the class. Teachers may also encourage their students to employ Spanish within the classroom setting and or in their assignments. However, it is a mistake to assume that all Latinos are fluent in Spanish. Many Latino students lack fluency in Spanish or may only possess some limited spoken communication skills. It is clear that teachers should avoid forming generalizations and, instead, gain specific knowledge and understanding of each of their student's language strengths and challenges.

# POTENTIAL BARRIERS IN LEARNING–TEACHING RELATIONSHIPS WITH DOMINANT-CULTURE TEACHERS AND SCHOOLS

As noted earlier in this chapter, a focus on interdependence and cooperation in the attainment of goals conflicts with dominant-culture emphasis on individualism (Vasquez, 1990). The result is Latino students' weakened achievement when conventional classroom teaching approaches are employed. Teaching styles and preferences that transmit information without engaging students in the learning process negatively affect Latino student achievement (Dunn, Griggs, & Price, 1993).

For example, Yong and Ewing (1992) reported that Latino/as' strongest perceptual strength tends to be kinesthetic. Thus, when placed in a classroom in which the teacher relies on lecture methods and or the use of PowerPoint or overhead presentations, as opposed to an actively engaging and experiential (hands-on) approach, Latino students may find themselves at an academic disadvantage. A related outcome, Black, Paz, and DeBlassie (1991) found that Latino secondary school students exhibited lower levels of self-esteem than did their dominant-culture counterparts.

On October 12, 2001, President George W. Bush signed Executive Order 13230, charging a presidential advisory commission with developing an action plan to close the educational achievement gap for Hispanic Americans. Unfortunately, the commission found that Latino/a students continue to be disadvantaged in U.S. schools. The report concluded:

- One of every three Hispanic American students fails to complete high school.

## Intercultural Communication Strategies for Teachers 7-2

### Classroom Applications: Beyond Content to the Sensitizing Process

Teachers must review the content of their curricula to make sure that it adequately incorporates the values, beliefs, traditions, and language of diverse students. Beyond a focus on content, it is important for teachers to review the way they enact the processes they employ.

Research suggests that the most effective communication processes are those that emphasize student-centered constructivist approaches to learning in which students build their own knowledge through discovery and hands-on exploration of subject matter. This same research would suggest that Latino students prefer kinesthetic modes of instruction, sufficient instructional structuring of assignment and activities, variety as opposed to routines, and an emphasis on cooperation and collaborative learning. Use this information to review your current preferred methods for learning or teaching. Ask yourself the following questions and use them to guide both *what* and *how* you teach:

1. Do I prefer telling rather than showing in instruction?
2. Do I prefer assignments that encourage individual achievement over collaborative work and cooperation?
3. Do I prefer to have time in which students can practice what has just been learned so feedback can be provided, or is there little time during instruction for guided practice and feedback?
4. Do I prefer the use of routine activities and assignments over variety and a change in pace and instructional activity type?
5. Do I prefer to model assignment expectations using demonstration, or do I prefer to explain what students are required to do when completing assignments?

- Only 10 percent of Hispanic Americans graduate from four-year colleges and universities, with fewer than 100,000 graduating each year.
- The federal government does not adequately monitor, measure, and coordinate programs and research to the benefit of Hispanic American children and their families, despite the rapidly growing Hispanic American population in the United States.

## FROM CONCEPTS TO LIVED EXPERIENCE

Many classroom barriers for Latino/as are obvious but are often ignored. An example is contained in the following excerpt, which brings to life the experiences of being Latina in the United States. These are the reflections of Carla Garcia upon entering her new American school.

### CARLA GARCIA

The day the Garcias were one American year old, they had a celebration at dinner. Mami had baked a nice flan and stuck a candle in the center. "Guess what day it is today?" She looked around the table at her daughters' baffled faces. "One year ago today," Papi began orating, "we came to the shores of this great country." When he was done misquoting the poem on the Statue of Liberty, the youngest, Fifi, asked if she could blow out the candle, and Mami said only after everyone had made a wish. "What do you wish for on the first celebration of the day you lost everything?" Carla wondered. Everyone else around the table had their eyes closed as if they had no trouble deciding. Carla closed her eyes too. She should make an effort and not wish for what she always wished for in her homesickness. But just this last time, she would let herself. "Dear God," she began. She could not get used to this American wish-making without bringing God into it. "Let us go back home, please," she half prayed and half wished. It seemed a less and less likely prospect. In fact, her parents were sinking roots here. Only a month ago, they had moved out of the city to a neighborhood on Long Island so that the girls could have a yard to play in, so Mami said. The little green squares around each look-alike house seemed more like carpeting that had to be kept clean than yards to play in. The trees were no taller than little Fifi. Carla thought yearningly of the lush grasses and thick-limbed, vine-laden trees around the compound back home. Under the amapola tree her best-friend cousin, Lucinda, and she had told each other what each knew about how babies were made. What is Lucinda doing right this moment? Carla wondered.

Down the block the neighborhood dead-ended in abandoned farmland that Mami read in the local paper the developers were negotiating to buy. Grasses and real trees and real bushes still grew beyond the barbed-wire fence posted with a big sign: PRIVATE, NO TRESPASSING. The sign has surprised Carla since "forgive us our trespasses" was the only other context in which she had heard the word. She pointed the sign out to Mami on one of their first walks to the bus stop. "Isn't that funny, Mami? A sign that you have to be good." Her mother did not understand at first until Carla explained about the Lord's Prayer. Mami laughed. Words sometimes meant two things in English too. This trespass meant that no one must go inside the property because it was not public like a park, but private. Carla nodded, disappointed. She would never get the hang of this new country.

Mami walked her to the bus stop for her first month at her new school over in the next parish. The first week, Mami even rode the bus with her, transferring, going and coming, twice a day, until Carla learned the way. Her sisters had all been enrolled at the neighborhood Catholic school only one block away from the house the Garcias had rented at the end of the summer. But by then, Carla's seventh grade was full. The nun who was the principal had suggested that Carla stay back a year in sixth grade, where they still had two spaces left. At 12, though, Carla was at least a year older than most sixth graders, and she felt mortified at the thought of having to repeat yet another year. All four girls had been put back a year when they arrived in the country. Sure, Carla could use the practice with her English, but that also meant she would be in the same grade as her younger sister, Sandi. That she could not bear. "Please," she pleaded with her mother, "let me go to the other school!" The public school was a mere two blocks beyond the Catholic school, but Laura Garcia would not hear of it. Public schools, she had learned from other Catholic school parents, were where juvenile delinquents went and where teachers taught those new crazy ideas about how we all came from monkeys. No child of hers was going to forget her family name and think she was nothing but a kissing cousin to an orangutan....

As the months went by, she neglected to complain about an even scarier development. Every day on the playground and in the halls of her new school, a gang of boys chased after her, calling her names, some of which she had heard before from the old lady neighbor in the apartment they had rented in the city. Out of the sight of the nuns, the boys pelted Carla with stones, aiming them at her feet so there would be no bruises. "Go back to where you came from, you dirty spic!" One of them, standing behind her in line, pulled her blouse out of her skirt where it was tucked in and lifted it high. "No titties," he snickered. Another yanked down her socks, displaying her legs, which had begun growing soft dark hairs. "Monkey legs!" he yelled to his pals.

"Stop!" Carla cried. "Please stop."

"Eh stop!" they mimicked her, "Plees eh-stop!" They were disclosing her secret shame: her body was changing. The girl she had been back home was being shed. In her place—almost as if the boys' ugly words and taunts had the power of spells—was a hairy, breast-budding grown-up no one would ever love. (Alvarez, 1991)

## SUMMARY

**Cultural Factor 1: Historical and Current Treatment in the United States**   The term *Hispanic* was used by the U.S. Bureau of the Census as an ethnic label to denote ethnically mixed combinations of European White, African Black, indigenous Indian, and Latin American ancestry. *Latino* is preferred by many members of this minority group as a way of emphasizing their Latin American background as opposed to the label (Hispanic) placed on them by dominant culture.

Latinos are the fastest-growing minority group in the United States. The Latino population is expected to surpass the African American population within this century and become the largest minority group in the United States. The Latino population is an ethnically diverse group comprised of Mexican Americans, Puerto Ricans, Cubans, and Central and South Americans, each representing a distinct land of origin. Yet, all are linked by a common language and cultural heritage.

**Cultural Factor 2: Initial Terms of Incorporation into U.S. Society**   Latino immigrants came to the United States from nonindustrial, agrarian-based countries. Many were monolingual, speaking only Spanish, and were unskilled for working in industrialized jobs in cities. The first wave of immigrants from Cuba were mostly highly educated, middle-class, skilled workers. Regardless of being skilled or unskilled, incorporation was not easy for Cuban immigrants because of the ways their traditions, customs, and language separated and, in some cases, isolated them from dominant culture.

**Cultural Factor 3: Shared Values and Traditions** One characteristic of paramount importance in most Latino cultures is commitment to family. *Familismo* (familism), which extends kinship beyond nuclear-family boundaries, is highly valued. It emphasizes interdependence over independence, affiliation over confrontation, and cooperation over competition. Other values extending from the emphasis on group and relationship include *simpatia*, the promotion of pleasant non-conflicting social relationships and *respeto* (respect). Males are expected to have *machismo*, that is, show chivalry, gallantry, courtesy, charity, and courage. Latinas are expected to be submissive, dependent, and pure.

*Marianismo*, which is a traditional Latina's socialized code of behavior, dictates that Latinas remember their docile and subjugated place in society, put their own needs below those of their husbands and families, refrain from criticizing their husbands, keep personal problems to themselves, and remain faithful to the marriage and family at all costs. However, Latina mothers are revered and are powerful family members.

**Cultural Factor 4: View of Spirituality and Humans' Relation to Nature** Spirituality, including a deep respect for nature and cultural fatalism, is highly valued in Latino/a culture. Cultural fatalism (which is closely linked to Latin American spirituality and religious convictions) is the belief that things are meant to happen and are beyond individuals' control.

**Cultural Factor 5: Acculturation and Experience with Exclusion and Alienation** Stages of acculturation may involve (1) initial joy and relief, (2) disillusionment with the new country, and (3) acceptance of the good and the bad in the host country. Evidence of movement through stages of acculturation and adaptation can be seen in both internal processes and external conflicts.

**Cultural Factor 6: Language Differences, Strengths, and Challenges** Sociolinguistic studies in the Latino/a community have shown the important ways in which language usage relates to issues of identity, racial stigma, and social power relations. Language for traditional Latino/as is inextricably linked to cultural identity. For them, language is not only an instrumental tool for communication but also an expression of cultural values. U.S. school and society's devaluation of the Spanish language negatively affects Latino/as' cultural integrity and academic achievement.

**Potential Barriers in Learning–Teaching Relationships with Dominant-Culture Teachers and Schools** One of every three Latino/a students fails to complete high school. Only 10 percent of Latino/as graduate from four-year colleges and universities, with fewer than 100,000 graduating each year. The federal government does not adequately monitor, measure, and coordinate programs and research to the benefit of Latino/a children and their families, despite the rapidly growing Latino population in the United States.

## Questions for Review

1. What are the significant traditional values commonly shared by Latino/as that would be in conflict with dominant-culture perspectives and practices?

2. How might machismo and marianismo influences be exhibited in the classroom?

3. Why is devaluation of the Spanish language a central concern for Latino/as?

## Important Terms

| | | | |
|---|---|---|---|
| collectivism | Hispanic | machismo | simpatia |
| cultural fatalism | Latinas | marianismo | |
| familismo | Latino | respeto | |

## Enrichment

Alvarez, J. (1991). *How the Garcia girls lost their accents*. New York: Penguin Group.

Augenbraum, H., & Stavans, I. (Eds.). (1993). *Growing up Latino: Memoirs and stories*. New York: Houghton Mifflin.

Burciaga, J. A. (1993). *Drink cultura: Chicanismo*. Santa Barbara: Joshua Odell Editions.

Cofer, J. O. (1990). *Silent dancing: A partial remembrance of a Puerto Rican childhood*. Houston: Arte Publico.

Cofer, J. O. (1996). *An island like you: Stories of the barrio*. New York: Puffin.

Palacios, A. (1994). *Standing tall: The stories of ten Hispanic Americans*. New York: Scholastic.

Pang, V. O. (2001). *Multicultural education: A caring-centered, reflective approach*. Boston: McGraw Hill.

Rodriguez, R. (2004). *Hunger of a memory: The education of Richard Rodriguez*. NY: Bantam Books.

Sanchez, B., Colon, Y., & Esparza, P. (2005). The roles of sense of school belonging and gender in the academic adjustment of Latino adolescents. *Journal of Youth & Adolescence*, 34(6), 619–628.

## Connections on the Web

http://lib.nmsu.edu/subject/bord/latino.html

This site features annotated links to Latino news, music, art, and community resources.

http://www.pbs.org/wgbh/amex/zoot/

This website provides for the viewing of the PBS movie, *Zoot Suit Riots* which explores the 1942 murder of a young Mexican-American man in LA that sparked a local rebellion.

http://chicanas.com/

This site is by, for, and about Chicanas—women of Mexican descent in the United States. It contains a variety of resources including biographies, poetry, cultural, and academic resources.

## References

Alvarez, J. (1991). *How the Garcia girls lost their accents*. New York: Penguin Group.

Arrendondo-Dowd, P. (1981) Personal loss and grief as a result of immigration. *Personnel and Guidance Journal*, 59, 376–378.

Baron, A., Jr. (1991). Counseling Chicano college students. In C. Lee & B. Richardson (Eds.), *Multicultural issues in counseling: New approaches to diversity* (pp. 1712–184). Alexandria, VA: American Association for Counseling and Development.

Barrett, S. E., Lau Chin, J., Comas-Diaz, L., Espin, O., Greene, B., & McGoldrick, M. (2005). Multicultural feminist therapy: Theory in context. *Women & Therapy*, 28(3/4), 27–61.

Bernal, G., & Guiterrez, M. (1988). Cubans. In L.Comas-Diaz & E. E. H. Griffin (Eds.), *Clinical guidelines in cross-cultural mental health*. New York: Wiley & Sons.

Black, C, Paz, H., & DeBlassie, R. (1991). Counseling the Hispanic male adolescent. *Adolescence*, 6, 223–232.

Burciaga, J. A. (1993). *Drink cultura: Chicanismo*. Santa Barbara: Joshua Odell Editions.

Cofer, J. O. (1990). *Silent dancing: A partial remembrance of a Puerto Rican childhood*. Houston: Arte Publico.

Cofer, J. O. (1996). *An island like you: Stories of the barrio*. New York: Puffin.

Dunn, R., Griggs, S., & Price, G. (1993). Learning styles of Mexican-American and Anglo-American elementary-school students. *Journal of Multicultural Counseling and Development*, 21(4), 237–247.

Falicov, C. J. (1982). Mexican families. In M. McGoldrick, J. K. Pearce, & E. E. H. Griffin (Eds.), *Clinical guidelines in cross-cultural mental health*. New York: Wiley & Sons.

Falicov, C. J. (2005). Emotional transnationalism and family identities. *Family Process*, 44(4), 399–406.

Garcia, O., Monn, J. L., & Rivera, K. M. (2001). How threatened is the Spanish of New York Puerto Ricans? Language shift with Vaiven. In J. A.Fishman, (Ed.), *Can threatened languages be saved? Reversing language shift, revisited: A 21st-century perspective* (pp. 44–73). Buffalo, NY: Multilingual Matters.

Gil, R. M., & Vazquez, C. I. (1990). *The Maria paradox: How Latmas can merge Old-World traditions with New-World self-esteem*. New York: GP Putnam's Sons.

Leslie, L. A., & Leitch, M. L. (1989). A demographic profile of recent Central American immigrants: Clinical and service implications. *Hispanic Journal of Behavioral Science*, 11(4), 315–329.

Moran, C. E., & Hakuta, K. (1995). Bilingual education: Broadening research perspectives. In J. Banks, & C. M. Banks (Eds.), *Handbook of research on multicultural education* (pp. 445–462). New York: Simon & Schuster.

Petuchowski, S. R. (1988). *Psychological adjustment problems of war refugees from El Salvador*. Unpublished doctoral dissertation, University of Maryland, College Park, MD.

Rodriguez, R. (2004). Hunger of a memory: The education of Richard Rodriguez. New York: Bantam Books.

Semour, M. N. (1977). Psychology of the Chicana. In J. C. Martinez (Ed.), *Chicano psychology* (pp. 329–342). New York: Academic.

Suarez-Orozco, C, & Suarez-Orozco, M. (1995). *Transformations: Immigration, family life, and achievement motivation among Latino adolescents*. Stanford, CA: Stanford University.

Torres, L. (1997). *Puerto Rican discourse: A sociolinguistic study of a New York suburb*. Mahwah, NJ: Lawrence Erlbaum.

Urciuoli, B. (1997). *Exposing prejudice: Puerto Rican experiences of language, race and class*. Boulder, CO: Westview.

U.S. Bureau of the Census. (2000). Resident population estimates of the U.S. by age and sex. Retrieved September 3, 2004, from http://www.census.gov/population/estimates/nation/umtfile2–1.txt

U.S. Bureau of the Census. (2003). Statistical abstracts of the United States: 2003 (123rd ed.). Washington, DC: U.S. Government Printing Office.

Vasquez, J. (1990). Teaching to the distinctive traits of minority students. *The Clearing House*, 63(7), 299–304.

Yong, F., & Ewing, N. (1992). A comparative study of the learning-style preferences among gifted African-American, Mexican-American and American-born Chinese middle-grade students. *Roeper Review*, 14(3), 120–123.

Zentella, A. C. (1997). *Growing up bilingual: Puerto Rican children in New York*. New York: Blackwell.

*I'm sick of knockin I'm sick of clockin*
*I'm sick of droppin in a hole never reaching my goal*
*It's got my soul separated into pieces*
*It just increases ...*
*So if you understood my attitude*
*Maybe you feel what I'm feeling*
*And then it start appealing*
*To ya intellect and aspect of dreams and aspirations*
*Death by temptations even got my heart basting*
*So I'm tracing the line where I can find a better path*
*And make it last, sit back and laugh before the aftermath*
*The tragic flaw is what makes it raw*
*So let it fall and I'll get through it even if I have to crawl*
*My way, I see the sun and there's no delay*
*And I'm a pray cause the lord will make a brighter day*
*Or will he keep me in his holding cell*
*But enough with the questions the only story to*
*tell is that [chorus:]*
*I'm stuck in between a rock and a hard place*
*Bad luck is what results from my paper chase*
*I keep looking it ain't no dough*
*So I don't wanna look no mo what*

**Ludacris**
"Rock and a Hard Place"

CHAPTER

# Learning from African American Stories

This chapter explores stories from African Americans that articulate cultural group values, struggles, and coping strategies. As with the previous chapters, personal narratives are presented to highlight the six major cultural factors explored in this text. Through understanding issues and cultural perspectives that are relevant to African Americans, you will increase your ability to make your classroom an effective learning community that includes and empowers members of this cultural group.

# CHAPTER OBJECTIVES

1. Describe common African American values and worldviews.
2. Identify the ways by which the people presented in the personal narratives in this chapter experienced and addressed the six cultural factors explored in this text.
3. Explain academic and intercultural interaction implications related to the six cultural factors for members in this cultural group.
4. Describe coping strategies utilized by members of this group.
5. Identify classroom strategies for cultivating the resources provided when traditional African American worldviews are integrated into your curriculum.

## CULTURAL FACTOR 1: HISTORICAL AND CURRENT TREATMENT IN THE UNITED STATES

*I try to find a way outta this maze*

*It's got me crazed I'm in a daze*
*So many ways to boost into a different phase*
*But I can't think I can't do nothing*
*You think I'm fronting*
*You hear me grunting*
*Lord you ain't even saying nuttin*

Ludacris, "Rock and a Hard Place"

The poignancy of these contemporary **hip hop** lyrics reveals a goal to confront societal barriers and to apply a history of coping skills to address injustice as well as an underlying belief that faith will provide strength, nurturance perseverance, and form the basis for survival. Dyson (2007) explained "… hip hop is important precisely because it sheds light on contemporary politics, history, and race" (p. xvi). Similarly, celebrated rapper, Jay Z said, in the foreward of the same work, that "Yes, our (hip hop) rhymes can contain violence and hatred. Yes, our songs can detail the drug business and our choruses can bounce with lustful intent. However, those things did not spring from inferior imaginations or deficient morals; those things came from our lives. They came from America." (p. x). Not unlike hip hop, slave songs (like the one presented below), passed down through oral tradition, reveal a history of African American treatment and survival at different points in U.S. history (Ogbar, 2007).

*Sumtimes I rocks my baby,*
*Sumtimes I sees him cry.*
*But we gon' have a good time*
*Way bye an' bye*

*Den I rocks my baby all the time*
*And keep the bad things 'way*
*So his little eyes will laugh at me*
*All the livelong day.*

*We gon' have a good time*
*Way bye an' bye*

Alice McGill (2000, p. 4), *In the Hollow of Your Hand: Slave Lullabies*

The words in this song describe overwhelming sorrow and hardship but also belief in a better time to come. Thus, "We gon' have a good time, way bye an' bye" communicates the message that current and future generations of African Americans will survive even in the midst of pervasive oppression and savage treatment at the hands of slaveholders.

> My ma was cook, an' used to clean house. I liked dustin' part best 'cause I could git my hands on de books and pictures dat ole Marse has spread out all over his readin' room. Ole Missus used to watch me mos' times to see dat I didn't open no books. Sometimes she would close up all de books an' put 'em on de shelf so's I couldn't see 'em, but Marse never liked her messin' wid his things. Dere was one book dat I was crazy about ... didn't know nothin' of what it was 'bout, but it had a lot of pictures, Injuns and Kings and Queens wid reefs on dere heads. Used to fly to dat book and hold it lookin' at de pictures whilst I dusted wid de other hand. One day while in de readin' room I heard a step comin' fum de kitchen. 'Fore I could move, de door opened an' someone came in. Thought sure it was Missus, but it was Marsa. He looked at me an' saw what I was doin', but he never said nothin'. I closed de book up an' put it back in place. Was scared fo' many a day dat I was gonna git a hidin', but guess he never tole Missus after all. Was a long time 'fore I teched any more books.

> *Negro in Virginia* quoted in Perdue, Barden, and Phillips (1976, pp. 97–98), *Weevils in the Wheat: Interviews with Virginia Ex-Slaves*

It is not surprising that slave narrative accounts and, more recently, hip hop music continue to be viewed with suspicion and sometimes disdain among members of dominant culture. These art forms have had their merit denied and their legitimacy questioned from their beginnings. However, it's important to note that like **slave accounts**, hip hop music "vocalizes the struggle of growing up black and poor in this country" (Dyson, 2007, p. xx). And while it's true that hip hop features stereotypes and parody, like other forms of art, they do so to make a point and to provide glimpses into "the complex varieties of black identity" (p. xxvi). And it is no wonder that dominant-culture individuals may express skepticism and fear when confronted with information flowing from these often unheard sources. For these truths challenge basic assumptions of entitlement, privilege, and access to opportunity (Sullivan, 2006). Once hidden from view, the realities of slavery, Jim Crow laws, and current racial injustice are, whether respected or not, brought to life in slave accounts and hip hop and other art forms.

> It's hard to tell small children about slavery, hard to explain that young Black men were lynched, and that police turned fire hoses on children while other men bombed churches, killing Black children at their prayers. This is a terrible legacy for all of us.

> **Elementary school teacher quoted in Tatum (1997, p. 41),** *Why are all the Black kids sitting together in the cafeteria?*

## Slavery

It is difficult to describe and discuss the experience of North American slavery—it is an experience of inhumanity that is almost impossible to grasp fully—so horrible that it would not be believed by many if it were not for books like Alex Haley's *Roots: The Saga of an American Family* and television miniseries that captured the public's attention in the 1970s while illuminating realities of slavery from the inside out and accounts (like the ones shared in this chapter) from slaves who found ways to learn to read and write and thus make their accounts a permanent part of American history whether visited or not. The knowledge that slaves were not permitted to learn to read and write and were punished if they were caught singing songs that did not meet with the approval of their masters makes their stories all the more valuable having succeeded in finding audience despite violent efforts to suppress them. It is well known that African slaves found ways to communicate with each other and their allies in secrecy—disguising their songs to sound harmless even when they were used to confront the oppression they endured or to help guide escaped slaves to safe places along the underground railroad in their search for freedom. When gathered together, African slaves might sing songs to strengthen one another, make plans, and to report news via the slave grapevine—similar to the role churches have played throughout African American history. These aspects of African American language and song still continue today as features of expression and meaning systems that facilitate African American discourse (Walters, 2008). Such forms of communication help to create a collective identity that slaveholders and oppression following slavery attempted to but could not erase.

Slavery resulted in a legacy that continues to shape the current social identities of African Americans *and* members of dominant culture. It provides context for the current sociopolitical landscape and affects all intercultural relationships in the United States.

U.S. society was in large part built on the backs of forced labor. Legal in all parts of the United States by the early 18th century, slavery was the dominant labor system of the Southern colonies. Colonists captured, imported, enslaved, battered, and killed hundreds of thousands of Africans in order to advance their economic and political goals. This inhumane treatment of an entire population was considered *highly successful* in that it brought wealth to slaveholders and so it continued for centuries resulting in racial and social class stratification based on consequent distributions of wealth that exists today. White slaveholders (taking the role of masters of slaves) soon developed a preference for African slaves over Native Americans who knew the terrain, which aided in their escapes and indentured European servants because, once purchased, Africans, by law, became their permanent property with African female slaves passing their slave status on to their children; whereas European **indentured servants** were held only for a few years until their debts or crimes were forgiven. Thus, although African slaves cost White colonists more to purchase than indentured servants, colonists found African slaves to be a *better long-term investment* for their use. "So much so, that by the 18th century, slavery became entrenched as a pervasive—and in many colonies central—component of the social order, the dark underside of the American dream" (Kolchin, 1993, pp. 3–4).

## Emancipation?

Slavery continued in the United States for more than 244 years. The process of freeing slaves, while mandated by President Lincoln's signing of the **Emancipation Proclamation** in 1863, continued until the passage of the Thirteenth Amendment to the Constitution in 1865, which barred slavery everywhere in the United States. However, the process of emancipation took a long time, leaving remnants that still exist today.

Many U.S. citizens are unaware that **Juneteenth** is recognized as a state holiday in 32 U.S. states. Also known as Freedom Day or Emancipation Day, Juneteenth is an American holiday honoring African American heritage that commemorates the announcement of the abolition of slavery in Texas in 1865. Celebrated on June 19th, recognition of this holiday is a preferred symbolic date for many African Americans instead of the July 4th North American Independence Day which does not reflect African American ancestors' access to freedom in the United States.

Additional amendments followed that were to help African ex-slaves obtain their rights in U.S. society. The Fourteenth Amendment proclaimed freed slaves to be U.S. citizens, and the Fifteenth Amendment provided African Americans with the right to vote. Yet, to this day, descendants of slaves continue to experience a lack of basic freedoms guaranteed to all citizens of the United States (Giddings, 2001). For example, the American Commission on Civil Rights found that African American voters in the crucial state of Florida were discriminated against in the 2000 Presidential election due to "injustice, ineptitude, and inefficiency". The investigation found that Black voters were 10 times more likely than Whites to have their ballots rejected. Their report confirmed that poor and minority citizens had much less chance of having their vote counted than their White counterparts. The report added that some Hispanic and Haitian voters were not provided with ballots in their native language, and there were no clear guidelines to protect the votes of eligible voters from being wrongly removed.

## Freedom—Yet Not Free

While legislation put a formal end to slavery, the reality of full inclusion in U.S. society continues to remain an obstacle for African Americans. Institutional racism serves as the primary means for limiting the opportunities of African Americans for economic advancement (White, 1999). Current employment and pay statistics reveal enduring inequities (see the section titled "Current Conditions" in this chapter).

Most African Americans in the antebellum South worked as agricultural laborers for Whites, just as they had worked as slaves. All the while, pervasive, racially inspired physical and psychological violence was inflicted on them—violence that especially targeted independent African Americans whose behavior seemed to their perpetrators to be insufficiently deferential. In the late 1800s, African American teachers, ministers, landowners, and politicians were special targets of abuse, burnings, whippings, and lynchings, which supported the existent widespread **institutional discrimination** against African Americans. Even though not all Whites supported the racist attacks, and some actively opposed them, the attacks set the tone for social relations in the Post-Reconstruction South. This set of circumstances let all "freed" slaves know that while they had been guaranteed "official freedom" via legislation, they were anything but "free" to live, work, or even move about in the environments in which they existed. Consider the experience of Booker T. Washington during his travels in the 1800s:

> While I was in charge of the Indian boys at Hampton, I had one or two experiences which illustrate the curious workings of caste in America. One of the Indian boys was

taken ill, and it became my duty to take him to Washington, deliver him over to the Secretary of Interior, and get a receipt for him, in order that he might be returned to his Western reservation.

At that time I was rather ignorant of the ways of the world. During my journey to Washington, on a steamboat, when the bell rang for dinner, I was careful to wait and not enter the dining room until the greater part of the passengers had finished their meal. Then, with my charge, I went to the dining saloon. The man in charge politely informed me that the Indian could be served, but that I could not. I never could understand how he knew just where to draw the color line, since the Indian and I were about the same complexion. The steward, however, seemed to be an expert in the matter. An illustration of something of this same feeling came under my observation afterward. I happened to find myself in a town in which so much excitement and indignation were being expressed that it seemed likely for a time that there would be a lynching. The occasion of the trouble was that a dark-skinned man had stopped at a local hotel. Investigation, however, developed the fact that this individual was a citizen of Morocco, and that while traveling in this country he spoke the English language. As soon as it was learned that he was not an American Negro, all the signs of indignation disappeared. The man who was the innocent cause of the excitement, though, found it prudent after that not to speak English. (Washington, 1965, p. 83)

In this excerpt, Booker T. Washington described how he was "careful to wait and not enter the dining room until the greater part of the passengers had finished their meal." And even then, he was instructed that he could not sit or be served! Before continuing on, reread the words of Booker T. Washington and complete Exercise 8-1. The exercise is intended to help you move from an understanding of this historical experience to an appreciation of the lived experience of discrimination and prejudice.

By 1880, Booker T. Washington had founded the first institution of higher education for Blacks, the Tuskegee Institute, which was an industrial school located in rural Alabama. Washington's philosophy and goals were not supported

---

**EXERCISE 8-1**

## Point of Reflection: Experiencing Discrimination— A Class Divided

Go to http://www.pbs.org/wgbh/pages/frontline/shows/divided/etc/view.html to watch five segments from *A Class Divided*, one of the most requested programs in Frontline's history. The video revisits Jane Elliott, whose first video, *Eye of the Storm*, presents this Iowa school teacher's lesson for her third grade students the day after Martin Luther King Jr. was murdered in 1968. Ms. Elliott gave her students a first-hand experience in the meaning of discrimination. The video series details the story of what she taught the children and the impact that lesson had on their lives.

After watching this video series, describe what you observed about the participants' behavior and feelings displayed. Reflect on your *own* reactions to the lesson. Answer the following questions:

1. Would you want to experience the lesson? Why or why not?
2. Did the lessons learned remain?
3. What effects were gained from the lesson?
4. What did you learn about discrimination, exclusion, and alienation effects on achievement?

Discuss your reflections with your classmates and instructor in small-group or large-group discussion in applying what you discovered from the video series to your own classroom practices.

by all African American intellectuals of the time. William E. Burghardt DuBois, the first African American to be awarded a Ph.D. and one of the founders of the **National Association for the Advancement of Colored People (NAACP)** challenged Washington's views that African Americans accept the inferior status of being trained for manual labor. DuBois, instead, called for the education of the most *talented tenth* (10 percent) of the African American population to equip them for leadership positions in the society. Rising from these early strategies to educate African Americans, there are currently 105 **historically Black colleges and universities (HBCUs)** in the United States including public and private, two-year and four-year institutions, medical schools and community colleges. The Higher Education Act of 1965 defines an HBCU as "… any historically black college or university that was established prior to 1964, whose principal mission was, and is, the education of black Americans, and that is accredited by a nationally recognized accrediting agency or association … or is, according to such an agency or association, making reasonable progress toward accreditation." Most HBCUs were established after the American Civil War and many worked to prepare their students for progress in agriculture and mechanics (Alabama A & M, North Carolina Agricultural and Technical State University, Prairie View A & M, Southern University and Agricultural and Mechanical College among them) while others provided higher education degrees in liberal arts and professional studies. Of the 105 HBCUs in the United States today, 27 of these universities offer doctoral programs and 52 schools provide graduate degree program at the Master's level. At the undergraduate level, 83 of the HBCU institutions offer the Bachelor's degree program and 38 of these schools offer associate degrees (African American Population, 2009).

## School Segregation

From the 17th to the late 20th century, schools were completely segregated by race. At the end of the American Revolution, nearly all African Americans in the United States were slaves who could neither read nor write. Literate slaves were likely to have been educated in the homes of their masters or in the company of missionaries through small church programs. One of the first schools created for African Americans was founded in New York in 1704. Near the end of the century, believing that slavery was a moral evil, Quakers started schools in Philadelphia to teach African and Native Americans. Officially, school segregation was mandated as early as the Massachusetts Supreme Court decision of 1850 that ruled that *equal but separate* schools were provided therefore preventing the Roberts family from sending their daughter, Sarah, to attend a White school in Boston (*Roberts v. City of Boston, 1850*).

School segregation continued when the Supreme Court upheld the **separate but equal doctrine** in educational facilities in the 1896 decision in the case of *Plessy v. Ferguson*. This ruling resulted in more than 50 more years of segregated schooling in the South and the migration of many African Americans to the North throughout the 1900s. **Jim Crow laws** were state and local laws in the United States enacted between 1876 and 1965 that mandated racial segregation in all public facilities, with a supposedly "separate but equal" status for African Americans. In reality, this led to treatment and accommodations that were inferior to those provided for White Americans, systematizing economic, educational, and social disadvantage.

At the height of this period, referred to as the *Jim Crow era,* African Americans were prevented by law from eating in White-only restaurants, staying in White-only hotels, or in any way assimilating in dominant culture.

It was not until the 1954 ***Brown v. The Board of Education of Topeka, Kansas*** court case declared racial discrimination in schools to be unconstitutional that African Americans were officially provided with access to all public educational facilities. As you may know from your studies of U.S. history, the process of desegregating U.S. schools and public facilities did not occur immediately or without an enormous amount of civil rights actions on the part of African Americans and their White allies. Opposition to school desegregation arose in school districts throughout the country. Many schools became battlegrounds characterized by boycotts, demonstrations, rallies, and violence. Currently, there remain concerns about the ability of *Brown* to bring about meaningful desegregation and equity in education (McNeal, 2009).

Likewise in broader society, African Americans have fought for their basic human rights. For example, after Rosa Parks' refusal to surrender her seat to a White man on a bus led to her arrest and Dr. Martin Luther King along with many other leaders in the African American community organized the Montgomery, Alabama bus boycott, seats on public buses finally were opened to African Americans. Because the boycott had deprived the bus company of 65 percent of its income, this type of social justice advocacy worked to affect dominant-culture economics in ways that were convincing and ultimately successful. It was almost a year later that the Supreme Court decided that bus segregation violated the Constitution. Similarly, two of the many courageous fights African Americans waged on a daily basis in order to gain rights they had been legally entitled by the Constitution were (1) the eventual desegregation at Little Rock Central High School in 1957, in which nine young African American school children walked into an all-White school to be educated amid screaming White rioters who yelled obscenities at them each day they returned to school, enduring the degradation of constant bullying and exclusion when White parents took their children out of the school rather than have their children seated next to African American children; and (2) the 1960 sit-in at the lunch counter of a Woolworth's in Greensboro, North Carolina, where teenagers fought for access to public facilities for all African Americans. The **Civil Rights Act**, passed over 45 years ago in 1964, declared basic human rights to fair housing, job opportunities, and the like for African Americans that had been denied them for more than 100 years after slavery ended. It was 14 years later still when the Supreme Court ruled that race could be a factor in making college admissions decisions. This was the start of affirmative action policy in the United States (Orfield & Kurlaender, 2001; Leach, 2004; Orfield & Lee, 2007).

## Current Conditions

It is estimated that 41.1 million U.S. residents self-identify as African American or African American in combination with one or more other races making up approximately 13.5 percent of the total population of the United States (U.S. Bureau of

## Intercultural Communication Strategies for Teachers 8-1

### Classroom Applications: Infusing Curriculum

For teaching to be effective, lessons need to be meaningful, incorporating the values, beliefs, traditions, and language of the students into the curricula. Such strategies increase the personal relevance of the material presented and help provide for an expanded knowledge base and diverse worldviews. Consider the following:

• Examine the content of your curricula to determine if it adequately and accurately reflects the rich history and contributions of African Americans.
• Review assignments to identify the degree to which they represent worldviews and perspectives of African Americans.

Ask yourself if your assignments, examples, resources, materials, and so on are relevant to students' out-of-school interests and knowledge domains.

the Census, 2007). In terms of educational, employment, and economic profiles, census data reveal the following:

• Among African Americans age 25 and over, 90 percent hold at least a high school diploma; 19 percent of African Americans age 25 or older earned a Bachelor's degree or higher compared to 32 percent of White Americans who have a Bachelor's degree or higher.
• Ten percent of African Americans were unemployed in 2008 (up from 7.6 percent in 2000) compared to 5 percent of Whites unemployed in 2008 (up from 3.5 percent in 2000).
• The annual median income in 2006 of African American households was $31,969 compared to the $50,673 median income for White households.
• About 24 percent of African Americans have incomes that fall below the poverty level in the United States compared to 8 percent of White Americans who live in poverty.
• An estimated 28 percent of Black males enter State or Federal prison during their lifetime, compared to 16 percent of Latinos and 4.4 percent of White males. Sixty-five percent of state prison inmates belonged to racial or ethnic minorities in 1991, up from 60 percent in 1986 and the of the persons convicted of drug trafficking in state courts in 1990, 57 percent were Black and 1 percent were persons from other racial groups.

These data reveal that African Americans continue to struggle for educational and economic equity in U.S. society (Oakes & Rogers, 2006, 2007; U.S. Bureau of the Census, 2007; Center for American Progress Action Fund, 2009) despite the fact that the first African American president of the United States was elected in 2008, Barack Hussein Obama's election as the 44th chief executive of the U.S. amounted to a national catharsis as his call for a change in the direction and the tone of the country was embraced by a majority of the voters. President Obama, who was also awarded the 2009 Nobel Peace Prize, previously served as a Senator from Illinois between January 2005 and November 2008. A graduate of Columbia

University and Harvard Law School, Obama worked as a community organizer in Chicago before earning his law degree and then worked as a civil rights attorney in Chicago and taught constitutional law at the University of Chicago Law School before becoming president.

Some would argue that based on the success some African Americans have carved out of the pervasive discrimination they have faced and the fact that an African American was elected to the highest office in the land that African Americans no longer experience institutional discrimination in the United States. After all, some say, "they [African Americans] can vote, live where their money permits them, eat where their appetites dictate, work at jobs for which their skills qualify them. They have civil rights" (Raspberry, 1990, p. 96) While many would like to believe that the problem of racism in the United States is solved, it is obvious when examining the current conditions of African Americans living in the United States that there is much work to do toward achieving social justice, cultural pluralism, and equity in schooling and job access.

## Intercultural Communication Strategies for Teachers 8-2

### Classroom Applications: Sensitivity to Involuntary-Minority Group Member History

Descendants of involuntary-minority groups are aware that when their ancestors were incorporated into the United States, it was not seen as a great escape into freedom, prosperity, and the pursuit of happiness. Instead, incorporation into U.S. society for African Americans meant imprisonment, enslavement, torture, degradation, and murder. Knowledge of the initial terms of incorporation into society of African Americans will help you prepare to create effective learning communities for these students. Specifically, you should do the following:

- Keep in mind that students and their families bring with them a history of experiences with discrimination brought about in schools and in larger society, and with these experiences may come caution and mistrust.
- Understand that for some, to "make it" means turning their backs on their cultural heritage and identity. Recognize the history that under-girds the pressure to resist "selling out," and acknowledge the strengths and contributions of African American culture and heritage.
- When discussing the history of immigrants in the United States, help the students recognize

the differential impact of voluntary and involuntary minority experiences with and orientations to dominant culture.

- Provide invitations to parents to work as collaborators in their child's education. Respecting their valuing of education, eliciting their input, and incorporating their resources and contributions make *partnership* more than just a word.
- Learn to read between the lines. When a student presents as rebellious or resistant, ask yourself if it is possible the student is responding to biased treatment and cultural codes of behavior.
- Show flexibility and adaptability to make your classroom open and accessible for all students. Make sure students are provided with choices and opportunities to achieve that do not require them to merely regurgitate information you have transmitted to them.
- Listen intently to the concerns expressed by students and make sure students know they are heard by you, that you understand their concerns, and that you will work with them to find ways to help correct problems related to their performance in your classroom

# CULTURAL FACTOR 2: INITIAL TERMS OF INCORPORATION INTO U.S. SOCIETY

African Americans and their ancestors, who suffered slavery and who historically have been denied true assimilation into U.S. society, are categorized as "involuntary minorities" in the United States based on their initial terms of incorporation into society (Ogbu, 1990). As stated previously in this text, voluntary-minority group members are said to believe that they will succeed in mainstream society through hard work and compliance with authority. These individuals' ancestors have chosen to enter the United States, often favorably comparing the treatment received in the United States to that in their countries of origin.

Involuntary minorities, however, keenly aware of the intergenerational oppression received since their ancestors were forcibly incorporated into U.S. society centuries ago, are less likely to adopt the compliant behaviors that have led to academic and economic success for voluntary minorities and members of dominant culture. Instead, involuntary-minority students are more likely to reject dominant-culture paths to success and to equate compliant behaviors with "**passing**" or "acting" White (Fordham, 1993; Ogbu, 1990).

# CULTURAL FACTOR 3: SHARED VALUES AND TRADITIONS

African Americans typically value family closeness (including extended-family members). As with Native American, Latino, and Asian American families, sometimes more than one generation in an African American family lives in one home. Grandparents, cousins, and other family members may live together in part to enable the pooling of resources and to combat economic disadvantages they face. Many African Americans are raised to rely on and care for family members, no matter what the circumstances. Respect for elders and devotion to parents is central in the lives of many African Americans. Even when family members do not live together in the same dwelling, loyalty between children and parents is often strong. In addition, a **fictive kinship** often exists among African Americans that forms close and lasting "family" relationships between African Americans who are not biologically related. In this way, African Americans are able to pull together as a community to care for one another.

Sibling responsibility for each other and family member support for all family members are stressed. Many African Americans strongly endorse the belief that one helps another and shares one's resources for the survival of the group. Elders are responsible for passing down the values, stories, and traditions of the group; as such, they play a key role in family and community systems. Elders of African American families often teach their children how to survive in dominant culture and how to respond to the racism they confront. Another system central to the maintenance and promulgation of these values is the church. The significance of the church to African Americans will be discussed in detail later in this chapter (see the discussion under Cultural Factor 4).

## Gender Treatment and Effects

Dominant culture in the United States has, throughout history, held a fascination and at the same time a particular disdain for African American women (Young, 1986). In many African cultures, women are independent in many ways because they work and often have complete control of their daily tasks and earnings. "Even though African women may be subordinate in their roles as wives, as mothers and sisters, they wield considerable authority, power, and influence. Wives may kneel before their husbands, but sons prostrate before their mothers. And, seniority is determined by age, rather than by gender" (Sudarkasa, 1991, p. 43). However, in the United States, a whole history of oppression has shaped the way African American men and women are treated and viewed by each other and by dominant-culture individuals.

The African slave trade and resulting concerted efforts to obliterate African culture, families, values, traditions, and institutions served to dehumanize African men *and* women in the eyes of dominant culture. Males were portrayed as oversexed beasts that would ravage White women if not controlled completely through force, using any means necessary. And whereas both African men and women were seen and generally treated as less-than-human savages throughout slavery, African women, perhaps for practical purposes, were ascribed some human qualities so as to exploit their usefulness as house servant and mammy. Males who worked as house servants seen as docile and known as "Uncle Toms" who had by definition sold out other slaves in order to win the masters' favor to reap their own personal rewards of safety and comfort. As such, they were seen both by Whites and African Americans as having no respect, real power or authority. African female slaves were often chosen for their skills or beauty (judged by White standards) to work and live in their masters' houses. This circumstance created opportunities for their masters to more easily rape them at will. To this day, the stereotype of African American women as promiscuous, immoral "jezebel" remains (Fordham, 1993). White men sought to exploit Black female eroticism and minimize sexual competition by forbidding slaves to marry and live in family constellations and later outlawing Black male sexual interactions with White women.

"The rise of lynching and castration stemmed from the White male attempt to control the conjured threat of Black male desire. Black women were depicted as hyper-sexed to justify the immoral acts of rape and harassment they experienced at the hands of White males while White women were projected as paragons of sexual virtue and placed on pedestals of purity" (Dyson, 2003, p. 218). DuBois (1969) wrote:

> I shall forgive the White South much in its final judgment day; I shall forgive its slavery, for slavery is a world-old habit ... but one thing I shall never forgive, neither in this world or the world to come: its wanton and continued and persistent insulting of the Black womanhood which it sought and seeks to prostitute to its lust. (p. 169)

However, the utility of the African female extended beyond that of their masters' sexual surrogates. When needed for child care, they were viewed as neutered "mammy," like the stereotyped Aunt Jemima, and when needed in the fields, the

African female was seen as an asexual field hand with work responsibility equal to that of African male slaves, as Sojourner Truth, who delivered her famous *Ain't I A Woman?* speech in 1851 at a Women's Convention in Akron, Ohio stated,

> That man over there says that women need to be helped into carriages, and lifted over ditches, and to have the best place everywhere. Nobody ever helps me into carriages, or over mud-puddles, or gives me any best place! And ain't I a woman? Look at me! Look at my arm! I have ploughed and planted, and gathered into barns, and no man could head me! And ain't I a woman? I could work as much and eat as much as a man—when I could get it—and bear the lash as well! And ain't I a woman? I have borne thirteen children, and seen most all sold off to slavery, and when I cried out with my mother's grief, none but Jesus heard me! And ain't I a woman?
>
> Sojourner Truth, *Ain't I a Woman?*, 1851

It is also significant to note that targeted discrimination and a highly publicized aspect of racism (the *absence of African American fathers*) in U.S. society has had devastating effects on the African American family and the ability of African Americans to develop economic resources sufficient to support their families. African American males are profiled by U.S. law enforcement to such an extent that they are arrested five times more often than dominant-culture males, even though the amount of illegal activity among both groups is similar. Yet, the fact that uncles, brothers, and grandfathers in the African American community often fill the roles of protectors and providers in families when needed is not featured in the media.

The pervasive depiction of the African American male as absent from the African American family does not take into account the legacy of slavery that prohibited African American males from protecting and providing for their families. This characterization exists despite the fact that 72 percent of African American households are headed by two parents.

Male slaves were so targeted for abuse and publicly attacked and slandered during slavery and thereafter that African American females have known for centuries that they must be able to provide for themselves and their children if they are to survive. These indelible marks on the African American family required African Americans to create a different and powerful sense of family (fictive kinship) among members in their community.

Today, broad archetypes continue to exist for African American males and females: African American males are widely seen as Uncle Toms who sell out their own kind and do the White man's bidding for acceptance, as athletic, oversexed, indulgent studs who exploit resources for wealth, or as shiftless, irresponsible fathers who are uncouth and uneducated and who do not provide for themselves or their families. African American females are seen as either promiscuous, dangerous temptations for White males who derive unearned benefits or as nonthreatening, unattractive, and compliant work horses valued only for their work products. All stereotypic roles stem from conditions of slavery in which African American male slaves were mythologized as oversexed to justify their torture and constraint and had no ability to protect themselves and their families from the brutality they endured and in which African American female slaves were forced to endure the sexual attacks of White male slave owners and the mistreatment and disdain of

White females for being the objects of White males' desire. Coping strategies for such treatment among African American male and female slaves often involved some form of acquiescence to Whites for their survival and for the survival of their family members. The male and female slaves who served in Whites' houses and benefited in part from such circumstances were largely perceived to be sellouts. To this day, *colorism* stemming from perceived approaches that African Americans have used to address their oppression creates divisions among members of the African American community. *Colorism* refers to the differential treatment people of color receive from dominant culture and other people of color based on the lightness or darkness of their skin. Because standards of beauty in U.S. society are predominantly defined as valuing physical features that are most like features prized in dominant culture and because people whose physical features more closely match those of dominant culture experience greater acceptance and related opportunities; other minority individuals who have features that are more different from members of dominant culture are further disadvantaged. As occurred during slavery, many African Americans who enjoy the unearned privileges bestowed upon them because of their lighter skin pigment may be treated with suspicion by other members of the ethnic group. The pervasive racism that shaped the lives of African Americans as slaves embraces the stereotypes of African Americans as drop-out dads, welfare mothers, prostitutes, cleaning ladies, criminals, and down-and-out laborers in U.S. society and reinforces the effects of colorism within the African American and other ethnic group communities. These conditions create serious challenges for African Americans.

African American women face unique barriers in attempting to advance in society (Spradlin, 1999). Throughout history and still today, African American women have not been able to benefit from the perceived virtuous characteristics of White womanhood nor can they gain acceptance for utilizing strategies that are effective for males in society.

"At a time when their white peers were riding the wave of moral superiority that sanctioned their activism, Black women were seen as immoral scourges. Despite their achievements, they did not have benefit of discriminating judgment concerning their worth as women … Black women were seen as having all the inferior qualities of White women without any of their virtues." (Giddings, 2001, pp. 81–82)

As such, networks and support systems for White women were not opened and to a great extent remain closed to African American women. At the same time, African American women are not often invited and welcomed to join country clubs, lunch groups, or knitting circles; they are not welcomed on the golf courses, on the basketball courts, or at the poker tables of White or African American men. African American women are not applauded for their decisiveness or abilities to command as men are, nor are they lauded for their demure and attractive demeanors as White women are. They seek to achieve in dominant culture without relying on the "softness" and linearity of White women (see Wade, 2001) and the power associated with being male.

Many successful African American women of today have carved out qualities stemming from their slave history and a history of discrimination that associates them with hard work, strength, creative problem-solving skills, and diligence. For many in dominant culture, African American women are those "loud Black voices"

(Fordham, 1993) that may offend the ears of dominant culture while demanding acknowledgement of their value and worth—presenting their cases with great passion and confidence borne of their conviction to achieve despite their discriminatory treatment. However, the sharp strength of their "loud voices" and all the strengths they bring to the U.S. classroom and work space are often eclipsed by the negative images that are painted of them in dominant culture.

Education is a highly prized value among African Americans as a way to achieve personal and family goals. However, the salience of education is often diluted by the realization that African American students experience systematic discrimination in U.S. schools—a knowledge that the deck is stacked against them (Ogbu, 1992). For example, overrepresentation of African American males in special education programs is a pernicious problem that continues to plague public schools in the United States (Hebbeler & Wagner, 2001). Placements begin early and have longstanding negative ramifications for students (Patton, 1991). "Labels have damaged many children, particularly minority group children whose cultures and lifestyles differ sufficiently from the 'norm' to make any measurement of their abilities and aptitudes by norm-biased scales a certain disaster for them" (Gorham, Des Jardins, Page, Pettis, & Scherber, 1976, p. 155). Labeling negatively affects their perceptions of themselves and their behavior. These perceptions and behavior then serve as the basis for the formation of lowered expectations for their performance in school (Ysseldyke, Algozzine, & Thurlow, 2000). Personal Narrative 8-1 serves as an example of these concerns.

## CULTURAL FACTOR 4: VIEW OF SPIRITUALITY AND HUMANS' RELATION TO NATURE

Many African American abolitionists, such as Frederick Douglass and those who followed, including Martin Luther King Jr., Jesse Jackson, Bishop T. D. Jakes and others, have worked within the community of African American churches to provide support and resources for African Americans in their march toward social justice and opportunity.

The African American church has been embraced by African Americans as a *rock in a weary land*—a shelter from societal mistreatment—often providing the only institution in society within which members feel safe, free to be themselves, and expect no discrimination. As might be expected, the church and religious teachings are central to meeting the spiritual needs of many African Americans. But the church has come to represent even more than a place of worship for its members. It has served as a vehicle for meeting many of the educational, political, economic, and social needs of African Americans. It has served as a meeting place for defense against discrimination and a launching pad for social and political reform.

For many African Americans, the church remains a place where everybody is somebody. Social class is largely de-emphasized in the church community. It may be one of the only public spaces where African Americans can expect to feel accepted and affirmed in the United States. But far more than a base for political activism or social freedom, the church for many is a place of shared values that provide the nutrients of life for its members. Entertainers like Tyler Perry have

## Personal Narrative 8-1

Langston Hughes, poet laureate, is one of the most controversial persons in the history of American poetry. His poems, which are committed to the ideal of social and political justice, are also criticized by some scholars as being too simple and unlearned. Such attempts to deny and belittle African American art forms may remind you of criticisms explored in this chapter of hip hop and slave accounts. Read a small portion of one of his poems, "The Bitter River," that was dedicated to the memory of Charlie Lang and Ernest Green, each 14 years old when lynched together beneath the Shubuta Bridge over the Chickasawhay River in Mississippi on October 12, 1942.

*... Wait, be patient," you say.*

"Your folks will have a better day."
But the swirl of the bitter river
Takes your words away.
"work, education, patience
Will bring a better day."
The swirl of the bitter river
Carries your "patience" away.

"Disrupter! Agitator!
Trouble maker! You say.
The swirl of the bitter river
Sweeps your lies away.
I did not ask for this river
Nor the taste of its bitter brew.
I was given its water
As a gift from you.
Yours has been the power
To force my back to the wall
And make me drink of the bitter cup
Mixed with blood and gall ...
Langston Hughes

*The Collected Poems of Langston Hughes'* p. 243–244

After reading this portion of the poem, reflect on what you've learned about slavery and the Jim Crow era in this chapter to add to your description of the different forms of oppression experienced by African Americans in the United States. Discuss your reflections with your classmates or instructor in large or small groups.

found ways to take the teachings of the church and make them more accessible to young and older African Americans alike in the form of morality plays, television shows, and movies which feature religious teachings that come to life in the perspectives, experiences, and solutions depicted by their characters.

Exercise 8-2 invites you to experience the encompassing sense of community that may be encountered at an African American church.

## EXERCISE 8-2    Field Experience: A Community Church

**Directions:** It is suggested that you consider this exercise only if church attendance is something that you value and not simply engage in this activity as an educational assignment or experimental task.

1. Locate a clearly identified African American church (for example, African Methodist Episcopal Church). Call the church (Pastor, Minister) and ask if it would be okay for you to attend services.

2. Following your attendance and participation in the church service, record your reflections on the experience, especially in light of how it was similar to and/or distinct from your previous church experiences. Share these reflections with a classmate, colleague, or your instructor.

# CULTURAL FACTOR 5: ACCULTURATION AND EXPERIENCE WITH EXCLUSION AND ALIENATION

Among involuntary-minority group members, instrumental adaptive responses are ways in which these individuals may try to cope with their limited access to jobs, wages, education, housing, and wealth in the United States and in their effort to make a space for themselves in dominant culture. Of course, not all members of minority groups react to institutional discrimination in the same ways. There is a full range of ways that members within the same minority group react to the derogatory treatment they receive. For example, civil rights activism, rioting, and assimilating to break racial barriers are all examples of instrumental adaptive responses. Variation in form may be influenced by differences in social class and individual coping and conflict-resolution styles (Ogbu, 1990; Alba & Nee, 2003).

Involuntary-minority group members may also utilize **expressive adaptive responses** to respond to societal discrimination. For example, *cultural inversion*—seeing certain ways of being as linked to dominant-culture and therefore inappropriate for them is an expressive adaptive response many African American students employ at some point in their development. Members of this cultural group may create systems of meaning—ways of dressing, speaking, and acting that unify them

## Intercultural Communication Strategies for Teachers 8-3

### Classroom Applications: Extending Curricula through Mentoring

A group mentoring approach can help you maximize community resources and decrease minority student resistance in schools. Organize mentoring meetings with three to five mentors from the African American community and five to seven students to discuss issues that pertain to school climate, community resources, African American history and current treatment in U.S. society, gender differences, and expectations. Meetings should take place weekly for a period of at least six weeks. Students should be asked to come prepared with questions for the group of mentors each week. By taking on this responsibility, they understand that they may direct the focus of the discussion when they feel the need. However, because mentors take responsibility for presenting information on predetermined topics, students are provided with an outline of the topics for each session that supports their personal and academic growth. Teachers provide a comfortable, consistent space complete with refreshments and arrange for all participants to have a copy of two books that also are discussed by the participants each week. Students and their mentors each pick out a book they would like the group to read and discuss. As such, the group mentoring sessions take on the feel of a book club. Students and mentors take turns facilitating the book discussions. This is another way to let the students know they are a critical component in their own education and support. Teachers must show their enthusiasm for the venture by taking responsibility for providing the consistent meeting space and refreshments and by encouraging regular attendance from students. This way all three constituents of the mentoring program demonstrate a vested interest in the success of the endeavor. Success should be measured through evaluations conducted at the end of each set of meetings. Finally, strengths and weaknesses of the program and personal gains from having participated in the group mentoring program can be shared with the parents of the students and members of the school community.

as a collective group while they subtly oppose dominant-culture expectations of them. Some African Americans may attempt, instead, to do the opposite. They may "pass," attempting to fit in with dominant culture by trying to be more like "them"—"acting white," in which case they play down their blackness and accentuate the dominant-culture values and behaviors they are able to exhibit. Passing, while not the only response to institutional discrimination, is certainly not rare. Ogbu (1991) noted that "some Blacks who benefited from the changes in opportunity structure since the 1960s chose to disaffiliate with the Black community and passed culturally into the White community" (p. 443).

While "passing" distances African Americans from other African Americans and African American culture, cultural inversion serves to unify African Americans and separate the group from dominant culture for the purpose of maintaining cultural identity, belonging, and networks that were damaged generations ago during slavery and remain under attack even today in broader society. As such, cultural inversion may be utilized by African American students to increase their feelings of personal and collective cultural integrity even though they conflict with behaviors that would lead to academic success in U.S. schools. Fordham (1982) has found:

> The subtle opposition of cultural inversion appears to be a frequent response to conquest and domination. Unable to overtly display their displeasure or opposition to the social structure which limits their obtainment of the most highly valued social goals, those social groups excluded from the cultural center of the social system frequently resort to methods which are considered inappropriate by the conquering group, but which at the same time enable the dominated group to retain some sense of self-respect and group identity. (p. 7)

## CULTURAL FACTOR 6: LANGUAGE DIFFERENCES, STRENGTHS, AND CHALLENGES

In general, African Americans tend to be more dramatic and expressive in their speech and language patterns than are members of dominant culture. During communication, African Americans may be more person-oriented than object- or topic-oriented. African Americans tend to be more affectionate than dominant-culture members and more direct and assertive during argumentation. African Americans also tend to enjoy interaction and integration in communication (Labov, 1973). As in many African American churches, a rhythmic volleying back and forth is often preferred over a monolithic dialogue.

Because African languages were taken from slaves when they were forcibly brought to the United States, a counter culture language system evolved that has been referred to most recently as **African American Vernacular English**, previously called *Ebonics*, which permitted a common language linked to cultural identity for the group (Wolfram & Thomas, 2002; Rickford & Rickford, 2000). Ebonics became a household word in the United States and in the world in the 1990s, when the school board of the Oakland, California, Unified School District (OUSD) passed what is now known as the "Ebonics Resolution." While the reactions of theoretical and applied linguists (for example, the Linguistic Society of America and the Board of Directors of Teachers of English to Speakers of Other Languages)

## Intercultural Communication Strategies for Teachers 8-4

### Classroom Applications: Responding to Language Differences

Inviting inclusion and participation of African American students within your classroom may be facilitated through the valuing and acknowledgement of different language systems. Specifically, you should do the following:

- Help students develop positive attitudes toward different language systems by teaching the history and components of cultural languages.
- Help students identify origins of variations in language used within the popular media (including music, poetry, and television).

- Assist students in learning to understand the importance of matching language type to settings and goals.
- Provide opportunities to learn, model, and practice different language systems within context (for example, in reading poetry and prose, in classroom presentations, with friends, during mock job interviews).

were generally in favor of the Ebonics Resolution, public reaction to this resolution was explosive.

It is often assumed that cultural language systems like African American Vernacular English (AAVE) represent incorrect pronunciations and grammar usage of the English language. Instead, such formats have been found to reflect a language system that incorporates patterns, symbols, and meanings that are elements in a specific linguistic system (Rickford & Rickford, 2000; Baugh, 2000; Green, 2002). The so-called grammar and pronunciation errors are instead variances in grammar and speech patterns that are not mistakes made by speakers but rather specific linguistic patterns repeated over and over in the use within the language system.

While the debate over the Ebonics Resolution has fallen silent, the issue remains to be addressed because many teachers continue to discriminate against students who employ cultural languages. Such treatment is another example and reflection of the devalued status of African Americans in the United States. Exercise 8-3 will help you reflect on the ways to handle such challenges when they arise.

Ogbu (1990) has contended that utilization of various coping strategies by involuntary-minority group members over time has shaped African American community's norms, values, and collective competencies. Because racial identity was and is jeopardized in the process of subordination experienced by involuntary-minority group members in the United States, he has hypothesized that a renegotiated collective cultural frame of reference emerged that often acts in opposition to dominant-culture behavioral expectations. The formulation of African American style to include the development of hip hop hairstyles from afros to corn rows, and the wearing of specific clothing styles and brands serve to support racial identity, supply integrity, and create symbolic differences in communication preferences and interaction styles. Interestingly, many of these elements created in opposition to dominant culture while not credited to African Americans have been co-opted by members of dominant culture (that is, the dominant-culture acquisition of African American clothing, hair, music, and communication preferences and styles).

## EXERCISE 8-3     Classroom Applications: A Professional Stance

**Directions:** Several approaches have been suggested to address concerns about minority students' use of familial language. Here you will find brief descriptions of other such proposals. Your task is to provide the descriptions to teachers in your school, at your field placement, or to a few professors in your field of study. Ask them to state their professional stance on these proposals. What do they see as the possible benefits (value) or detriments (costs) of these programs? What alternatives to the programs do they suggest? Finally, after reflecting on their comments, identify your position along with the rationale and research upon which it is based.

1. **The Oakland Ebonics Resolution:** (a) The language patterns of African American students are genetically based, do not constitute a dialect of English, and originated in West and Niger Congo African Language Systems; (b) these language patterns should be officially recognized as the primary language of African American students, who should have access to the same types of programs and funding that are available to other students whose primary language is not English; and (c) an academic program should be designed and implemented to instruct African American students in their primary language and facilitate the acquisition and mastery of SAE (Standard American English).

2. **Bridge:** This reading curriculum originally developed by Gary Simpkins, Grace Holt, and Charletta Simpkins in the 1970s is based on contrastive readings and exercises in the language and culture of AAVE (African American Vernacular English) and SAE.

3. **Bidialectal Communication:** This program employed in the Dekalb County, Georgia, school district program teaches fifth- and sixth-grade students to switch from their "home speech" to "school speech."

In terms of school adaptation, Ogbu (1992) described five roles that African American students may adopt to allow for achievement within the confines of racially antagonistic conditions often experienced in U.S. schools. These roles include (1) the **assimilator role**, (2) the **emissary role**, (3) the **alternator role**, (4) the **regular role**, and (5) the **ambivalent role** (see Table 8-1).

## POTENTIAL BARRIERS IN LEARNING–TEACHING RELATIONSHIPS WITH DOMINANT-CULTURE TEACHERS AND SCHOOLS

Relating, as they may, from the perspective of those who have been marginalized, African American families and students may display suspicion related to the ways African American students are treated in schools. For example, parents may resist forcing their children to rigidly adhere to school rules and codes of conduct simply because they are school policies. Their mistrust of the system is formed by what has been called a *healthy paranoia* when it comes to their interactions with society's institutions—including schools. Ever mindful that they are the same institutions that disadvantaged them and generations of their family members, parents may be careful to look out for the psychological safety of their children even if that means refusing to require them to comply with school rules—rules that may be unintentionally biased, devaluing, or unfair. Yet, even with this suspicion and desire to protect their children, parents of minority students are also called to make the best of the school experience and thus are likely to be strong advocates for quality

**Table 8-1**　Adapting to Antagonistic Conditions of U.S. Schools

| | |
|---|---|
| **The assimilator role** | Adopted by academically successful African American students who opt to attempt to disassociate themselves from African American cultural elements in order to adopt dominant-culture cultural elements. |
| **The emissary role** | Adopted by African American students who play down racial identity and cultural elements in order to succeed but do not completely reject African American culture and identity. |
| **The alternator role** | Employed by African American students who opt to deliberately follow school rules of behavior and standard practices while attempting to participate in African American culture within their communities and at home. |
| **The regular role** | Utilized by African American students who have been accepted as members of African American culture but who do not abide by all African American cultural norms (for example, these students may maintain close family ties and camouflage academic abilities from their peers). |
| **The ambivalent role** | Endorsed by African American students said to be caught between the desire to fit in with African American peers and the desire to achieve in school. School success for these students is often erratic as they pivot back and forth between attempting to be perceived as good students by school officials and being seen as true members of African American teen subculture by their peers. |

education for their children. Their ambiguity about whether or not to support school officials in their mandates—whether to, in fact, join with the school—is often interpreted by school authorities as a lack of care and concern for their children's education.

If minority parents do not attend PTA meetings or enroll their children in after school activities, these actions may be perceived as a lack of interest or an unwillingness to do all that is recommended for school success. Instead, this refusal to be part of a system that marginalizes them may represent their lack of trust that their children will be treated fairly and that their children will, in fact, actually benefit from playing by the rules set for them in school.

# FROM CONCEPTS TO LIVED EXPERIENCE

The reason I want to teach is based on my history as a student. During my elementary through high school years, I felt like all the teachers had it out for me. It seemed like I couldn't do anything without getting in trouble. There were often times when it seemed like a confrontation was imminent with my teachers whether it was me instigating it or not. I would say that I was responsible for starting trouble seventy percent of the time. I was an intelligent student but I was very active and sought to have the attention of my classmates on me. It's funny because now I am a person who doesn't want to ever be at the center of attention. Most of the teachers I had seemed out of touch with students and almost as if they did not really care either way if students were having trouble or whether they passed or failed. I believe that because all students are not the same, different methods must be used to get through to them. Many of my teachers never made an effort to get through to me and I was labeled as a troublemaker. That may have been true but there are positive ways of address students' misbehavior and being sent out of class should be the last option because after a few times of that happening, a student can get immune to the meaning of it. At the end of middle school, I graduated from the in-school suspension program. The last three weeks of school when everyone else was doing fun activities, including making graduation plans and enjoying the last few weeks with their fellow students, I was in ISAP writing definitions with the other "bad kids". The day of graduation, I had to meet everyone in the gym because I could not walk down the halls with my classmates. I barely made it out of middle school and my problems did not stop there. However, there was something that really saved me from my reputation as a "bad kid" and that was my desire to have a reputation as an athlete. I know that everyone is not able to be an athlete; but I think it is important to find something positive that can help to form a student's identity to create a positive reputation. My goal is to become a teacher who relates to his students and helps them find their niche in school and life. I'm a person who understands students whose backgrounds are similar to mine. I know what it is like to be cast out and characterized by a certain perception, and what impact that has on a student. After being told that you are a certain "type" of student, it becomes easy to take on the qualities of that kind of student. It's easy to become comfortable with the "bad kid" reputation no matter what the repercussions are. I know from personal experience that early experiences shape futures. I intend to be a positive experience in the lives of my students.

*Michael F., Education Student at Kentucky State University, an HBCU, personal communication, November, 2009.*

## SUMMARY

**Cultural Factor 1: Historical and Current Treatment in the United States** Slave accounts and hip hop have had their merit denied and their legitimacy questioned from their beginnings. It is important to note that these art forms vocalize the struggle of African American oppression in the United States as their truths challenge basic assumptions of entitlement, privilege, and access to opportunity. Slavery resulted in a legacy that continues to shape the current social identities of African Americans and members of dominant culture. It provides context for the current sociopolitical landscape and affects all intercultural relationships in the United States. Slavery was legal in the United States for more than 244 years. The process of freeing slaves, while mandated by President Lincoln's signing of the Emancipation Proclamation in 1863, continued until the passage of the Thirteenth Amendment to the Constitution in 1865, which barred slavery everywhere in the United States.

However, the process of emancipation left remnants that still exist today. In the late 1800s, African American teachers, ministers, landowners, and politicians were special targets of abuse, burnings, whippings, and lynchings, supported by Jim Crow laws that maintained widespread institutional discrimination against African Americans. The 1954 *Brown v. The Board of Education of Topeka, Kansas* court case that declared racial discrimination in schools to be unconstitutional and civil rights actions and legislation that followed paved the way for the end of the hold of the Jim Crow era.

It is estimated that currently 41.1 million U.S. residents self-identify as African American or African American in combination with one or more of other races making up approximately

13.5 percent of the total population of the United States. African Americans continue to struggle for educational and economic equity in the United States despite the fact that Barack Obama was elected the first African American president of the United States in 2008. An African American family's median income is almost $20,000 per year lower than that of White Americans, while unemployment, first incarceration, and poverty rates are twice as much or higher than for White Americans (Bureau of Labor Statistics, 2009).

**Cultural Factor 2: Initial Terms of Incorporation into U.S.** Society African Americans are considered involuntary minorities. Voluntary-minority group members are descendents of those who were said to believe that they would succeed in mainstream society through hard work and compliance with authority. Involuntary minorities are less likely to adopt compliant behaviors that have led to academic and economic success for voluntary minorities and members of dominant culture because they are descendents of those who were involuntarily incorporated into U.S. society through conquest, slavery, or colonization. As such, they may have experienced generations of oppression that result in a knowledge that the deck is stacked against them.

**Cultural Factor 3: Commonly Shared Values and Traditions** Respect for elders and devotion to family (including fictive kinship) is central in the lives of many African Americans. Sibling responsibility for siblings and family member support for all other family members are stressed. Slavery and oppression in the United States prohibited African American men from protecting and providing for their families. Current negative images of African American males and females stem from injustices endured during slavery and racism that still exists today. To this day, colorism, a word that stemmed from the perceived approaches that African Americans have used to address their oppression, creates divisions among members of the African American community. African American women face unique barriers in attempting to advance in society. Throughout history and still today, African American women neither benefit from the perceived virtuous characteristics of White womanhood, nor can they, as women, gain acceptance for utilizing strategies that are effective for males in society.

Education is another value prized by African Americans as a way to achieve personal and family goals. However, the salience of education is often diluted by the realization that African American students experience systematic discrimination in U.S. schools—a knowledge that the deck is stacked against them.

**Cultural Factor 4: View of Spirituality and Humans' Relation to Nature** The church and religious teachings are central to meeting the spiritual needs of many African Americans. But the church has come to represent even more than a place of worship for its members. It has served as a vehicle for meeting many of the educational, political, economic, and social needs of African Americans. It serves as a meeting place for defense against discrimination and a launching pad for social and political reform.

**Cultural Factor 5: Acculturation and Experience with Exclusion and Alienation** Instrumental adaptive responses are cultivated by African Americans to oppose institutional discrimination and to enable their participation in dominant culture. For example, civil rights activism and rioting are both examples of instrumental adaptive responses. Categorized as involuntary-minority group members based on their ancestors' initial terms of incorporation into society, African Americans may also utilize expressive adaptive responses that are distinct, personal ways of responding to the societal discrimination they face. For example, involuntary-minority group members may attempt to fit in with dominant culture by trying to be more like Whites ("passing" or "acting" White.) or utilize cultural inversion. Because racial identity is jeopardized in the process of subordination experienced by involuntary-minority group members, a renegotiated collective cultural frame of reference emerges that often acts in opposition to dominant-culture behavioral expectations. Cultural inversion is involuntary-minority group members' regard of certain forms of behavior, symbols, and meanings as inappropriate for them because they are seen as characteristic of White America.

**Cultural Factor 6: Language Differences, Strengths, and Challenges** Because the African languages were taken from slaves when they were brought to North America, a language system, African American Vernacular English (AAVE), that is commonly referred to as Ebonics has permitted a common language linked to cultural identity for the group. It is often assumed that cultural language systems like African American Vernacular English represent incorrect pronunciations and grammar usage of the English language. Instead, AAVE incorporates patterns, symbols, and meanings that are specific elements in a legitimate linguistic system.

Ogbu (1992) described five roles African American students may adopt to allow for achievement within the confines of racially antagonistic conditions often experienced in U.S. schools. These roles include: (1) the assimilator role, (2) the emissary role, (3) the alternator role, (4) the regular role, and (5) the ambivalent role.

**Potential Barriers in Learning–Teaching Relationships with Dominant-Culture Teachers and Schools** Relating, as they may, from the perspective of those who have been marginalized, African American families and students may display caution related to their treatment in schools. In cases where parental involvement seems limited, this refusal to be a part of a system that marginalizes them may represent their lack of trust that they will be treated fairly and that their children will, in fact, actually benefit from playing by the rules set for them in schools.

## Questions for Review

1. How might historical treatment of African Americans in the United States affect current African American student orientations to schooling?

2. What is cultural inversion and how might it affect African American student achievement?

3. Is it conceivable that African American teachers would not be received well by African American students? Explain.

## Important Terms

African American
   Vernacular English
   (AAVE)
alternator role
ambivalent role
assimilator role
aversive racism
*Brown v. the Board of
   Education of
   Topeka, Kansas*

Civil Rights Act
cultural inversion
Ebonics
Emancipation
   Proclamation
emissary role
expressive adaptive
   responses
fictive kinship
hip hop

historically Black
   universities and
   colleges (HBCU)
indentured servants
institutional
   discrimination
involuntary minorities
Jim Crow laws
Juneteenth

National Association
   for the
   Advancement of
   Colored People
   (NAACP)
passing
regular role
separate but equal
   doctrine
slave accounts

# Enrichment

Baugh, J. (2000). *Beyond Ebonics: Linguistic pride and racial prejudice.* Oxford, UK: Oxford University.

Cole, J. B. (2003). *Gender talk: The struggle for women's equality in African American communities.* New York: Ballantine.

Dyson, M. E. (1997). *Race rules: Navigating the color line.* New York: Vintage Books.

Dyson, M. E. (2003). *Why I love Black women.* New York: Basic Civitas Books.

Dyson, M. E. (2004). *The Michael Eric Dyson reader.* New York: Basic Civitas Books.

Dyson, M. E. (2007). *Know what I mean?: Reflections on hip hop.* New York: Basic Civitas Books.

DuBois, W. E. B. (1965). The souls of Black folk. In J. H. Franklin (Ed.), *Three Negro classics* (pp. 207–389). New York: Avon.

Franklin, J. H. (Ed.). (1965). *Three Negro classics.* New York: Avon.

Giddings, P. (2001). *When and where I enter: The impact of Black women on race and sex in America.* New York: Perennial.

Grant, J. (Ed.). (1968). *Black protest: History, documents, and analyses, 1619 to the present.* New York: Fawcett Premier.

Green, L. (2002). *African American English: A linguistic introduction.* Cambridge, UK: Cambridge University.

Guinier, L., & Sturm, S. (2001). *Who's qualified?* Boston: Beacon.

Hacker, A. (1992). *Two nations: Black and white, separate, hostile, unequal.* New York: Charles Scribner's Sons.

Halsall, P. (1997). Modern history sourcebook: Sojourner Truth: "Ain't I a woman?", December 1851. Retrieved 17 December 2009, from http://www. fordham.edu/halsall/mod/sojtruth-woman.html

Harris, F. R, & Wilkins, R. W. (Eds.). (1988). *Quiet riots: Race and poverty in the United States.* New York: Pantheon.

Hayre, R. W., & Moore, A. (1997). *Tell them we are rising: A memoir of faith in education.* New York: John Wiley & Sons.

Ogbar, J. O. (2007). *Hip-hop revolution: The culture and politics of rap.* Lawrence, Kansas: University Press of Kansas.

Perdue, C. L., Barden, T. E., & Phillips, R. K. (Eds.). (1976). *Weevils in the wheat: Interviews with Virginia ex-slaves.* Charlottesville: University of Virginia.

Rampersad, A. & Roessel, D. (1994). *The collected poems of Langston Hughes.* New York: Alfred A. Knopf, Inc.

Sullivan, S. (2006). *Revealing whiteness: The unconscious habits of racial privilege.* Bloomington and Indianapolis, IN: Indiana University Press.

Tatum, B. D. (1997). *"Why are all the black kids sitting together in the cafeteria?" and other conversations about race. A psychologist explains the development of racial identity.* New York: Basic Books.

U.S. Bureau of the Census. (2003). *Statistical abstracts of the United States: 2003* (123rd ed.). Washington, DC: U.S. Government Printing Office.

West, C. (1999). *The Cornel West reader.* New York: Basic Civitas Books.

White, D. G. (1999). *Too heavy a load: Black women in defense of themselves 1894–1994.* New York: Norton & Company.

Williams, L. (2000). *It's the little things: Everyday interactions that anger, annoy, and divide the races.* New York: Harcourt.

## Connections on the Web

http://www.blackamericaweb.com/

BlackAmericaWeb.com is a site that features African American perspectives on news, travel, entertainment, business, technology, and sports.

http://www.blackplanet.com/

BlackPlanet.com is an online social-networking site for African Americans. Launched in 1999, it was the fourth highest trafficked social-networking site in 2007.

http://www.blackvoices.com/

Blackvoices.com presents African American family, health, entertainment, culture, and community news.

http://www.library.vcu.edu/jbc/speccoll/vbha/school/school.html

Fourteen oral history interviews with Richmond, Virginia African American residents conducted by Virginia Commonwealth University students as part of a course. Participants were interviewed about their education experiences.

http://www.slavenarratves.com/

This site features a collection of slave narratives.

http://www-dept.usm.edu/~mcrohb/

The University of Southern Mississippi's Center for Oral History and Cultural Heritage in conjunction with the Tougaloo College Archives compiled this oral account of the Civil Rights era.

http://www.africa.upenn.edu/K-12/menu_EduAFAM.html

The University of Pennsylvania African Studies Center provides this resource site for Internet African American teaching resources.

http://www.splcenter.org/center/tt/teach.jsp

Founded in 1991 by the Southern Poverty Law Center, Teaching Tolerance provides K-12 educators with educational materials that promote respect for differences and appreciation of diversity in the classroom.

## References

African American Population (2009). 2010 Census Multimedia Center: Black Population. Retrieved from http://2010.census.gov/mediacenter/portrait-of-america/black-population.php

Alba, R., & Nee, V. (2003). *Remaking the American mainstream: Assimilation and contemporary immigration.* Cambridge, MA: Harvard University.

Baugh, J. (2000). *Beyond Ebonics: Linguistic pride and racial prejudice.* Oxford, UK: Oxford University.

Bureau of Labor Statistics (2009). *African American history month spotlight.* United States Department of Labor. Retrieved from http://www.bls.gov/spotlight/2009/african_american_history/ on 12/16/2009.

Center for American Progress Action Fund. (2009). *Wage gap by numbers.* Retrieved 17 December 2009, from http://www.americanprogress.org/issues/2009/01/wage_gap_numbers.html

DuBois, W. E. B. (1969). The domination of women. In *Darkwater: Voices from within the veil.* New York: Schocken.

Dyson, M. E. (2007). *Know what I mean?: Reflections on hip hop.* New York: Basic Civitas Books.

Dyson, M. E. (2003). *Why I love Black women.* New York: Basic Civitas Books.

Fordham, S. (1982, December). *Cultural inversion and black children's school performance.* Paper presented at the annual meeting of the American Anthropological Association, Washington, DC.

Fordham, S. (1993). Those loud black girls: Black women, silence, and gender "passing" in the academy. *Anthropology and Education Quarterly, 24,* 3–32.

Giddings, P. (2001). *When and where I enter. The impact of Black women on race and sex in America.* New York: Perennial.

Gorham, Des Jardins, Page, Pettis, & Scherber. (1976). Effect on parents. In N. Hobbs (Eds.), *Issues in the classification of children* (pp. 154–188). West Lafayette, IN: Jossey-Bass.

Green, L. (2002). *African American English: A linguistic introduction.* Cambridge, UK: Cambridge University.

Hebbeler, K., & Wagner, M. (2001). *Representation of minorities and children of poverty among those receiving early intervention and special education services: Findings from two national longitudinal studies.* Washington, DC: Stanford Research Institute.

Hollingsworth, L. A., Didelot, M. J., & Smith, J. O. (2003). REACH beyond tolerance: A framework for teaching children empathy and responsibility. *Journal of Humanistic Counseling, Education & Development, 42*(2), 139–152.

Kolchin, P. (1993). *American slavery, 1619–1877.* New York: Hill & Wang.

Labov, W. (1973). *Language in the inner city: Studies in Black English vernacular.* Philadelphia: University of Pennsylvania.

Leach, B. W. (2004). Race as mission critical: The occupational need rationale in military affirmative action and beyond. *Yale Law Review, 113*(3), 1093–1143.

McGill, A. (2000). *In the hollow of your hand: Slave lullabies.* Boston: Houghton Mifflin.

McNeal, L. (2009). The re-segregation of public education now and after the end of Brown v. Board of Education. *Education and Urban Society, 41*(5), 562–574.

Oakes, J., & Rogers, J. (2006). *Learning power: Organization for education and justice.* New York: Teachers College Press.

Oakes, J., & Rogers, J. (2007). Radical change through radical means: Learning power. *Journal of Educational Change, 8*(3), 193–206.

Ogbu, J. U. (1990). Minority education in comparative perspective. *Journal of Negro Education, 59,* 45–55.

Ogbu, J. U. (1991). Minority coping responses and school experience. *The Journal of Psychohistory, 18,* 433–456.

Ogbu, J. U. (1992). Understanding cultural diversity and learning. *Educational Researcher, 21,* 5–24.

Ogbar, J. O. (2007). *Hip-hop revolution: The culture and politics of rap.* Lawrence, Kansas: University Press of Kansas.

Orfield, G., & Kurlaender, M. (Eds.). (2001). *Diversity challenged: Evidence on the impact of affirmative action.* Cambridge, MA: Harvard Education.

Orfield, G., & Lee. C. (2007). *Historic reversals, accelerating resegregation, and the need for new integration strategies.* A report of the Civil Rights Project. Retrieved from http://www.civilrightsproject.ucla.edu/research/deseg/reversals_reseg_need.pdf.

Patton, J. M. (1991). The Black male's struggle for education. In L. E. Gary (Ed.), *Black men* (pp. 199–214).

Perdue, C. L., Barden, T. E., & Phillips, R. K. (Eds.). (1976). *Weevils in the wheat: Interviews with Virginia ex-slaves.* Charlottesville: University of Virginia.

Raspberry, W. (1990). The myth that is crippling Black America. *Reader's Digest,* 96–98.

Rickford, J. R., & Rickford, R. J. (2000). *Spoken soul: The story of Black English.* New York: Wiley & Sons.

Rumbaut, R. G., & Portes, A. (2001). *Ethnicities: Children of immigrants in America.* Berkeley: University of California.

Spradlin, L. K. (1999). Taking black girls seriously: Addressing discrimination's double bind. In L. Alvine & L. Cullum (Eds.), *Breaking the cycle: Gender, literacy, and learning* (pp. 7–12). Peterborough, NH: Heineman Boynton-Cook.

Sudarkasa, N. (1991). Absent! Black men on campus. *Essence*, 22(7), 140.

Sullivan, S. (2006). *Revealing whiteness: The unconscious habits of racial privilege*. Bloomington and Indianapolis, IN: Indiana University Press.

U.S. Bureau of Census. (2007). *Economic Census*. Retrieved 21 December 2009, from http://www.census.gov/econ/census07/

Wade, M. E. (2001). Women and salary negotiation: The costs of self-advocacy. *Psychology of Women Quarterly*, 25, 65–76.

Walters, R. (2008). *Race in education 1954–2007*. Columbia, Missouri: The Curators of the University of Missouri.

Washington, B. T. (1965). Up from Slavery. In J. H. Franklin (Ed.), *Three Negro classics*. New York: Doubleday/Random House.

Wolfram, W., & Thomar, E. R. (2002). *The development of African American English*. Maiden, MA: Blackwell.

Young, C. (1986). Afro-American family: Contemporary issues and implications for social policy. In D. Pilgrim (Ed.), *On being Black: An in-group analysis*. Bristol, IN: Wyndham Hall.

Ysseldyke, J. E., Algozzine, B., & Thurlow, M. L. (2000). *Critical issues in special education* (3rd ed.). Boston: Houghton Mifflin.

*I need life, close-up, tooth and claw. Alive, real, power, exercise. There are more real, fulfilling, and satisfying things to do than sit around talking to a bunch of good old boys about the same old things, year after year. I don't want to talk about doing things, I want to be doing things and I want to know the realities and limits of life by their measure! I don't want my life to be nothing, to not make a difference ... And life is so short, I could be gone tomorrow ... There is only one way—destiny, destiny. To trust destiny.*

**Eustace Conway**
*Source:* **Elizabeth Gilbert's The Last American Man, 2003, p. 83.**

CHAPTER

# 9 Learning from the Poor and Working-Class Stories

The values, perspectives, and views of what constitutes "*the good life*" expressed in Conway's brief narrative, which appears in Gilbert's (2003) biography, of his self-sufficient life lived in the Appalachian Mountains provide insight into significant aspects of the culture of individuals who make up the poor and **working class** in the United States. Gilbert (2003) explains

> ... while the classic European coming-of-age story generally featured a provincial boy who moved to the city and was transformed into a refined gentleman, the American tradition evolved into the opposite. The American boy came of age by leaving civilization and striking out toward the hills. There, he shed his cosmopolitan manners and became a robust and proficient man. Not a gentleman, mind you, but a man. This (Eustace Conway) was a particular kind of man, this wilderness-bred American. He was no intellectual. He had no interest in study or reflection. He had, as de Toqueville noticed, "a sort of distaste for what is ancient." Instead, he could stereotypically be found, as the explorer John Fremont described the uber-frontiersman Kit Carson, "mounted on a fine horse, without a saddle and scouring bare-headed over the prairies." Either that or whipping his mighty ax over his shoulder and casually, "throwing cedars and oaks to the ground." (p. 5)

This account, presenting a rural perspective, has in common values and perspectives often shared by poor and working-class individuals and families who live in urban and suburban areas as well. Members of this group exist in all regions of the United States. Some live in poverty; some are homeless; some live in homes with mortgages while working work in various service positions and in other industries to provide for themselves and their families; and there are many more who live varying lifestyles with wide-ranging incomes, family constellations, and views of what "the good life" entails. It might seem obvious that economic comfort is better than economic discomfort for people across cultural groups. However, it must also be noted that affluence does not guarantee healthy self-development of happiness. The ability to purchase goods is certainly an asset for a person. However, societal judgments about the amount of goods needed to constitute a good life are debatable. This reality is seldom recognized given the considerable societal emphasis on opulence and ownership of abundant material goods.

This chapter explores the wide-ranging poor and working-class culture in the United States and how daily economic struggles and associated social class may clash, even if sometimes imperceptibly, with middle-class ideals and standards commonly endorsed within schools and dominant culture—a clash that is detrimental for poor and working-class student development and achievement and, ultimately, for all members of society (Collins & Veskel, 2004). Many people may believe that poverty is merely the extent to which individuals *do without*—some people and families struggling more than others to survive and endure daily challenges of living with little to no income. However, members of the poor and working class, a vastly diverse cultural group, may, instead, view their lack of material means as less important than their ability to live in beautiful natural surroundings in harmony with nature and having only themselves to which to answer and on which to depend. Conversely, others may identify the poverty of the poor and working-class people as the culmination of insurmountable societal injustices and impediments to the very survival of members of this group.

## CHAPTER OBJECTIVES

1. Describe common values and worldviews of the vastly diverse population of poor and working-class individuals in the United States.
2. Identify ways in which the individuals profiled in this chapter experienced and addressed the six cultural factors explored in this text. Explain academic and intercultural interaction implications related to the six cultural factors for members of the working class.
3. Describe coping strategies that may be utilized by members of this group.
4. Identify classroom strategies for cultivating positive relationships with students from poor and working-class families to facilitate their full participation and academic achievement in school.

## CULTURAL FACTOR 1: HISTORICAL AND CURRENT TREATMENT IN THE UNITED STATES

### Historical Background

From the country's very beginnings, dominant-culture citizens in the United States have coerced subordinates to do their labor. "By the early 18th century, slavery, legal in all of British America, was the dominant labor system of the Southern colonies. During the century and a half between the arrival of 20 Blacks in Jamestown in 1619 and the outbreak of the American Revolution in 1776, slavery—nonexistent in England itself—spread through all the English colonies that would soon become the United States" (Kolchin, 1993, pp. 3–4). Because the colonists came from a hierarchical society, they apparently saw nothing particularly problematic about some people working, even in bondage, for the well-being of others. **Indentured servitude** was a booming institution in the colonies. White individuals who were either kidnapped, sentenced, or simply too poor to afford passage to North America were sold or sold themselves into temporary slavery. Most adults ended up serving four or five years of servitude. Children, however, often served seven years or more. But even when the original terms of their bondage were met, many adults and children found their servitude extended for so-called criminal behaviors (including disobedience, attempted escape, and childbearing).

> During their indenture, servants were essentially slaves, under the complete authority of their masters. Masters could (and readily did) apply corporal punishment to servants, forbid them to marry, and sell them (for the duration of their terms) to others. In short, indentured servitude provided the emerging colonial gentry with relatively cheap labor, more land and wealth, and the honor to pose authority over other humans. (Kolchin, 1993, p. 9)

## Who Are the Middle Class?

The **middle class** in the United States is ambiguously defined. While the term is commonly used, there is little agreement about what it entails. Contemporary sociologists commonly divide the middle class into two subgroups: (1) the **upper or professional middle class**, constituting 15 to 20 percent of households, includes educated, salaried professionals, and managers; and (2) the **lower middle class**, constituting roughly one-third of all households in the United States, includes mostly semiprofessionals, skilled craftsmen and lower-level managers. Members of the middle class are commonly believed to have a comfortable standard of living, significant economic security, considerable work autonomy, and rely on their expertise rather than their labor to sustain themselves. Depending on the class model used, the middle class may constitute anywhere from 25 to 66 percent of the households in the United States.

In the United States most people want to believe that they are members of the middle class and, in fact, often identify themselves as such. However, the income for middle class families ranges between $25,000 and $100,000, which clearly represents a wide variety of economic well-being and security. In general, middle-class persons, especially upper middle-class individuals tend to be characterized by their jobs which require them to conceptualize, create, and consult—that explains why a college education is seen as one of the main indicators of middle-class status. Largely attributed to the nature of middle-class occupations, middle-class values tend to emphasize independence, adherence to intrinsic standards, valuing innovation and respecting nonconformity. It is important to note that one way in which middle-class desirability and mystique is maintained is through the social promotion of the nobility of the middle class for its strong work ethic and so-called "self-made" success. It is hard to argue with these virtues and there is little wonder why most U.S. citizens see themselves as belonging to this group whether they earn the associated income, have occupations that fit the profile, or benefit from the associated social-class status. Such deceptions disguise social-class stratification and

**EXERCISE 9-1**   **Point of Reflection: Social-Class Values and Conventions**

Think about what social class means and entails, and identify your social class based on your family's circumstances. Using information from this chapter, describe how you know that your family has the social-class position you identified. Finally, discuss what social-class status you hope to attain someday. If it is different than your family's social-class status, discuss what you believe it will take for you to obtain your desired social-class position in society and why it is important for you. Share your insights with your colleagues, classmates, or teacher in a small-group discussion.

obscure institutional classism while quietly maintaining and justifying poor and working-class individuals' subordinate positions in society. Members of the middle and capitalist classes are, thus, advantaged while escaping the watchful eye and judgment of the populace and media. Complete Exercise 9-1 to identify your social-class values and characteristics.

Given the challenging economic times, the size of the middle class decreases daily with high rates of unemployment concentrated among working-class and poor males. Approximately 5 percent of college-educated women and men were unemployed in 2009, while almost 9 percent of women and 11 percent of men holding a high school degree were also unemployed (Wilcox, 2009).

## Current Conditions

While slavery no longer exists and formal indenture has ended, the structures, policies, and practices found within U.S. institutions that sprung from these early human injustices continue to support class stratification and differential treatment for different classes of U.S. residents (Collins & Veskel, 2004; Rose, 2000). With such unequal beginnings, it is easy to see how the United States has maintained a society comprised of those who have and those who have not.

While the United States is largely viewed as a **classless society**, the truth is, there are enormous differences in the economic status and conditions of U.S. residents as a function of individuals' positions in the socioeconomic strata. The United States is actually a highly stratified society in which social-class distinctions operate in every aspect of life, determining the nature of one's work, the quality of schooling, and the health and safety of one's family. Currently, over 35 million U.S. residents are poor. A family of four with an income at or below $16,018 a year lives in poverty. In the United States, one out of every four children is born into poverty, while at the same time, families holding the top 1 percent of the country's wealth doubled their share of wealth in the last 30 years. During that same period, the percentage of children living in poverty in the United States also doubled. Since 1980, the percentage of children living in families with medium income fell from 41 percent to 34 percent, while the percentage of children living in families in extreme poverty rose from 17 percent to 24 percent. (U.S. Bureau of the Census, 2003).

Consider, for example, the decrease in minimum-wage earnings over the past 40 years. In 1955, the average minimum wage was $0.75 an hour; with adjustment taking into account the value of the dollar today, it was $4.39 an hour. In 1965, the minimum wage was $1.25 ($6.23 with adjustment for the value of a dollar today). In 1975, the minimum wage in the United States was $2.10 (with adjustment: $6.12). In 1985, the minimum wage was $3.35 (with adjustment: $4.88). In 1995, minimum wage was set at $4.25 (with adjustment: $4.38). And in 2004, the minimum wage in the United States was $5.15 (with adjustment: $4.42) per hour. It is clear from these statistics that the country's economic policies and institutionalized practices have kept the lowest wage earners in their working-class and poor positions in society. These structural barriers to advancement have nothing to do with the amount of motivation and hard work—so-called boot-strap pulling—that working-class and under-class workers demonstrate.

There have been some improvements in the state of poverty in the United States. In 2008, 13.2 percent of all persons lived in poverty compared to the 1993 poverty rate of 15.1 percent. Between 1993 and 2000, the poverty rate fell each year, reaching 11.3 percent in 2000. However, the poverty rate for all persons masks considerable variation between racial/ethnic subgroups. Poverty rates for African Americans and Latinos greatly exceed the national average. In 2008, 24.7 percent of Blacks and 23.2 percent of Latinos were poor, compared to 8.6 percent of non-Hispanic Whites and 11.8 percent of Asian Americans. In addition, poverty rates are highest for families headed by single women, particularly if they are African American or Latino. In 2008, 28.7 percent of households headed by single women were poor, while 13.8 percent of households headed by single men and only 5.5 percent of married couple households lived in poverty.

It is important to realize that children represent a disproportionate share of the poor in the United States; they are 25 percent of the total population, but make up 35 percent of the poor population. In 2008, 14.1 million children, or 19 percent, were poor. The poverty rate for children also varies substantially by race as shown in Table 9-1.

A chief concern for school officials, revealed by these statistics, is that children in low-income families fare more poorly than children in more affluent families in the areas of economic security, health, and education. Children living in poor families are more likely to have difficulty in school than children living in other families and, as adults, earn less and are unemployed more often than dominant-culture individuals (Federal Interagency Forum on Child and Family Statistics, 1998).

**Table 9-1**    Children Living in Poverty

| Category | Number | Percentage |
|---|---|---|
| All children under 18 | 14,068 | 19.0 |
| White only, non-Hispanic | 4,364 | 10.6 |
| Black | 4,202 | 33.9 |
| Hispanic | 5,010 | 30.6 |
| Asian | 494 | 13.3 |

*Source:* U.S. Bureau of the Census. (2008). *Income, Poverty, and Health Insurance Coverage in the United States: 2008,* Report P60, n. 236, Table B-2, pp. 50–55.

Further, because public school budgets are based on property taxes, allowing higher-income school districts to spend more than poorer ones, the country's school system is rigged in favor of the already privileged, with lower-class students often tracked into economically and academically deficient classrooms, thus continuing the cycle of oppression (Sklar, 1998; Kozol, 1991).

## CULTURAL FACTOR 2: INITIAL TERMS OF INCORPORATION INTO U.S. SOCIETY

The colonists' institution of indentured servitude that began in the 1600s in colonial America created the structures that define the current social classes in the United States. **Social-class** differences have a profound impact on the way people live. Class differences affect how much time it takes to accomplish daily tasks in life (for example, doing laundry, shopping for food and clothing, travel, treatment for illness, and child care). Class differences determine where one lives, how one is educated, who one's friends are, what one does for a living, and even what one may expect out of life. There have always been huge differences between the haves and have nots in the United States (Manstios, 1998). However, the United States is perceived by most to be a **meritocracy** in which all people have equal opportunities to be successful—to live the so-called *American dream*. It is widely believed that all it takes is for people to "pull themselves up by their bootstraps" in order to succeed. After all, it is often argued, "poor and working-class people find themselves in their positions because they made bad choices."

With such sentiments as the societal backdrop, those who are poor often find themselves blamed for social problems that oppress them. However, it is clear that people do not choose to be working class, poor, or homeless. Rather, social systems and institutions exist that maintain the **cycle of poverty**. Consider, for example, the impact and process of inheritance. Wachtel (1984) likened inheritance to "a series of Monopoly games in which the winner of the first game refuses to relinquish his or her cash and commercial property before the start of subsequent games. With such an arrangement, it is not difficult to predict the outcome of subsequent games" and resulting economic options (pp. 161–162). Those who are unable to play or those who attempt to play but are hampered by their lack of capital and institutionally curtailed opportunity structures find that they are limited, and even prohibited from upward social mobility—limited not by their desire, choices made, merit, or effort but by the reality of the fact that they were born into working-class or poor families.

The image of the "American family" or the lived experience of the "average" American lifestyle that is depicted in television shows such as *The Hills, iCarly, Privileged, MTV Cribs,* and *Gossip Girl,* and in soap operas, sitcoms, and reality shows present lives of comfort in which individuals are free to make a variety of choices about how to spend their days and enjoy all aspects of life. These shows depict lives filled with luxury, opportunity, freedom, all the disposable time one desires, and abundant life choices.

In fact, the problems of the poor are often hidden from mainstream America's view, or when presented, they are greatly distorted. For example, the poor are portrayed as undeserving; having only themselves to blame; and lacking motivation,

## EXERCISE 9-2    Point of Reflection: Social Problem or Individual Failure

*Directions:* Interview five different individuals and record their responses to the following:

1. What is the most likely explanation for the current state of life for homeless people and what is one thing you feel needs to be done to change their situation?

2. Share your findings with your colleagues, classmates, or teacher in small-group discussion. Do you find any common themes present among the responses? Is blame assigned? If so, where? Are the suggested interventions reasonable, given what you know about poverty in the United States?

intelligence, and skills to address their struggles. Or they are portrayed as people who are temporarily down on their luck, in which case a holiday gift basket or some trips to a soup kitchen are all they need to rebound and turn their lives around. At other times, the poor are presented as an inconvenience and an irritation, as in the case of those living in homeless shelters, collecting welfare, or surviving as panhandlers. Dominant culture in the United States has blamed the poor and working class for their struggles rather than the government polices and institutionalized practices that serve to disadvantage the poor and working class keeping them in their social class while advantaging the middle and capitalist classes (Manstios, 1998). Exercise 9-2 will help you examine your personal biases regarding the poor and working class in the United States.

## CULTURAL FACTORS 3 AND 4: SHARED VALUES, TRADITIONS, AND SPIRITUALITY

Living lives filled with daily economic struggles and often having experienced generations of economic deprivation may provide the poor and working class with perspectives that are different from those in the middle and capitalist classes.

Some early research (for example, Kahl, 1968; Lengermann, 1982; Nisan, 1973) suggested that the poor typically share a preference for (1) present-time orientation, (2) action versus reflection, (3) linear social relations, and (4) subjugation to or at least harmony with nature.

> Eustace would say, "Don't destroy the entire plant! Be considerate of limited resources. Take one leaf, nibble a little bit of it, pass it around. Remember that the whole world isn't here for you to consume and destroy. Remember that you aren't the last person who will walk through these woods. Or the last person who will live on this planet. You've got to leave something behind."
>
> *Source:* Elizabeth Gilbert's *The Last American Man*, 2003, p. 111.

In addition, working-class and poor individuals may value tightly knit family life and conventionality. They are said to embrace a type of solidarity and to share ambitious attitudes toward education. However, it is important to recognize that while these values may be shared by some members of the working class and poor, it is difficult to identify clear aspects that truly typify members of this cultural

**Table 9-2**  Comparison of Working-Class and Middle-Class Values

| Working Class | Middle Class |
|---|---|
| Believe that one must make as much money as one can to pay for as good a life as one can afford. | Possess "cultural capital" and engage in networking. Use cultural information and contacts to advance. Identify with brand name clothing, cars, and so on. |
| Believe in a "whatever it takes" work ethic. Speak in a forthright manner—open and honest. Are proud of cultural customs. Employ the use of nonverbal communication skills. | Have a sense of belonging among members of dominant culture. Speak the language of dominant-culture authorities with fluency. |
| Have respect for parents and close contact with extended-family members. Exhibit a sense of loyalty and solidarity with family and community members. Experience limited choices in school. | Receive privileged education. Expect extra and special treatment from authorities. Emphasize individuality. Children have a say in what they do. Seek intellectual challenges and choices in school. |
| Confront limited images in the media that portray cultural group members in a positive light. Mistrust "eggheads." Prefer logic that encompasses common sense and intuition. | Relate to predominant images in popular culture. Prefer analytical and logical approaches to problem solving. |
| Are emotionally expressive. Tend to be tough and loud. | Exercise emotional restraint. Emphasize surface appearances and getting along with dominant-culture authorities. |
| Seek work that pays well. | Seek work that is fulfilling and pays well. |
| Respect parents' accomplishments and efforts.<br>Acquiesce to authority when needed, yet refuse to be dominated on one's own turf. | Feel pressured to achieve more than their parents.<br>Protest, question, and challenge authority. |
| Believe "I am what I am." | Believe "I must be someone important." |
| Experience overt prejudice and oppression. | Largely unaware of social-class oppression. |
| Expect to be a worker. | Expect to be a manager. |

*Source:* Adapted from Lubrano, A. (2004). *Limbo, Blue Collar Roots, White Collar Dreams.* Hoboken, NJ: John Wiley & Sons.

group because there is abundant fluidity in the social consciousness among poor and working-class persons (Ozum, 1995). An interesting comparison of working-class versus middle-class values was outlined by Lubrano (2004) (see Table 9-2).

In school, working-class and poor students may demonstrate resistance to dominant-culture values that underlie certain school practices. It is not uncommon to find working-class and poor (particularly male) students who are less willing to follow dominant-culture timetables, routines, and expected forms and degrees of participation or who take informal control of classrooms by limiting work production or finding forms of expression that may seem disrespectful or disrupt teachers' agendas. White working-class and poor male students are currently the worst performers on English tests compared to all other groups by age 11. Ethnic minority pupils, on the other hand, as a whole, from similar backgrounds are not only ahead but also improving more quickly even though thousands in this group do not speak English at home. Poor white male students are also among the worst performers in math and science, according to statistics published by the Department for Children, Schools, and Families (Clark, 2009).

## Valuing the Practical

Working-class and poor males, in particular, may reject school due to the forces of social-class oppression which promote the realization that practical job skills may prove to be more useful than the obtainment of degrees and a knowledge of theory Willis, 1977). For them, "an ounce of keenness is worth a whole library of certificates" (Willis, 1981, p. 254).

## Gender Roles

While working- and under-class males may resist schooling, working-class females (less likely than working-class males to be held responsible by the group for upholding the integrity of the working class) are not seen as sell-outs to the group when they achieve in school. In addition, working-class and poor females are typically staunch supporters of their male counterparts in the home and in schools, even when they are treated as subordinates by them. It is commonly understood that because the men are forced to fend off the harsh realities of the workplace—laboring in unpleasant conditions so they can provide for their families amid social-class injustice—the women's place is to create a warm and supportive home environment; take most, if not all, responsibility for child care and family obligations; and in all ways help the men in their lives to achieve and produce for the family.

**Chauvinism** frequently reigns in poor and working-class culture where women may be assigned roles that do not provide them with high status. The roles of homemaker and helper, while strongly needed and called upon in society, are not usually compensated with outward displays of respect, income, and value. In addition, both working-class and poor families commonly extend enormous and continual efforts to maintain their survival, often requiring all family members, including children, to work to contribute to the family's finances and development.

## CULTURAL FACTOR 5: ACCULTURATION AND EXPERIENCE WITH EXCLUSION AND ALIENATION

Working-class and poor students and their parents continue to be excluded in numerous ways in schools and society. The media routinely depicts the "normal" lifestyles of the middle class in which people are portrayed as living in affluent residences while working in white-collar jobs, and having discretionary time to pursue their hobbies and interests (Manstios, 1998). Working-class and poor citizens are excluded by such portrayals of "normal" lifestyles that do not reflect their life circumstances and realities. This type of exclusion also exists in U.S. schools—schools established and designed to perpetuate social-class stratification through the preparation of young people for their roles in those social classes (Carnoy, 1974). In fact, school performance (grades and test scores) and educational attainment (level of schooling completed) strongly correlate with socioeconomic class status.

> Through the inequality of resources and practices in schools serving communities of different regions, ethnic groups, and socioeconomic levels, and through the unequal treatment of children of varying backgrounds within the same schools, schooling teaches children both their place in society and how to behave in that place. The gradual accumulation of differential experience in the early years of schooling leads mainstream children to believe that education will ultimately bring rewards and success, while non-mainstream children frequently come to view education as a humiliating and fruitless pursuit. (Eckert, 1989, p. 7)

As with racial stratification influences, Brookover and Erickson (1975) maintained that social-class stratification creates role expectations that define student behavior expectations; that is, role expectations specify how a student should behave in school based on his or her social-class status. Similarly, Eckert's (1989) research on social-class relations among White high school students identified two distinct social-class categories of students: (1) burnouts—coming from the working class and enrolled primarily in general and vocational courses; and (2) jocks—coming from the middle class, moving along a college-bound educational track, playing or participating in school sports and activities, and receiving respectable grades. Eckert found that burnouts had an adversarial relationship with the school, while jocks had a cooperative relationship.

According to Eckert (1989), adolescent social structure characterizes the opposition that integrates the forces of family, neighborhood, and society. The structure and norms of school and peer social interaction, according to Eckert, explain polar social-class orientations to school achievement. Eckert concluded that jocks and burnouts are embodiments of the middle and working classes, respectively; the two separate cultures are in many ways social-class cultures, and opposition and conflict between them define social-class relations and differences that exist in society.

Schools both formally and informally encourage and maintain social-class distinctions. For example, researchers have found that teachers' classroom expectations for working-class and poor students are often lower and that they tend to discourage these students and under-evaluate their work. It is also a common practice of school officials to steer children of the working class into general education and vocational programs, thus limiting their future options (Becker, 1952; Cicourel & Kitsuse, 1963; Eckert, 1989; Rist, 1970; Bloom, 2001).

A rigid form of exclusion often encountered by working-class and poor students in U.S. schools involves the process of tracking. **Tracking,** or grouping students in schools based on their so-called ability, contributes to differential school outcomes and unfairly sorts students for subsequent social and economic roles (Oakes & Lipton, 1990). In fact, numerous research studies have found that tracking and rigid ability grouping are generally ineffective and, for many children, are

## EXERCISE 9-3    Field Experience: Setting the Direction Early

**Directions:** Interview three school principals.

1. Ask the principals if tracking is employed in their schools. If so, ask how students are assigned to tracks and how change in their tracks occurs when students' achievement improves.
2. Conduct research to identify statistics on the demographic profiles of the students placed in lower tracks (that is, identify socioeconomic status (SES), gender, race, and ethnicity) of low, average, and high tracks in schools.
3. Share your findings with your teacher, colleagues, or classmates in small-group discussion. Are there any apparent connections between track placement and SES? Gender? Race? Ethnicity? Discuss implications for student outcomes and opportunities.

harmful (Goodlad & Marshall, 1984; National Commission on Excellence in Education, 1983; Noland, 1985).

Tracking is predicated on a belief that prospects for school performance are readily identifiable and, for all practical purposes, unchangeable. This assumption is false (Oakes & Lipton, 1990). The fault of this assumption and the damage it can create are especially noticeable when tracking is employed in the early grades. Employing this line of thinking and the practice of tracking in the early grades in reading and math groups may severely restrict the educational options available to those placed in low and average tracks. Just as children are being presented for the first time with academic material, they are also being judged severely by their primary-grade school teachers in order to be placed into tracks that will most likely endure for their entire lives. Students placed in the highest reading groups will be expected to achieve and will be attended to as achievers in ways that will ensure the best of all educational experiences. Not so for those placed in the lowest reading groups. For many of these students, their educational experience will be characterized by the teaching and learning of rote skills rather than critical-thinking or decision-making skills. Even though without tracking the so-called gifted, average, and low-achieving students can fare as well or even better academically, the practice of tracking continues because it benefits those who favor it (occupants of the higher tracks)—mostly middle-class students and their parents (Sennet & Cobb, 1973; Oakes & Lipton, 1990). Exercise 9-3 invites you to look at the issue of tracking as a mechanism through which class distinctions within U.S. schools are maintained.

## The Digital Divide

A concept that springs from social-class inequity associated with tracking students and typical funding school practices is the digital divide. The term **digital divide** refers to the gap between people with effective access to digital and information technology and those with very limited or no access at all. It is the unequal access of some members of society to communicate using information technology that is not enjoyed by economically disadvantaged members of society and includes the imbalances in physical access to technology as well as the imbalances in resources and skills needed to effectively operate that technology. One area of significant focus is school computer access whereby wealthy school districts and college prep classrooms are much more likely to provide students with regular high-quality computer access than poor schools and remedial classrooms.

## CULTURAL FACTOR 6: LANGUAGE DIFFERENCES, STRENGTHS, AND CHALLENGES

Labov and Robins (1969), in studying social class in casual conversation, found a correlation between "g"-dropping (for example, *drinking* to *drinkin'*) and social class. In their study, 80 percent of those in the lower class exhibited g-dropping, whereas only 5 percent in the upper middle class exhibited this behavior.

Bernstein (1962) and others have suggested that members of the working class employed restricted codes in their language use. For example, tag clauses, such as "you see" or "you know," are phrases that were found to be more often employed by the working class because they tend to reinforce the social relationship between the speaker and listener rather than to simply convey information (Cook & Gurr, 1981).

In addition, research has demonstrated that middle-class parents tend to talk more, have longer utterances, label more, and provide more information about objects to their children than do working-class and poor parents (Hart & Risley, 1992; Lawrence & Shipley, 1996). Many theorists believe that this distinction of parent-speak results in middle-class students having communication patterns that more closely match those of middle-class teachers (Goldfield, 1987, 1993). As such, teachers should utilize a variety of resources that feature varied cultural language use as well as develop effective ways to help students encounter meaningful and relevant language variances in a variety of assignments in the classroom in efforts to increase their linguistic awareness and the legitimacy of cultural languages (for example, Brown, Palincsar, & Purcell, 1986; Snow, 1991).

## POTENTIAL BARRIERS IN LEARNING–TEACHING RELATIONSHIPS WITH DOMINANT-CULTURE TEACHERS AND SCHOOLS

When working-class and poor parents receive inferior educations and/or drop out of school for reasons that include alienation and mistreatment in schools, conflict between needs and requirements at home and school, and the economic realities for their families, they end up with less formal education. This in turn restricts them to lower-paying jobs in society. Such conditions may negatively affect their ability to provide the best possible opportunities to advance their academic goals and provide for themselves and their families.

On average, the achievement of students from low-income families is below the achievement of students from middle-class families. And while some students from low-income families are successful in school, their achievement does not negate the existence of barriers that curtail their achievement. As such, both school improvement and social and economic reform are needed (Rothstein, 2004).

Research identifies that young children of highly educated parents are read to consistently and are encouraged to participate in school activities that increase their academic achievement (Eckert, 1989). These students are more likely to pass an age-appropriate reading test in kindergarten, and so the achievement gap begins. Middle-class parents have been found to ask more questions that require their children to think when they read to them than do working-class and poor parents. There are other stark differences in the ways dominant-culture and working-class parents converse with their children. Children of dominant-culture parents develop a sense of entitlement from an early age that may stem from knowledge of the authority and responsibility their parents enjoy in their occupations. The understanding that a person can control her or his own environment is passed down to dominant-culture children and becomes an important variable in achievement. In addition, children from dominant-culture families gain increased self-assurance when they participate in extracurricular activities that require transportation and sometimes fees that children from low-income families may not be able to provide. The confidence that comes from having the opportunity to participate in organized sports and extracurricular activities, coupled with the other advantages such as numerous and varied educational resources, leads to increased self-confidence for dominant-culture students. Students with greater self-confidence in these areas face unfamiliar school challenges with less fear and anxiety. In addition, homework exacerbates achievement differences between dominant-culture and working-class students. Middle-class parents are more likely to have the time, knowledge, and resources to help their children with their homework.

Not surprisingly, middle-class professional parents tend to associate with and be friends with similarly educated professionals. Such acquaintances provide their children with academic and occupational role models that motivate them to achieve. In addition, these connections serve as resources for their children as academic and professional network systems are formed. Working-class students come from families that generally have fewer middle-class friends working as professionals. Working-class and poor students, therefore, often must struggle harder to motivate themselves to obtain high-paying professions than students who assume, on the basis of their parents' social circle, that they will someday be doctors, lawyers, managers, and business executives.

Overall, lower-income children are in poorer health. They have poorer vision, poorer nutrition, poorer oral hygiene, and higher instances of asthma, which partly stems from living in substandard housing containing high-sulfur heating systems or in neighborhoods with heightened air pollution. Each of these health issues contributes to weakened abilities to perform in school, energy deficits, and absenteeism. In addition, transient living conditions and difficulties in finding adequate, affordable housing among low-income families contribute to the underachievement of poor and homeless students. Students whose families have difficulty finding stable, affordable housing are more likely to be mobile, and student mobility is a significant cause of underachievement.

In addition, parental involvement is correlated with student success. As such, schools have high expectations for parental involvement in their children's education. Parents are expected to attend parent–teacher conferences, respond to the many requests sent home by schools, chaperone field trips, volunteer in classrooms, provide treats for birthday parties, and organize or contribute to fund-raisers. They are expected to make sure that their children are developmentally prepared for school, to provide supervision and help with homework and school projects, and to read to their children on a daily basis. Certainly all of these activities should prove helpful in the education of students. However, a question remains: To what degree can poor and working-class parents engage in these activities? What seem to be reasonable expectations for families who have ample economic resources may be unrealistic expectations for families who do not (see Exercise 9-4).

**EXERCISE 9-4**  **Field Experience: Hidden Alienation**

*Directions:*

1. Contact a school in your area and speak with a counselor or administrator. Identify the various programs, services, activities, and so on that the school employs in an attempt to inform and engage parents in the process of their children's education (for example, back-to-school nights, open houses, PTA meetings, booster club events, newsletters, advisory groups). Be sure to get the description of what these forms of communication entail, when they meet, what is expected of and from parents, and so on.

2. With your classmates, colleagues, and/or instructor, review the data, looking for explicit or hidden barriers working-class and poor parents face in their attempts to partner with schools.

3. Generate recommendations for removing these barriers and engaging all parents across socioeconomic levels in schools.

Schools must understand the economic hardships encountered by working-class and poor families who are struggling to make ends meet, and must take steps to facilitate these students' and their families' involvement in school activities and curriculum development.

## FROM CONCEPTS TO LIVED EXPERIENCE

The following is a portion of a story provided by Jay Shaft (2003), entitled "Living on the Edge of Disaster: Being a Poor Working Mother in America" that offers a glimpse into the life of Dana. As you read of Dana's work and economic struggles, consider the impact of her circumstances on her daughter's relationships and academic achievement. Think about the readiness with which her daughter is able to approach each new day of learning. Imagine the many mandates her daughter encounters in school that seem realistic for children who come from families with access to many resources yet seem unrealistic for her, given her life conditions. Think about the disenfranchisement and restricted resources both she and her mother may experience as a result of their poverty.

**DANA'S STORY**

Dana is a 36-year-old white mother, who has lost five jobs in the last 10 months. She moved from up north to Florida on word of mouth about all the jobs available. Little did she know before moving that the jobs she heard about were vanishing into thin air. The factory jobs and manufacturing jobs that were so prevalent just two years ago have been eliminated or moved to other cities or sectors.

All that seems to be available are low-income service industry jobs or temporary fill-in jobs. What little jobs that become available are sought by hundreds of unemployed workers desperate for any position.

She has struggled to be hired, only to be eliminated due to economic cutbacks within weeks of getting into the job and setting herself up for some sort of job security. After getting the prospect of financial security and the hope of catching up with her bills, she sees the job disappear and has to start her employment search all over again.

"It's an exercise in tenacity at best," she sighs. "Thank you George Bush, we're really seeing our bright future and prosperity!" As she puts on a dim and vague smile she describes her worries and fears. You can see her desperation and fear for tomorrow etched in the worried lines of her face.

She has rarely found reason to smile in the last year and the laughs are few and far between. The ability to relax and have a truly enjoyable time has been yanked out from under her, and her good times have dried up.

"I have never had to live like this in my life. This never seemed possible to me before I moved down here. I had to live in a motel for two months and in various shelters before I got a permanent apartment." She now lives in a two-room studio that is barely big enough for her and her daughter.

"This is no way for my kid to live. No kid should have to go through this. I mean I feel so bad sometimes that I can't give her more security and the things she really needs. I tried to file bankruptcy after being forced to live on my credit cards rather than be homeless and have my kid out on the street. I am so broke that I can't even afford to pay the lawyer the filing fee for the bankruptcy, so the bills keep coming in.

"My neighbors watch out for me and it embarrasses me, like I can't take care of my kid. I never had it where my neighbors have to help me, but I'm not going to turn it down. Everybody has to take help sometimes and it helps me get by with a little extra food to feed my kid."

# SUMMARY

**Cultural Factor 1: Historical and Current Treatment in the United States** While the United States is largely viewed as classless, the truth is that there are enormous differences in the economic status and conditions of life as a function of one's position in the socioeconomic strata of the United States. Children in low-income families fare more poorly in the areas of economic security, health, and education than children in more affluent families.

The *middle class* in the United States is ambiguously defined. While the term is commonly used, there is little agreement about what it entails. Contemporary sociologists commonly divide the middle class into two subgroups: (1) the upper or professional middle class, constituting 15 to 20 percent of households, includes educated, salaried professionals, and managers; and (2) the lower middle class, constituting roughly one-third of all the households in the United States, includes mostly semiprofessionals, skilled craftsmen, and lower-level managers.

Because public-school budgets are based on property taxes, allowing higher-income school districts to spend more than poorer ones, the country's school system is rigged in favor of the already privileged, with lower-class students tracked into deficient classrooms, thus continuing the cycle of oppression.

**Cultural Factor 2: Initial Terms of Incorporation into U.S. Society** The colonists' institution of indentured servitude created conditions for the establishment of social-class stratification in the United States. Social-class differences affect how much time it takes to accomplish daily tasks in life. They determine where one lives, how one is educated, who one's friends are, what one does for a living, and even what one expects out of life. People do not choose to be poor or working class. Rather, social systems and institutions exist that maintain this cycle of poverty.

**Cultural Factors 3 and 4: Shared Values, Traditions, and Spirituality** The poor may share a preference for (1) present-time orientation, (2) action versus reflection, (3) linear social relations, and (4) subjugation to or at least harmony with nature. Members of the working class tend to value tightly knit family life and conventionality. They may also exhibit solidarity and share ambitious attitudes toward education.

**Cultural Factor 5: Acculturation and Experience with Exclusion and Alienation** School performance (grades and test scores) and educational attainment (level of schooling completed) strongly correlate with economic class. The gradual accumulation of differential experience in the early years of schooling leads mainstream children to believe that education will ultimately bring rewards and success, while nonmainstream children frequently come to view education as a humiliating and fruitless pursuit. Tracking or grouping students in schools based on their so-called ability contributes to differential school outcomes, and unfairly sorts students for their subsequent social and economic roles.

**Cultural Factor 6: Language Differences, Strengths, and Challenges** Members of the working class may employ restricted codes of spoken English that feature tag clauses that reinforce the relationship between the speaker and the listener rather than simply convey information. Middle-class parent–child communication patterns more closely match communication patterns and expectations found in U.S. schools.

**Potential Barriers in Learning–Teaching Relationships with Dominant-Culture Teachers and Schools** When working-class and poor parents receive inferior educations and/or drop out of school for reasons that include ostracism in schools, conflicts between needs and requirements at home and school, and the lack of opportunity for their families, they end up with less education. On average, the achievement of students from low-income families is below the achievement of students from middle-class families. The structure and scheduling of school meetings, outings, and parent associations may preclude the involvement of working-class and poor parents.

## Questions for Review

1. What constitutes the middle, working, and under (poor) class in the United States and why is it a difficult concept to define and agree upon?

2. How is tracking related to social class?

3. What school practices have a hidden social-class bias (for example, senior proms; class trips to Washington, DC; school assignments about "What I did on my summer vacation;" and so on)?

## Important Terms

chauvinism
classless society
cycle of poverty

digital divide
Indentured servitude
lower middle class

meritocracy
social-class
tracking

upper or professional
middle class
working class

## Enrichment

Eckert, P. (1989). *Jock and burnouts: Social categories and identity in high school.* New York: Teachers College.

Gilbert, E. (2003). *The last American man.* New York: Penguin Books.

Handel, G. (2000). *Making life in Yorkville: Experience and meaning in the life course narrative of an urban working class man.* Westport, CT: Green wood.

Hook, B. (2000). *Where we stand: Class matters.* New York: Routledge.

Kozol, J. (1991). *Savage inequalities: Children in America's schools.* New York: Crown.

Rogers, J., & Teixeira, R. (2000). *America's for-gotten majority: Why the White working class still matters*. New York: Basic Books.

Sanders, M. G. (2000). *Schooling students placed at risk: Research, policy, and practice in education of poor and minority adoles-cents*. Mahwah, NJ: Lawrence Erlbaum.

Shipler, D. K. (2004). *The working poor: Invisi-ble America*. New York: Alfred A. Knopf.

## Connections on the Web

http://EzineArticles.com/?expert=Jeff_Maide

As many as 3.5 million Americans are home-less each year. Of these, more than 1 million are children. This site provides accurate infor-mation about homeless people.

http://web.worldbank.org/WBSITE/EXTERNAL/TOPICS/EXTPOVERTY/0,,menuPK:336998~pagePK:149018~piPK:149093~theSitePK:336992,00.html

PovertyNet is a site that provides information on poverty and associated conditions in the United States. It also features resources, statis-tics, and worldwide poverty assessments.

## References

Becker, H. S. (1952). Social class variation in teacher–pupil relationship. *Journal of Educa-tional Sociology*, 25, 451–465.

Bernstein, B. (1962). Social class, linguistic codes and grammatical elements. *Language and Speech*, 5, 221–240.

Bloom, L. R. (2001). "I'm poor, I'm single, I'm a mom and I deserve respect": Advocating in schools and with mothers in poverty. *Educa-tional studies*, 32(3), 300–316.

Brookover, W. B., & Erickson, E. L. (1975). *Sociol-ogy of education*. Homewood, IL: Dorsey.

Brown, A., Palincsar, A., & Purcell, L. (1986). Poor readers: Teach, don't label. In U.Neisser (Ed.), *The school achievement of minority children* (pp. 105–143). Hillsdale, NJ: Erlbaum.

Carnoy, M. (1974). *Education as cultural impe-rialism*. New York: McKay.

Cicourel, A. V., & Kitsuse, J. I. (1963). *The edu-cation decision-makers*. New York: Bobbs-Merrill.

Clark, L. (2009). White working class boys are schools' worst performing ethnic group by age of 11. Retrieved from http://www.daily-mail.co.uk/news/article-1163212/White-working-class-boys-worst-performing-ethnic-group-schools-age-11.html#ixzz0iXGfBp61

Collins, C., & Veskel, F. (2004). Economic apartheid in America. In M. L. Andersen, & P. H. Collins (Eds.), *Race, class, and gender: An anthology* (5th ed., pp. 127–139). Belmont, CA: Wadsworth/Thomson.

Cook, M., & Gurr, P. J. (1981). Social class and ritualized speech. *Language and Speech*, 24 (4), 373–376.

Eckert, P. (1989). *Jock and burnouts: Social cat-egories and identity in high school*. New York: Teachers College.

Federal Interagency Forum on Child and Family Statistics. (1998). America's Children. Re-trieved from http://www.childstats.gov

Gilbert, E. (2003). *The last American man*. New York: Penguin Books.

Goldfield, B. (1987). The contributions of child and caregiver to referential and expressive language. *Applied Psycholinguistics*, 8, 267–280.

Goldfield, B. (1993). Noun bias in maternal speech to one year olds. *Journal of Child Language*, 20, 85–99.

Goodlad, T. L., & Marshall, S. (1984). Do students learn more in heterogeneous or homogeneous groups? In P. P.Peterson, I. C. Wilkinson, & M. T.Hallman (Eds.), *The social context of instruction* (pp. 13–28). New York: Academic.

Hart, B., & Risley, T. (1992). American parenting of language-learning children: Persisting differences in family-child interactions observed in natural home environments. *Developmental Psychology, 28,* 1096–1105.

Kahl, J. A. (1968). *The measurement of modernism: A study of values in Brazil and Mexico.* Austin: University of Texas.

Kolchin, P. (1993). *American slavery: 1619–1877.* New York: Whill & Wang.

Kozol, J. (1991). *Savage inequalities: Children in America's schools.* New York: Crown.

Labov, W., & Robins, C. (1969). A note on the relation of reading failure to peer-group status in urban ghettos. *Record, 70*(5), 395–405.

Lawrence, V. W., & Shipley, E. F. (1996). Parental speech to middle- and working-class children from two racial groups in three settings. *Applied Psycholinguistics, 17,* 233–255.

Lengermann, P. M. (1982). The debate on the structure and content of West Indian values: Some relevant data from Trinidad and Tobago. *British Journal of Sociology, 23,* 298–311.

Lubrano, A. (2004). *Limbo, blue collar roots, white collar dreams.* Hoboken, NJ: John Wiley & Sons.

Manstios, G. (1998). Class in America: Myths and realities. In P. S. Rothenberg (Ed.), *Race, class, and gender in the United States: An integrated study* (4th ed., pp. 202–214). New York: St. Martin's.

National Commission on Excellence in Education. (1983). *A nation at risk.* Washington, DC: U.S. Government Printing Office.

Nisan, M. (1973). Perceptions of time in lower-class Black students. *International Journal of Psychology, 8*(2), 109–116.

Noland, T. K. (1985). *The effects of ability grouping: A meta-analysis of research findings.*

Unpublished dissertation, University of Colorado, Boulder.

Oakes, J., & Lipton, M. (1990). Tracking and ability grouping: A structural barrier to access and achievement. In J. I.Goodlad & P. Keating (Eds.), *Access to knowledge: An agenda for our nation's schools* (pp. 187–202). New York: College Entrance Examination Board.

Ozum, A. (1995). The representation of the working class and masculinity and Alan Sillitoe's *Saturday Night and Sunday Morning. Journal of English Languages and Literature, 3,* 39–50.

Rist, R. C. (1970). Student social class and teacher expectations. *Harvard Educational Review, 40,* 411–51.

Rose, S. J. (2000). *Social stratification in the United States.* New York: New Press.

Rothstein, R. (2004). *Class and schools: Using social, economic, and educational reform to close the Black–White achievement gap.* New York: Teachers College.

Sennet, R., & Cobb, J. (1973). *The hidden injuries of class.* New York: Vintage.

Shaft, J. (2003). *Living on the Edge of Disaster: Being a Poor Working Mother in America.* Retrieved from http://www.scoop.co.nz/stories/HL0310/S00074.htm

Sklar, H. (1998). Imagine a country. In P. S. Rothenberg (Ed.), *Race, class, and gender in the United States: An integrated study* (4th ed., pp. 192–201). New York: St. Martin's.

Snow, C. E. (1991). The theoretical basis of the home-school study of language and literacy development. In C. E. Snow (Chair), *The social prerequisites of literacy development: Home and school experiences of preschool-aged children from low-income families.* Symposium presented at the meeting of the American Educational Research Association, Chicago.

U.S. Bureau of the Census. (2003a). *Money income in the United States.* Retrieved from http://www.census.gov

U.S. Bureau of the Census. (2003b). *Employment characteristics of families in 2003.* Retrieved

15 September 2004, from http://www.bls. gov/news.release/famee.rro.htm

U.S. Bureau of the Census. (2008). *Income, Poverty, and Health Insurance Coverage in the United States: 2008*. Report P60, n. 236, Table B-2, pp. 50–55.

Wachtel, H. (1984). *Labor and the economy*. Orlando, FL: Academic.

Wilcox, B. (2009). The great recession's silver lining. *The State of Our Unions*. National Marriage Project at the University of Virginia.

Willis, P. (1977). *Learning to labour*. Westmead, Farnborough, Hants, UK: Saxon House.

Willis, P. (1981). *Learning to labor: How working class kids get working class jobs*. New York: Columbia University.

*What is the girls' movement? Well, we're girls. But we—and most other girls—don't talk about a "Girls' Movement." We just think life should be fair, and things should be equal between girls and guys. And we still have a long way to go to reach that goal.*

*So, who are we? And who are we to tell you what the Girls' Movement is to girls? We're Ana and Emma; we're both fourteen years old as we write this; and we've been friends since—forever! We're also both editors for New Moon: The Magazine for Girls and Their Dreams. That means we hear from a lot of girls. We hear what girls are doing and thinking. We hear girls' opinions on what they find unfair, and on what they do to change things in their daily life.*

*We don't actually call ourselves "The Girls' Movement," because we just don't feel there is a large organized girls' movement going on, like there is with adult feminism. Also even though we know there's a long way to go, we feel we've already come a long way, because of feminism. Compared to how things were thirty years ago, we feel very lucky to be girls now. We define feminism in terms of our everyday actions: how we react to unfair situations and what we do to change them. ...*

**Source:** Anna Grossman and Emma Peters-Axtell, at the age of 14.
Girls: "We are the ones who can make a change!" In *Sisterhood is forever: The women's anthology for a new millennium*, 2003, New York: Washington Square Press, pp. 121–123.

CHAPTER

# 10 Learning from Girls' and Women's Stories

In the personal narrative that begins this chapter, Anna Grossman and Emma Peters-Axtell describe not only struggles they encounter as 14-year-old girls living in the United States but also progress made by feminist activists from which they know they have benefitted. So, while progress for women's rights has taken place in various societal contexts and domains, Grossman and Peters-Axtell remind us that there remains much work to do to gain equality for women and girls.

Sports is one area where things have really gotten better for girls (because of Title IX). But there's still unfairness. Last year, Emma's soccer team was discriminated against because they're girls. Her school has one good playing field and the girls weren't allowed to scrimmage there—while the boys' teams were allowed. The female coach didn't fight the decision because she was worried about retaliation later from the Director of Athletics. Even though we were inspired by our country's huge excitement about the U.S. Women's Soccer Team triumphs in 2000, when it comes closer to home, we're still struggling ... like ... media image—that's a huge issue for girls. When we see unrealistic, "perfect" images over and over, telling us that looking that way will make us popular, we start to think those images are the "right" ones. And if that isn't enough, the faces and bodies of models and celebrities are airbrushed to make them even more perfect! Many girls then see these impossible images, and strive to be just like them. This creates self-consciousness and low self-esteem. Some girls even end up hurting their bodies, trying to become thinner to look different, in order to fit those images.

But things are better for girls and women than they were, and we thank feminism for that. It shows that real change can happen—and that women and girls can make it happen. In the future, we want women and girls to be treated equally with men and boys; to get the respect men and boys get. We want girls to be encouraged to become scientists and mathematicians. We want girls to be allowed to play any sport a guy can. We want equality in the workplace, at school, and in sports. We want equal opportunity and equal pay. We also want equal representation. Women should be expected and encouraged to take political positions. We want to walk down the halls at school and the streets of our city and feel safe from violence against us. We want to end stereotypes against girls and women. Equality will not only improve society's view of girls and women; equality will help us speak up—for ourselves and for other people.

Source: Anna Grossman and Emma Peters-Axtell

It is important to bring into focus the personal, political, and professional sacrifices women have made along with the challenges that remain.

What are current challenges, opportunities, and conflicting demands for women in the United States? Who serve as role models for success? Who support women's achievements? If educators are to foster and support the development of girls and women, they must have a thorough understanding of the impact of gender socialization and bias on learning, teaching, and classroom dynamics.

## CHAPTER OBJECTIVES

1.  Describe values and worldviews commonly shared by women and girls in the United States.
2.  Identify ways in which the women and girls profiled in the case narratives experienced and addressed the six cultural factors explored in this text.
3.  Explain academic and intercultural interaction implications for women and girls related to the six cultural factors.
4.  Describe coping strategies commonly utilized by women and girls as they confront sexism and gender bias in society.
5.  Identify classroom strategies for integrating feminist perspectives and values within your curricula.

## CULTURAL FACTOR 1: HISTORICAL AND CURRENT TREATMENT IN THE UNITED STATES

In the United States, **sexism** is grounded on the assumption that women are inferior to men. The history of sexism is long, and though the specific manifestations have changed over time, outcomes from this ideology remain today.

In Ancient Greece, Aristotle is said to have regarded women as defective men. In his writings, he classed women and children together, concluding that neither had fully developed rationality. Similarly, during medieval times, Christian doctrine was a strong source of support for views proclaiming the inferiority of women; beliefs that positioned the man as the *head* and the women as the *heart* of families were used to support beliefs of male superiority. Historically, women who attempted to move out of their subordinate roles were labeled evil and rebellious, and were even burned as witches for their acts of resistance (Adkinson & Hackett, 1995).

One key to understanding women's status in a society is their degree of participation in the economy as well as their control over the products they produce. Every society employs some type of **sexual division of labor**. However, it is important to recognize that the nature of the division of labor by sex greatly affects the relative status of men and women and influences their power and rights and defines their relationships in society. For example, the plow changed agriculture from a female occupation to a male occupation in many agricultural societies. Before the invention of heavy farming machinery, females tended to crops while males hunted or worked in other ways to provide for their families. The earliest division of labor resulted in a more or less equal contribution to the family's (and society's) economy. Eventually, surpluses of food produced wealth that became the property of men. This wealth was passed down from father to son. As wealth and property became the birthright of males, women came to be viewed as powerless male possessions (Adkinson & Hackett, 1995).

Historically, innate qualities have been used as the basis for the differential valuing and treatment of men and women. And while many continue to assume that there are widespread intellectual, personality, and behavioral differences between males and females, very few sex differences have actually been identified in research (Ferree, 1990; Williams, 2000). In fact, there are many more similarities than differences between boys and girls and between men and women (Matlin, 1987). Further, those differences identified are now generally believed to be caused by differential treatment of males and females from before birth and throughout development rather than derived from innate abilities and temperaments (Richardson, 1981). Society's **gender-based norms** and expectations account for assumptions of male intellectual and leadership superiority and female nurturance and interpersonal superiority (Albee & Perry, 1998; Coltrane, 1996). However, these social constructions are not based on biological evidence.

Gender-role expectations for women and men continue to prohibit all members of the society from routinely questioning stereotypical gender expectations, specifically those that disadvantage women. What is defined as "normal" and therefore as *right* and *correct* for women and men often goes unchallenged. **Gender stereotyping** functions to support the status quo that maintains the marginalization of women (see Exercise 10-1).

Males are socialized in culturally defined masculine ways that preserve the dominance of men as a group, and women are socialized to think and behave in ways that preserve their inferior status in society. This process of placing differential value and status on the various characteristics associated with each gender results in social and economic inequality (Kobrynowicz & Biernat, 1997). The women's movement began by challenging assumptions that asserted the inferiority of women.

## EXERCISE 10-1  Point of Reflection: Stereotyping: Maintaining the Status Quo

*Directions:* Prescribed gender-role expectations for women and men prohibit all members of society from questioning stereotypical expectations. What is defined as normal, and therefore as right and correct, goes unchallenged. In this exercise, you are invited to reflect on the accuracy of the following common gender-related beliefs:

- Women make better childcare workers.
- Women seek love and romance; while men seek sex and physical stimulation.

- Women are better communicators than men.
- Women are overly emotional and sensitive.
- Men are analytical; while women are intuitive.
- Women are more nurturing than men.

Discuss the accuracy of each statement and possible societal implications associated with believing each statement with your classmates, colleagues, and/or your instructor.

## The First Wave of the Women's Movement

The progression from the treatment of White women as possessions and property to treating them as individuals with rights is said to have begun when Elizabeth Cady Stanton questioned the rights White women were permitted in the 1800s. Stanton's questioning is believed to have initiated the **women's rights movement** in the United States on July 13, 1848 when Stanton and some of her close friends met for tea. The women discussed their discontent with the limitations placed on them in the new democracy following the American Revolution. Stanton reasoned that because White women had endured dangers in the New World equal to White men, they should experience the same freedom gained by men. With her friends' agreement, days later, Stanton organized a convention to discuss the social, civil, and religious conditions and rights of White women at the Wesleyan Chapel in Seneca Falls on July 19 and 20, 1848. The **Seneca Falls Convention** is now seen as the starting point for the women's equal rights movement in the United States (Eisenberg & Ruthsdotter, 1998).

Stanton later used the Declaration of Independence as the framework for writing what she titled a **Declaration of Sentiments** in which she stated: "The history of mankind is a history of repeated injuries and usurpations on the part of and toward women, having in direct object the establishment of an absolute tyranny over her. To prove this, let facts be submitted to a candid world" (Eisenberg & Ruthsdotter, 1998, pp. 2–3). The evidence she provided included the following:

- Women had no legal rights and were not allowed to vote.
- Women had to submit to laws that they had no voice in forming.
- Women had no property rights.
- Husbands had the power to imprison and beat wives as well as hold all legal power over and responsibility for women.
- Women had no rights to the custody of their own children.
- Women were not allowed to enter the professions of law or medicine.
- Colleges and universities were not open to women. (Eisenberg & Ruthsdotter, 1998, pp. 2–3)

Laws and politics acted to keep women in their subordinate position in families and in the broader society. With the help of Frederick Douglass, African American abolitionist and orator, Stanton and others were able to convene the first Women's Rights Convention at which the delegates unanimously endorsed her *Declaration of Sentiments*. Afterward, women's rights conventions were held regularly to discuss women's issues. Women like Susan B. Anthony, Lucy Stone, Ida B. Wells-Barnett, and Sojourner Truth traveled across the country during this time lecturing and organizing to promote women's rights for the next 40 years. Amid great opposition and ridicule from dominant culture, the women's suffrage movement of the 19th century persevered, and 72 years after those initial meetings in Seneca Falls, women won the right to vote in 1920 (Eisenberg & Ruthsdotter, 1998).

In 1919, as the suffrage movement ended, the **National American Woman Suffrage Association (NAWSA)** reconfigured itself into the **League of Women Voters**, and in 1920, the Women's Bureau of the Department of Labor was established to advocate for changes in the workplace. A few years later in 1923, Alice Paul, the leader of the National Woman's Party, drafted the **Equal Rights Amendment (ERA)** for the United States Constitution. At about the same time, the birth-control movement initiated by public health nurse Margaret Sanger sought women's rights to control their own bodies, sexuality, and reproduction, thus adding a new dimension to women's emancipation. Eventually, in 1936, the Supreme Court declassified birth-control information as *obscene*. But it was not until 1965 that married couples in all states could legally obtain contraceptives (Eisenberg & Ruthsdotter, 1998).

## The Second Wave

The 1960s ushered in what is commonly referred to as the *second wave of the women's rights movement*. During that time, President Kennedy convened a Commission on the Status of Women, naming Eleanor Roosevelt as chair. The commission issued a report in 1963 that documented widespread discrimination against women in virtually every area of U.S. life. To begin to address identified injustices, Title VII of the 1964 **Civil Rights Act** was passed, which prohibited employment discrimination on the basis of race, sex, religion, and national origin. With its passage, the Equal Employment Opportunity Commission (EEOC) was established to investigate complaints of work discrimination. By 1966, the **National Organization for Women (NOW)** was organized to address the specific needs and treatment of women in society. And with the inclusion of **Title IX** in the education codes of 1972, equal access to higher education and professional schools became the law. The ERA also became law in 1972 stating: "Equality of rights under the law shall not be denied or abridged by the United States or by any state on account of sex" (Eisenberg & Ruthsdotter, 1998; Whalen & Whalen, 1985).

## Current Conditions

Some people now believe that women have achieved equality and that sexism no longer exists. Many are young women who do not believe that they have ever in their lives encountered sexism. These women do not acknowledge, and therefore address, female objectification, gender bias, and employment discrimination that may be beyond their awareness. In order for work toward equality for women to continue, all individuals, including women and girls, must engage in proactive advocacy to promote and support women's rights and realize that despite the real gains made by women over time on numerous fronts, compelling evidence exists that demonstrates that inequality and sexism continue to thrive in the United States (Hallock, 1994; Kirchmeyer, 1998; Schneer & Reitman, 1995).

The objectification of women is viewed by many as one of the main indicators of women's subordination within a sexist society. **Sexual objectification** of women involves disregarding their personal abilities and capabilities, and focusing instead on attributes relevant to women's role as a sexual partner including her physical attractiveness, sex appeal, and submissiveness. Objectification has been found to lead to negative psychological effects including female depression and negative self-image. Because their intelligence and competence are not acknowledged through this process, women and girls may come to believe that they are only valued for their physical beauty. Examples of female objectification include sexual depictions of women in advertising and media, images of women in pornography, the preponderance of strip clubs and prostitution that exist in most cities, as well as the pressure some women feel to have cosmetic surgery, particularly breast enlargement.

Throughout history, in fact, women have been highly valued for their physical attributes over their intelligence or capabilities. The precise degree to which objectification has affected women's development and achievement is a topic of great debate. However, it must be recognized that sexual objectification forces women and girls to place a heavy emphasis on the importance of their appearance in society—which more often than not leads to their feelings of fear, shame, inadequacy, and even depression.

For example, in most films, television shows, and music videos, men are in control of the camera's gaze (that is, the audience sees the world through their eyes) while women are typically on the receiving end of that gaze. They are looked at, objectified, and sexualized by male protagonists (Peters, 2008). Some people may believe that women should take control of their own bodies and benefit from their sexuality by using it to derive a competitive edge. Such an approach suggests a rekindling of power over their bodies that was lost through their objectification by men and male-dominated industries. You have seen a surge of skimpy or sexual clothing styles worn by women and even by girls as young as five years old, and female music video and film performances in which women seem to objectify themselves. Madonna, Beyonce, Britney Spears, Rihanna, and Lady Gaga—to name a few—seem to sanction their own highly sexualized images. It is important to realize, however, that dominant pop culture has encouraged sexualized images of women and girls throughout history and that objectification has worked to advantage males over females such that males garner greater respect and status and women are more often seen as submissive objects used for male pleasure.

In addition, after significant and far-reaching legal and social advances made in the 1960s and 1970s, powerful groups in the 1980s and 1990s used considerable force to stall and reverse women's rights. Some opposed affirmative action programs and other programs established to reduce discrimination against women and other minority groups. As such, women of today are still employed primarily in jobs that are not equally valued by society (Agars & Kottke, 2004; Heilman, 1983). Women continue to experience hiring discrimination, **glass ceilings**, and

**maternal walls**. Affordable quality child care is not available for many working mothers, and women receive lower wages for the same work performed by men. In addition, **mommy tracking** is a widespread practice that reflects women's lost career opportunities and advancement when they have children.

Even though equal pay has been the law since 1963, women are still paid less than men—even though they have similar education, skills, and experience. In 2007, women were paid only 77 cents for every dollar a man was paid, according to the U.S. Bureau of the Census. These figures are even worse for African American women and Latinas. While Asian American women earned 88 cents for every dollar earned by men, African American women earned only 72 cents; and Latinas earned only 60 cents for every dollar that men earned (U.S. Bureau of the Census, 2007). In addition, women continue to face widespread sexual abuse and sexual harassment at their workplace.

The American Federation of Labor and Congress of Industrial Organizations (AFL-CIO) and the Institute for Women's Policy Research (IWPR) jointly undertook a national study to analyze income data. According to the study:

- America's working families lose a staggering $200 billion of income annually to the wage gap—an average loss of more than $4,000 each for working women's families every year because of unequal pay, even after accounting for differences in education, age, location, and the number of hours worked.
- If married women were paid the same as comparable men, their family incomes would rise by nearly 6 percent, and their families' poverty rates would fall from 2.1 percent to 0.8 percent.
- If single working mothers earned as much as comparable men, their family incomes would increase by nearly 17 percent, and their poverty rates would be cut in half, from 25.3 percent to 12.6 percent.
- If single women earned as much as comparable men, their incomes would rise by 13.4 percent, and their poverty rates would be reduced from 6.3 percent to 1 percent.

The study also found that:

- Women *lawyers'* median weekly earnings are nearly $206 less than those of male attorneys, and women *in office and administrative support* receive about $71 a week less than male administrative support;
- Women *physicians'* median earnings are nearly $688 less each week than men's earnings, and the 90 percent of *nurses* who are women earn $119 less each week than the 10 percent of nurses who are men;
- Women *professors'* median pay is $233 less each week than men's pay, and women *elementary school teachers* receive about $86 less each week than men;
- Women *food service supervisors* are paid about $122 less each week than men in the same job, and *waitresses'* weekly earnings are about $67 less than waiters' earnings.

It is clear that sexism, including job discrimination, affects women and their families in all income brackets (Bonder, 2008). Research further suggests that between 35 percent and 50 percent of women in the workforce will be sexually harassed at some point in their careers (Gutek, 2001). The increasing awareness of pay differences and the ongoing experience of sexual harassment have led to the implementation of antidiscrimination and sexual harassment policies for virtually all employers in the United States. However, not even these changes have resulted in equality for women in the workplace.

The gap between men and women in obtaining college degrees has not closed completely, but the percentage is closer: 25 percent of women versus 29 percent of men age 25 and older hold a bachelor's degree or higher. In fact, since 1979, 56 percent of all college students are women. A record 65 women were elected to the U.S. House of Representatives in the November 2004 election, including 57 incumbents and 8 newcomers. In the Senate, all female incumbents held onto their seats, keeping the number of women steady at 14 (Mitchel, 2005).

However, many women continue to be employed in traditionally feminine jobs that pay less and are less prestigious and less influential than traditionally male professions (Agars & Kottke, 2004). In the 1970s, 1980s, and 1990s women who were married and/or mothers of young children flooded into the labor market (Bianchi & Casper, 2001). What was thought to be a glass ceiling for all women has turned out to be, in large part, a problem that might more accurately be termed *the maternal wall* for women with children (Williams, 2000). Increasingly, the gender gap in compensation has become an issue of "mother" versus "other," causing some analysts to describe motherhood as the worst economic decision a woman could make (Crittenden, 2001). While the wages of women without children are approaching those of men, mothers' wages lag far behind. Mothers earn 60 percent of the wages of fathers (Waldfogel, 1998).

Working part time is often seen as a viable choice for women with children. However, part-time workers are rarely provided with healthcare benefits, competitive wages, and advancement opportunities. In 2001, 65.6 percent of the part-time work force in the United States was made up of women; and of all employed women, 27 percent worked part time, compared to 12.6 percent of employed men. Two out of three mothers aged 25 to 44 work less than 40 hours per week year round (U.S. Bureau of the Census, 2002). Most women who work part time do so for family reasons (Institute for Women's Policy Research, 2001). Further, in desirable professions where full time often means overtime, mothers have trouble competing for positions (Williams, 2000). Employers of high-status jobs continue to seek a traditionally defined ideal worker who starts work in early adulthood and works full time and full force for 40 years straight, taking no time off for childbearing and childrearing (Crosby, 2004; Mintz, 2000).

## The Third Wave

Today, many women's rights advocates think of themselves as members of the "third wave" of the women's rights movement. Those active in the fight for women's rights address issues such as women's admissions and treatment in military academies; women's reproductive rights (still contested more than 25 years after the Supreme Court's ruling in *Roe v. Wade* affirmed women's choice during the first two trimesters of pregnancy); women's leadership in religious worship; affirmative action backlash and actions to repeal affirmative action; mommy tracking; sexual harassment; violence against women; the maternal wall; glass ceilings; and other forms of institutional discrimination that subordinate women in the United States.

## CULTURAL FACTOR 2: INITIAL TERMS OF INCORPORATION INTO U.S. SOCIETY

The early treatment of women in the United States resembled the treatment of children. Prior to the industrial era of the 19th and 20th centuries, women were denied rights and privileges now considered part of adulthood. Prior to this time, women were not allowed to have ownership of any kind and were not even considered the legal guardians and custodians of their own children. Originally, some women came to the United States as indentured servants or slaves; and married women failed to legally exist apart from their husbands.

According to Adkinson and Hackett (1995), at least four major themes have characterized dominant culture's historical treatment and incorporation of women in the United States: (1) neglect—women's health and social issues were ignored; (2) blatant sexism—including searches for the presumed mental and psychological mechanisms of women's inferiority; (3) pathologizing women's concerns—including diagnoses of hysteria and depression assigned to women whom male doctors believed were "overreacting" to their life conditions; and (4) circumstances—in which women's needs and issues are more a part of dominant-culture awareness.

## CULTURAL FACTOR 3: SHARED VALUES AND TRADITIONS

Gender stereotypes greatly influence male and female behavior. While males are expected to be boldly active in pursuing their convictions and rights, task-oriented, and self-assertive, females in the United States are socialized to be passive, dependent, demure, relationship-oriented, and selfless (Eagly, 1987). This attitude of regarding men's assertiveness and the more constraining expectation that women act selflessly is a major factor in gender disparity outcomes. If women must be selfless to be approved, when they emerge as social leaders, they are punished and maligned (Eagly & Karau, 1991, 2002). Bem (1974) identified masculinity as being independent, assertive, forceful, dominant, and aggressive. Individuals known or assumed to possess this gender-role orientation are perceived to be strong and effective leaders (Wiley & Crittenden, 1992). Women, on the other hand, are socialized to be feminine. Femininity involves being dependent, submissive, quiet, and unassuming. Women who embrace female gender socialization stereotypes (feminine females) have been found to experience lower levels of career advancement when compared with men and women who behave in masculine ways as well as men who act in feminine ways (Kirchmeyer, 1998).

It is true that external societal forces have created precise value systems for both men and women in dominant culture. By a young age, females voice a preference for toys and traits that are consistent with society's definition of femininity. It is not clear where females' real values along the aggressive–submissive continuum lie because they cannot be measured outside the social context within which they exist. Females learn early on that they must choose between enhancing their achievements or their gender identities (Gilligan, 1982). Adding to their oppression, when women act in non-normative (ways that are considered masculine, by definition), their likeability decreases. Because decreased likeability is related to decreased influence, women's decreased influence leads to their weakened achievement and career success and advancement (Carli, 1990; Rudman & Glick, 1999).

# Female Student Identity Development

Belenky, Clinchy, Goldberger, and Tarule (1986) have described five positions that females adopt in their approach to knowledge acquisition. Yet these researchers caution that although these positions reflect female development, they are not necessarily experienced by all female students in a linear or hierarchical progression. Girls in the first position of silence do not perceive themselves as competent learners. They lack confidence in themselves and doubt their abilities. Girls in the second position experience received knowledge by listening to authorities. They emphasize external learning and seek gratification by attempting to measure up to the truths they have been given. At the third position, the uncertainty of external authority is acknowledged. They engage in a quest for self-understanding and personal knowledge. At the fourth position, procedural knowledge is emphasized. Females use objective thought and reason to learn procedures that give them the power to apply knowledge using their own problem solving. They also seek opportunities for personal sharing of information within climates where they feel supported and understood. Finally, at the fifth position, females begin to integrate intuitive, subjective knowledge with objective, external reason. At this stage, they are active constructors of their own knowledge and accomplished in their abilities to critically analyze and challenge what is presented to them by others as knowledge. Belenky, Clinchy, Goldberger, and Tarule (1986) noted that not all females progress through all five stages of development. As a result of the negative influences of **gender socialization** in U.S. society, many may remain throughout their lives in the earlier positions of silence and acquiescence.

Behaviors, values, and characteristics associated with females and males are neither universal nor timeless; they are socially constructed, reflecting the society and time in which they appear. For example, women during World War II (WWII) were seen as strong, capable, and independent when they were needed to replace men in the factories when the men went to war. However, with the return of the men from the war back into the labor force, the image of what women are capable of dramatically changed. They were again expected to be weak and submissive to suit the dominant culture's preferences of the time.

The following gender attitudes are currently prescribed for members of U.S. society:

- **Men (or masculinity):** Including exhibiting strength, aggression, ambition, competitiveness, rational, unemotional thought, independence, intelligence, emotional detachment, and toughness;
- **Women (or femininity):** Involving the opposite of what it means to be male; thus, women are expected to be weak, passive, unambitious, cooperative, relationship-oriented, dependent, uninterested and uninvolved in intellectual endeavors, emotional, gentle, and caring.

While it is clear that assimilating such values for the fulfillment of distinct roles and functions in society can serve individuals and society, they also serve as a hindrance to male and female development. For example, women attempting to emerge as social leaders find themselves sanctioned by a society that expects them to be selfless (Eagly & Karau, 1991, 2002) or simply ignored because they are perceived to lack those traits typically associated with masculinity (Wiley & Crittenden, 1992).

Teachers and other school officials have been found to respond negatively to "overly assertive" girls who display behaviors that would seem acceptable if the same behaviors were presented by male students. As such, female students are seen as inferior or lose opportunities if they act in stereotypically female ways (passive, dependent, and so on) and are demeaned and disciplined for acting in stereotypically male ways. In either case, female students are disadvantaged (Jones, 1997; Heilman, 1983).

Hopefully, the day will come when *both* women and men will be supported for having nurturing and achieving capacities and ambitions and a knowledge will prevail that neither gender has unique abilities that are suitable only for one particular societal role, function, or life arena (Coltrane, 1996; Gilbert & Rader, 2001).

## Intercultural Communication Strategies for Teachers 10-1

### Classroom Applications: Gender in the Classroom

As noted, women in the United States are viewed as feminine when they act in ways considered by gender definitions to be appropriate for women in U.S. culture. This is also true for female students. Often, what it is to be "feminine" can interfere with female students' active participation in the classroom. To counter this, teachers should do the following:

- Consciously and intentionally call on boys and girls equally. Research suggests that in whole-class teaching, where the teacher decides who should contribute, boys make more contributions than girls do, and their contributions are usually more elaborate. It has been suggested that this happens partly through activities within discussions, for example, hand-raising, and partly because boys' reputations for misbehavior lead to greater monitoring of them by teachers. Therefore, be mindful of calling on children of each gender equally. Use index cards or Popsicle sticks with your students' names on them to keep track of whom you actually call on during class discussions.
- Be sure to monitor the degree to which students interrupt others who may be attempting to contribute. Research shows that boys tend to interrupt and dominate in class discussion.
- Be sure to call on girls for assistance in class, as research shows that teachers more typically call on boys for help.

- Girls both seek and give help more frequently than boys; therefore, provide them the opportunity to use their helping skills to demonstrate competence.
- When working in small groups, encourage students to take turns being recorders and reporters, because some research on mixed-sex groups suggests that girls tend to direct their input through boys.
- While noting the valuable contributions of those offering ideas, answers, and recommendations, be mindful of the value of those (typically girls) who contribute to groups through supportive behavior such as empathic repetition or building upon another's idea. Use effective questioning methods to help female students further develop their positions.
- At least twice per year, set up a video camera in your classroom to observe the gender dynamics and discover the reason for silences and the lack of involvement for some members of your class. If students are quiet but engaged, an encouraging gesture may be all that is needed to include them. If students are being intimidated or interrupted by others in the class, an intervention may be called for in a way that gives them strength. This will provide you with an opportunity to observe your own teaching behaviors as well, so you can analyze the effectiveness of your nonsexist teaching strategies.

# CULTURAL FACTOR 4: VIEW OF SPIRITUALITY AND HUMANS' RELATION TO NATURE

Historically, within the Judeo-Christian religious tradition and other religions that endorse a "higher power," the higher power has been and continues to be portrayed using masculine form in both iconographic presentations and in literary descriptions. Typically, the higher power is presented as Father, King, Judge, or Master. The masculine image of the higher power has been advanced through creations such as Michelangelo's *The Creation of Adam* (in the Sistine Chapel) or William Blake's *God Creating the Universe,* which depicts God as a white-haired, bearded man, and serves as a potent source of influence for defining God's image for millions of individuals worldwide.

**Feminists** criticize such patriarchal depictions of God, noting that such practices continue in spite of the theoretical recognition that the higher power transcends gender and that religious worship need not be patriarchal. Further, the practices and languages that emanate from such patriarchal perspectives have served to isolate many women from their own spirituality. Fiorenza (1979) gave voice to this sense of isolation when she wrote:

> We are all used to hearing: God the Father loves you, and if you join the brotherhood and fellowship of all Christians, you will become sons of God and brothers of Christ who died for all men. Such exclusive language has communicated to women for centuries that they are nonentities, subspecies of men, subordinated and inferior to them not only on a cultural, but also on a religious plane. Feminists hold that the combination of male language for God with the stress on the sovereignty and absolute authority of the patriarchal God has sanctioned men's drive for power and domination in the Church as well as in society. (p. 139)

Most feminist thinkers postulate images of a higher power that encompass the full humanity of men and women (Johnson, 1989). In this light, *feminist spirituality* is not restricted to a female point of view but rather refers to a perspective, an approach to life, that is relevant and empowering to women and men alike.

---

**EXERCISE 10-2**    ## Field Experience: Religious Depictions of Higher Power Beings

*Directions:* The following exercise requires you to interview a person who is affiliated with some form of religious organization, faith, or spirituality.

1. Ask the individual the following questions:

   - How would you describe your higher power?
   - When you think of the image of your higher power, what image comes to your mind?
   - If you have a formal or structured prayer (for example, the Our Father [Lord's Prayer] in Christian religions) that you feel is central to your faith, would you recite it for me?

2. If the description, image, or prayer appears to be particularly male referent, ask the individual if he or she would be willing to do the following:

   - Describe the feminine qualities of your higher power.
   - Envision or image your higher power with feminine characteristics.
   - Say the prayer, replacing male referents with female referents.

3. Share your observations with your classmates, colleagues, and your instructor in small-group discussion.

While there are variations within feminist theology, most often holism, connectedness, and interdependence are emphasized, similar to Native American, Asian, Latino, and other nature-based spiritual traditions. Another characteristic of female spirituality is that it tends to go beyond the traditional rigorous asceticism of male spirituality to include acceptance of one's deepest feelings, affectivity, creativity, and mysticism (Kolbenschlag, 1982).

## CULTURAL FACTOR 5: ACCULTURATION AND EXPERIENCE WITH EXCLUSION AND ALIENATION

Women have been acculturated in dominant culture in the United States to meet the needs prescribed for her in society. From colonial times to the present, females have been socialized to serve husbands and children in self-sacrificing ways, to the detriment of their own personal and professional development. Simultaneously, women have been hindered in the obtainment of and alienated from the highest realms of social status and positions of power (for example, president of the United States) in society. As was discussed earlier in this chapter, women have been segregated into low-paying, traditionally "female" professions and alienated in various ways that have resulted in their subordination in society (Chodorow, 1974; Kossoudi & Dresser, 1992). But the experience of exclusion and alienation is not limited to their roles in society and lost opportunities presented. For some women, the experience of oppression in a male-dominated society has resulted in alienation from themselves, as they have been found to lose their voices (that is, connection and attention to their own ideas and knowledge about the world) during their entry into adolescence (Gilligan, 1982) (see Personal Narrative 10-1). In this personal narrative, the description of morality, quoted in Brown (1990), is that of Kate, an adolescent who was interviewed by Brown in her investigation of adolescent female morality. Gilligan's (1982) research found that girls exhibit a kind of political resistance up until the age of about 11 or 12 in which they stand up for what they believe and insist on being heard. Those actions are replaced by psychological

---

**Personal Narrative 10-1    Kate**

"… I have certain sets of maybe principles that I have never really sat and defined. They aren't—morals frequently have religious connotations and things like that … I don't have morals that are just for the sake of morals: Someone says this is how it is. I have principles of my own that shift as I get older. But I am always, you know, I live according to [principles]. … But they are flexible. I would weigh any given situation and … it is never a black-and-white, right-and-wrong situation. … It [her moral decision-making] is never something I think of as a moral. Because in my mind

I think of morals as being structured, binding kind of— and the principles I have for myself aren't that way, so I never really call them morals. … So, it's hard to know where and what they [her moral principles] are just because they are such an integral part of my actions and my everything." (p. 95)

*Source:* Brown, L. (1990). When is a moral problem not a moral problem? In *Making Connections: The Relational Worlds of Adolescent Girls at Emma Willard School.* Gilligan, C., Lyons, N. P., and Hanmer, T. J. Eds. pp. 88–109. Cambridge, Massachusetts: Harvard University Press.

resistance that occurs around age 13 to 14 in which girls may silence themselves in an effort to meet the gender expectations prescribed by dominant culture.

# CULTURAL FACTOR 6: LANGUAGE DIFFERENCES, STRENGTHS, AND CHALLENGES

For this marginalized group, it is the language of dominant culture, and not group members themselves, that presents barriers and challenges. Linguistic theory notes that the language one speaks not only reflects one's view of the world but also determines one's power in it (Bolinger, 1968). "Whatever a particular culture considers to be the 'real world' is really constructed, unconsciously for the most part, by the language spoken in that culture. Language then both inculcates and reflects cultural beliefs about, among other things, women and men" (Barnouw, 1963, p. 1). Consider the connotations for the following terms: *tenderness, weakness, vulnerability,* and *timidity.* Each typically brings to mind femininity and womanliness. These qualities are actually harmful to women's opportunities and status in society when viewed in contrast to the following qualities associated with masculinity: *determination, strength, decisiveness,* and *courage* (Miller & Swift, 1988). Additionally, the use of pronouns (for example, he, she, him, her) in instances when gender specificity is not essential has led many authors to refer to unspecified or hypothetical persons or things using male pronouns, assuming *he* or *him* implies a generalization for both genders. Such an assumption is akin to the use of *man* as the equivalent for *human being.* Failure to recognize the impact of intentional and inadvertent sexism in language furthers the pervasive absence of females in written and oral discourse (Wilcoxion, 1989).

## Intercultural Communication Strategies for Teachers 10-2

### Classroom Applications: Sexist Language in the Classroom

When we think of sexist language, our attention may be drawn to the overuse of the pronouns *him* and *he* as generic terms for any person of any gender or perhaps to the sexist nature of more informal greetings, such as "How are you guys all doing?" (when referring to a mixed-gender classroom). Think about it. You would probably never dream of addressing a mixed-sex group of students by asking, "How are you gals doing?"—right?

The teacher who wishes to create a nonsexist classroom needs to go beyond monitoring such verbal references. You should review all materials—including verbal examples you use within your classroom—for sexist language that may occur in one of the following forms.

- Omission: Review all materials: readings, case illustrations, examples, and word problems. Are males and females equally represented?
- First: In referring to both females and males, as might be the case when providing an example of Tom and Joan, is the male typically or exclusively first? Is that necessary for the meaning of the illustration?
- Activities and Occupations: When mentioning various activities and occupations or using an illustration, are some activities or occupations more often assigned specifically to a male or to a female? For example, when making reference to nurses, secretaries, or teachers, is there a tendency to employ a female's name? How about when the reference is to a doctor, police officer, or an athlete?

Sexist language also excludes and objectifies females in U.S. society in the following ways: (1) labeling the supposed exception to the rule (for example, woman doctor, male nurse); (2) trivializing female gender forms (for example, poetess, suffragette); (3) using terminology that refers to women as children (for example, baby, doll); and (4) using terminology that refers to women as food (for example, tomato, sugar, cupcake). These terms single out women as different from and unequal to men. Further, where there is an understood and clear demarcation between the words *boy* and *man,* there is no such distinction (linguistically) between *girl* and *woman* (Unger, 1979). Not only must teachers examine their own language use but they must also thoroughly search for gender bias in print and other media materials they introduce in the classroom.

## POTENTIAL BARRIERS IN LEARNING–TEACHING RELATIONSHIPS WITH DOMINANT-CULTURE TEACHERS

Many teachers believe that teaching should be neutral and gender blind. However, when teachers adopt a neutral stance, the result is often inadvertent sexism. Teachers must be aware of and continually review their own values and biases toward females in order to be advocates for equality and equal opportunities for women and girls in schools (see Exercise 10-3).

### Intercultural Communication Strategies for Teachers 10-3

#### Classroom Applications: A Nonsexist Learning Environment

Children, when they come to school, may well be armed with gender-differentiated patterns of social interaction. These gender-differentiated patterns can be encouraged, practiced, and consolidated within the classroom. For the teacher interested in expanding social interaction patterns to reflect the uniqueness of individuals and not gender differentiated roles, the following should be considered.

- For students who are quiet, allow them to journal or provide input in written form, and refer to their comments in an affirming way.
- Allow for variation in pace. Some question-and-answer exchanges can occur in rapid-fire order, whereas at other times, require a few moments of reflection prior to calling on students for their participation.
- While it is often pleasing to respond to the most animated student, resist always calling on the most aggressive; rather, look for subtle indications that a more quiet student is interested in contributing.

- Break up gendered monopolies by calling on those who have yet to respond.
- Affirm through the conception and implementation of your instructional activities that the value of engaged listening and supportive reflection are as valuable to a classroom exchange as the initiation of a response.
- With the goal of equality, be sure not to overreact by calling exclusively on girls in a class. Seek a balance.
- Eliminate gender-typed activities and assignments (for example, boys will help move the desks, girls can collect the papers).
- Be mindful and monitor all examples and illustrations employed in class. Do they speak to the specific experiences of all children, boys and girls?
- Be careful with gendered forms of address. For example, refer to great writers, scientists, and astronauts as "he or she," as is now more commonly done with teachers, lawyers, and so on.
- Arrange activities so that both girls and boys have opportunities for leadership.

## EXERCISE 10-3    Field Experience: Perspectives on Gender

*Directions:*

1. Observe an instructor teaching a lesson in her or his classroom. Make note of gender-biased language or references (illustrations, examples, anecdotes, and so on).

2. Following the observation, ask the teacher the following questions, recording his or her response.

   - In your years of teaching, have you noted any *consistent* differences between your male and female students? Please explain.

   - In developing your lesson plans, what steps, if any, do you take to ensure the use of male and female representation? Can you provide references and illustrations?

   - Have you taken any specific steps in designing your classroom environment, your specific lessons, lesson activities, or the ways you interact with your students to insure a nonsexist learning environment?

3. Share your observations with your classmates, colleagues, or your instructor in small-group discussion.

Teaching, for the most part, operates to conceal the existence of social conflict and to preserve the status quo. Thus, female students in the classroom (who often constitute the numerical majority of students) are consumers of practices that often work against their best interests. For example, authoritarian instructional approaches work against female students' best interests because they do not incorporate collaborative and discovery-learning approaches found to engage and empower female students. Thus, teachers cannot be gender blind or neutral; they must be feminists in that they identify ways to reverse the effects of sexism and gender bias that exist in schools and society.

Feminists (both male and female) are advocates for equality between the sexes. Anyone who seeks equal opportunities for males and females is considered a feminist. Teachers must be active feminists in their work with their students. Their teaching strategies must be informed by a comprehensive knowledge of gender socialization and its effect on human development and learning.

Ethical teachers should be knowledgeable about social issues (including violence against women, eating disorders, objectification, sexual harassment, and so on) that have particular impact on girls and women. For example, teachers, in their work with female students, must be keenly aware of the place in which women find themselves in society—need to be perceived as beautiful and sexy in order to be accepted (even for girls as young as age 7 or 8) yet also needing to remain chaste lest they be considered promiscuous and therefore undesirable. These and other social issues create great confusion and unrest for female students and affect their interactions in classrooms. Socialized from birth in a society that institutionalizes the devaluation of females and severely limits their choices and opportunities, no female is untouched by sexism.

Ethical teachers are aware of all forms of sexism and oppression and how they affect female students' academic performance. The effects of sexism place female students at a great disadvantage that is not merited (Allport, 1954). Teachers need to be aware of the ways that gender attitudes and school practices restrict the lives of female students. They must encourage and support nontraditional gender roles in order to counteract the harmful impact of sexism, as well as examine their own gender attitudes and preferences.

In addition, they must be aware of their power and its use in the classroom and how male and female students experience power differently. The act of teaching implies an unequal power relationship between the teacher and the student, although the degree of this power differential varies depending on the theoretical orientation of the teacher (that is, behavioral, cognitive, neo-behavioral, or constructivist). For a female student, experience with a commanding authoritative teacher in the classroom may magnify her experience of inequality in society and represent another opportunity for her to be rewarded for expressing submission. When submission in the classroom is required, it may negatively affect female students' sense of adequacy and self-esteem. While it is difficult, and many would say undesirable, to eliminate all power differentials in the classroom, teachers can and should ensure that they use power in educationally supportive ways that benefit their students and do not maintain stereotypic dependency behaviors among their students. Teachers who make their students aware of choices; encourage autonomy; and teach their students critical analysis and decision making skills exhibit expertise in this area (Bonder, 2008). Such practices pave the way for female student achievement and empowerment to compete in traditionally male-dominated professions as well as lead to enhanced career opportunities. The following narrative describes the job discrimination that Brenda Berkman experienced in the process of attempting to fulfill her nontraditional career goals. In doing so, she helped make progress in the fight for the rights of all female firefighters.

## FROM CONCEPTS TO LIVED EXPERIENCE

The overwhelming impetus for me to become a firefighter was exactly what the world witnessed the day of the 9/11 attacks: the opportunity to help somebody in the direst hour of need. After practicing law for five years, I became the named plaintiff in a lawsuit challenging the physical abilities exam for firefighters as being discriminatory and not job-related. ... About forty of us went into the Fire Academy at the same time. There was a great deal of questioning about women's physical abilities, about "watering down" physical standards—even though we'd taken a test based on standards being met by men already on the job who set the performance level. Then they proceeded to re-test us, using it as a field day for harassment. About a dozen of us were allowed to graduate on time; the rest were held over for "re-training," since they kept changing the requirements. We were in danger of being picked off one by one. So we formed an organization, the United Women Firefighters. The only support we got was from the Vulcan Society, the organization of African American firefighters. The Firefighters' Union stood with the city defending against our lawsuit; in fact, after we'd won, the city surrendered at district court—but the union appealed to the second circuit.

Meanwhile they were trying to kick women out of the Academy one by one, some of us graduates went into the field as probationary firefighters. But nothing was done to prepare firefighters in the field for the fact that women were on the way. The women were going out, one per firehouse, with no accommodations in terms of bathrooms or changing areas. No one bothered to make the guys aware that they shouldn't be walking around naked in front of us. During this period, some women never changed or went to the bathroom in the firehouse—and I'm convinced that their reaction to the lack of privacy actually damaged their health because they weren't performing normal bodily functions and also were unable to shower, so dangerous materials and chemicals stayed on their skin.

*Source:* Brenda Berkman, Lieutenant, New York City Fire Department, Ladder Company 12

In *Sisterhood Is Forever: The Women's Anthology for a New Millennium 2003,* New York: Washington Square Press, p. 331.

## SUMMARY

**Cultural Factor 1: Historical and Current Treatment in the United States**   One key to understanding women's status in a society is their degree of participation in the economy of the society as well as their control over the product they produce. Every society employs some type of sexual division of labor. The progression from White women being treated as possessions and property to being treated as individuals with rights has occurred in three waves, starting with Elizabeth Cady Stanton's writing of the *Declaration of Sentiments* and the subsequent rise of the National American Woman Suffrage Association (NAWSA). The second wave of the European American women's rights movement included the passage of Title VII of the 1964 Civil Rights Act, which prohibited employment discrimination on the basis of race, sex, religion, and national origin.

Sexual objectification of women involves disregarding their personal abilities and capabilities, and focusing instead on attributes relevant to women's role as a sexual partner including her **physical attractiveness**, sex appeal, and submissiveness which has been found to lead to negative psychological effects including depression and negative self-image. Because women and girls' intelligence and competence are not acknowledged, they may come to believe that they are only valued for their physical beauty.

Today, the third wave of the women's rights movement operates with a focus on issues such as women's admission and treatment in military academies; women's reproductive rights (still contested 25 years after the Supreme Court ruling in *Roe v. Wade* affirmed women's choice during the first two trimesters of pregnancy); women's leadership in religious worship; affirmative action; mommy tracking; sexual harassment; violence against women; the maternal wall; glass ceilings; and other forms of institutional discrimination against women in the United States.

**Cultural Factor 2: Initial Terms of Incorporation into U.S. Society**   At least four major themes have characterized dominant culture's historical treatment and incorporation of women in the United States: (1) neglect—women's health and social issues were ignored; (2) blatant sexism—including searches for the presumed mental and psychological mechanisms of women's inferiority; (3) pathologizing women's concerns; and (4) current circumstances in which women's needs and issues are coming into dominant-culture consciousness.

**Cultural Factor 3: Shared Values and Traditions**   Behaviors, values, and characteristics associated with females and males are neither universal nor timeless; they are socially constructed, reflecting the society and time in which they operate. While women are presented as passive and submissive, it is not clear where females' real values along the aggressive–submissive continuum lie because they cannot be measured outside the social context within which they reside. Within the existing social context, females are socialized to be passive, dependent, relationship-oriented, and selfless.

**Cultural Factor 4: View of Spirituality and Humans' Relation to Nature**   The practices and languages that emanate from the presentation of religious higher power figures in masculine form have resulted in patriarchal perspectives that have often isolated women from their own spirituality. Most feminist thinkers postulate images of God that encompass the full humanity of men and women; thus, *feminist spirituality* is not restricted to a female point of view but rather refers to a perspective—an approach to life.

**Cultural Factor 5: Acculturation and Experience with Exclusion and Alienation** Women have been acculturated in dominant culture in the United States to meet the needs of society. From colonial times to the present, females have been socialized to serve husbands and children in self-sacrificing ways, to the detriment of their own personal and professional development.

**Cultural Factor 6: Language Differences, Strengths, and Challenges** Failure to recognize the impact of intentional and inadvertent sexism in language furthers the pervasive absence of females in written and oral discourse. Sexist language excludes, objectifies, and sets apart females in U.S. society in the following ways: (1) labeling the supposed exception to the rule (for example,

woman doctor, male nurse); (2) trivializing female gender forms (for example, poetess, suffragette); (3) using terminology that refers to women as children (for example, baby, doll); and (4) using terminology that refers to women as food (for example, tomato, sugar, cupcake).

**Potential Barriers in Learning–Teaching Relationships with Dominant-Culture Teachers** Teachers must be aware of and continually review their own values and biases toward females in order to be advocates for equality and equal opportunities for women and girls. Teachers must be active feminists in their work with their students, where *feminist* refers to all (both male and female) who advocate for equality between the sexes.

## Questions for Review

1. In what ways has the *maternal wall* been found to disadvantage female workers even more so than *glass ceilings*?

2. How is it that males may be considered feminists?

3. What does the following mean: Females, particularly adolescent females, may *lose their voices* through process of subordination in society?

## Important Terms

| | | | |
|---|---|---|---|
| Civil Rights Act | gender stereotyping | Association | sexism |
| Declaration of | glass ceiling | (NAWSA) | sexual division of |
| Sentiments | League of Women | National | labor |
| Equal Rights | Voters | Organization for | sexual objectification |
| Amendment (ERA) | maternal wall | Women (NOW) | Title IX |
| feminist | National American | Seneca Falls | women's rights |
| gender-based norms | Woman Suffrage | Convention | movement |
| gender socialization | | | |

## Enrichment

Crittenden, A. (2001). *The price of motherhood: Why the most important job in the world is still the least valued.* New York: Metropolitan.

Gay, G. (2000). *Culturally responsive teaching: Theory, research, and practice.* New York: Teachers College.

Gilligan, C. (1982). *In a different voice.* Cambridge, MA: Harvard University.

Haag, P. (2002). Single-sex education in grades K–12: What does the research tell us? In *The Jossey-Bass reader on gender education* (pp. 647–676). San Francisco: Jossey Bass.

Morgan, R. (2003). *Sisterhood is forever: The women's anthology for a new millennium.* New York: Washington Square Press.

Pipher, M. (1994). *Reviving Ophelia: Saving the selves of adolescent girls.* New York: Ballantine Books.

Richardson, L. W. (1981). *The dynamics of sex and gender: A socialized perspective* (2nd ed.). Boston: Houghton Mifflin.

Ward, J. (2002). *School rules. In The Jossey-Bass reader on gender in education* (pp. 510–542). San Francisco: Jossey Bass.

## Connections on the Web

http://www.aauw.org/

This website promotes education and equity for all women and girls, and features gender equity statistics and current women's issues and struggles.

http://www.feminist.org/

This is the site for the Feminist Majority that was founded to promote women's empowerment through research, education, and action. It provides advocacy resources.

www.now.org

This site of the National Organization for Women is an excellent resource for information on women's rights legislation.

## References

Adkinson, D. R., & Hackett, G. (1995). *Counseling diverse populations.* Madison, WI: Brown & Benchmark.

Agars, M. D., & Kottke, J. L. (2004). Models and practice of diversity management: A historical review and presentation of new integration theory. In M. Stockdale & F. J. Crosby (Eds.), *The psychology and management of workplace diversity* (pp. 55–77). Maiden, MA: Blackwell.

Albee, G. W., & Perry, M. (1998). Economic and social causes of sexism and the exploitation of women. *Journal of Community and Applied Social Psychology, 8,* 145–160.

Allport, G. W. (1954). *The nature of prejudice.* Cambridge, MA: Addison Wesley.

Barnouw, V. (1963). *Culture and personality.* Home-wood, IL: Dorsey.

Belenky, M. F., Clinchy, B. M., Goldberger, N. R., & Tarule, J. M. (1986). *Women's ways of knowing.* New York: Basic Books.

Bem, S. L. (1974). The measurement of psychological androgyny. *Journal of Consulting and Clinical Psychology, 42,* 155–162.

Berkman, B. (2003). Breaking barriers: Firefighters. In Morgan, R. (Ed.) *Sisterhood is forever: The women's anthology for a new millennium* (p. 331). New York: Washington Square Press,.

Bianchi, S. M., & Casper, L. M. (2001). American families. *Population Bulletin, 55,* 2–43.

Bolinger, D. (1968). *Aspects of language.* New York: Harcourt Brace Jovanovich.

Bonder, G. (2008). *Gender equity in education: A renewed commitment.* Retrieved from http://www.aflcio.org/issues/jobseconomy/women/links.cfm.

Carli, L. L. (1990). Gender language and influence. *Journal of Personality and Social Psychology, 59,* 941–951.

Chodorow, N. (1974). *The reproduction of mothering: Psychoanalysis and the sociology of gender.* New York: Columbia University.

Coltrane, S. (1996). *Family man: Fatherhood, housework, and gender equity.* New York: Oxford University.

Crittenden, A. (2001). *The price of motherhood: Why the most important job in the world is still the least valued*. New York: Metropolitan.

Crosby, F. J. (2004). *Affirmative action is dead: Long live affirmative action*. New Haven, CT: Yale University.

Eagly, A. H. (1987). *Sex difference in social behavior: A social role interpretation*. Hillsdale, NJ: Erlbaum.

Eagly, A. H., & Karau, S. J. (1991). Gender and the emergence of leaders: A meta-analysis. *Journal of Personality & Social Psychology*, 60(5), 685–710.

Eagly, A. H., & Karau, S. J. (2002). Role congruity theory of prejudice toward female leaders. *Psychological Review*, 109(3), 573–597.

Eisenberg, B., & Ruthsdotter, M. (1998). Living the legacy: The women's rights movement 1848–1998. *The National Women's History Project*. Retrieved on February 6, 2005, from http://www.legacy98.org/move-hist.html.

Ferree, M. M. (1990). Beyond separate spheres: Feminism and family research. *Journal of marriage and the family*, 52, 866–884.

Fiorenza, E. S. (1979). Feminist spirituality, Christian identity, and Catholic vision. In C. P. Christ & J. Plaskow (Eds.), *Women spirit rising* (p. 139). San Francisco: Harper & Row.

Gilbert, L. A., & Rader, J. (2001). Current perspectives in women's adult roles: Work, family, and life. In R. K. Unger (Ed.), *Handbook of the psychology of women and gender* (pp. 156–169). New York: John Wiley & Sons.

Gilligan, C. (1982). *In a different voice*. Cambridge, MA: Harvard University.

Grossman, A., & Peters-Axtell, E. (2003). Girls: "We are the ones who can make a change!" In Morgan, R. (Ed.), *Sisterhood is forever: The women's anthology for a new millennium* (pp. 121–123). New York: Washington Square Press.

Gutek, B. A. (2001). Women and paid work. *Psychology of Women Quarterly*, 25(4), 379–394.

Hallock, P. (1994). Promoting diversity on campus: Thoughts to action. *Thought and Action*, 10, 65–78.

Heilman, M. E. (1983). Sex bias in work settings: The lack of fit model. In L. L.Cummings & B. M.Staw (Eds.), *Research in organized behavior* (Vol. 5, pp. 269–298). Greenwich, CT: JAI.

Institute for Women's Policy Research. (2001, May). *Today's women workers: Shut out of yesterday's employment insurance system* (Pub. No. A127). Washington, DC: Author.

Johnson, E. A. (1989). Mary and the female face of God. *Theological Studies*, 50, 500–520.

Jones, J. M. (1997). *Prejudice and racism* (2nd ed.). New York: McGraw Hill.

Kirchmeyer, C. (1998). Determinism and managerial career success: Evidence and explanation of male/female differences. *Journal of Management*, 24, 673–692.

Kobrynowicz, D., & Biernat, N. (1997). Decoding subjective evaluations: How stereotypes provide shifting standards. *Journal of Experimental Social Psychology*, 33, 579–601.

Kolbenschlag, M. (1982, July–August). Feminist, the frog Princess and the New Frontiers of Spirituality. *New Catholic World*, 160.

Kossoudi, S. A., & Dresser, L. J. (1992). Working class rosies: Women industrial workers during World War II. *The Journal of Economic History*, 52, 431–447.

Matlin, M. W. (1987). *The psychology of women*. New York: C & S College Publishing.

Miller, C., & Swift, K. (1988). *The handbook of nonsexist writing* (2nd ed.). New York: Harper & Row.

Mintz, S. (2000). From patriarchy to androgyny and other myths: Placing men's family roles in historical perspective. In A. Booth & A. C. Crouter (Eds.), *Men in families: When do they get involved? What difference does it make?* (pp. 3–30). Mahwah, NJ: Lawrence Erlbaum Associates.

Mitchel, P. (2005). Feminism fits busy schedules. *Herizons*, 6.

Peters, M. (2008). *Women, sex and film: The objectified woman and her guest for subjectivity*. Retrieved from http://filmtvindustry.suite101.com/article.cfm/women_in_film#ixzz0iXQTzXR0.

Richardson, L. W. (1981). *The dynamics of sex and gender: A socialized perspective* (2nd ed.) Boston: Houghton Mifflin.

Rudman, L. A., & Click, P. (1999). Feminized management and backlash towards agentic women: The hidden costs of a kinder, gentler image of middle management. *Journal of Personality and Social Psychology*, 77, 1004–1010.

Schneer, J. A., & Reitman, F. (1995). The import of gender as managerial courses unfold. *Journal of Vocational Behavior*, 47, 290–315.

Unger, R. K. (1979). *Female and male: Psychological perspectives*. New York: Harper & Row.

U.S. Bureau of the Census. (2002). *Historical income tables—People Table. Work experience of workers by median earnings and sex: 1967–2001*. Washington, DC: U.S. Government Printing Office.

U.S. Bureau of the Census. (2007). Washington, DC: U.S. Government Printing Office.

Waldfogel, J. (1998). Understanding the "family gap" in pay for women and children. *Journal of Economic Perspectives*, 12, 137–156.

Whalen, C., & Whalen, B. (1985). *The longest debate: A legislative history of the 1964 civil rights act*. Washington, DC: Seven Locks.

Wilcoxion, S. A. (1989). He/she/they/it?: Implied sexism in speech and print. *Journal of Counseling & Development*, 68, 114–116.

Wiley, M. C., & Crittenden, K. S. (1992). By your attributions you shall be known. *Sex Roles*, 27, 259–276.

Williams, J. (2000). *Unbending gender: Why work and family conflict and what to do about it*. New York: Oxford University.

*As most know, pledging a fraternity takes up a great deal of time, so as pledging went on, I spent more and more time with my pledge brothers and the active members. This was when I began to notice their attitudes about homosexuality. I had become aware that I was gay, but they did not suspect because I did not give off any of the stereotypical gay signals. I did not talk with a lisp, swish my hips from side to side, or give any sexual glances. This was not because I was trying to hide anything from them but simply because it was not me. As time went on, I started to notice the little jokes they made about gays. I joke with my gay friends about being gay, but we never cross the line of being offensive to each other. My brothers, unlike my gay friends, did not see this line.*

*Over the next few weeks, my ears became attuned to the references that were made about gays. Never once did I hear a positive one. The word, "fag" came up as a derogatory term in every other sentence with certain brothers. Never once did I hear something that made me want to stand up and say, "Hey, I'm like that—I'm gay." The more comments I heard, the more I did not want to tell anyone. I asked myself: Do I want to join an organization that condemns someone who is gay?*

**Source:** David Anglikowski, *Family and the Bond of Brotherhood, Out on Fraternity Row: Personal Accounts of Being Gay in a College Fraternity*, pp. 195–196.

CHAPTER

11

# Learning from Lesbian, Gay, Bisexual, Transgendered, and Questioning (LGBTQ) Individuals' Stories

There is much to celebrate in acknowledging lesbian, gay, bisexual, transgendered, and questioning (**LGBTQ**) students' identities. At the same time, discrimination against and exclusion of members of this cultural group occurs every day in the United States. The derogatory views and exclusion reflected in Anglikowski's story persists in U.S. society and schools.

I asked our pledge-class president, Chris, a question one night when we were driving over to one of the fraternity's houses. "What would it take for the fraternity to kick someone out?" There was only one thing that he could think of. The only reason that someone might be kicked out would be if he was gay. This was the answer I feared. They would kick out a pledge, Chris told me, but maybe not a brother. They would only make it so that he would not want to be a member anymore. When I think about it, there are plenty of ways the fraternity could make a person want to leave. Part of me can understand why. Many of the events that happen are geared for straight couples, thus it would seem out of place at something like a date dash to have two guys there together. Why does that have to be?

I had to think about what my integrity meant to me. Part of me thought that it was none of their business what my sexual orientation was. But then another part of me kept thinking that I was being dishonest with them. The fact that I am gay is part of who I am, and I was not sharing that part with them. I know they would not have accepted me if they knew I was gay when I pledged. Even if some of my brothers did not have a problem with me personally being gay, they might have a problem with having a gay man in their fraternity. The last thing they wanted to be known as was the "gay fraternity." It would kill the house.

This chapter explores the lives and perspectives of LGBTQ students. As is true for all cultural groups presented within this text, it is important to remember that there is wide variance between the perspectives and experiences of each member of this group. While this chapter highlights the struggles of LGBTQ individuals within a society that marginalizes their status, it is important to remember that this discussion is presented with the knowledge that LGBTQ individuals perceive and address **heterosexism** differently. As such, oppression that marginalizes the status of LGBTQ people may cause some members of the group to feel conquered, limited, and depressed while others may react through resistance, advocacy for the group, and liberation that is accompanied by pride and joy. The spectrum of reaction to oppression among members of this group is wide. Therefore, it is important not to assume that all LGBTQ students are victims, but rather to understand that as with all other oppressed groups, most lead full, satisfying, and successful lives despite the oppression they face. Even so, it is important to explore the challenges and barriers confronted by members of this group in an effort to reveal institutionalized discrimination as well as group member resilience and advocacy that serve to advance the progress to provide for the establishment of equal rights for LGBTQ individuals.

This chapter will explore oppression, struggles, resistance, and successes of LGBTQ individuals in the United States.

## CHAPTER OBJECTIVES

1. Define sexual orientation.
2. Describe common values and worldviews of gay and lesbian people in U.S. society.
3. Identify ways in which the people profiled in the personal narratives experienced and addressed the six cultural factors explored in this text.
4. Explain academic and intercultural interaction implications relevant for working with LGBTQ students and their families.

5. Describe some coping strategies utilized by members of this cultural group.
6. Identify classroom strategies for cultivating the resources provided when gay and lesbian individuals' and families' realities and worldviews are integrated in curricula.

## SEXUAL ORIENTATION

Human sexuality is complex in that individuals engage in a variety of sexual activities that are viewed differently by various members of society. Sexual identity is the degree to which one identifies with or endorses social and biologically prescribed aspects of being male or female. Some perceive sexual identity to be a simple, straightforward product of biology. Such a position, often termed an *Essentialist position,* argues that sexual orientation is a part of an individual's core being. This stance often leads to the conclusion that **heterosexuality** is the "right and correct" form of sexuality and thus **homosexuality** is "improper." However, Katz (1997) explained, "[B]iology does not settle our erotic fates. The common notion that biology determines the object of sexual desire or that physiology and society together cause sexual orientation, are determinisms that deny the break existing between our bodies and situations and our desiring, [j]ust as the biology of our hearing organs will never tell us why we take pleasure in Bach or delight in Dixieland" (p. 64).

**Sexual orientation** is an integral part of one's sexual identity and is defined by to whom individuals are emotionally and physically attracted. One's sexual orientation may be lesbian, gay, bisexual, transgender, heterosexual, or questioning. **Questioning** is included in this list because people may *question* their sexual orientations at any point in their lives. During time periods when individuals question their sexual orientation, feelings and objects of their emotional and physical attraction may vary. It is important to note that each sexual orientation is considered to be *normal* by all prominent mental health organizations, such as the American Psychiatric Association and the American Psychological Association.

LGBTQ individuals are people in all age, gender, social-class, ability, and racial/ethnic groups. A conservative estimate identifies LGBTQ individuals as representing at least 10 percent of the total population in the United States. Population estimates of members of this group are conservative because many LGBTQ individuals remain **closeted** (that is to say, they do not divulge their sexual orientation) in order to have access to rights and fair treatment that would be denied to them if members of dominant culture knew their sexual orientation—as David Anglikowski described in the personal narrative presented at the beginning of this chapter. In fact, not all LGBTQ individuals identify or affiliate with LGBTQ culture. Reasons can include geographic distance, a lack of awareness of the culture's existence, fear of social stigma, and personal preference to remain unidentified by sexuality or community. The way LGBTQ persons experience life and their identities varies widely and is influenced by cultural and social variables, including regional residence, social class, race, religion, family, and other forces. As such, all generalizations about members of the LGBTQ communities must be viewed within context.

# CULTURAL FACTOR 1: HISTORICAL AND CURRENT TREATMENT IN THE UNITED STATES

Gay and lesbian individuals are often described as having an *invisible* history. Historical records that chronicle gay and lesbian lives and experiences are sketchy at best with most information derived from religious and legal actions exercised to eradicate homosexual behavior (Bullough, 1976, 1979). However, the history of gay and lesbian individuals is ultimately one of movement toward recognition and the establishment of human rights.

Bullough (1979), in Adkinson and Hackett (1995), identified major societal reactions to gay people throughout history as having ranged from tolerance to societal and religious condemnation of homosexual behavior as sinful, criminal, and even medically pathological; to widespread societal discrimination; and finally to a more contemporary treatment that recognizes varying degrees of rights and acknowledgement of gay and lesbian culture.

## Acceptance and Tolerance

During Greek times, homosexuality was described by some as the only form of pure and lasting eroticism. Plato's view was that only love between persons of the same gender (*Platonic* love) could transcend sex. Even still, women in Ancient Greece were not encouraged, as men were, to have same-sex attachments; women of all classes led severely restricted lives. Some of the earliest information known about the lives and perspectives of lesbians is from sixth-century female poet, Sappho from the Greek island of Lesbos, who wrote poetry that celebrated love between women. However, Sappho was married to a man, and there is not much information left about her sexuality following the purposeful destruction of most of her poetry during the Christian era (Bullough, 1979).

## Homosexuality Viewed as Religious Sin and Crime

Christian religious tradition has been one of the most forceful opponents of gay and lesbian lifestyles. Attempts to categorize homosexuality as a sin that is not to be tolerated continue today. Much of the evidence for such claims comes from biblical scriptures in which homosexuality is depicted as a crime against nature. Those taking this position were often less concerned with the sins of adultery and divorce, as well as women who engaged in so-called unnatural sexual behavior. Historically, great emphasis was placed on the condemnation of gay men who were wasting their semen (that is, "spilling their seed"), which was perceived to be vital for procreation—the "true" reason for sex. Bullough (1979) identified a 390 AD Roman law that prescribed the death penalty for anal intercourse. The law was intended to halt male prostitution and "later became the foundation for the laws of the Christian Church canon as well as European and English civil law" (Adkinson & Hackett, 1995, p. 61).

## Homosexuality Viewed as Sickness

Even in the "enlightened" arena of medicine, homosexual behavior was defined as deviant. While Freud believed homosexuality was "assuredly no advantage," he stated that it was not wrong. Freud's followers, however, interpreted homosexuality as a flight from incest in the absence of a father or in the presence of a weak one. It was believed that the boy suppressed his desire for all women and sought to be like his mother in accepting the father in other roles (Bullough, 1979). For years, professionals in the field of psychology focused on "curing" gay and lesbian individuals rather than on understanding gay men's and lesbian women's counseling issues (Adkinson & Hackett, 1995).

## Harassment, Discrimination, and Exclusion

As noted earlier in this chapter, most of what is known pertaining to the history of this cultural group is scantily reported, and many of the historical events are contested by some on the grounds that they may not truly reflect incidences particular to LGBTQ individuals. The following is a list of historical events adapted from an excerpt in *The Reader's Companion to American History* (1991) that identifies harassment, discrimination, and exclusion of gay and lesbian individuals in the United States:

### 1920s–1950s

- Urban gay subculture became visible in the United States as early as the 1920s and 1930s.
- The Chicago Society for Human Rights became the country's earliest known gay rights organization, and many cities had public gay bars during the 1940s.
- Alfred Kinsey published *Sexual Behavior in the Human Male* in 1948, which found that homosexual behavior was far more common among U.S. men than was previously believed. These findings provoked widespread discrimination against gays.
- Consistent with the sentiments of the time, President Eisenhower issued an Executive Order in 1953 that barred gays and lesbians from being hired by the federal government. This federal mandate encouraged state and local governments to harass gay citizens through surveillance programs and regular police raids on gay bars.
- In 1950, Harry Hay, Charles Rowland, and others formed what would be called the Mattachine Society, which was created to address discrimination against gays in the United States.
- Five years later, the Daughters of Bilitus, a lesbian organization founded by Del Martin and Phyllis Lyon, joined the Mattachine Society to work to advance the rights and liberties of gay and lesbian people. Chapters of both organizations were established in several cities in the United States, and journals were published to provide resources and organization for gay and lesbian political action.

**1960s–1990s**

- The LGBT rights movement, fueled by the Civil Rights movement in the 1960s, led to activists such as Franklin Kameny and Barbara Gittings protesting discriminatory government employment policies.

- In 1962, Illinois became the first state in the United States to decriminalize homosexual acts between consenting adults in private.

- In 1969, the New York City police raided a Greenwich Village gay bar, the now-famous Stonewall Inn. Several days of rioting following this incident ignited a large-scale, mostly grassroots, gay liberation movement.

- The American Psychiatric Association removed homosexuality from its official list of psychiatric disorders, and there were at least 750 registered gay and lesbian organizations in the United States by 1973.

- In 1977, a popular singer at the time, Anita Bryant, led a campaign to repeal a gay rights ordinance in Dade County, Florida. Her actions spurred a Christian-led discrimination movement in the United States in the 1980s against gays and lesbians.

- Civil rights actions from the gay rights movement that followed resulted in federal and state governments not only decriminalizing homosexual behavior but also outlawing discrimination based on sexual orientation.

- In 1982, Wisconsin became the first state in the United States to outlaw discrimination based on sexual orientation.

- When HIV/AIDS took center stage in the 1980s (with the first cases identified in the United States in 1981), the prevalence of the disease among gays was used to strengthen antigay sentiments. HIV/AIDS was perceived by many in dominant culture to be a "gay disease" and was used as justification for discrimination against gay and lesbian people. The epidemic and ensuing propaganda linking HIV/AIDS to the so-called evils of homosexuality motivated many gay and dominant-culture advocates to join the gay rights movement. By 1986, more than 38,000 worldwide had been diagnosed with the disease, though the Reagan Administration had only officially recognized the disease in September 1985. By the end of the decade, more than 8 million people worldwide would have HIV/AIDS. Reagan himself, in 1990, would eventually apologize for his administration's failure to respond to the disease. As of June 2007, according to the Center for Disease Control, 71 percent of those in the United States infected with HIV/AIDS were "men who have sex with men."

- In 1987, more than 600,000 LGBT people and their allies marched in Washington, demanding equality and social justice.

- By 1990, the number of registered gay and lesbian organizations increased to several thousand.

- A critical moment in the history of gay rights that also helped dominant-culture Americans understand the violence against gay and lesbian people was the murder of Matthew Shepherd in 1998. Shepherd, a gay college student at the University of Wyoming, was kidnapped, beaten, and left tied to a fence for 18 hours. Because the circumstances of his death received extensive media coverage and even took the form of a play and movie, *The Laramie Project*, U.S. citizens were provided with evidence of the existence of acts of violence that target gays and lesbians and were persuaded to consider the morality of the treatment of gays and lesbians in the United States (Brewer, 2003).

## Current Conditions

**Marriage Equality?**   Marriage between same-sex couples was first made legal in the Netherlands in 2001. Since then, six additional countries have passed legislation to recognize marriage rights for LGBT citizens. Spain is the only country in the world that recognizes same-sex marriage and heterosexual marriage under the same law.

Marriage equality statistics in the United States change rapidly. Currently, five U.S. states: Massachusetts (2004), Connecticut (2008), Iowa (2009), Vermont (2009), New Hampshire (2009 vote, 2010 enactment), as well as the District of Columbia (2009 vote, 2010 enactment) recognize marriage equality. Two states, Maine and California, had recognized marriage equality at one point, but passed ballot initiatives rescinding marriage rights for gay and lesbian couples. One state, New Jersey, recognizes civil unions between same-sex couples, and several states such as Oregon, Maine, and Washington have domestic partnership laws that grant certain benefits to same-sex couples.

However, thirty states have passed constitutional amendments or laws explicitly banning same-sex marriage. Prohibiting marriage protection to same-sex individuals denies them 1,000 federal protections and responsibilities granted to heterosexual individuals. Opponents of same-sex marriage have also been championing Proposition 8 in California, a statewide ballot measure that would rescind marriage rights for LGBT citizens in that state. These marriage equality statistics provide evidence that the gay rights movement is garnering strength, resulting in a growing sense of pride and liberation of LGBTQ individuals along with evidence of mounting dominant-culture acts to curtail the movement and continue discriminatory policies and practices against gay and lesbian citizens.

**Employment Equality?**   There are currently 13 states, as well as the District of Columbia, that have enacted policies to protect against gender identity and sexual orientation discrimination in employment. Seven states, meanwhile, have laws that prohibit employment discrimination solely based on sexual orientation. However, in thirty states, LGBT citizens can be fired on the basis of their sexual orientation and/or gender identity without any legal recourse, and as many as 39 percent of LGBT workers continue to experience some sort of workplace discrimination or harassment (Jones, 2008).

**LGBTQ Culture in the Media**   Public attitudes about homosexuality changed dramatically during the 1990s, and a decrease in publicized hostility toward homosexuality was observed (Wilcox & Norrander, 2002). Yet, in U.S. politics, gay rights support has typically been divided along party lines, with support for gays and lesbians associated with liberalism and the Democratic Party, whereas opposition to gay rights has typically been associated with conservatism and the Republican Party (Haeberle, 1999; Wilcox & Norrander, 2002). LGBTQ movement's gains have also been reflected in the media. In 1997, the title character of the television show *Ellen* (played by an openly lesbian actor, Ellen Degeneres), along with other television shows like *Will and Grace,* the popular, *Queer Eye for the Straight Guy,* and the *Rosie O'Donnell and Ellen Degeneres Shows* and films like *Birdcage* and *Brokeback Mountain,* have provided a positive view of lesbian and gay life, thus paving the way for mainstream awareness and recognition of LGBTQ cultural issues and perspectives (Brewer, 2003).

As LGBTQ citizens continue to struggle against discrimination in employment, housing, child custody, adoption, and health insurance as well as confront violence and negative stereotyping in wider society, in some cities, LGBTQ individuals live in so-termed gay villages within which LGBTQ community members may organize a number of events to celebrate their cultures, such as Pride parades, the Gay Games, and Southern Decadence.

Discrimination at both the macro level (for example, health insurance and partner-benefit laws) as well as at the micro level (involving daily personal interactions) is equally damaging. Gays and lesbians face economic discrimination as well as a result of heterosexism in hiring, promotion, and firing practices. The movie *Philadelphia* provided an insightful illustration of the overt and covert discrimination gay and lesbian people may encounter in the workplace and the struggles gays and lesbians may confront when they attempt to secure their rights as citizens through legal action. In addition, gay and lesbian students are all too often harmed by teachers, students, and other members of dominant culture who trivialize their gay identity. Members of this cultural group continue to be disadvantaged by having their problems attributed to their sexual orientation, being assumed to be heterosexual, suffering gross insensitivity with regard to the importance of their close relationships, being alienated or absent in children's literature and academic curricula, experiencing physical assaults, and in other ways having their status marginalized in dominant culture (see Personal Narrative 11-1).

Dominant-culture male attitudes toward homosexuality are more unfavorable than female attitudes toward gay citizens, and attitudes toward gay men are often less favorable than attitudes toward lesbians (Herek, 1994; Kite & Whitley, 1996; Steffens & Wagner, 2004). Particular disdain held for gay men by members of dominant culture was found even among professionals (Berkman & Zimberg, 1997).

Further, with regard to economics, it is accurate to say that lesbian wages are closer to heterosexual women's wages compared to openly gay men's wages in relationship to the wages of heterosexual men. Berg and Lien (2002) found, for example, using a model that controlled for factors such as level of education, years of experience, and place of residence, that lesbians earned some 30 percent more than heterosexual women, while gay men earned around 22 percent less than their heterosexual male counterparts.

# CULTURAL FACTOR 2: INITIAL TERMS OF INCORPORATION INTO U.S. SOCIETY

The concept of homosexuality began to take shape toward the end of the 19th century when a biomedical view of homosexuality was presented (Miller, 1995). The Kinsey Heterosexual-Homosexual Scale (KHHS) was the first sexual-response scale created (Kinsey, Pomeroy, Martin, & Gebhard, 1953). Kinsey et al. used the

KHHS to categorize individuals in a static way based on variable aspects of sexual orientation, such as attraction, behavior, fantasy, lifestyle, emotional preference, social preference, and self-identification. In their study, 50 percent of males were found to be exclusively heterosexual, 4 percent were categorized as exclusively homosexual, and the remaining 46 percent fell somewhere in between. Later, the Klein Sexual Orientation Grid (KSOG) (Klein, Sepekoff, & Wolf, 1986) extended the scope of the Kinsey model. This grid configured sexual orientation along seven components: (1) sexual behavior (With whom do you have sex?); (2) emotional preference (Whom do you like or love?); (3) sexual fantasies (Whom do you fantasize about?); (4) sexual attraction (To whom are you attracted?); (5) social preference (With whom do you socialize?); (6) lifestyle, social world, and community (Where do you tend to spend time and with whom?); and (7) self-identification (How do you identify yourself?). Klein et al. asked respondents to rate their positions on each component using a scale of 1 (other sex only) to 7 (same sex only). The researchers contended that using this measure for defining sexual orientation reveals that one's sexual orientation is an ever-changing aspect of oneself.

## Personal Narrative 11-1   There Is No Lesbian Barbie

In heterosexual families, both parents are sanctioned. They are legally the parents of the children, with the myriad of rights and daily sense of entitlement that confers. They don't have to think about it. They adopt or conceive their children together. Both their names are on the adoption documents or birth certificate. Each parent can travel with the child or take her or him to an emergency room for medical treatment. Both have titles that are recognized, carry meaning, and validate their relationship to the child a thousand times a day. They each think that she and he are the real parents. And everyone else thinks so too. Our situations are different. We have to deal with legal, practical, and psychological issues that arise out of the fact that society does not automatically recognize and honor our families, and that in "double-mommy" families we are not both legally sanctioned parents. In many states, the status of lesbian parents as sexual partners and/or parents is illegal or highly vulnerable. In Georgia, a sodomy statute is still on the books. In New Hampshire, the "Live Free or Die" state, a known lesbian cannot adopt a child or become a foster parent. In New York, an "unmarried couple" (and lesbians are still not permitted to marry) cannot adopt jointly. We may have to struggle for the right for both parents to be present when our child is born, and we rarely have the right to have both names on our child's birth certificate. In most cases of domestic adoption, and always in international adoption, we cannot present ourselves both as parents. Once we have our children, lesbians still face the very real threat of losing them. Although progress has been made, a lesbian in a custody dispute with a biological father is still likely to lose in most states, and in some cases may be permitted visitation only outside her lesbian household and not in the presence of her lesbian partner. A lesbian mother can lose custody of her children to biological grandparents or another biological relative who stakes a claim.... Every form we ever fill out for our child, from preschool application to college application, calls our authenticity into question ... At school we must say that our family requires two Mother's day cards to be made.... We never see our families validated by the culture that inundates our children. Families like ours are not on *Sesame Street* or *Barney,* not in most children's books, not in movies. There are no songs about us on Raffi's albums. There are no marketing campaigns to celebrate or merchandise the wedding of Ariel to Snow White. There is no lesbian Barbie.

*Source:* Segal-Sklar, S. (1995). Lesbian parenting: Radical or retrograde? In K. Jay (Ed.), *Dyke life: From growing up to growing old. A celebration of the lesbian experience* (pp. 174–175). New York: Basic Books.

But with all of the investigations and interest in defining sexual orientation, an obvious question goes widely overlooked: Why is there a need for a definition of sexual orientation? The very process of attempting to define sexual orientation amounts to a subtle form of discrimination and oppression (Hubbard, 1997; Katz, 1997).

A dichotomous portrayal of sexual identity was introduced over 40 years ago by Kinsey. Foucault (1978), instead, maintained that homosexuality is a *social construct* that is little more than 100 years old, stating there was no definition for homo- versus heterosexuality until there was a sociopolitical need to do so. There was no definition for heterosexuality as normative and correct until homosexuality was identified and defined as different and incorrect (Katz, 1995). Foucault explained that the ongoing quest to define sexual orientation is also an ongoing insidious process that continues to present one form of identity (that is, heterosexual) as right and normal and another (that is, homosexuality) as wrong.

## CULTURAL FACTORS 3 AND 4: SHARED VALUES, TRADITIONS, AND SPIRITUALITY

It is important to note that there is as much variation among members of LGBTQ culture as there is within the identified heterosexual population. The vast majority of gay and lesbian people live much the same as their heterosexual counterparts, seeking long-term relationships and raising families. As such, in attempting to define common or generally held cultural values, one must remember that members of the LGBTQ community are also members of a number of communities and cultural groups. When speaking of the gay and lesbian community, especially in terms of shared values and traditions, it is important to highlight that for all gay or lesbian individuals, values they embrace may be more reflective of and aligned with gender, social-class, racial, or ethnic groups than with values prevalent among members of gay or lesbian communities. However, on the macro level, discrimination and violence against gays (**hate crimes**) and the prohibition of gays and lesbians to marry create a common cause for advocacy that brings the gay community together—making up an important element of gay culture (Button, Rienzo, & Wald, 2000; Haider-Markel, 2000).

### Gay Culture

During the 19th and early 20th centuries, gay culture was highly covert and relied upon secret symbols and codes woven into an overall heterosexual context. Gay influence initially was limited, for the most part, to high culture. Association of gay men with opera, couture, fine cuisine, musical theater, and interior design began with wealthy homosexual men using the straight themes of these media to send their own signals. For example, in the heterocentric film *Gentlemen Prefer Blondes,* a musical number features Jane Russell singing "Anyone Here for Love" in a gym while muscled men dance around her. The film's costumes, choreography, and screen play, were all created by men. While gay men may have enjoyed the film for these aspects, Russell's presence provided the heterocentric focus needed to popularize the film among dominant-culture members of the time.

Current descriptions of gay males are more accurately ambiguous even though damaging stereotypes and generalizations about gays from the past still linger on today. Gay men are a diverse and broad group of individuals, who come in all shapes, sizes, personalities, and styles of dress. Although it is common for dominant culture individuals to automatically associate gay men with stereotypes that involve feminine behavior and certain types of clothing, for every gay man who exhibits those qualities, there is another who does not.

## Lesbian Culture

Lesbian culture includes elements both from the larger LGBTQ culture and elements that are more closely specific to the lesbian community. The history of lesbian culture over the last half-century has also been tightly entwined with the evolution of *feminism*. Old stereotypes of lesbian women stressed a dichotomy between women who adhered to stereotypical male gender stereotypes (*butch*) and stereotypical female gender stereotypes (*femme*), and that typical lesbian couples consisted of a butch/femme pairing. Today, some lesbian women adhere to being either *butch* or *femme,* but these categories are much less rigid and are now uncommon. There is a subculture within some lesbian communities called *Aristasia,* in which lesbians adhere to exaggerated levels of femininity. In this culture, there are two genders, blonde and brunette, although the labels are unrelated to actual hair color. Brunettes are femme, and blondes are even more so. Also notable are *diesel dykes*—women who are said to be extremely butch and may use "male" forms of dress and *lipstick lesbians*—women who exhibit "femininity" and are attracted to women.

## Bisexual Culture

Bisexual culture has evolved around a common cause emphasizing opposition to *monosexism* (discrimination against bisexual and pansexual people) and *biphobia* (hatred and/or distrust of bisexual people). Many bisexual, fluid, and *pansexual* individuals consider themselves to be part of the LGBTQ or Queer community. In an effort to create both more visibility, and a symbol for the bisexual community, a bisexual flag, featuring a pink or red stripe at the top to represent homosexuality, a blue one on the bottom for heterosexuality and a purple one in the middle to represent bisexuality, as purple is from the combination of red and blue, has been created. Additionally, *Celebrate Bisexuality Day* has been observed on September 23rd by many members of the bisexual community and their allies since 1999.

## Transgendered Culture

**Transgendered individuals** are people who, to varying degrees, adopt male and female personas in the expression of aspects of their gender. Transgendered individuals are usually comfortable with their biological sex but experience both masculine and feminine selves and express this by adopting male and female personas. The study of transgendered culture is complicated by the many and various approaches to living as a transgendered individual. There are several different groups of individuals with different concerns who are often categorized within this group, for example, intersexed individuals and transsexuals are often described as members of this group. **Intersexed individuals** are people who are born with atypical combinations of male and female genitalia or reproductive organs and/or hormonal or chemical constitutions. **Transsexuals** are individuals who experience a clash between their biological sexual identity and their gender identity. Some transsexuals choose to have sexual reassignment surgery in order to bring about congruence in their biological and gender identities. Some transgender women and men, however, do not classify as being part of any specific *trans* culture. In addition, there are transgender individuals who make their past known to others and those who, instead, live according to their gender identity and do not reveal their past, believing that they should be able to live in their gender role in a normal way choosing to disclose their sexuality to others at their own discretion.

As a whole, LGBTQ community members tend to value that which is valued by many in society—authenticity, acceptance, safety, freedom, and community. Taking into account the wide-ranging variation among members in this cultural group, it is fair to say that perhaps the most noticeable common values and traditions of this group have been created in response to the discrimination members of this group face and the need for solidarity and unity to promote advocacy for their group. **Intentional families** may be formed to replace families created through biology that may be absent or impaired due to homophobia and discrimination. In fact, this cultural group is one of the only groups that cannot necessarily rely on members of their own families to help them understand the oppression they experience. Family members not only are likely to have little to no experience with similar discrimination faced by gay and lesbian individuals but also may engage in discrimination against their own gay and lesbian family members. Therefore, understanding, support, and coping strategies for addressing discrimination may not be provided by gay and lesbian citizens' biological family members.

Similarly, members of this group are aware that, due to heterosexism that pervades society and therefore all aspects of life, they may not have access to their chosen religious practices that they may have enjoyed before coming out as gay and lesbian individuals. It is widely known that many organized religions' policies and practices denounce, exclude, and/or otherwise alienate gay and lesbian people. Not surprisingly, advocacy, liberalism, sexual freedom, gender diversity, and human rights are principles that tend to be valued among members of this group.

## CULTURAL FACTOR 5: ACCULTURATION AND EXPERIENCE WITH EXCLUSION AND ALIENATION

Identifying oneself as an LGBTQ individual and disclosing this to other people is often referred to as **coming out**. Coming out may be a positive or negative experience depending on the level of acceptance and supports present. In addition, coming to terms with typical confusion about one's identity can have both positive and negative effects on many aspects of a person's life, including social relationships, school or work, and self-esteem.

Many LGBTQ individuals fear negative reactions, rejection, and damaging friendships and family relationships when they come out. In many regions of the country, strong cultural attitudes and discriminatory laws make coming out even harder. The Cass Identity Model (1979) is one of the foundational theories of gay and lesbian identity development. This model was the first to treat gay people as normal in a homophobic society instead of treating homosexuality as a problem to be cured. Cass described a process of six stages of gay and lesbian identity development explaining that while the stages are sequential, some people might revisit stages at different points in their lives.

## The Cass Six Stages Homosexual Identity Model

**Stage One: Identity Confusion**    In the first stage, which might also be called the *Questioning* stage, the individual is surprised to think of himself or herself as a gay person. This stage begins with the person's first awareness of gay or lesbian thoughts, feelings, and attractions. The person typically feels confused and experiences turmoil. To the question "Who am I?", answers might involve acceptance, denial, or rejection. Individuals in this stage may avoid information about lesbians and gays; inhibit homosexual behavior; and deny of homosexuality saying they were experimenting; it was an accident; or they were just drunk. Males may keep emotional involvement separate from sexual contact; females may have deep relationships that are nonsexual, though strongly emotional. To cope, the individual may explore internal positive and negative judgments; allow himself or herself to be uncertain regarding sexual identity; find support in knowing that sexual behavior occurs along a spectrum; and may receive permission and encouragement to explore sexual identity as a normal experience.

**Stage Two: Identity Comparison**    In this stage, the person accepts the possibility of being gay or lesbian and examines the wider implications of that tentative commitment. Self- or social-alienation may lead to isolation. The individual may begin to grieve for losses and the things she or he will give up by embracing his or her sexual orientation. She or he may compartmentalize her or his sexuality believing that it is only temporary, or maybe she or he is just in love with this particular woman or man. To cope, the individual will develop his or her own definitions; acquire information about sexual identity, lesbian and gay community resources; and talk about the loss of heterosexual life expectations.

**Stage Three: Identity Tolerance**    In the third stage, the person comes to the understanding that she or he is not the only one and acknowledges that he or she is likely gay or lesbian and seeks out other gay and lesbian people to combat feelings of isolation. To cope, the individual may talk and think about the issue dealing specifically with feelings of shame; recognize options; accentuate difference between himself or herself and heterosexuals; seek out lesbian and gay culture contacts; and may try out variety of stereotypical roles.

**Stage Four: Identity Acceptance**    During this stage, the individual accepts herself or himself and attaches a positive connotation to his or her gay or lesbian identity—accepting rather than tolerating it. There is continuing and increased contact with the gay and lesbian culture while the person struggles to deal with the inner tension of no longer subscribing to society's norm, attempt to bring congruence between the private and public view of self. To cope, the individual may compartmentalize his or her gay life; maintain less contact with heterosexuals; attempt to "fit in" within the gay community; and begin selective disclosures of sexual identity.

**Stage Five: Identity Pride**    In this stage, the individual is coming out of the closet. She or he may divide the world into heterosexuals and homosexuals, become immersed in gay and lesbian culture while minimizing contact with heterosexuals by possibly developing an us–them quality to political/social views. To cope, the individual may receive support for exploring anger issues; find support for exploring issues of heterosexism; and develop skills for coping with reactions and responses to disclosure of sexual identity.

**Stage Six: Identity Synthesis**    In the last stage, the individual integrates his or her sexual identity with all other aspects of the self, and his or her sexual orientation becomes only one aspect of the self rather than the focus of one's entire identity. Coping strategies might include fighting against heterosexism alongside allies which is liberating and may increase trust of dominant-culture others.

The Cass model has been criticized for not taking into account sociocultural factors that can affect identity development; not addressing the nature of the stigma and stigma management practices that have changed since the inception of the model; and not acknowledging that the linear nature of the model suggests that anyone who abandons the model or fails to go through each of the six stages would not be able to be considered a well-adjusted homosexual (Kaufman & Johnson, 2004). Contemporary models build on the Cass model and typically comprise the following five stages.

**Stage One: Self-Recognition as Gay**    More than just an awareness of attraction to members of the same sex, it involves confusion, some attempt at denial and repression of feelings, anxiety, trying to "pass," counseling, and often religious commitment to "overcome" sexuality. Eventually, acknowledgment and acceptance of one's sexual orientation develops. There may be some grief over "the fall from paradise" and feelings of loss of a traditional heterosexual life. Gay and lesbian people may be fairly closeted at this point. However, most seek out the information about being gay.

**Stage Two: Disclosure to Others**    Sharing one's sexual orientation with a close friend or family member is the first step in this stage. Rejection may cause a return to the Self-Recognition stage, but positive acceptance can lead to better feelings of self-esteem. Usually disclosure is a slow process.

Some gays and lesbians come out in "gentle" ways, admitting they are gay if asked but not volunteering it. Others do it in "loud" ways, proclaiming their sexuality to others to end the invisibility of being gay. As this stage progresses, a self-image of what it means to be gay develops, and the individual studies stereotypes and incorporates some information about gays while rejecting other information.

**Stage Three: Socialization with Other Gays**   Socializing with other gays and lesbians provides the experience that the person is not alone in the world, and there are other people like him or her. A positive sense of self, indeed pride, develops, and is strengthened by acceptance, validation, and support. Contact with positive gay or lesbian role models can play a big role in this stage.

**Stage Four: Positive Self-Identification**   This stage entails feeling good about oneself, seeking out positive relationships with other gays or lesbians, and feeling satisfied and fulfilled.

**Stage Five: Integration and Acceptance**   This stage entails an openness and non-defensiveness about one's sexual orientation. One may be quietly open, not announcing one's sexual orientation, but available for support to others. Couples live a comfortable life together and generally seek out other couples. Openness is often mitigated by age. Older men may be less open in their lives, and may see no need to change. Younger men may be more open, politically active, and visible in the gay community.

The decision and process of closeting reflects the experience of pressure to acculturate in dominant culture and/or anxiety tied to the projected discriminatory consequences of "coming out." Gay and lesbian people in the United States are shown through violence and other heterosexist acts that "coming out" as gay or lesbian may place them at great risk for disapproval and discrimination from family members and the larger society. President Clinton instituted the "Don't Ask, Don't Tell" policy in the U.S. military in 1993. While at face value one could argue that this was a step toward acceptance because it "permitted" gays and lesbians to serve in the military, others maintain that such a mandate further stigmatized gays and lesbians by forcing them to hide their sexual identities and therefore indicating that gay and lesbian lifestyles are unacceptable. In addition, the policy met with such stiff opposition from dominant culture that it eventually led to the discharge of thousands of men and women from the armed forces (Miller, 1995).

As is often true for members of other minority groups, gay and lesbian citizens have, out of necessity, become adept at passing as dominant-culture others—in this case as heterosexuals in order to survive and to be accepted. For some, the choice to "come out," while ultimately liberating, may involve significant fear forged with great effort and courage through careful planning, and that requires frequent and repeated explanations in defense of sexual identity—one of the most personal and private aspect of oneself—to others (often strangers). As such, "coming out" is clearly a conscious decision to become a target of oppression (Parker, 2001). For many, the path of least resistance is to play the role expected in dominant culture (that of a heterosexual) and struggle with the psychological and emotional consequences of not being true to oneself (see Personal Narrative 11-2).

While it is clear that many members of the LGBTQ community have made great strides to stand up and be counted, being known as openly gay or lesbian continues to lead to alienation and exclusion in the dominant culture in that openly LGBTQ individuals continue to face widespread institutional discrimination; are

## Personal Narrative 11-2

My name is Carly and I am a 27 year old biology teacher. I grew up in a small town in Northeastern KY. This small town possessed many small-minded beliefs and prejudices. Growing up I had many friends that is until I realized I looked at women more affectionately than my other female friends. In high school I was in my first lesbian relationship but I tried to remain in the closet. Once other students began to find out my secret, I started being picked on and I lost most of my friends. As a high school student this alone is a traumatic experience but to add to it an evolving sexual identity, it became disastrous. My relationship with my girlfriend progressed for nearly two years and we were ridiculed constantly, but that was not all. I lived with my father during this time and when he found out that I was gay not only did I get kicked out of the house in the middle of a February night but he also tried to "beat some sense into me." This resulted in an emergency protective order and a displaced relationship with my father. I remained in the closet throughout high school and up until my sophomore year in college. College was a whole new experience for me because there were many other gay students and because discrimination there was prohibited. I began to slowly come out to various friends at a time and then finally to my mother. My mother was raised with a strong religious background in which she was taught that homosexuality is wrong. It took my mother nearly seven years to finally accept me for who I was in relation to my sexual identity. After my mother passed away, I came out to all of my family finally trying to emerge from the never-ending "closet".

I decided to become a teacher for a variety of reasons including trying to open the minds of my students and end discrimination. So I began teaching at a high school with 1,500 students. Even though this school was much larger than the one that I went to there were many things that discriminated against LGBTQ students and families. During my interview with the school I was told there's several "gays" that go there and the faculty doesn't have to accept it but they can't show prejudice either. I had a feeling that I was off to a great start here, because even though that was a very homophobic way to word their policy, it was better than the high school I went to.

The first day of school, the first thing I told my students is I will not tolerate hate language at all including passive statements such as "that's so gay". I even had a student ask if they could say "that's so rainbow" instead, making reference to the symbol for gay pride. The students immediately assumed I was gay because I was the only teacher who enforced this rule. Nevertheless, I would catch them saying it and I would send them to the office or have them rephrase it to me. When the students rephrased it they would say I meant that's so stupid. My immediate question back was so are you saying that being gay is stupid? This brought the subject to attention a little more clearly and they quit saying it. I was happy that the students were getting it and that the staff had to be supportive.

Reality set in for me after that when some of the staff found out that I am a lesbian. I was instructed I was never to be alone with a female student, male students did not matter but a female student had to be accompanied by another student or a teacher. I was not rehired needless to say and I cannot get a good reference from them now. It is against the law for an employer to discriminate against a person for being gay but proving that that was the reason is an entire new story.

At prom and homecoming, gay students were not allowed to bring a date that was of the same sex, they could buy two separate tickets but not a couples ticket. This meant that these students had to pay more to enjoy the same activities as heterosexual students. During sexual education it was always enforced that a married couple had a baby, a man and his wife. I taught biology and even caught myself saying mommy and daddy when it came to explaining genetics. For my LGBTQ students this had to be hard. For one I messed up by making those comments, some of my students had lesbian and gay parents. Did I make them feel that their parent's relationship was not a valid one? Some students wanted to confide in me after they found out (I never told my students or the faculty) because they were trying to deal with the overwhelming emotions concerned with their sexual identity. They wanted to tell me how they could not bring their date, or how other kids were picking on them or were waiting to beat them up after school. These

### Personal Narrative 11-2   Continued

things they felt comfortable telling me because it made them feel safe, I was one of them. I however could not be alone with them so I had to tell them to go to the counselor, leaving them feeling abandoned by one of their own. Further, my LGBTQ students saw how the staff treated me and how I had a different set of rules than the other heterosexual teachers. Were they always going to be treated like that? Could they ever be themselves living or working without being segregated? I did try to make a difference by cutting down on the language associated with negativity towards homosexuals in

hopes that this small step would help prevent some levels of discrimination. All of these things can negatively influence a child's emotions and identity development. Children who are struggling with their sexual identity often think that it is wrong due to the reaction from parents, friends, churches, and schools. By trying to help by not denying my sexual orientation (although not directly admitting it) I may have actually done more damage because my students saw how some kids, staff and principals made fun of me and although I'm used to it, it had to be scary for them.

not represented in children's literature and academic curricula; and are often discounted by teachers and others. Many openly LGBTQ persons in the United States experience isolation and treatment as second-class citizens.

The discounting of an LGBTQ presence comes in many shapes and forms. Consider the impact of a constant barrage of seemingly benign questions posed to LGBTQ students from their earliest years in school: "Do you have a girlfriend yet?" "Who do you want to marry when you grow up?" "Who are you taking to the prom?" In addition, alternative family constellations continue to be largely ignored in schools. When students have families that include two mothers, two

### EXERCISE 11-1   Increasing Awareness

*Directions:* As noted in the text, members of the gay and lesbian community continue to be alienated and excluded from the dominant culture. Sometimes the process of exclusion and discrimination is apparent, while at other times it goes unrecognized. The goal of this exercise is to increase your awareness of the subtle ways perhaps you or those with whom you work may discount the value and presence of members of the gay and lesbian community.

Observe the various messages you see and hear that involve sexual orientation. Record your observations and share them with your classmates, colleagues, or teacher in small-group discussion. Consider the impact these incidents may have on a person who is gay or lesbian.

Examples of things to observe:

- Heterosexual privilege (for example, heterosexuals exhibiting public displays of affection in television commercials and TV shows, on billboards, in movies, and so on)
- Language (for example, the use of derogatory descriptions of gay and lesbian people)
- Assumptions made, such as the assumption that one is dating a member of the opposite sex (for example, when a male says to another that "he should bring her along" without knowing if the partner is male or female)
- Negative reactions (responses to same-sex individuals holding hands, hugging, and so on)

fathers, or any other variation, they experience marginalization and alienation in classrooms and schools that have yet to decide whether or not it is appropriate to be advocates for the equal treatment of LGBTQ families. These actions illustrate the exclusion and deeply embedded discrimination that LGBTQ citizens face in schools and in wider dominant culture.

## CULTURAL FACTOR 6: LANGUAGE DIFFERENCES, STRENGTHS, AND CHALLENGES

### Language as Weapon, Tool, and Liberation

Language brings both problems and empowerment to many marginalized groups. It is used to discriminate against members of the LGBTQ group. Terms like, *fag, queer, dyke,* and *butch* have been used to denigrate LGBTQ individuals. But, like the other oppressed peoples, gay and lesbian people have reclaimed terms that are used to discriminate against them, and have redefined slurs through double entendre with new meanings that serve to lift up rather than tear down members of this group. When gay and lesbian people call themselves "queer" or "dyke," they do it in such a way that not only helps take the sting out of the slurs they hear from dominant culture but also provides them with a tool for uniting through various forms of communication while celebrating their identities. It is important to note that such language use is considered appropriate only among members of the group and their trusted allies. When members of the group use these terms aimed at themselves, they understand the particular purpose and opposite meanings they represent. In this way, language that is used against them is both a weapon and a tool of liberation for members of this group.

In public high schools, 97 percent of students regularly hear homophobic remarks from their peers (Parker, 2001). The use of antigay slurs in U.S. schools is rampant, and each time an antigay slur is uttered, it is likely to be heard by a gay or lesbian student. It is, for the most part, commonplace and accepted by students and teachers alike for students to show disdain for some action by stating: "That's so gay." Yet, consider the reaction to a student who would state, "That's so Asian." Would such a remark be condoned if uttered in public? A student who makes such a statement would surely be labeled a racist. Why, then, are gay jokes and demeaning comments accepted in dominant culture?

Teachers are slow to intervene when derogatory comments about gay and lesbian students are made. In one study, 77 percent of prospective teachers stated that they would not encourage a class discussion on homosexuality (Parker, 2001). And among the reasons students use to explain why they do not stand up for gay and lesbian students when they hear slurs is "My friends will assume that I am gay if I do" (Parker, 2001).

Beyond being the recipients of hate crimes and hate language, members of the gay and lesbian community have, according to some, developed a distinct cultural language. Polari is a gay slang language, which has now almost died out. It was more common in the 1960s when gays had more need for a private slang to conceal their homosexuality in the face of the repressive society of the time. **Lavender**

## Intercultural Communication Strategies for Teachers 11-1

### Language That Helps

- Avoid heterosexist language. Avoid examples or language that reinforces peoples' assumptions that everyone is heterosexual. For example, rather than saying, "If a girl wants to bring her boyfriend to the dance ..." we can say, "If a girl brings her partner ..."
- Help students become aware of their own use of heterosexist/homophobic language in their comments in the classroom. This includes eliminating obviously derogatory use of words like "that's gay" or "fag" but also statements that presume the universality of heterosexuality (for example, "Any guy would like to date her!").
- Intercede when others are using hurtful, heterosexist remarks. Students are sometimes fearful of challenging these comments and need an adult model.
- Use respectful terminology when discussing LGBTQ issues. Your knowledge of appropriate terms conveys intercultural competence and helps you to be perceived as an ally.
- If you identify yourself as heterosexual when introducing yourself to your individuals or a class or if you discuss your family/lifestyle, refer to your significant other as your partner rather than as your wife, husband, or spouse. Such activism shares heterosexual privilege with gay and lesbian individuals who do not have the right to legally marry in most states and serves to signal to your students that you are aware of and have an appreciation for alternative family constellations.

**language** is a modern adaptation of Polari. Today's lavender language terminology is widely Americanized while Polari was based on languages such as Italian, French, Yiddish, and the slang of particular social groups such as sailors or fairground people. Some key Polari lexical items still in use today are *bona,* meaning "good" or "well," *ajax,* meaning "next to," *eek,* meaning "face," and *vada,* meaning "to look." Lionel Tiger, Darwin Professor of Anthropology at Rutgers University, explained that lavender language is a language comprised of distinct and independently developed linguistic constructions with distinct vocabulary that is specific to the LGBTQ community. Lavender language is not slang nor dialect but an actual language that, in fact, some gay and lesbian people struggle to master (Betsch, 2003).

In addition, after the Stonewall riots in the United States in 1969, gay male culture began to be publicly acknowledged for the first time. Some gay men formed *The Violet Quill* society, which focused on writing about gay experience as something central and normal in a story for the first time.

## COPING STRATEGIES FOR ADDRESSING OPPRESSION

While LGBTQ individuals may experience joy and empowerment upon "coming out," for others who may experience less acceptance and social support, the experience of embracing nonconformist sexual identities may be difficult. And if LGBTQ individuals ingest heterosexism and negative stereotyping perpetuated in dominant culture, they internalize hatred directed at themselves in ways that may lead to anxiety and depression (Sayce, 1995). Anxiety, depression, and suicide have been linked to the effects of prejudice and discrimination and internalized negative feelings associated with living as a gay or lesbian person in U.S. society (Health Education Authority, 1998).

While not the experience for all gay and lesbian citizens, more LGBTQ individuals attempt suicide, suffer from depression, and misuse substances than non-LGBTQ individuals (Bridget, 1994). Further statistics on the use of alcohol indicate that alcoholism affects the gay and lesbian community at a rate of 20–33 percent, which far exceeds the general population rate of 10 percent. The most often cited reason for drug and alcohol use in the gay and lesbian community is that it is a means for coping with depression and societal oppression (Herbert, Hunt, & Dell, 1994).

Coping strategies and styles for addressing oppression vary as much as the individuals who employ them. The following two narratives demonstrate a part of the spectrum of responses and varied coping styles exhibited by gay and lesbian persons as they address discrimination (see Personal Narratives 11-3 and 11-4).

## Personal Narrative 11-3    Paul

Sixth grade at Central: the Irish toughs led by Vinnie O'Connor, a bully's bully, huge hulking with a blood-lust sneer that made even Kite look like a choirboy. It happened in the basement corridor, just outside the boys' lavatory, where the sixth grade had its lockers. Vinnie and a group of three or four others had somebody pinned in a corner. Vinnie was snarling and shoving. "Yeah, you're a homo, ain't ya? Little fairy homo. Ain't that right?" Then he shot out a fist and slammed his victim's head against the wall. A bustle of students streamed past to their lockers, eyes front and pretending not to see.

But my locker was just a few feet away; I couldn't help but hear it all if I wanted to get my lunchbox. Besides, I was drawn to it now, as to a wreck on the freeway. "Homo, homo, homo," Vinnie kept repeating, accompanying each taunt with a savage rabbit punch. The victim pleaded, terrified but trying not to cry. It was Austin Singer, a meek, nervous kid who was always working too hard to make friends; the son of a math teacher at Phillips Academy. He vigorously denied the homo charge, choking it out between punches, which only made Vinnie angrier. He growled at two of his henchboys, who pinned poor Austin's face to the wall. Vinnie made a hawking sound and spit a glob of phlegm on the brick beside Austin's face. "Come on, homo— lick that off." Austin whimpered and tried to pull back. Vinnie brought up his knee into Austin's kidney, making him cry out. Where were the teachers? All old

maids, two floors away in the teachers' room, eating their own bird lunches. "Lick it, homo," Vinnie hissed. One of the brute lieutenants pushed Austin's face along the brick, scraping it raw. And now Austin, broken, surrendered whatever dignity was left. His tongue lolled out, and he licked up the phlegm while the bullies cheered. "Swallow it!" Vinnie commanded. From where I stood, by my locker, I saw a daze of horror, the self-disgust in Austin's face as he got it down without retching. Vinnie and his boys sprang away, shrieking with laughter. Instantly I busied myself with my lunchbox, terrified they would notice me. As they swaggered away, neither I nor anyone else made a move toward Austin—slumped in the corner as if it would have been easier to die than survive this thing. We all went hurrying away to eat our waxed-paper lunches. I never, never talked to Austin again. But, as I hastened to assure myself, we hadn't been friends anyway. The cold truth I took from the scene of Austin Singer's humiliation was this: At least I could still pass. I never gave a thought to the evil of what Vinnie had done, how sick with confused desire, the carnal thrill of degradation. The only reality lesson in it for me was not to be recognizably Other. At all costs I would discipline myself to appear as regular as Vinnie's boys, lest he suspect me and pin me to the wall.

*Source:* Monette, P. (1992). *Becoming a man: Half a life story.* New York: HarperCollins.

**Personal Narrative 11-4**   **Tales of a Suburban Columnist**

For a year, in Palo Alto, birthplace of Hewlett Packard and Silicon Valley, I had the rare opportunity to write for a straight audience as a lesbian. My vehicle was the *Palo Alto Weekly,* a free newspaper delivered to homeowners in five surrounding towns. When the paper actively solicited people of color to write a column, I proposed that they spice up the attempt to diversify and offered myself as a woman of "some color" who was willing to write from a lesbian perspective. It was a measure of the paper's liberal stance that they took me on.

My first column was entitled "Tales of a Media Slut," an account of my search for role models in the media as a young, biracial, lesbian immigrant. I was thrilled to have a voice in the community I had lived in since I was 10 years old. The local lesbian and gay population wrote me letters of praise, just for being visible, especially since the column included a photograph. Strangers stopped me on the street with friendly hellos. My co-workers were amused to be able to tell their friends they worked with the notorious town queer. My boss, who had participated in the civil rights movement of the 1960s, drew parallels in support of my activism. Homophobes wrote anonymous letters quoting the usual biblical passages and phoned the newspaper demanding that it stop publishing the opinions of a pervert. My parents had mixed feelings. Though I had been out to them for some years, they didn't know whether to be proud of me or apologetic when their friends mentioned having seen my column.

My second column, "Ten Good Reasons to Be a Lesbian," generated a handful of protest letters, mostly from men who were outraged that I had pointed out that lesbians didn't have to take care of men. The paper was delighted at the response. But when I addressed more serious issues of identity versus assimilation, I exceeded the paper's tolerance level. The editor asked me to cut out the personal details of "motorcycles vibrating between our legs" and stick to the issues the public would understand, like Clinton's waffling on gays in the military. When I continued to write about lesbian life rather than political issues, the paper terminated my column. Somehow it was permissible to have strong political opinions, but the line was drawn at descriptions of queer folk living their "radical" lives.

*Source:* Kovattana, A. (1995). Tables of a suburban columnist. In K. Jay (Ed.), *Dyke life: From growing up to growing old. A celebration of the lesbian experience* (p. 273) New York: Basic Books.

## POTENTIAL BARRIERS IN LEARNING–TEACHING RELATIONSHIPS WITH DOMINANT-CULTURE TEACHERS AND SCHOOLS

As noted throughout this chapter, LGBTQ students and their families may celebrate their identities and feel accepted in their homes, communities, and school environments. In that case, it is imperative that existing facilitative conditions in schools be broadened and enhanced to provide support for values and perspectives of LGBTQ individuals, including the recognition and inclusion of alternative family structures and participation in advocacy for the rights of LGBTQ students and families. LGBTQ students often feel invisible in their schools. Their invisibility, alienation, and isolation are typically reinforced by heterosexism that permeates the schools and larger society. The following statistics illustrate some of the reasons educators should be concerned about the experiences LGBTQ students encounter in schools:

- Students hear antigay epithets 25 times a day, and teachers fail to respond to these comments 97 percent of the time.
- More than 91 percent of LGBT students say they hear homophobic slurs or expressions frequently or often.

- Fifty-three percent of students report hearing homophobic comments made by school staff.
- Forty-five percent of gay males and twenty percent of lesbians report having experienced verbal harassment and/or physical violence as a result of their sexual orientation during high school.
- Gay and lesbian youth are two to three times more likely to commit suicide than other youths, and 30 percent of all completed youth suicides are related to the issue of sexual identity.
- LGBT are five times more likely to miss school because of feeling unsafe. Twenty-eight percent are forced to drop out.
- Twenty-six percent of gay and lesbian youth are forced to leave home because of conflicts with their families over their sexual identities. (Gay, Lesbian, and Straight Education Network, 2003; Uribe & Harbeck, 1992)

Many gay students go through the school day fearing violence and harassment from school staff and their peers. For these students, the stress and anxiety encountered inhibit their ability to learn.

As is true for adult members of the LGBTQ community, some gay and lesbian students try to pass as heterosexual dominant-culture others in schools so their sexual orientation will not be detected, and as a result, the energy required to create such a disguise hinders a focus on school work needed for effective learning. LGBTQ students, on the whole, also tend to have a more difficult journey through adolescence (a time when identity and sexuality are explored) than dominant-culture students because they may feel even more confined by the pressure to

## Intercultural Communication Strategies for Teachers 11-2

### Supporting Your Students

- Make no assumption about sexuality. If a student has not used a pronoun when discussing a relationship, do not assume one.
- Do not assume that all your students are straight. Such an assumption reinforces the invisibility that most gay and lesbian students already suffer.
- Identify yourself as a safe person to speak with. It helps to identify yourself as a safe person to talk with by using a safe-zone sticker, a rainbow ribbon/button, and so on.
- Confidentiality is important. Students need to believe that their privacy will be respected. They should not be encouraged to "come out." This is always an individual's own right to decide.
- Be a role model—exhibiting respect, concern, and advocacy for all students.

- Challenge homophobia and heterosexism among students and colleagues.
- Develop a list of referral resources for students and families needing information.
- Work for the development of antidiscrimination policies that include sexual orientation.
- Monitor your curricula and advocate for anti-heterosexist materials and texts.
- Do not simply include gay and lesbian issues into the curriculum as a token of your own liberal, culturally sensitive orientation. Instead, involve alternative family issues and examples and the perspectives/voices of members of this cultural group in your curricula in meaningful ways.
- Create safe and effective guidelines for classroom discussions of sexual orientation.

conform to societal roles and believe it is highly likely that they will be dismissed, despised, or deleted from school life if they do not meet society's expectations (Khayatt, 1994). Along with these factors potentially interfering with their personal and academic development, LGBTQ students' social and emotional needs and concerns often go unrecognized and unmet in schools.

Perhaps one of the biggest barriers to a LGBTQ student's learning and development of a facilitative relationship with a dominant-culture teacher is the teacher's potential lack of awareness and experience with diversity. Either through ignorance or denial, teachers are often unaware of the reality and experiences of gay and lesbian students within their classes. Further, once they are aware, they are often ill-prepared to respond in ways that create safe, facilitative learning environments.

Suggestions found within Intercultural Communication Strategies 11-2 are provided as ways to reduce heterosexism in schools and to help students feel safe and accepted in the classroom. Teachers are likely to ignore heterosexist comments, refrain from setting guidelines for respectful discussions, and ask questions that denote their beliefs that all of their students or their students' parents are heterosexual (for example, "When you get married, you'll probably" or "Ask your mom and dad for help with this assignment."). These types of student–teacher interactions leave a lasting impression that teachers believe the only correct sexual orientation is heterosexual. Whether intentional or not, this is a form of oppression and exclusion that serves to alienate gay and lesbian students from their teachers, their classes, and their schools. When no one speaks up when teachers make such seemingly harmless remarks, gay and lesbian students may believe everybody in the room shares the same heterosexist viewpoints. These gay and lesbian students often feel isolated and sometimes paralyzed by fear of what might happen if anyone in the room knew that they are gay or lesbian.

## FROM CONCEPTS TO LIVED EXPERIENCE

In this narrative, Deborah Perkins describes her resolve when confronting heterosexism during the process of *coming out* to her mother.

### WHAT I SHOULD HAVE SAID

"I'm gay. I'm sorry. Please don't hate me." "I think you're very sick," Mom replied. Then she turned and walked away. I sat there on her mountain of rejection, calling out, "I'm still your daughter and I love you," and hearing only the echo of my own voice. My heart broke like a pane of glass. If only I could do it over again, I wouldn't search day after day, trying to find just the right words to ward off her anger and quell her disgust.

"You don't know," I would tell her, "how it feels to discover you're not who you think you are. You don't know what it's like to learn at the age of 32 that you've fallen in love with a woman, and nothing in your fundamentalist, heterosexual background has prepared you for that. You don't know how it feels to realize after all those years that you're a lesbian."

"You don't know what it's like to sit in a classroom or an office with people who are supposed to be your friends and listen to their sneering comments about 'dykes and faggots.' You don't know what it's like not daring to speak the truth about yourself. You don't know what it's like to have to learn how to be and how to hide."

"You don't know the fear of being backed into a corner by a man bigger and stronger than you, who is trying to convince you that he can turn you back into a 'real' woman."

"You don't know what it's like to be judged for who you love instead of for who you are. You can't imagine the never-ending ache of wanting to tell your parents the one thing you know will hurt them most of all. And you can't begin to know the depth of that pain when you see the disappointment in their eyes."

If I could go back and do it again, I wouldn't try to find the words that are the easiest to say and the easiest to hear. This time, I would just tell the truth. (quoted in Jay, 1995, p. 45)

## SUMMARY

**Cultural Factor 1: Historical and Current Treatment in the United States** Gay and lesbian individuals have a largely invisible history. Most of what we know about gay and lesbian people historically comes from legal actions that were leveled against LGBTQ individuals. Urban gay subculture existed in the United States as early as the 1920s and 1930s. Five U.S. states recognize marriage equality. However, 30 states have passed constitutional amendments or laws explicitly banning same-sex marriage. There are currently 13 states, as well as the District of Columbia, that have enacted policies to protect against gender identity and sexual orientation discrimination in employment. Seven states have laws that prohibit employment discrimination solely based on sexual orientation. However, in 30 states, LGBT citizens can be fired on the basis of their sexual orientation and/or gender identity without any legal recourse. Discrimination at both the macro level (for example, health insurance and partner-benefit laws) as well as at the micro level (involving daily personal interactions) is equally damaging.

**Cultural Factor 2: Initial Terms of Incorporation into U.S. Society** The dichotomous portrayal of sexual identity was introduced over 40 years ago, by Kinsey's (1948) *Sexual Behavior in the Human Male,* which revealed to the U.S. public that homosexuality was far more widespread than previously believed. Prior to the widespread stigma associated with having an "alternative" lifestyle or sexual identity, the definition for homo- versus heterosexuality was not significant.

**Cultural Factors 3 and 4: Shared Values, Traditions, and Spirituality** Taking into account the wide-ranging variation among members in this cultural group, it is fair to say that perhaps the most noticeable common values and traditions of this group have been created in response to the discrimination that members of this group face and the need for solidarity and unity. During the 19th and early 20th centuries, gay culture was highly covert and relied upon secret symbols and codes woven into an overall heterosexual context. Gay influence initially was limited, for the most part, to high culture. Association of gay men with opera, couture, fine cuisine, musical theater, and interior design began with wealthy homosexual men using the straight themes of these media to send their own signals. Lesbian culture includes elements both from the larger LGBTQ culture and elements that are more closely specific to the lesbian community. The history of lesbian culture over the last half-century has also been tightly entwined with the evolution of *feminism*. Bisexual culture has evolved around a common cause emphasizing opposition to *monosexism* (discrimination against bisexual and pansexual people) and *biphobia* (hatred and/or distrust of bisexual people). The study of transgender culture is complicated by the many and various approaches to living as a transgender individual. Advocacy, liberalism, sexual freedom, gender diversity, and human rights are principles that tend to be valued among members of this group.

**Cultural Factor 5: Acculturation and Experience with Exclusion and Alienation** Identifying oneself as an LGBTQ individual and disclosing this to other people is often referred to as *coming out*. Coming out may be a positive or negative experience depending on the level of acceptance and supports present. Many LGBTQ individuals fear negative reactions, rejection, and damaging friends and family relationships. The Cass Identity Model (1979) is one of the foundational theories of gay and lesbian identity development. The decision to be closeted (hiding one's gay or lesbian identity) is a product of the pressures of acculturation. Gay and lesbian people in the United States know that "coming out" places them at great risk for disapproval and discrimination from family and the larger society, and as such have become adept at "passing." Members of the gay and lesbian community continue to be alienated and excluded from the dominant culture. Issues regarding unique health and psychological needs, legal rights, and social support networks remain unaddressed.

**Cultural Factor 6: Language Differences, Strengths, and Challenges** Beyond being the recipients of hate language, members of the gay community have, at least according to some, developed their own language. *Lavender language* is described as a form of lesbian/gay discourse that is comprised of distinct and independently developed linguistic constructions.

**Coping Strategies for Addressing Oppression** Coping both with the discrimination and oppression of the dominant culture, as well as with internalized homophobia, can be highly detrimental to LGBTQ individuals' mental health. There appears to be no single or universal pattern of coping that members of the gay and lesbian community have employed as they address the oppressive power of the dominant culture. Coping strategies and coping styles vary, as do the individuals employing them.

**Potential Barriers in Learning–Teaching Relationships with Dominant-Culture Teachers and Schools** Many gay and lesbian students go through their school day fearing violence and harassment from their peers, and this constant anxiety inhibits their ability to learn. Either through ignorance or denial, teachers are often unaware of the reality and existence of gay and lesbian students within their classes. Further, once they are aware, they are often ill-prepared to respond in ways that create a safe, facilitative learning environment.

## Questions for Review

1. To what does the Q in LGBTQ refer and why it is included in the acronym.

2. What does the process of "coming out" involve?

3. What experiences that LGBTQ students commonly confront in schools negatively affect their development and achievement?

## Important Terms

| | | | |
|---|---|---|---|
| closeted | heterosexuality | lavender language | transgendered |
| coming out | homosexuality | LGBTQ | individuals |
| hate crimes | intentional families | questioning | transsexuals |
| heterosexism | intersexed individuals | sexual orientation | |

## Enrichment

Badgett, M. V. (1999). Assigning care: Gender norms and economic outcomes. *International Labour Review*, 138(3), 311.

Blackburn, M. V. (2005). *Sexual identities and schooling*. New York: Lawrence Erlbaum Associates.

Due, L. (1995). *Joining the tribe: Growing up gay & lesbian in the 90s*. New York: Doubleday.

Epstein, D., & Johnson, R. (1998). *Schooling sexualities*. Buckingham, UK: Open University.

Foucault, M. (1978). *History of sexuality, Vol. I: An introduction*. New York: Pantheon.

Fradenburg, L., & Freccero, C. (1996). *Premodern sexualities*. New York: Routledge.

Gay, Lesbian, and Straight Education Network. (2003). *The 2003 national school climate survey: The school related experiences of our nation's lesbian, gay, bisexual and transgender youth*. New York: Author.

Jay, K. (Ed.). (1995). *Dyke life: From growing up to growing old. A celebration of the lesbian experience*. New York: Basic Books.

Katz, J. N. (1995). *The invention of heterosexuality*. New York: Dutton.

Kinsey, Alfred C. et al. (1948/1998). *Sexual Behavior in the Human Male*. Philadelphia: W. B. Saunders; Bloomington: Indiana U. Press. [First publication of Kinsey's Heterosexual-Homosexual Rating Scale. Discusses Kinsey Scale, pp. 636–659.]

Kumashiro, K. (2001). *Troubling intersections of race and sexuality: Queer students of color and anti-oppression education*. Lanham, MD: Rowman & Littlefield.

Marcus, E. (2002). *Making gay history: The half-century fight for lesbian and gay equal rights*. New York: Perennial.

Monette, P. (1992). *Becoming a man: Haifa life story*. New York: HarperCollins.

Roscoe, W. (1988). *Living the spirit: A gay American Indian anthology*. New York: St. Martin's.

Savin-Williams, R. (1998). *And then I became gay: Young men's stories*. New York: Routledge.

Sonnie, A. (2000). *Revolutionary voices: A multicultural queer youth anthology*. Los Angeles: Alyson.

## Connections on the Web

http://www.glsen.org/

The Gay, Lesbian, and Straight Education Network (GLSEN) is a national organization that brings together teachers, parents, students, and concerned citizens to work together to end homophobia in U.S. schools.

http://www.iglhrc.org/cgi-bin/iowa/home/index.html

This website features information and resources geared to protect and advance the human rights of all people and communities subject to discrimination or abuse on the basis of sexual orientation, gender identity, or HIV status.

http://www.safeschoolscoalition.org/safe.html

This site provides information and resources for the purpose of addressing school climate issues and promoting safe schools for all students.

# References

Adkinson, D. R., & Hackett, G. (1995). *Counseling diverse populations*. Madison, WI: Brown & Benchmark.

Berkman, C. S., & Zimberg, G. (1997). Homophobia and heterosexism in social workers. *Social Work*, 42, 319–332.

Berg, N., & Lien, D. (2002). Measuring the effect of sexual orientation on income: Evidence of discrimination? *Contemporary Economic Policy*, 20(4), 394–414.

Betsch, M. L. (2003). *University conference focuses on "gay language."* Retrieved from http://www.conservativenews.org/ViewCulture.asp?Page=/Culture/archive/200302/CUL20030206c.html.

Brewer, P. R. (2003). The shifty foundation of public opinion and gay rights. *The Journal of Politics*, 65(4), 1208–1220.

Bridget, J. (1994). *Treatment of lesbians with alcohol problems in alcohol services in Northwest England*. Lesbian Information Service.

Bullough, V. L. (1976). *Sexual variance in society and history*. New York: Wiley & Sons.

Bullough, V. L. (1979). *Homosexuality: A history*. New York: New American Library.

Button, J. W, Rienzo, B. A., & Wald, K. D. (2000). The politics of gay rights at the state and local level. In G. A. Rimmerman, K. D. Wald, & C.Wilcox (Eds.), *The politics of gay rights* (pp. 347–376). Chicago: University of Chicago.

Cass, V. C. (1979), Homosexual identity formation: A theoretical model, *Journal of Homosexuality*, 4(3).

Haeberle, S. H. (1999). Gay and lesbian rights: Emerging trends in public opinion and voting behavior. In E. D. B. Riggle & B. L. Tadlock (Eds.), *Gays and lesbians in the democratic process* (pp. 146–169). New York: Columbia University.

Haider-Markel, D. P. (2000). Lesbian and gay politics in the states: Interest groups, electoral politics, and policy. In G. A. Rimmerman, K. D. Wald, & C. Wilcox (Eds.), *The politics*

of gay rights* (pp. 347–376). Chicago: University of Chicago.

Health Education Authority. (1998). *Sexual identity*. World Mental Health Day.

Herbert, J. T., Hunt, B., & Dell, G. (1994). Counseling gay men and lesbians with alcohol problems. *Journal of Rehabilitation*, 60(2), 52–57.

Herek, G. M. (1994). Assessing heterosexuals' attitudes toward lesbians and gay men: A review of empirical research with the ATLG scale. In B. Greene & G. M. Herek (Eds.), *Lesbian and gay psychology: Theory, research, and clinical applications. Psychological perspectives on lesbian and gay issues* (Vol. 1, pp. 206–228). Thousand Oaks, CA: Sage.

Hubbard, R. (1997). The social construction of sexuality. In P. S. Rothenberg (Ed.), *Race, class, and gender in the United States: An integrated study* (4th ed., pp. 52–55). New York: St. Martin's.

Jay, K. (Ed.). (1995). *Dyke life: From growing up to growing old. A celebration of the lesbian experience*. New York: Basic Books.

Jones, M. A. (2008). A few statistics on LGBT issues. Employment NonDiscrimination Act, HIV/AIDS, Marriage Equality. Retrieved from http://gayrights.change.org/blog/view/a_few_statistics_on_lgbt_issues.

Kaufman J. & Johnson, C. (2004). Stigmatized individuals and the process of identity. *The Sociological Quarterly*, 45(4), 807–833.

Khayatt, D. (1994). Surviving school as a lesbian. *Gender and Education*, 6(1), 47–61.

Kinsey, A. C, Pomeroy, W. B., Martin, C. E., & Gebhard, P. H. (1953). *Sexual behavior in the human female*. Philadelphia: Saunders.

Kite, M. E., & Whitley, B. E, Jr. (1996). Sex differences in attitudes toward homosexual persons, behaviors, and civil rights: A meta-analysis. *Personality and Social Psychology Bulletin*, 22, 336–353.

Klein, F., Sepekoff, B., & Wolf, T. J. (1986). Sexual orientation: A multivariate dynamic process. *Journal of Homosexuality*, 11, 35–49.

Kovattana, A. (1995). Tables of a suburban columnist. In K. Jay (Ed.), *Dyke life: From growing up to growing old. A celebration of the lesbian experience* (p. 273). New York: Basic Books.

Leap, W. (Ed.). (1995). *Beyond the lavender lexicon: Authenticity, imagination, and appropriation in lesbian and gay languages.* Luxembourg: Gordon & Breach.

Miller, N. (1995). *Out of the past: Gay and lesbian history from 1869 to the present.* New York: Vintage.

Monette, P. (1992). *Becoming a man: Haifa life story.* New York: HarperCollins.

Parker, J. (2001). Language: A pernicious and powerful tool. *English Journal*, 74–78.

*The Reader's companion to American history* [Electronic version]. (1991). New York: Houghton Mifflin. Retrieved from http://pnnt.infoplease.com/ipa/A0194028.html.

Sayce, L. (1995). *Breaking the link between homosexuality and mental illness: An unfinished history.* MIND Discussion Document.

Segal-Sklar, S. (1995). Lesbian parenting: Radical or retrograde? In K.Jay (Ed.), *Dyke life: From growing up to growing old, a celebration of the lesbian experience* (pp. 174–175). New York: Basic Books.

Steffens, M. C., & Wagner, C. (2004). Attitudes toward lesbians, gay men, bisexual women, and bisexual men in Germany. *Journal of Sex Research*, 41(2), 137–149.

Uribe, V., & Harbeck, K. M. (1992). Project 10 addresses needs of gay and lesbian youth. *Education Digest*, 58(2), 50–54.

Wilcox, C., & Norrander, B. (2002). Of moods and morals: The dynamics of opinions on abortion and gay rights. In B. Norrander & C. Wilcox (Eds.), *Understanding public opinion* (2nd ed., pp. 121–148). Washington, DC: Congressional Quarterly.

*Using a wheelchair provides a visual identification of what appears to be the main problem a person has in being unable to ambulate or walk. But while being in a wheelchair may identify one of the problems, there are usually many other problems that coexist for the individual and there will be many problems that will be faced in the future because the human body was not made to sit or lay for many hours of the day. The human body was made to walk, run, jump, and play in this world that we live in.*

*It was for that reason that I was taken aback at many of the statements that were made to me by "educated people" on this campus (two of which were my academic advisers). The very first and I think the most mean spirited was, "If you lose weight you could get up and walk again, right?" The same person told me later that my physical health would prevent me from finishing the Masters degree to which I was aspiring. I requested that this issue be clarified in writing and presented to me. Check out the American Disabilities Act. Remarkably my grades began to drop.*

*Source:* **Kai, The Wheelchair Lady.**

CHAPTER

# Learning from the Stories of People with Disabilities

Disability affects us all. At some point, every human being will experience either physical or mental disabilities or both. This chapter explores stories of persons with disabilities, a history of oppression, strengths, resiliency. In this chapter, you will encounter the voices of people with disabilities. Kai's story reminds us that viewing the world from different perspectives and hearing the voices of those whose voices are often silenced, stifled, or misunderstood can make a huge difference in the lives of individuals and creating welcoming equitable environments.

I wish that I could say that being mobility challenged was the only handicap that I am faced with in this part of my life, but, it is not. I am one of the lucky ones in that I use an electric wheelchair. There are others on campus that use hand propelled wheelchairs and still others that count every step to and from class.

This campus is not built for people who are handicapped. There are electronic door openers that were placed on the slope of the on–off ramp which are difficult at best for people who would be using canes, walkers, or wheelchairs (one of the first things to disappear is the sense of balance when using any form of assistance to ambulate). There are other electronic door openers that sit out in the elements. Think about this, the expectation is to reach out and touch a steel button attached to electric cables while the rain is running down the arm to the button. There are buttons that only work when an inside person is rung up and then they yell back, "OK, IT'S OPEN NOW." There are many book racks in the library that are not accessible to a person in a wheelchair. I was told once that I was just "S-O-L," after asking for a book that was on a floor accessible only by steps. My comment back was, "Well, I think you picked the wrong person, on the wrong day, at the wrong time to make that remark to; now get up and go get my book."

There are many more things on campus that are not in compliance. Computer labs are designed in such a manner that a wheelchair cannot possibly get up to a table. Swimming pools are designed so that a mobility challenged person cannot use the dressing rooms, or get in or out of the pool (the lift is designed for a person who is 6' and 110 pounds). I have to jump to get on the seat that is as wide as a balancing beam (I am not). As I was trying to get on the lift, unknowingly, there was bleach put in the water and it ate a hole through my swim suit, sweats, and towel. The jarring from jumping and actually making it on to the seat ended up really hurting my back as well. Restrooms on this campus are a joke. There may be one in the entire building that is designed for a wheelchair.

Many of the problems on this campus could be fixed easily, just ask a person in a wheelchair what they need. Listen to them when they make a complaint and then ask, "What would be a positive outcome?"—A novel idea, a positive outcome. Extend an awning to cover the button in the rain. Let the mobility-challenged ride the bus. Place electronic book shelves in the basement of the library (like the ones used in medical record filing). Turn the tone down on loud speakers. Just ask a handicapped person and listen.

In the winter, a snow storm (electric wheelchairs are not supposed to be out in the wet weather; it says so in the instruction manual) hit. I had gotten tired of trying to traverse the campus and having the wheelchair stall on me. I began a one person pro-test march. Figuring, that if I had to be out in the snow that I might as well put the time to good use (until I froze to death and I was bronzed to make a rather large piece of yard art). I carried signs. The one in front said that I was not allowed to ride the campus bus, between the buildings, in the bad weather. The sign on my back was where many people signed in support of my plight. It really was not JUST my plight. I was eventually sent to the multicultural advisor. I do not remember how I got there. I do remember that the Office of Disability wanted me to sign consent forms so that they could tromp through my medical records for whatever they wanted. I refused to do it. HIPPA is a small insignificant federal law that says I did not have to do that. If the school needed any documentation of my physical needs all they needed to do was to ask me and it would be provided. It was not good enough for them (understand this—if you are not registered with the Office of Disability on campus, the school is under no obligation to make accommodations for you, physically or otherwise). It saves them a lot of money right? The person who headed the Office of Multicultural Affairs listened and then offered the comment, "Well, my doctor told me to walk and that would help with the pain. You do walk right?" I sat there stupefied. They had missed the part where I talked about the damage done to both of my knees (my right ankle beyond repair,) how the repair was to be done, and then how the damage to my spine negated any thought of fixing my knees. People hear what they want to hear.

The second advisor flatly told me that I would never make a good counselor and that I needed to go be tested to see what my aptitude was good for. This conversation would have been better discussed in private. However, the issues were discussed in front of my peers (who happened to be decades younger than I). It was evident that this person knew nothing about who I was as a walking person. When I told them that I have been doing counseling, case management, crowd control, staffing, in-servicing, and admission assessment for many years because I was the registered nurse supervisor of a psychiatric hospital; this person was astonished and said, "You were a registered nurse?"

I have even had an instructor take information out of context, and embellish it with "hunches" and then repeat it to my academic advisor. This was totally unprofessional. There was no need to do what was done as I would have clarified anything necessary. There was no dignity or respect offer in these scenarios.

Several times I have been met with statements and actions (chased through the student life building and admonished for a possible infringement of a campus policy, at no time was I addressed by name or requested to personally come and talk about the issue. Instead, I was threatened with academic sanctions). It was not until the threats were put in writing and delivered by letter, that I was ever addressed by name—no dignity and respect there either.

Even now I am listed as a "non-traditional student." That term means any student that does not come to college straight from high school, is married, or has children. If that is not discriminatory I do not know what is.

I wish I could say that is the wheelchair that poses the only discrimination that I face, but, it is not. I am an old, fat (and I use the term because most everyone uses that term when talking about large women, unless the large woman has money) woman in a wheelchair. There are many people who feel that teaching the older students is about as useless as teaching a dead cat. Being a fat woman to many means that I should hide myself indoors in shame because of what I have become. Being in a wheelchair is just plain fun right? RIGHT?

Oh yes, there is a little matter of being out in an electrical storm; think, two batteries and a solid steel frame: Lightning Rod!!

A closer look at the shared experiences, distinct challenges, and strengths found among members of this group will increase your ability to make your classroom an effective learning community in which students with disabilities achieve.

## CHAPTER OBJECTIVES

After reading this chapter you will be able to:

1. Define disability, impairment, handicap, exceptionality, and giftedness;
2. Describe cultural perspectives and values shared by persons with disabilities;
3. Discuss significant socio-political changes which have occurred in the process of incorporating persons with disabilities in dominant culture;
4. Identify ways in which the people profiled in the personal narratives in this chapter experienced and addressed the six cultural factors explored in this text;
5. Explain academic and intercultural interaction implications related to the six cultural factors for members in this group;
6. Describe coping strategies commonly utilized by members of this group; and

7.  Identify classroom strategies for cultivating resources provided when the needs and strengths of students with disabilities are integrated in your curricula.

# DEFINITIONS

## Exceptionality

**Exceptionalities** are created by differences among students. Exceptional students are defined as students who require supplemental services to effectively facilitate their academic development. Students with disabilities and gifted students are two groups of exceptional students.

## Disability

A **disability** is an observable, measurable characteristic of an individual that interferes with the individual's functioning. The Education for All Handicapped Act of 1975 identified disabilities as involving mental retardation or hearing, visual, speech, learning, emotional, orthopedic, or other health impairment including:

| | |
|---|---|
| Autism | Deaf–blindness |
| Deafness | Emotional disturbance |
| Hearing impairment | Mental retardation |
| Multiple disabilities | Orthopedic impairment |
| Other health impairment | Special learning disability |
| Speech or language impairment | Traumatic brain injury |
| Visual impairment | |

> "If a student is identified as having one of these conditions (or a condition that is subsumed under one of these categories—such as attention deficit hyperactivity disorder), s/he is a student with a disability" (Smith, 2004. p. 8).

The Education for All Handicapped Act of 1975 defined disabilities as involving mental retardation or hearing, visual, speech, learning, emotional, orthopedic, or other health impairment (Fagan & Wallace, 1979). Amendments to this act in 2004 expanded the list of recognized **impairments** to include students who have physical or mental impairments that substantially limit one or more major life activities, students who have a record of impairment, and/or students who are regarded as having impairment(s). Physical or mental impairments were defined as any physiological disorder or condition, cosmetic disfigurement, or anatomical loss affecting one or more of the following body systems: neurological; musculoskeletal; special sense organs; respiratory, including speech organs; cardiovascular; reproductive; digestive; genitor-urinary; hemic and lymphatic; skin; and endocrine; or any psychological disorder, such as mental retardation, organic brain syndrome, emotional or mental illness, and specific **learning disabilities**.

Nevertheless, defining *disability* continues to be a matter of social debate and construction as it is contrasted with *impairment and handicap*. *Disability* has been defined as a functional limitation within the individual caused by physical, mental, or sensory impairment. Recently, *disability* has come to refer to a restriction or lack of ability to perform an activity in the manner or within the range considered "normal" for humans, while *impairment* is defined as the loss or abnormality of psychological, physiological, or anatomical structure or function. **Handicaps**, on the other hand, involve the loss or limitation of opportunities to take part in the "normal" life of the community on an equal level with others due to physical or social barriers. Handicaps may be considered barriers, demands, and environmental pressures placed on people by various aspects of their environments, including other people.

The medical model of disability focuses on individuals' functional limitations (impairments) and identifies impairments as the cause of disadvantages experienced by **persons with disabilities**. The social model, in contrast, shifts the focus from impairment to disability. In this case, *disability* refers to the disabling social, environmental, and attitudinal barriers rather than on individuals' "lack of ability." Thus, the only way to rectify conditions using the medical model is through treatments and cures, while social change and the removal of disabling barriers are solutions for those who support the social model.

## Giftedness

There was a time when gifted students were included with students with disabilities as a group of students who required special education services. At that time, the category that included both groups of students was called "Students with Exceptionalities." With the passage of the No Child Left Behind Act of 2001, Congress reauthorized the Elementary and Secondary Education Act (ESEA)—a principal federal law that affects school-aged children. No Child Left Behind was created to increase accountability, flexibility, and federal support for education. Rather than including gifted students as students with exceptionalities, this legislation currently defines gifted students as students who provide evidence of high achievement capability in artistic, intellectual, creative, or leadership capacities, or in specific academic fields who require services or activities not ordinarily provided by the school in order to fully develop their capabilities. If this definition sounds to you like it might include all students, you are not alone in your thinking.

Most researchers in the field today believe that **giftedness** is multidimensional, with high aptitude being only one factor (Renzulli & Reis, 1997). These researchers have identified multiple intelligences within individuals that help us to recognize talents present in all students (Gardner, 1993). So, how are gifted students identified and then singled out for special services? Grades and test scores should not be the only identifiers of gifted students. When schools limit their identification efforts to test scores and grades, they contribute to one of the most pernicious problems that schools face: the under-representation of minority students in gifted programs (National Center for Education Statistics, 1994; Brown, 1997). To effectively identify gifted students, schools should use multiple sources of data that include a variety of other forms of assessment to provide more accurate demonstrations of students' strengths and abilities, such as teacher observations, interviews with students, information from parents, and portfolios of student work (Hunsaker, Finley, & Frank, 1997). It is also important for teachers to realize that gifted students may not fit common stereotypes of high-ability students. For example creativity (a form of intelligence that is characterized by divergent thinking and the production of original ideas) and task commitment may also be significant aspects of giftedness. These definitions of giftedness are clearly more inclusive than previous ones. In fact, gifted students may have disabilities that accompany their talents as well as exhibit high ability in some academic areas but not in others (Nielsen, Higgins, & Hammond, 1993).

Common myths about gifted students include beliefs that these students do not need help, have fewer problems than other students due to their intellect, are self-directed, have the same social and emotional development experiences of other same-age students, are social isolates, have families who prize their abilities, and are naturally creative. Gifted students share some common characteristics, including performing at high academic levels, thinking abstractly and connecting ideas easily, demonstrating effective problem-solving skills, persevering in academic pursuits, tending to equate achievement with self-worth, struggling with heightened sensitivity with regard to their performance, and experiencing academic problems that result from curricula that do not meet their needs (Freeman, 1994; Roberts & Lovett, 1994). While these are some common qualities, gifted students are members of a highly diverse group. Teachers must develop methods for continually assessing all students in attempting to identify their strengths rather than weaknesses. It is imperative that teachers advocate for and provide opportunities that meet the needs of their students. Most schools employ an **enrichment** (the addition of topics and skill development activities to traditional curricula) and/or an **acceleration** (moving students through curricula or years of schooling in a shortened time period) approach to address the needs of gifted students. Tracking ("ability" grouping) is another popular approach in which schools offer advanced placement and honors courses to address the needs of gifted students (Kulick & Kulick, 1997). However, such strategies are highly criticized because research consistently confirms evidence that gifted students perform equally well in heterogeneous learning groups while so-called average students are disadvantaged by such practices (McDaniel, 1993; Oakes & Lipton, 1990; Sapon-Shevin, 1996). Teachers must take responsibility for creating environments in which students at all levels achieve. To accomplish this goal, they must become expert and collaborative curriculum designers who know all of their students well; value and build on students' strengths; and provide strategies, tools, and opportunities that will enhance all students' academic development, while simultaneously monitoring the effectiveness of their methods.

## CULTURAL FACTOR 1: HISTORICAL AND CURRENT TREATMENT IN THE UNITED STATES

From the earliest written records, there is evidence that people with disabilities existed and were an important part of society. For example, Aesop, the blind Greek poet, was so successful that his morality lessons are still revered today. While some persons with disabilities were treated humanely, others served as court jesters in palaces and courts of the Middle Ages. People with disabilities have been treated inconsistently throughout history but typically they were victims of discrimination and cruelty (Smith, 2004). Kai's personal narrative, that opens this chapter, illustrates the disregard, discrimination, and depersonalization that many persons with disabilities have and continue to experience.

## Historical Background

Hohenshil and Humes (1979) explained that throughout history, persons with disabilities have been ignored, exiled, exploited, tortured, and even destroyed. Nomadic societies saw persons with disabilities as problems—actual barriers to the group's productivity because people with disabilities were viewed as being unable to contribute to their communities. During the agricultural era, persons with disabilities received some acceptance in mainstream society. However, physical differences were seen as deformities which were often explained as resulting from evil or sin dwelling in the individual or individual's family. As Western Civilization progressed and Christianity spread, persons with disabilities continued to be seen as unproductive in terms of what was believed they could contribute to their society. Adults and children with disabilities were commonly placed in institutions and mental asylums whether or not their individual differences and needs could be positively affected by such treatment. In effect, they were "warehoused"—kept out of the way and out of the sight of dominant culture—their needs largely disregarded and unmet. Persons with disabilities were seen as people deserving of pity and charity. Later, persons with disabilities were labeled *handicapped*—a term that implies dependence—as they continued to be seen as needy and deficient.

During the 1960s, rehabilitative counseling was developed to try to help persons with disabilities adapt and "fit" into society. This often meant that persons with disabilities had to find a way to meet the demands of the environments they were seeking to enter rather than changing the environments to incorporate them and their differences. Liz's story echoes Kai's experiences that appeared at the beginning of this chapter in illustrating the effects of assimilation in structures that prohibit functioning and accessibility.

> It wasn't my body that was responsible for all my difficulties, it was external factors, the barriers constructed by the society in which I live. I was being disabled—my capabilities and opportunities were being restricted—by prejudice, discrimination, inaccessible environments and inadequate support. Even more important, if all the problems had been created by society, then surely society could un-create them.... As individuals, most of us simply cannot pretend with any conviction that our impairments are irrelevant because they influence so much of our lives. External barriers create social and economic disadvantage and our subjective experience of our bodies is also an integral part of our everyday reality.
>
> Liz Crow (1996)
>
> "Including All of Our Lives: Renewing the Social Model of Disability."

Kai's narrative provides insights into the ways by which societal environments continue to fail persons with disabilities while blaming them for not "fitting in" and conquering the demands of their environments on their own. Civil rights actions have helped pave the way for the assimilation of persons with disabilities. Yet, currently access and equality battles continue to be fought by members of this group.

## Current Conditions

The 2000 Census identified more than 33 million adult persons with disabilities living in the United States. 18.5 million of these individuals reported being employed.

Both persons with disabilities who were working and those not working stated a need for similar types of accommodations. One-third of nonworking persons with disabilities reported the need for some type of accommodations. The other two-thirds could work without accommodations or were unaware of specific accommodations that might make work possible. The most common accommodations cited were the need for:

- Accessible parking or accessible public transit stop nearby—19 percent
- An elevator—17 percent
- Adaptations to work stations—15 percent
- Special work arrangements (reduction in work hours, reduced or part-time hours, job redesign)—12 percent
- Handrails or ramp—10.4 percent
- A job coach—5.6 percent
- Specific office supplies—4.5 percent
- A personal assistant—4.0 percent
- Braille, enlarged print, special lighting, or audiotape—2.5 percent
- Voice synthesizer, teletypewriter (TTY), Infrared System, or other technical device—1.8 percent
- Reader, Oral or Sign Language Interpreter—1.8 percent

Even if the definition of disability was restricted to those having health problems or disabilities which prevent persons from working or which limit the kind or amount of work one can do, there are an estimated 16 percent civilian adult men and women in the United States categorized as disabled with regard to work limitations. This would amount to about 1 in 13 civilian citizens (Houtenville, 2005). And, even with advances in medicine, education, and laws attempting to remove barriers that exclude individuals with disabilities, these individuals continue to encounter discrimination ranging from outright intentional exclusion and access to substandard services, programs, activities, benefits, jobs, or other opportunities. Read Paul Orfalea's story to identify the ways by which he was able to turn around the disadvantages he confronted.

Not surprisingly, women with disabilities are additionally disadvantaged. Data from the *Disabled Women's International Newsletter, No. 5, October 1991* and the work of Esther Boylan (1991) illustrate the greater degree of discrimination faced by women with disabilities in the workforce. She found that women with disabilities have higher levels of unemployment and were paid significantly lower wages than men with disabilities.

## CULTURAL FACTOR 2: INITIAL TERMS OF INCORPORATION INTO U.S. SOCIETY

Prior to 1975 there was little if any public or governmental attention that concerned the education of students with disabilities (Thomas & Russo, 1995) (see Table 12-1). Students who were identified as having special needs were regularly excluded in public education. Education for these students was either nonexistent or was the responsibility of the students' families or caretakers. Examples include

## Personal Narrative 12-1    Paul

In second grade, I was in a Catholic school with 40 or 50 kids in my class. We were supposed to learn to read prayers and match letter blocks to the letters in the prayers. By April or May, I still didn't know the alphabet and couldn't read. I memorized the prayers so the nun thought I was reading. Finally, she figured out that I didn't even know my alphabet, and I can remember her expression of total shock that I had gotten all the way through second grade without her knowing this.

My parents offered my brother and sister $50 to teach me the alphabet but that didn't work. So I flunked second grade. I had the same nun again, and she was mean. She paddled me for two years, but I still didn't learn the alphabet or how to read.

After that, my mother had me tested everywhere, at this college, that clinic. For two years they thought I couldn't read because I had bad muscles in my eyes. I went to an eye doctor to do eye exercises. Then I went to a speech teacher who thought I had a lazy tongue because I switched my R's and W's.

Every summer I went to summer school, and during the school year I was in every little special group. I was in the speech group, the corrective posture group, the purple reading group, the green reading group. In third grade, the only word I could read was "the." I used to keep track of where the class was reading by following from one "the" to the next.

Finally my mother found a famous remedial reading teacher who knew I needed to learn phonetics and who understood my dyslexia. By seventh and eighth grade, I still had barely learned how to read. I wasn't too worried about it then because I somehow knew I'd have my own business one day, and I figured I'd hire someone to read to me.

By the time I was 15 or 16, I could get by in class with reading. But I could never spell. I was a workshop major in high school, and my typical report card was two C's, three D's, and an F. I just got used to it.

When I graduated from high school, I had a 1.2 grade-point average. I was eighth from the bottom of my class of 1,500 students. To be honest, I don't even know how seven people got below me.

Everyone in my family and all my parents' friends had their own businesses. So, for me, college was just for fun because I knew I was going to own my own business. In college, I majored in business and "loopholes." I knew who all the easy teachers were. Once, I had to take a literature class in which we had to read 13 books. That's like a lifetime of reading for me! So, to get by, I read *Cliff Notes* and watched great plays on TV.

In my investment strategies class, my teacher almost failed me because I made so many spelling errors on his tests. When he found out I had a learning disability, he announced to the class that I was "on the brink of brilliancy" because he looked at my ideas instead of the spelling. The students were impressed after that, and they thought I saw the world a little differently.

While I was in college, I rented a little garage for $100 a month on the main road of campus, which was the perfect location for my business. I sold notebooks, pens, pencils, and had a small copying machine. I made $1,000 some days.

Though reading is still difficult for me, I do like reading. I like the written language because I like photocopying. I believe in double-spacing, since it helps my business.

When I talk to college students about all this, I tell them to work with their strengths, not their weaknesses. Go where you're strong.

*Source:* Paul Orfalea, founder and chairperson of Kinkos, Inc. Retrieved from http://www.ldonline.org/firstperson/6994

early court cases like a 1893 ruling by the Massachusetts Supreme court which upheld the exclusion of a student diagnosed with mental retardation from the public school system (*Watson v. City of Cambridge, 32 N.E. 864,864 (Mass.1993)*) and a 1919 Wisconsin supreme Court ruling that determined that a student can be excluded from public education when the presence of that child is harmful to the best interest of the school (*State ex rel Beattie v. Board of Education, 1972, N.W.*

**Table 12-1**  Persons with Disabilities: Educational History

| | |
|---|---|
| **Before 1800** | • Children with disabilities are kept at home, and few, if any, receive a formal education. |
| **1800 to 1850** | • In 1817, William Gallaudet creates the first formal special education program in the United States. |
| | • Education programs for children with disabilities are created, primarily as residential institutions. While [these programs] claim to "educate," most of these children are simply removed from society's view and contribute to a growing segregation in the educational system. |
| **1850 to 1950** | • Special schools for children with visual, hearing, and cognitive disabilities are created, including many residential schools or institutions for children with disabilities. Unfortunately, most children with disabilities are still uneducated. |
| | • By 1918, all individual states mandate state-financed education for [their] citizens, creating a nationwide public school system that guarantees a free education for all citizens. |
| | • Minorities and children with disabilities are almost always excluded from this emerging public school system. |
| | • As more children attend public schools, teachers notice more pupils who are "slow" or "backward." Teachers begin to call for special classes and persons with special training to take care of these students. |
| | • Some parents pool their resources to start a school or program for children with developmental disabilities. While sporadic, these attempts prove that children with disabilities can be educated in the community. |
| | • Rhode Island opens the first public special education class in the United States in 1896. |
| | • By 1923, almost 34,000 students are in special education classes. |
| | • By the mid-1920s, professional views of persons with disabilities are changing. Superintendents begin to see the positive results of education and community interaction for people with disabilities. |
| | • Special education classes are offered primarily in large cities. Many families send their children to institutions because they believe that is the only place the children will receive training. |

(*continued*)

**Table 12-1**   Continued

| 1950 to 1975 | • In 1954, the landmark *Brown v. Board of Education* decision rocks the educational system. The U.S. Supreme Court decides that schools cannot discriminate on the basis of race, establishing that a "separate" education is not an equal education. |
| --- | --- |
| | • During the 1960s and 1970s, the parents' movement works to improve conditions in state institutions; to create community services, educational, and employment opportunities; to initiate legislation; and to challenge the conventional wisdom that persons with disabilities cannot be helped. |
| | • Only one in five students with disabilities in the United States is educated. More than 1 million students are excluded from public schools and another 3.5 million do not receive appropriate services. Many laws specifically exclude students with certain disabilities. |
| | • In 1973, Congress enacted Section 504 of PL 93-112 as part of the Rehabilitation Act. This legislation and the amendments of 1986 and 1992 guarantee the rights of individuals with disabilities in employment and in educational institutions that receive federal funding. |
| 1975 to mid-1980s | • In 1975, the Education for All Handicapped Children Act, PL 94-142, is passed. This is the first major legislation to require all school districts to develop and provide a free, appropriate public education (FAPE) for all children and youths with disabilities. |
| | • An important provision of the legislation requires that the education of children with disabilities be provided in the least restrictive environment (LRE) for each child, opening the door for children to be educated in general education classrooms in their neighborhood schools. |
| | • The legislation challenges educators to reassess the way they view children with disabilities and their potential to learn. |
| Mid-1980s to 1999 | • The *Timothy v. Rochester School District* ruling establishes that "all means all." The U.S. Court of Appeals decision requires all school districts to assume responsibility for educating every child, including those with disabilities—no exceptions. |
| | • Inclusive education begins to take root in neighborhood schools across the nation. However, system-wide endorsement of inclusion is years away. |

(*continued*)

**Table 12-1**  Continued

|  |  |
|---|---|
|  | • In 1990, the Individuals with Disabilities Education Act (IDEA) and PL 101-336, the Americans with Disabilities Act (ADA), are passed, expanding services to include individuals aged 3 to 21 and ensuring that school-aged children with disabilities are also protected outside of school—including employment and access to a range of public and private services. |
|  | • For school districts that have embraced the idea of inclusion, children with physical limitations now have physical access to neighborhood schools for the first time. |
|  | • In 1993, an unequal education is still the rule for children with developmental disabilities. Fewer than 7 percent of school-aged children with disabilities are educated in general education classrooms. |
|  | • In 1997, the Reauthorization of IDEA passes. This law ensures that children with disabilities have the right to more than access to education—they have the right to a quality education and quality outcomes. |
| 2000 to present | • Significant progress has been made but there's still room for improvement. During the 2000–2001 school year, 6.3 million children aged 3 to 21 receive[d] some form of special education, according to the U.S. Department of Education. That's over 10 percent of the total student population! |
|  | • Among students with disabilities aged 14 and over, the high school graduation rate is more than 56 percent. |
|  | • The idea of full inclusion is beginning to take hold and students with disabilities can now be found in an increasing number of regular classrooms on at least a part-time basis. |
|  | • In the 1999–2000 school year, 96 percent of students with disabilities [were] served in regular school buildings and nearly half spent 80 percent of their day in a regular classroom. |
|  | • In 2004, IDEA was reauthorized, [with] changes including modified definitions, policies, and procedures for implementing services for students with disabilities with the newest regulations distributed in July 2006. |

*Source:* Partners in Education. (n.d.). Retrieved from http://www.partnersinpolicymaking.com/education/history_overview.html

*153 (Wis. 1919))*. The 1919 case cited that the physically paralyzed student was excluded because his frequent drooling was deemed to interfere with other students' education. Such exclusion continued late into the 1960s with many states implementing laws that excluded children who were categorized as deaf, blind, emotionally disturbed, and mentally retarded (Yell, 1998).

It has been suggested (Wodatch, 1990) that the modern disability rights movement began more than 40 years ago during the 1960s when people with disabilities around the world successfully challenged dominant social stereotypes. In the United States, Ed Roberts, a post-polio quadriplegic who used a ventilator to assist his breathing, broke American educational barriers when he became the first person with such a significant disability to attend college. Roberts entered the University of California at Berkeley in 1962. During a lifetime of fighting for equality he became an international representative of human rights to challenge discrimination against persons with disabilities. And yet even though the 1960s were a time of heightened political action, during which the Civil Rights Act of 1964 was passed, it must be noted that this legislation did *not* include protections for persons with disabilities. While prohibiting discrimination on the basis of race, religion, and national origin, disabilities were not included and would not be included or addressed in legislation until almost a decade later with the passage of PL 93-112, Section 504 of the Rehabilitation Act in 1973 which provided a link between disability and antidiscrimination laws (Wodatch, 1990). Of course, legislation is only a part of the struggle for equality. Overt and subtle forms of discrimination continued to exist in schooling, employment, hiring, access, and political representation.

Unlike the Civil Rights Act of 1964, Section 504 of PL 93-112, part of the Vocational Rehabilitation Act, did not mandate compliance or public accommodations by employers in the private sector or for those programs that did not receive federal financial assistance. The mandates found within Section 504 applied only to federal and federally funded programs. In 1975, **PL 94-142**, the Education for All Handicapped Children Act, mandated a free and appropriate education for all children, including the right to the following:

- Learning in the least restrictive environment (**LRE**)
- Learning with the aid of an individualized education program (**IEP**) designed to meet the student's unique needs
- A plan to screen and identify students with disabilities
- Full-service schooling at no cost to their families
- **Due process**
- A nondiscriminatory evaluation
- Confidentiality
- Services performed by personnel who receive ongoing training

In 1990, the **IDEA** and subsequent revisions of its regulations amended PL 94-142, including replacement of the word *handicapped* with the word *disabilities* and expanding services to include individuals aged 3 to 21 (Yell, 1998).

Passage of PL 94-142 was highly significant for students with disabilities and their families in that it requires that all children with disabilities receive a free, appropriate public education with specific criteria to define the process. Changes implicit in the law included efforts to improve how children with disabilities were identified, evaluated, and educated. This mandate resulted in dramatic changes in the public school education of students with disabilities (Sarason & Doris, 1979).

Confounding the problem of securing equal rights and educational services for students with disabilities, institutional racial and social-class discrimination have affected the evaluation practices that have identified disabilities where they did not exist. Students of color are disproportionately placed in special education classes. These students are disproportionately male, African American, and working class or poor. Referrals are typically made by teachers who are mostly white, middle-class females whose definitions for acceptable behaviors and cultural values are frequently incongruent with those of minority students. Such outcome reflect a bigotry of low expectations and biased interpretations of behaviors (Losen & Orfield, 2002) as these placements occur when minority students do not actually have a disability which results in their stigmatization and severely limited opportunities for academic success (Artiles & Harry, 2004).

In the more than 30 years since the passage of Public Law 94-142, significant progress has been made toward meeting national goals for developing and implementing effective programs and services for early intervention, special education, and related services. But the passage of IDEA signaled more than change in the American educational system, it also prompted change in the national perspective and treatment of persons with disabilities. IDEA forced a revaluation of the role of persons with disabilities in American society for decades to follow. As such, stronger and broader base political support for persons with disabilities came into existence in the late 1980s (Wodatch, 1990).

## EXERCISE 12-1   Field Experience: Identifying Disabilities Commonly Found in Schools

**Directions:** You may want to consult Heward (2003) and/or other sources to research and define the disabilities listed here to improve your knowledge of disabilities that teachers often encounter in schools. After listing functional definitions for each term, write an academic strength that you imagine would exist among persons who have these disabilities.

### Physical and Sensory Challenges

Epilepsy

Cerebral palsy

Hearing impairment

Visual impairment

### Communication Disorders

Articulation disorders

Stuttering

Voicing problems

Language disorders

### Other Learning Challenges

Attention-deficit disorder (ADD)

Attention-deficit hyperactivity disorder (ADHD)

Autism

Cancer

Diabetes

Dyslexia

HIV/AIDS

A significant focus that took center stage in the 1980s was on developing services and resources necessary to support independent living for people with disabilities—an independence that would allow for more options for participating fully in society. Such actions have resulted in the formation of a national network of Centers for Independent Living which combine self-help services and advocacy; the elimination of custodial institutions, the development of adaptive equipment and the passage of the Air Carriers Act (1986) which provides rights for persons with disabilities to use air transportation (see Table 12-2).

While the **ADA** has opened doors to provide for the rights of persons with disabilities, there is much to be achieved (Wodatch, 1990). Progression from reinforcing the dependency of persons with disabilities to facilitating their independence and from forcing persons with disabilities to adapt to inadequate environments to adapting environments to meet the needs of persons with disabilities is substantial; however, dominant-culture attitudes and beliefs about persons with disabilities are slow to change.

We are only beginning to harness the resources available through Universal Design principles. **Universal Design** began largely as physical accommodation practices that revolutionized the way people thought about access issues to create a more inclusive world and involves the design of products and environments to be usable by all people, to the greatest extent possible, without the need for adaptation or specialized design. Universal Design benefits those who identify as persons with disabilities as well as those who may not identify as such, and the organizations that adopt accessibility principles. The seven principles of Universal Design include:

1. Equitable Use—designs that are useful and marketable to people with diverse abilities. Furthermore, it means providing services equally to all users, with no segregation, with individuals' privacy secured, and assuring that the design is generally considered appealing.

2. Flexibility in Use—ensures that the design accommodates a wide range of individual preferences and abilities including choice in methods for using the service and adaptability to the user's pace.

3. Simple and Intuitive Use—makes the design or service easy to understand, regardless of the user's experience, knowledge, language skills, or current concentration level by eliminating unnecessary complexity, providing information

**Table 12-2** Legislated Support for Independent Living

- The Fair Housing Amendments Act was passed in 1988, bringing people with disabilities under the protection of the Fair Housing Act of 1968. This act prohibited discrimination toward people with disabilities in the sale or rental of properties.
- The U.S. Department of Housing and Urban Affairs (HUD) issued regulations covering federally funded public housing and other recipients of HUD funds, including Community Development Block Grant Programs. These policies required design standards that opened entrances and passageways to persons with disabilities and provided access to facilities.

in a consistent fashion, and accommodating a range of literacy and language skills all help to ensure the simplicity of design.

4. Perceptible Information—transferring knowledge effectively regardless of ambient conditions or the user's sensory abilities using different modes of information delivery, highlighting essential information, giving clear and easy instructions, and providing information in an accessible way that can be absorbed by people with sensory limitations all help to improve the quality of perceptible information.

5. Tolerance for Error—such that the product or service minimizes hazards and adverse consequences of accidental or unintended actions. This concept applies more to universal accessibility of products. However, in service delivery this concept would discourage actions that may have adverse consequences; for example, insensitivity to a person's disability and lack of respect for that person's right to privacy may have unintended consequences.

6. Low Physical Effort—participants can use the product or service efficiently and comfortably with a minimum of fatigue. In specific terms, the user will minimize repetitive actions and minimize sustained physical effort.

7. Size and Space for Approach and Use—the service or product meets the needs of all users, regardless of body size, posture, or mobility. Specifically, this principle requires a clear line of sight for all users, assumes comfort for a seated or standing user, and provides adequate space for use of assistive devices and personal assistance.

These seven principles have broad implications for improved accessibility for persons with disabilities as well as for persons who do not have identified disabilities. They improve the functionality of environments without compromising durability, aesthetics, or intended use (Leydorf, 2004).

## CULTURAL FACTORS 3 AND 4: SHARED VALUES, TRADITIONS, AND SPIRITUALITY

Print media may be one of the clearest indications that a disability culture exists. Hundreds of books have been written that feature disability culture and political newsletters. Organizations that promote the independence for persons with disabilities have sprung up in huge numbers, giving form to shared values and experiences that constitute culture for members of this group.

People with disabilities forged a group identity, as have other minority groups, to increase their visibility and resources for advocacy to confront the differential and pejorative treatment they experience as a group (Dworkin & Dworkin, 1976). Members of this group share a common history of oppression and a common bond of resilience yet vary greatly in terms of their views of themselves and the discrimination they confront. Brown (1994) surveyed a number of disability activists and reported references to the legacy of customs and values that represent the common experiences of disabled people and the reality of their different ways of coping, relating, and expressing themselves as evidence in support of the notion of disability culture.

Persons with disabilities have created a body of art, music, literature, and traditions embodying expressions of their lives that form the "matter" of their culture built around their experiences with disability. Most importantly, as noted in Brown, persons with disabilities stated that they were proud of themselves as people with disabilities—explaining, "we claim our disabilities with pride as part of our identity. We are who we are: we are people with disabilities." (Brown, 1996, p. 7)

Having encountered negative stereotypes depicting those with disabilities as deficient, deformed, weak, and incompetent, many persons with disabilities have been motivated to create awareness centering around their positive attributes and abilities. As such, **disability culture** may be most visible in artistic expressions and other work produced by and about members of the group. In 1995, a youth dance ensemble, Restless Dance Company, created a dance theatre performance that reflected cultures of disability. Similarly, *Talking Down*—a troop composed of teens with and without physical disabilities—was created by the Restless Dance Company. It explored the idea that Down Syndrome not only existed but was long overdue for exposition and celebration. Other artists including performance artists (e.g., Cheryl Marie Wade, Wry Crips Women's Theatre), dancers (e.g., the Axis Dance Troupe), playwrights (e.g., Neil Marcus), and musicians (e.g., Jeff Moyer, Jane Field) illuminate disability culture. Their work celebrates their uniqueness and challenges along with their talents and skills of persons with disabilities.

# CULTURAL FACTOR 5: ACCULTURATION AND EXPERIENCE WITH EXCLUSION AND ALIENATION

## Acculturation in Schooling

**Inclusion** in schooling involves integrating students with disabilities in regular classrooms whenever possible *with* the supports necessary for them to succeed. It is mandated as a byproduct of PL 94-142 (Turnbull, Turnbull, Shank, & Smith, 2004). This sometimes controversial educational policy differs greatly from **mainstreaming** which involves the placement of students with identified disabilities in some "regular education" classes when they have demonstrated that they can function academically with those classes without additional help or resources. Supporters of inclusion criticize mainstreaming for the following reasons:

1. A disproportionate number of students currently placed in special education are from oppressed groups in the United States.
2. Curriculum pull-out programs are often poorly integrated with the curricula of general education classes.
3. Special education students who are pulled out generally do not feel and are not treated as though they are a part of the school.
4. Entrance criteria into special education are often vague and inconsistently applied.
5. Special education has become a dumping ground for students who do not actually have learning, physical, or **mental disabilities**, and it is often used to "warehouse" students whose first language is not English or who do not have academic skills and knowledge compared to their same-age counterparts due to educational failures.

To add to the confusion and resistance associated with inclusion, in 1986, Madeline Will, Assistant Secretary of Special Education and Rehabilitative Services, suggested a delivery approach (targeting mostly students with mild disabilities) to correct the perceived deficiencies of mainstreaming and the special education system. Special education services were criticized from their inception as ineffective, excessively costly, segregating, and stigmatizing (Hocutt, Martin, & McKinney, 1990). This approach evolved into the most extreme form of advocacy for students with disabilities in schooling, known as the Regular Education Initiative (REI), which argues for a major reorganization of educational services that would emphasize the regular classroom, restructure the relationship between regular, special, remedial, and compensatory education programs, and eliminate segregated schooling for special education students (Salend, 1994; Fuchs & Fuchs, 1994). Proponents of this approach believe that all special education support should be provided in the context of the general education classroom and in other integrated environments. Many people mistakenly believe that inclusion advocates are proponents of the REI. The current thrust for the delivery of education for persons with disabilities emphasizes **full inclusion**—the commitment to educate each student in the school and classroom he or she would otherwise attend to the maximum extent appropriate (Rogers, 1993).

## Experience with Exclusion and Alienation

As evidenced by the historical treatment of persons with disabilities, dominant culture has ignored, ridiculed, and excluded members of this group, defining their differences as deficiencies to be feared. Fear may be one of the greatest barriers that members of this group face in their interactions with dominant culture. One reason they may be alienated is the vulnerability and mortality that members of dominant culture may associate with disability (Funk, 1987). Because humans tend to choose to associate with what they perceive to be strength as opposed to weakness, persons with disabilities often have trouble being accepted because members of dominant culture may be reminded that they, too, someday will be vulnerable and face disability. The fear of having a disability and of being treated with neglect, condescension, and disrespect all contribute to dominant-culture group members' tendencies to alienate and exclude persons with disabilities.

It is common for school officials and dominant-culture families to oppose inclusion in schooling fearing that "regular" students' education will be harmed when teachers must place "special" attention on students with disabilities when they are enrolled in "regular" classrooms. Such claims ignore the fundamental rights of persons with disabilities to experience full participation in schooling and society. Inclusion initiatives provide supports for students to enable them to achieve in "regular classrooms"; to meet the needs created by their disabilities be they in the form of modified instruction, adaptations, or aides who may accompany them to "regular" classrooms; and to work with classroom teachers to meet their needs. Inclusion is a reality that is long overdue for students with disabilities (Turnbull, Turnbull, Shank, & Smith, 2004). However, if teachers and other school officials hold negative views of students with disabilities and oppose inclusion initiatives, educating students with disabilities in "regular" classrooms may result in underachievement and tacit abuse of these students. It is imperative that teachers and school officials embrace the mission of schools and work with diversity advocates to help students with disabilities actualize their academic potentials in "regular" classrooms. Explore your beliefs about inclusion and the rights of students with disabilities by completing the assignment in Exercise 12-2.

## EXERCISE 12-2   Point of Reflection: Inclusion Values Clarification

### Part I

**Directions:** You have 10 minutes to work alone to rank (not rate) the items listed from 1 to 10 (1 = least appropriate and therefore most problematic for you to condone). After finishing your individual ranking, work together with your classmates or colleagues in a small group to come to agreement in reranking the top three items, using the same ranking system (that is, identify the three most problematic and inappropriate statements for the group). You have 15 minutes to complete the group-consensus ranking.

| Individual Ranking | Group Ranking | Items |
|---|---|---|
| _____ | _____ | A. Having a regular student's education impaired because you have included students with disabilities (SWD) |
| _____ | _____ | B. Limiting a student who has the ability to succeed in "regular" classes by enrolling her or him in a special education classroom |
| _____ | _____ | C. Requiring teachers to work twice as hard in order to provide quality education for SWD and all other students |
| _____ | _____ | D. Requiring taxpayers to pay for expensive in-service training for teachers to learn to work effectively with SWD |
| _____ | _____ | E. Exposing an included SWD to potential ridicule in the "regular" classroom |
| _____ | _____ | F. Using funding to finance programs for included SWD |
| _____ | _____ | G. Creating the potential for included students to feel frustrated when included in "regular" classrooms because they can't do the same work as "regular" students |
| _____ | _____ | H. Exposing SWD to ridicule in school hallways and cafeterias because they are excluded and taught in special education classrooms and other students do not have a chance to get to know them |
| _____ | _____ | I. Requiring parents to pay for learning opportunities not provided for their SWD who are attending separate segregated "special" schools |
| _____ | _____ | J. Causing teachers to feel frustrated because they have to learn new ways to teach SWD that they never wanted to teach when they chose the teaching profession |

### Part II

**Directions:** When your group has finished ranking the items, review the ranked list and identify those assumptions, principles, or criteria that the group used to determine rankings. In other words, why was letter X ranked number 10? Do this for four to five of the assumptions. You have approximately 10 minutes to complete this task.

# CULTURAL FACTOR 6: LANGUAGE DIFFERENCES, STRENGTHS, AND CHALLENGES

Language not only reflects attitudes but can also give shape to attitudes and actions. Many of the terms employed to describe persons with disabilities serve to exclude and unfairly characterize them. Words like *retard, spaz,* and *crippled* are characterizations of persons with disabilities that are widely used among members of dominant culture. In fact, it is still considered acceptable in dominant-culture comedy to mock mentally retarded persons and make fun of physical and psychological disabilities. Attitudes demonstrated in the use of these terms also exist in subtle, more pervasive, characterizations of persons with disabilities. For example, when a term like *blind* is used as a synonym for ignorant, unaware, or unknowing (e.g., "They robbed him blind") one may conjure up images of a pitiful, naïve, incompetent person who has been duped (Hayes, 2001, p. 14).

In addition, some forms of body language that are equally disrespectful include touching someone's assistive device (e.g., walker, wheelchair, or prosthetic) without permission (Hayes, 2001, p. 80); speaking loudly to a person with visual impairment; and communicating with a caretaker who accompanies a person with a disability rather than communicating with the person with whom the interaction is directed. Such actions send the message that persons with disabilities are dependent and do not have rights, thoughts, and feelings of their own.

It is important to the more than 33 million Americans with disabilities that they be portrayed realistically and spoken to respectfully. For example, the word *disabled* ignores the fact that persons with disabilities are people who have disabilities. Focusing on disability through the use of the labels like *disabled* and *handicapped* reflects a stereotype of persons who had no other means of support than to take off their hats (caps) and beg for help from dominant culture in order to survive—*cap in hand* became *handicapped*. Such terminology does not represent the reality of persons with disabilities.

Persons with disabilities prefer identifications which reference them as persons first. An emphasis on characteristics of a person rather than on a person as a human being is not only disrespectful but also inaccurate. Thus describing someone as a *person with a disability* is more accurate than referring to her or him as a *disabled person*. Saying that someone "uses" a wheelchair or other assistive device avoids the assumptions embedded in terms like *confined to a wheelchair* or *wheelchair-bound* which imply that persons and their wheelchairs are inseparable (Hayes, 2001, p. 16). In addition, emotionally neutral terms are preferable to those with negative connotations (Maki & Riggar, 1997). The terms *visually impaired* and *hearing impaired* are more accurate then *blind* or *deaf*, because the latter terms do not recognize the range of impairments that people with disabilities have. Further, many persons with hearing impairment do not consider themselves to have a disability at all. It is widely believed among members of this group that it is the hearing world's ignorance of their language that creates disability (Olkin, 1999).

# COPING STRATEGIES FOR ADDRESSING OPPRESSION

Throughout this text, you have seen how various minority groups have addressed oppression and responded to their exclusion in dominant culture. In addition to facing isolation, persons with disabilities may also find themselves treated like children or treated with disdain. When they are assumed to be incompetent or totally dependent, when they are pitied or not taken seriously, when they are ridiculed and avoided, they are oppressed. Imagine the circumstances described by Kai at the beginning of this chapter, as she has come to understand if she wants to attend courses held on a college campus, she must be able to conquer any barriers in the physical environment of the school that would prohibit her attendance. Consider as well students with learning disabilities, like Paul, whose narrative appears in this chapter, who may be constantly told to try harder as they try to make sense of language as Paul does—language which he sees through the lenses of a person with a dyslexia, a perceptual learning disability that causes letters and numbers to appear scrambled. Fortunately, through approaches like Universal Design and efforts from Offices for Students with Disabilities that now exist at universities, emphasis has changed in many ways from "helping" persons with disabilities to exist in a world that denigrates their differences and prohibits their inclusion to one that facilitates accessibility and acceptance. Ramps and other physical support devices are widely manufactured and installed while schools are required to provide instruction that addresses students' individual needs. Simultaneously, to address the challenges of their oppression, persons with disabilities have united and formed supportive communities that provide information, resources, and advocacy similar to that of other minority groups. Such alliances not only shed the light of awareness on the needs and issues of the group but also facilitate changes in society that positively affect the welfare of members of the group.

Many persons with disabilities have coped with oppression by calling attention to their *abilities* and making themselves visible as people who exist beyond their *disabilities*. Rather than trying to fit into a world that often rejects them, many persons with disabilities have created standards and values that are different from those embraced by dominant culture. Some believe that "real integration ... can be achieved only on the basis of a full recognition of our[their] differences and this in turn will depend a great deal on us[them] making the free choice to identify ourselves[themselves] as a social group" (Finkelstein, 1987). The tables must turn to recognize that persons with disabilities must be accepted as they are and not made to feel that they are inadequate because they do not move, perceive, learn, and communicate in the same ways members of dominant culture do. Standards must be reshaped to include values and skills embodied by persons with disabilities that are often overlooked and undervalued. Standards for optimum physical movement, expression, learning style, and existence must be re-envisioned to include the physical movements of persons with physical disabilities; the communication strategies of persons with vision and hearing impairment; the learning styles of students with learning disabilities; and the lives of a myriad of people who lead lives that function differently from others in dominant culture. American society must perceive and applaud the beauty of sign language and skillful wheelchair locomotion. They must marvel at the strength and creativity of students who put meanings together in ways that defy customary logic. Until such changes occur, persons with disabilities will continue to be marginalized.

## POTENTIAL BARRIERS IN LEARNING–TEACHING RELATIONSHIPS WITH DOMINANT-CULTURE TEACHERS AND SCHOOLS

The history of exclusion and oppression of persons with disabilities is long. While significant steps have been taken to remove barriers to inclusion, work must continue. Initially, the IDEA emphasized the process of mainstreaming students with disabilities with those who did not have identified disabilities. The process of "mainstreaming" entailed placing students with disabilities in "regular" classes to the "maximum extent appropriate". Typically, "mainstreaming" was implemented by having students with disabilities participate in the some portions of the general education program, usually in art, music, and physical education as opposed to math, reading, and science courses. It was believed that enrolling students into these types of classes would not interfere with the education of "regular" students in the "more important" academic subjects. Most students with disabilities were, however, still enrolled in self-contained special education classes throughout most of their school day. These initial attempts to include students with disabilities were, in many ways, ill-conceived and ineffective and served to squelch students progress toward equal rights by contributing to the stigma and exclusion associated with self-contained special education, lowered expectations for and watered-down instruction, and in presenting the appearance that the needs of students with disabilities were being adequately and equitably met.

In order for inclusion to occur, more than policies and practice must change. Inclusion strategies rest, first and foremost, on individuals' mindsets and perspectives. Stereotypes, misconceptions, bias, ignorance, and anxiety can serve as a basis to resist inclusion. Faculty, parents, and staff, all involved must understand the concept of inclusion as fundamental right. Attitudes, facilities, policies, practices, and services all need to be assessed to ensure that those necessary to facilitate inclusion are in place. An example of policy changes that have developed to reduce bias experienced by students with disabilities is the current criteria for defining mental retardation (see Table 12-3). Whereas in the past, persons were labeled mildly, severely, and profoundly retarded, current definitions are based on services utilized by individuals in placing a focus on individuals' capabilities rather than their disabilities (Drew & Hardman, 2004).

Funding for coordinated services and individual support mechanisms for ensuring adequate transportation and access not only serve to facilitate inclusion but also create an environment in which equality is possible. Finally, and most importantly, the programs and curricula offered to all students must be tailored to students' accurately identified and regularly monitored and assessed specific educational needs (see Intercultural Strategies 12-1).

**Table 12-3** Mental Retardation

According to the American Association on Mental Deficiency (AAMD), *mental retardation* (MR) refers to substantial limitations in intellectual functioning as measured by an IQ test with a score between 70 and 75 *and* significantly subaverage functioning in two or more adaptive skill areas (that is, communication, self-care, social skills, self-direction, health and safety, leisure, functional academics, and work). It manifests by age 18. About 1 to 2 percent of the U.S. population fit this description. Those classified as MR are placed into one of four categories:

1. *Intermittent:* Requires support on an as-needed basis
2. *Limited:* Requires time-limited treatment, few staff members, employment training, and transitioning from school to adult world
3. *Extensive:* Requires regular involvement (daily) in some treatment environments
4. *Pervasive:* Requires highly intensive care provided across environments, potentially life-sustaining treatments, and many staff members

*Source:* Drew, C. J., & Hardman, M. L. (2004). *Mental retardation: A life cycle approach* (8th ed.). Upper Saddle River, NJ: Prentice Hall.

# FROM CONCEPTS TO LIVED EXPERIENCE

In the following story, Liz Bogod (2006) describes her struggles in coming to terms with her disability.

### FINDING MY LD PRIDE

This is the story of how I came to accept that my learning disability is nothing to be ashamed of. Through a long, painful journey to arrive at this acceptance, I have come to know my many strengths and to find skills that I did not know I possessed. I offer my story to other LD children, youth, and adults, in the sure knowledge that, if they can come to the realization of their own true abilities and talents, like me, they can shed the sense of shame which all too often leaves LD people feeling dumb, stupid and altogether incapable.

I was six years old. It was September and the long, hot summer had come to an end. When I got to school, I knew something was not quite right. I was returning to the same classroom and the same teacher but there were none of the same students. I was in Kindergarten again. My parents told me that my birth date was in the wrong month which meant I could not go into first grade and would have to repeat Kindergarten. At that time, I accepted the explanation.

It was not until the following year in grade one that I had an inclination that the excuse my parents used for my repeating Kindergarten was a lie. I did not know that the real reason was because I could only count to ten while my classmates were counting to one hundred; I could not tie my shoes while classmates were tying them and I could not write my name.

I have vivid memories of my parents meeting my grade one teacher to discuss my school difficulties. After being sent out of the room fully aware of the topic of conversation, I was mad! How dare you, I thought, have a conversation about me without including me! My attempts to eavesdrop failed; but, I did not need to hear what they were saying. I knew exactly what they were talking about—me and my unfinished math book! I had tried to hide the fact that I could not cope with math and had hidden the math book in my desk.

Soon I was faced with one of the most traumatic experiences of my childhood. I found myself with my mother in an interview with a scary doctor who seemed to have no rapport with children. I was commanded to answer her questions. She frightened me and I instantly took a dislike to her. I shut up like a clam and was totally uncooperative. I remember my mother arguing with her so evidently things did not go well. Many years later, I discovered this scary dictator was a very eminent child psychiatrist at a major children's hospital.

The next thing that happened to me was that I was moved into a special education class. I wondered what was so special about me? I was just a normal kid who wanted to fit in, do well in school, and make my parents proud of me, but somehow my inability to do math and other learning disabilities seemed to make me "special." So, the "special" kid went into "special" class with seven other "special" kids with other "special" problems. I felt different and abnormal.

I remained in the special education class for two years. During this time, I was slowly reintegrated back into the mainstream class. My academic reintegration went fairly smoothly, but my social reintegration was a disaster. On my first day, I went to class wanting to make friends, but I really did not know how. My poor social skills made it difficult for me to relate to people. I had trouble understanding humor, keeping up with conversations, and using and understanding body language. As a result, children did not want to play with me.

The memories I have of my early school years are isolation, loneliness, and the many recesses when I sat alone on the school steps. When I set out to find a friend the kids ran away from me. One well-meaning, but misguided, teacher took pity on me sitting by myself and decided to assign me a "friend." News of this assigned friend got around and I was told, "You are such a loser, you had to be assigned a friend." Throughout my elementary school years, I experienced this kind of social rejection over and over again. This was the part of my learning disability nobody understood.

In high school to help with my learning disabilities in math, science and French, I would spend one period a day in the school learning Center, often referred to as the Romper Room! Math and French were compulsory in grade nine and I had a lot of difficulty with these credits, but coping socially weighed much more heavily on my mind. I dreaded group work because I was always the last one to be picked to join a group. I was very unhappy—totally isolated and soon became depressed. I was labeled mentally ill and passed from one psychiatrist to the next. Many interpretations were made to explain my problem. I was told that I had a depressive mental illness and was put on medication. I was told I was too dependent on my parents which I have since learned is very common among children with learning disabilities.

With hindsight, I know all my pain could have been prevented [if I had known that I had a learning disability and learned how to cope with it. As an adult,] I filled out a learning disabilities checklist, I was amazed to find out how much on the list applied to me. I realized that I had a reason for being as I am. I was not mentally ill, retarded or stupid. As I continued to explore the subject, I found out how many famous people have learning disabilities, and as I was able to speak to others about the topic, I found how many people there are who have a learning disability…. I decided that much more was to be gained by shouting out my learning disability and making others aware that though it takes us longer, is more difficult, those of us with learning disabilities get there in the end and can be successful, productive members of society.

*Liz Bogod*

*Source:* http://www.ldonline.org/firstperson/Finding_My_LD_Pride!

## Intercultural Communication Strategies for Teachers 12-1

### Strategies for Facilitating the Academic Achievement of Students with Disabilities

Utilize the following strategies to adapt your instruction to help students with disabilities achieve in your classroom:

1. Collaborate with special education teachers to help screen and identify students with disabilities and then identify appropriate strategies and curriculum revision to meet the needs of students with disabilities.
2. Participate actively in the Individualized Education Program Planning Committee at your school.
3. Provide a structured written overview before each lesson.
4. Use visual aids, demonstrations, simulations, and manipulatives frequently to ensure that students understand the concepts presented.
5. Use transparencies and an overhead projector to outline course concepts and keep each transparency for later review by students who need it.
6. Color-code outlines with chalk or pens to add emphasis.
7. Provide a copy of teacher or peer notes for students to allow students to focus on listening during instruction.
8. Provide "turn and talks" or other interactive activities to assist students' abilities to understand and refine their understandings of concepts before learning new material.
9. Enable students to tape-record material presented orally, if needed.
10. Use computer-assisted instruction when appropriate.
11. Include a variety of activities integrating students' multiple intelligences to help students understand and apply content learned in each lesson.
12. Break assignments into smaller parts and provide feedback as each part is completed.
13. Provide additional time to complete assignments or tests when needed.
14. Provide checklists, outlines, and advanced organizers to assist comprehension.
15. Supply reading materials at various reading levels.
16. Enable students to demonstrate understanding using a variety of media, including oral presentations, creative projects, audio- or video-taped assignments, bulletin board displays, dramatizations, written assignments, and demonstrations.
17. Allow students to word-process rather than hand-write assignments, if needed.
18. Give frequent, shorter quizzes rather than longer tests that require a great deal of memorization.
19. Give tests and exams orally or on audio tape when needed.
20. Assist students in setting short-term goals and provide opportunities for self-evaluation of progress toward those goals.
21. Teach students to organize and keep track of materials.
22. Set up a regular communication system to provide consistent structure and support between parents and teachers.
23. Provide instruction and practice in using study skills.
24. Provide instruction and practice in using self-monitoring strategies.
25. Identify students' strengths, skills, and interests.
26. Establish effective and efficient routines in the classroom.
27. Establish positive rapport with students and model respectful behavior.
28. Provide opportunities for student selection of learning materials and assignments.
29. Minimize classroom clutter and distractions.
30. Work individually with students frequently.
31. Do not view lack of student participation as lack of motivation or student resistance.
32. Re-examine the notion of what is fair. Fair does not mean that every child gets the same treatment but that every child gets what he or she needs.
33. Research information, state and federal laws, and school policies pertaining to working with students with diabetes, HIV/AIDS, epilepsy, autism, cancer, and so on (see Exercise 12-1 for topics). Summarize information and related

> ## Intercultural Communication Strategies for Teachers 12-1  Continued
>
> educational strategies and place it in a handy file for quick reference. Follow suggestions you identify in your research (for example, keeping orange juice on hand for diabetic students, and so on).
>
> **Links**
>
> http://www.allabilities.com/society.html
>
> www.dpi.org

# SUMMARY

**Definitions**   Exceptionalities are created by differences among students. Exceptional students require supplemental services to facilitate their academic development. Students with disabilities and gifted students are two groups of exceptional students.

A *disability* is a restriction or lack of ability to perform an activity in the manner or within the range considered "normal" for humans, while *impairment* is defined as the loss or abnormality of psychological, physiological, or anatomical structure or function. Handicaps involve the loss or limitation of opportunities to take part in the "normal" life of the community on an equal level with others due to physical or social barriers.

**Cultural Factor 1: Historical and Current Treatment in the United States**   Throughout history, persons with disabilities have been ignored, exiled, exploited, tortured, and even destroyed. The focus was on individuals' disabilities rather than on persons' lived experiences. Throughout the 1960s, the provision of rehabilitative counseling simply extended the view that the disabled needed to adjust—to fit in, rather than have society adjust to incorporate them. The 2000 Census identified more than 33 million adult persons with disabilities living in the United States. 18.5 million of these individuals reported being employed. Both persons with disabilities who were working and those not working stated a need for similar types of accommodations. One-third of nonworking persons with disabilities reported the need for some type of accommodations.

**Cultural Factor 2: Initial Terms of Incorporation into American Society**   Prior to 1975 there was little if any public or governmental concern and attention regarding the education of students with disabilities. While the Civil Rights Act of 1964 prohibited discrimination on the basis of race, religion, and national origin, disabilities were not included and it would not be included or addressed in legislation until almost a decade later with the passage of Section 504 of PL 93-112, the Rehabilitation Act in 1973. In 1975, Public Law 94-142, the Education for All Handicapped Children Act mandated a free and appropriate education for all children. A significant focus that took center stage in the 1980s was on developing services and resources necessary to support independent living for people with disabilities—an independence that would allow for more options for participating fully in society. Universal Design began largely as physical accommodation practices that revolutionized the way people thought about access issues to create a more inclusive world and involves the design of products and environments to be usable by all people, to the greatest extent possible, without the need for adaptation or specialized design. Universal Design benefits those who identify as persons with disabilities as well as those who may not identify as such, and the organizations that adopt accessibility principles.

**Cultural Factors 3 & 4: Commonly Shared Values, Traditions and Spirituality**   Print media may be one of the clearest indications that a disability culture exists. A legacy of customs and values that represent the common experiences of disabled people and the reality of their different ways of coping, relating, and expressing themselves is evidence supporting the notion of disability culture. Persons with disabilities have created a body of art, music, literature, and other expressions of their lives that form the "matter" of a culture built around experience with disability.

### Cultural Factor 5: Acculturation and Experience with Exclusion and Alienation

The fear of having a disability and of being treated with neglect, condescension, and disrespect all contribute to dominant-culture group members' tendencies to alienate and exclude persons with disabilities. Inclusion in schooling is mandated as a byproduct of PL 94-142. The most extreme advocacy for students with disabilities in schooling comes in the form of the Regular Education Initiative (REI) which argues for the elimination of segregated special education classes altogether.

### Cultural Factor 6: Language Differences, Strengths, and Challenges

The word *disabled* ignores the fact that persons with disabilities are people who have disabilities. Focusing on disability through the use of the labels like *disabled* and *handicapped* reflects a stereotype of persons who had no other means of support than to take off their hats (caps) and beg help from dominant culture in order to survive—*cap in hand* became *handicapped*. Preferred identifications are those which reference a person first. Thus describing someone as a *person with a disability* is more accurate than referring to her or him a *disabled person*; saying someone *uses* a wheelchair or other assistive device avoids the assumptions embedded in terms like *confined to* or *wheelchair bound*.

### Coping Strategies for Addressing Oppression

The emphasis has changed in many ways from "helping" persons with disabilities exist in a world that denigrates their differences to creating accessibility and acceptance. To address challenges of their oppression, persons with disabilities have united and formed communities for information, resources, support, and advocacy similar to other minority groups. Many persons with disabilities have coped with oppression by calling attention to their abilities and making themselves visible as people who exist beyond their disabilities.

### Potential Barriers in Learning–Teaching Relationships with Dominant Culture Teachers and Schools

The Individuals with Disabilities in Education Act emphasized the process of mainstreaming students with disabilities with those who did not have identified disabilities. The process of "mainstreaming" entailed placing students with disabilities in "regular" classes to the "maximum extent appropriate." In order for inclusion to occur, more than policies and practice must change. Inclusion strategies rest, first and foremost, on individuals' mindsets and perspectives. Stereotypes, misconceptions, bias, ignorance, and anxiety can serve as a basis to resist inclusion. Faculty, parents, and staff, all involved must understand the concept of inclusion as fundamental right. Beyond attitudes—facilities, policies, practices, and services all need to be assessed to ensure that those necessary to facilitate inclusion are in place.

## Questions for Review

1. How is *disability* defined differently from *handicap*?

2. In what ways does *inclusion* advance rights for students with disabilities?

3. What are the principles of *Universal Design* and how do they enhance accessibility for all individuals?

## Important Terms

| | | | |
|---|---|---|---|
| ADA | giftedness | learning disabilities | PL 93-112 |
| disability | handicaps | LRE | PL 94-142 |
| disability culture | IDEA | mainstreaming | Universal Design |
| due process | IEP | mental disabilities | |
| exceptionalities | impairments | persons with | |
| full inclusion | inclusion | disabilities | |

## Enrichment

Bowe, F. (1978). *Handicapping America: Barriers to disabled people*. New York: Harper Row.

Bowe, F. (1980). *Rehabilitating America*. New York: Harper Row.

Charlton, J. I. (1998). *Nothing about us without us, disability, oppression and empowerment*. Berkeley: University of California.

Engel, D. M., & Munger, F. W. (2003). *Rights of inclusion: Law and identity in the life stories of Americans with disabilities*. University of Chicago Press.

Lipsky, D. K., & Gartner, A. (1997). *Inclusion and school reform: Transforming America's classrooms*. Baltimore: Paul H. Brooks.

Murdick, N., Gartin, B., & Crabtree, T. (2002). *Special education law*. Upper Saddle River, NJ: Prentice Hall.

Sailor, W. (Ed.). (2002). *Whole-school success and inclusive education: Building partnerships for learning, achievement, and accountability*. New York: Teachers' College.

Salend, S. J. (1994). *Effective mainstreaming: Creating inclusive classrooms*. New York: Macmillan.

Smith, D. (2004). *Introduction to special education: Teaching in an age of opportunity* (5th ed.). Needham Heights, MA: Allyn & Bacon.

Turnbull, R., Turnbull, A., Shank, M., & Smith, S. (2004). *Exceptional lives: Special education in today's schools*. Upper Saddle River, NJ: Prentice Hall.

## Connections on the Web

http://arch-online.org/tag/types-of-disabilities

This website provides information on disability rights and advocacy.

http://www.wapd.org/

This Voices of Positive Ability website features issues and personal stories of persons with disabilities along with resources and legal information.

http://www.ada.gov/

This ADA website presents information to assist persons with disability and includes ADA standards for accessible design.

http://www.childdevelopmentinfo.com/learning/teacher.shtml

This site features suggested classroom interventions for students with learning disabilities.

# References

Artiles, A. J., & Harry, B. (2004). *Addressing culturally and linguistically diverse student overrepresentation in special education: Guidelines for parents.* Denver: National Center for Culturally Responsive Education Systems.

Bogod, L. (2006). First person: Finding my LD pride. LD online. Retrieved from http://www.ldonline.org/firstperson/Finding_My_LD_Pride!

Boylan, E. (1991). *Women and disability.* London: Zed Press.

Brown, C. N. (1997). Legal issues and gifted education: Gifted identification as a constitutional issue. *Roeper Review*, 19, 157–160.

Brown, S. E. (1994). *Investigating a culture of disability: Final report.* Las Cruces, NM: Institute on Disability Culture.

Charlton, J. I. (1998). *Nothing about us without us, disability, oppression and empowerment.* Berkeley: University of California.

Crow, L. (1996). Including all of our lives: Renewing the social model of disability. In J. Morris (Ed.), *Encounters with strangers: Feminism and disability* (pp. 55–72). London: The Women's Press.

Demographics and Statistics (Stats RRTC). (2005, April 4). Retrieved from http://www.disabilitystatistics.org on November 16, 2005.

Drew, C. J., & Hardman, M. L. (2004). *Mental retardation: A life cycle approach* (8th ed.). Upper Saddle River, NJ: Merrill.

Dworkin, A. G., & Dworkin, R. J. (1976). *The minority report.* New York: Praeger.

Fagan, T., & Wallace, A. (1979). Who are the handicapped? *Personnel and Guidance Journal*, 58, 215–220.

Finkelstein, V. (1987). Disabled people and our culture development. Retrieved from http://www.independentliving.org/docs3/finkelstein87a.html.

Frasu, A. (2004). Which is correct: Deaf, deaf, hard of hearing, or hearing impaired? Deaf Linx. Retrieved from http://www.deaflinx.com/label.html on May 8, 2006.

Freeman, J. (1994). Some emotional aspects of being gifted. *Journal for the Education of the Gifted*, 17, 180–197.

Fuchs, D., & Fuchs, L. S. (1994). Inclusive schools movement and the radicalization of special education reform. *Exceptional Children*, 60, 294–309.

Funk, R. (1987). Disability rights: From caste to class in the context of civil rights. In A. Gartner & T. Joe (Eds.), *Images of the disabled, disabling images* (pp. 7–30). New York: Praeger.

Gardner, H. (1993). *Multiple intelligences: The theory in practice.* New York: Basic Books.

Hayes, P. A. (2001). *Addressing cultural complexities in practice: A framework for clinicians and counselors.* Washington, DC: American Psychological Association.

Heward, W. L. (2003). *Exceptional children* (7th ed.). Upper Saddle River, NJ: Merrill/Prentice Hall.

Hocutt, A. M., Martin, E. W., & McKinney, J. D. (1990). Historical and legal context of mainstreaming (Inclusion). In J. W. Loyd, N. N. Singh, & A. C. Repp (Eds.), *The regular education initiative: Alternative perspectives on concepts, issues & models* (pp. 17–28). Sycamore, IL: Sycamore Publishing.

Hohenshil, T. H., & Humes, C. W. (1979). Roles in counseling in ensuring the rights of the handicapped. *Personnel and Guidance Journal*, 58, 221–227.

Houtenville, A. J. (2005). *Disability statistics in the United States.* Ithaca, NY: Cornell University Rehabilitation Research and Training Center on Disability.

Hunsaker, S. L., Finley, V. S., & Frank, E. L. (1997). An analysis of teacher nominations and student performance in gifted programs. *Gifted Child Quarterly*, 41, 19–24.

Kitano, M. K. (1997). Gifted Asian American women. *Journal for the Education of the Gifted*, 21, 3–37.

Kulick, J. A., & Kulick, C. L. C. (1997). Ability grouping. In N. Colangelo & G. A. Davis

(Eds.), *Handbook of gifted education* (2nd ed., pp. 230–242). Boston: Allyn & Bacon.

Leydorf, D. (2004). Integrating universal design principles in asset development programs, World Institute on Disability. http://www.wid.org/publications/integrating-universal-design-principles-in-asset-building-programs/.

Losen, D. J., & Orfield, G. (2002). *Racial inequality in special education*. Cambridge, MA: Harvard Education.

Lupart, J. L., & Pyryt, M. C. (1996). "Hidden gifted" students: Underachiever prevalence and profile. *Journal for the Education of the Gifted*, 20, 36–53.

Maki, D. R., & Riggar, T. F. (1997). Rehabilitation counseling: Concepts and paradigms. In D. R. Maki & T. F. Riggar (Eds.), *Rehabilitation counseling* (pp. 3–31). New York: Springer.

McDaniel, T. R. (1993). Education of the gifted and the excellence–equity debate: Lessons from history. In C. J. Maker (Ed.), *Critical issues in gifted education: Programs for the gifted in regular classrooms* (pp. 6–18). Austin, TX: Pro-Ed.

National Center for Education Statistics. (1994). *Digest of education statistics*. Washington, DC: U.S. Government Printing Office.

Nielsen, M. E., Higgins, L. D., & Hammond, A. E. (1993). The twice-exceptional child project: Identifying and serving gifted/handicapped learners. In C. M. Callahan, D. A. Tomilson, & P. M. Pizzat (Eds.), *Contexts for promise: Noteworthy practices and innovations in the identification of gifted students* (pp. 145–196). Charlottesville, VA: National Research Center on the Gifted and Talented.

Oakes, J., & Lipton, M. (1990). Tracking and ability grouping: A structural barrier to access and achievement. In J. I. Goodlad & P. Keating (Eds.), *Access to knowledge: An agenda for our nation's schools* (pp. 187–202). New York: College Entrance Examination Board.

Olkin, R. (1999). *What psychotherapists should know about disability*. New York: Guildford.

Renzulli, J. S., & Reis, S. M. (1997). The school-wide enrichment model: New directions for developing high-end learning. In N. Colangelo & G. A. Davis (Eds.), *Handbook of gifted education* (2nd ed., pp. 136–154). Boston: Allyn & Bacon.

Roberts, S. M., & Lovett, S. B. (1994). Examining the "F" in gifted: Academically gifted adolescents' psychological and affective responses to scholastic failure. *Journal for the Education of the Gifted*, 17, 241–259.

Rogers, J. (1993). The inclusion revolution. *Phi-Delta-Kappa-Research Bulletin*, 11, 1–6.

Salend, S. J. (1994). *Effective mainstreaming: Creating inclusive classrooms*. New York: Macmillan.

Sapon-Shevin, M. (1996). Beyond gifted education: Building a shared agenda for school reform. *Journal for the Education of the Gifted*, 19, 192–214.

Sarason, S. B., & Doris, J. (1979). *Educational handicap, public policy and social history: A broadened perspective on mental retardation*. New York: Free Press.

Smith, D. (2004). *Introduction to special education: Teaching in an age of opportunity* (5th ed.). Needham Heights, MA: Allyn & Bacon.

Thomas, S., & Russo, C. (1995). *Special education law: Issues and implications for the '90s*. Topeka, KS: NOLPE.

Turnbull, R., Turnbull, A., Shank, M., & Smith, S. (2004). *Exceptional lives: Special education in today's schools*. Upper Saddle River, NJ: Prentice Hall.

Wodatch, J. (1990). *The ADA: What it says*. Worklife, 3, 3.

Yell, M. L. (1998). *The law and special education*. Upper Saddle River, NJ: Prentice Hall.

### PART 3

# Promoting Change and Achievement

*From colonial times to today, educators have preached equality of opportunity and good citizenship while engaging in acts of religious intolerance, racial segregation, cultural genocide and discrimination against immigrants and minorities.*
**Spring, 2004, p. 3**

CHAPTER

13

# Understanding the Achievement Gap between Minority and Dominant-Culture Students

## Stratification Effects

Schools continue to reproduce a sorting system based on caste that prevails in society. Whether it is through structural barriers like tracking (so-called ability grouping) or through more informal social interactions that separate people based on race, gender, social class, sexual orientation, or ability, sorting students for rewards or discrimination occurs every day in the United States. Students are either privileged or marginalized in schools based on race, gender, sexual orientation, ability, and socioeconomic status. The differential treatment of those who systematically encounter discrimination has resulted in stratified educational resources, opportunities, and outcomes.

Race and social-class achievement gaps have been widely researched, discussed, and well documented in the literature Brown-Jeffy, 2010 (Coleman et al., 1966; Irvine & Irvine, 1995; Jensen, 1969; Kozol, 1991; Oakes, 1985; Persell, 1977; Pollard, 1989). In spite of the improvements made in the United States in civil rights and race relations since 1960, minority students generally continue to exhibit lower levels of achievement than dominant-culture students in U.S. schools (Fordham, 1982; Fordham & Ogbu, 1986; Irvine & Irvine, 1995; Ogbu, 1992b, 1994; Spring, 2004).

Various theories and models have been presented to explain achievement differences between minority and dominant-culture students. This chapter presents three theories—cultural deprivation, cultural difference, and oppositional cultures—and discusses the forms and processes of differential treatment and stratification of students within U.S. schools.

## CHAPTER OBJECTIVES

1. Describe cultural deprivation and cultural differences theory explanations for minority student underachievement.
2. Describe Ogbu's oppositional cultures theory.
3. Explain the difference between voluntary and involuntary minorities and the impact of these different orientations on academic achievement.
4. Discuss the effects of gender and socioeconomic stratification on academic achievement.
5. Discuss the effects of heterosexism and ableism on academic achievement.
6. Describe what is meant by the term *opportunity structures* and the role they play in the reduction of stratification effects on minority students.

## CULTURAL DEPRIVATION THEORY

**Cultural deprivation theory** blames minority student underachievement on cognitive or linguistic deficiencies that supposedly exist within impoverished minority student community environments. This theory assumes that the fundamental educational practices and skills that White middle-class children learn are not represented and taught in minority student homes and thus disadvantage children from these communities in schools (Ausubel, 1964; Bloom, Davis, & Hess, 1965; Coleman et al., 1966). Interventions stemming from the cultural deprivation model seek to supplement existing school curricula with remedial education programming. These approaches have not been consistently successful in closing the achievement gap between minority and dominant-culture students.

Reasons for the failure of such programs are many, including the fact that in general, these programs are not designed to maintain academic achievement once it has been boosted by temporary singular programs. In addition, remediation programs often teach students basic academic skills that, if learned, will not prepare students to function in classes that require critical thinking and problem-solving skills. The failure of such programs, especially in relation to African American student education, has resulted in the strengthening and further endorsement of an old myth that achievement gaps are reflections of the inadequacy of minority students' genetic backgrounds (Jensen, 1969).

While this line of reasoning enjoyed a surge in popularity (Murray & Herrnstein, 1994), the claims posited by genetic theorists are unsubstantiated to the extent that they are discredited by most educators and researchers (Hirsch, 1987; Hudley & Graham, 1995; Valentine & Lloyd, 1989). We now know that genetic explanations are baseless. For example, they do not explain why some African American students succeed in U.S. schools and why racially mixed students do not necessarily perform better academically than students who are classified solely as African American (Ogbu, 1974).

# CULTURAL DIFFERENCE THEORY AND SOCIAL STRATIFICATION: AN UNJUST CYCLE OF BLAME

Cultural difference (Moll & Diaz, 1987; Trueba, 1987) and **multicultural educa-tion** (Banks, 1987; Banks & Banks, 1989) theories have also been used to explain and guide attempts to improve minority student achievement. These perspectives move from blaming minority students for their underachievement in U.S. schools to blaming the schools for their general lack of sensitivity to the different learner needs of culturally diverse student populations. However, interventions developed and implemented as an outgrowth of these approaches have come up short. Vari-ous school reform strategies employed by schools, in efforts to address recommen-dations emphasized by cultural difference and multicultural approaches, have not resulted in the closing of racial achievement gaps (Ogbu, 1992a).

> [M]ulticultural approaches to curriculum reform really do not offer a viable explana-tion for or "solutions" to the problem of racial inequality in schooling. Proponents of multiculturalism fail to take into account the differential structure of opportunities that help to define minority relations to dominant white groups and social institutions in the United States. (McCarthy, 1990, p. 56)

It is no surprise that schools continue to be blamed for the consistently unsat-isfactory academic performance of minority students. Americans have historically placed emphasis on the role of the school in preparing the nation's students for their jobs in society (Anyon, 1981; Apple, 1989; Bowles & Gintis, 1976; Good-lad, 1984; Spring, 1989, 2004; Wise, 1979). Most Americans agree that desirable jobs are acquired by those who are successful in school and are, therefore, more qualified to attain the highest-paying positions in the economy. "Americans of all classes send their children to school to prepare them to get jobs and high wages, as well as to achieve fine lifestyles and to be able to live in better neigh-borhoods when they grow up [They] do not send their children to school because they want them to become intellectuals" (Ogbu, 1974, p. 5). However, the logic of confidence (Meyer & Rowan, 1977) at work in this line of reasoning assumes that students have equal and fair opportunities to succeed in schools. Meyer and Rowan (1977) argue that organizations incorporate societally rationalized proce-dures to achieve legitimacy, independent of the practices' actual efficacy. A review of the **social stratification** structures and associated outcomes that exist in U.S. schools demonstrates not only does inequality exist for dominated cultures but also that school policies and practices support that inequality (Downey, 2008; Spring, 2004).

Because the same **opportunity structures** present in society are replicated in schools, societal stratification that assigns status and rewards to individuals not only places and maintains minority students in subordinate positions in society but also justifies their stratified placement in those positions in school. Rothenberg (1995) noted, "[O]ur society is organized in such a way as to make hierarchy or class itself appear natural and inevitable. We grade and rank children from their earliest ages and claim to be sorting them according to something called natural ability. The tracking that permeates our system of education both reflects and cre-ates the expectation that there are A people, B people, C people, and so forth. Well before high school, children have come to define themselves and others in just this way and to accept this kind of classification as natural" (pp. 11–12).

So, A people are placed in rich learning environments that provide the best possible resources, and C people are located in skeletal learning environments that stress the basics in order to "help them catch up." But will students who are placed in remedial programs ever catch up through their enrollment in remedial programs? Probably not, if they are never presented with the same content and instruction that fuel college-preparation programs of study. When remedial programs do not work to reduce the academic achievement gap between minority and dominant-culture students, school success, once again, is equated with individual student ability, effort, and responsibility. So, in effect, **cultural difference theory** (like cultural deprivation theory) removes the responsibility for minority student underachievement from schools, school systems, and society at large and again places it squarely on the shoulders of minority students. Minority students thus become more intensely blamed each time another school reform plan fails to result in overall minority student success.

## OGBU'S OPPOSITIONAL CULTURES THEORY AND RACIAL STRATIFICATION

According to Ogbu (1974), race alone does not explain minority student variability in school achievement. Ogbu developed a structural model of racial stratification to explain why subjugated minority groups achieve poorly in schools. His model begins with an articulation of minority student "type" as an outgrowth of the form of their initial terms of incorporation into U.S. society.

### Types of Minority Students

Two types of minority students were identified by Ogbu (1974) as determined by their initial terms of incorporation into U.S. society: (1) immigrant or voluntary minorities and (2) caste-like subordinate or involuntary minorities. While we have previously introduced the concepts of voluntary and involuntary incorporation, they are worth reviewing to help illuminate the ways racial stratification affects minority student achievement.

**Voluntary minority** students are defined as persons whose ancestors came into this country by choice, probably because they believed the change would lead to better opportunities for success. Meanwhile, involuntary or subordinate minority students' ancestors were initially brought into U.S. society against their will, through slavery or conquest.

This **oppositional cultures theory** suggests that now—generations later—the descendents of voluntary minority students may see the discrimination they receive from members of the dominant culture in the United States as an obstacle that can be overcome through hard work and compliance with rules established by dominant culture. Precisely because voluntary minorities' ancestors chose to take part in U.S. society, voluntary minority students tend to be more willing to play by dominant-culture rules. In contrast, subordinate or involuntary minorities' ancestors have historically received inferior education in the United States and may have been forced by the effects of racial stratification to terminate their educations early. In addition, subordinate minorities continue to have access to jobs and wages below those extended to members of dominant culture. Therefore, having experienced an entire history of discrimination and injustice from dominant culture in the United States (including dominant-culture school interactions), subordinate minorities often display distrust of traditional paths (schooling) to success.

Similarly, Spring (2004) explained the negative effects of deculturalization on minority student development and achievement. **Deculturalization** is the educational process of destroying a people's culture and replacing it with a new culture. Spring reminds us that **cultural genocide**—attempts to destroy other cultures—has been an important part of the history of violence in the United States. In fact, abundant examples of cultural genocide are presented throughout this text in exploring the treatment of each cultural group explored. Deculturalization synthesizes the effects of cultural prejudice, racism, religious bigotry, and democratic beliefs that result in cultural genocide.

## To Achieve Is to Be White

Under the forces of deculturalization, subordinate minority students often feel compelled in many ways to change their attitudes and behaviors and, in truth, surrender their cultural and racial identities in order to succeed in the United States and in U.S. schools. They may feel they must publicly abandon characteristics that they generally equate with their racial identity so that they may be more readily accepted and rewarded for their efforts within dominant-culture schools.

One way this may appear is in the imitation of the behavior of dominant culture which can take various forms: Some may try to treat other members of their minority group as destructively as dominant-culture members treat them. A few may develop enough of the qualities valued by dominant culture to be partially accepted. Usually they are not wholly accepted, and even if they are, it is only if they are willing to forsake their own identification with other members of their cultural group. Consider women in a profession which does not accept and view them as successful; it is not unusual to hear them praised with phrases like "She thinks like a man" (Miller, 1995).

Whereby voluntary minority students may view education in the United States as one of their main means for achieving opportunities for success, **involuntary minority** students often see U.S. education as being partially responsible for the loss of their racial and cultural identities. Involuntary minority students, having experienced generations of discrimination and prejudice in the United States, may have determined that they cannot succeed by following the traditional educational routes to economic success. They may be convinced that they must choose between taking one of two major paths on their educational journeys. One involves assimilation and, in turn, estrangement from other involuntary minority students and results in academic achievement. The other involves resistance toward dominant culture, public expression of self and racial identity, alignment with other involuntary minority students, and resultant academic underachievement. In reality, there are more than two ways involuntary minority students can respond, but often the choice is one that ultimately costs them in terms of their own academic

**Table 13-1**  A Continuum of Adaptive Strategies

Ogbu (1992b) described the following strategies as those often employed by African Americans in order to promote school success:

1. **Emulation of Whites or cultural passing:** Adopting "White" academic attitudes and behaviors or trying to behave like middle-class White students.
2. **Accommodation without assimilation:** An alternation model, a characteristic strategy among voluntary minorities. A student adopting this strategy behaves according to school norms but at home in the community behaves according to African American norms.
3. **Camouflage:** Disguising true academic attitudes and behaviors, using a variety of techniques. One technique is to become a jester or class clown. Since peer group members are not particularly interested in how well a student is doing academically, the student claims to lack interest in school and that schoolwork/homework or getting good grades is not important. The camouflaging student studies in secret. The good grades of camouflaging students are attributed to their "natural smartness." Another way of camouflaging is to become involved in "African American activities." For example, if an African American athlete gets A's, there is no harm done.
4. **Involvement in church activities:** Promotes school success.
5. **Attending private schools:** For some, a successful way to get away from peer groups.
6. **Mentors:** Another success-enhancing strategy.
7. **Protection:** A few students secure the protection of bullies from peer pressures in return for helping the bullies with their homework.
8. **Remedial and intervention programs:** Help some students succeed.
9. **Encapsulation:** May become encapsulated in peer group logic and activities. These African American students do not want to do the "White man's thing" and as a result, often fail.

achievement and/or social adjustment. Ogbu (1992b), for example, has indicated that a rather complex continuum stretches between the two extremes noted (see Table 13-1). The variety of strategies that subordinate minority students may use to reject dominant-culture expectations for educational standards of behavior or to put forth academic achievement efforts are often the means by which these students survive within racially stratified school environments.

The strategies appear to be those employed by involuntary minority students in an attempt to survive the barriers they confront in schools. While such coping responses may be advantageous for addressing psychological survival needs and enhancing one's racial identity, many of these tactics have an unfortunate side effect: The rejection of many or all behaviors and values endorsed by dominant culture also serve to undermine achievement and achievement-striving in school. In addition, the safety that emerges from withdrawal from competition for teachers' praise may also preclude assimilation. In this sense, the opposition expressed toward dominant-culture practices, including participation in school activities, greatly hinders involuntary minority student achievement. So, while a rejection of the dominant-culture frame of reference may help to defend against prejudice and enhance minority student identity, it simultaneously prohibits involuntary minority students from using traditional academic success strategies that have typically been beneficial for White and voluntary minority students.

## GENDER STRATIFICATION EFFECTS ON ACHIEVEMENT: TO ACHIEVE IS TO BE MALE

Gender, when used as a class distinction, is also a factor that contributes to a caste-like or subordinate minority positioning within schools. It is a position that can negatively affect achievement. Gilligan (1982) and other contemporary researchers (Bowker, 1993; Brown, 1991; Debold, Wilson, & Malave, 1993; Kerr, 1985; Robinson & Ward, 1991) emphasized how the different (often neglectful) treatment of female students in schools affects female student identity and academic development.

Since the early 1970s, researchers have documented the inequitable expectations, insensitive and/or inadequate teacher-approval behaviors, and unfair patterns of teacher–student interaction that sustain gender bias in schools (Keating, 1990). Belenky, Clinchy, Goldberger, and Tarule (1986) maintain:

> [F]emale students more often express the existence of gaps in their learning and doubt their intellectual competence than do male students. For many women, the real and valued lessons learned did not necessarily grow out of their academic work but from their relationships with friends and teachers, life crises, and community involvements. Women may feel alienated in academic settings and experience formal education as either peripheral or irrelevant to their central interests and development. (p. 4)

Belenky et al. (1986) contend that education, as traditionally defined and practiced, does not adequately serve the needs of females. "The commonly accepted stereotypes of women's thinking as emotional, intuitive, and personalized ha[ve] contributed to the devaluation of women's minds and contributions, particularly in Western technologically oriented cultures, which value rationalism and objectivity" (p. 6).

In order to achieve, female students may, therefore, engage in **gender passing** by acting more like male students in order to be accepted and promoted (Fordham, 1993). Lever (1976) concluded after studying 181 fifth- and sixth-grade White, middle-class student academic behaviors that "if a girl does not want to be left dependent on men, she will have to learn to play like a boy" (cited in Gilligan, 1982, p. 10). Fordham (1993) agreed that female students are compelled to pass as male dominant others. "Gender passing or impersonalization suggests masquerading or presenting a persona or some personae that contradicts the literal image of the marginalized or doubly refracted self" (p. 3). Fordham argued that gender passing is a reality for both African American and White women in finding that the first and only commandment for all women in the academy is "Thou shalt be taken seriously." For these female students, to achieve is to be male. Gains made are easily reversed when females who succeed and take on leadership roles in schools and society feel the need to replace feminist goal perspectives with ones that disadvantage female development and achievement. (See Personal Narrative 13-1.)

## Personal Narrative 13-1

We have made large gains in our status and rights. With rights comes responsibility: to keep the pressure on for more change. Despite individual exceptions, women in science and technology have not been in the vanguard of the Women's Movement. One of the goals of feminists, inside and outside scientific and technology fields, should be to connect the success of women in these fields to the success of feminist activism. They are intricately linked. The waning of feminism as a societal force allows men to reassert their sense of entitlement to jobs (and entire fields), to keep women out or marginalized in the lower ranks. This is what happened in computer science, when men seized the opportunities of that high-tech industry in the 1900s: they built a masculinist culture that excluded and dissuaded girls and women from entering; this eventually created a climate in which the new industry could be misused to promote the sexual trafficking and exploitation of women and girls; that in turn has brought about a serious global women's rights crisis. This is a cautionary lesson about what happens when women are excluded from participating in the technological and commercial development of a new field.

Feminists are learning that we need to understand, critique, and act on issues that didn't yet exist or seem relevant at the beginning of this feminist wave—issues like genetic engineering, agribusiness, and food security. Furthermore, feminists are just beginning to grasp fully the impact that new communication and information technologies have on women and children. Globalization has brought new issues to the fore that require analysis and action on local, national, regional, and global levels.

To respond to these challenges, the Women's Movement needs more women in science, engineering, and technology—women who can help mold the research questions, as well as help determine the uses to which scientific and technological findings are put. We need more women and girls taking courses in science, engineering, technology, and women's studies, so that they can learn, understand, and strengthen the connections between these fields and women's rights and status—in the lab, and in the world.

Donna Hughes, Professor of Genetics

## SOCIAL-CLASS STRATIFICATION EFFECTS OF ACHIEVEMENT: TO ACHIEVE IS TO BE WEAK

U.S. society is stratified not only according to race and gender classifications but also largely on the basis of social-class distinction. Within U.S. society, each social-class culture is not equally valued. Furthermore, because the societal standard of respectability in the United States is middle class, to be from the working class is to be defined as inferior and subordinate (Gardner, 1993). Sennett and Cobb (1972) suggested that *resistance* and *conformity* are central to understanding the process by which parental attitudes toward school are shaped. The probability that parents will conform to or resist the meritocratic ideology of pursuing educational attainment to help ensure occupational and therefore economic success tends to depend on their social-class background and on whether they have experienced "hidden injuries of class" which helps explain the attitudes of parents toward education based on their class-specific experiences in their own family, at school, and in the workplace.

Differences between rich and poor individuals in society are socially constructed by the differential opportunities and related experiences made available to different classes of people. In a cyclical reinforcing fashion, these differences are, then, used to rationalize and justify the unequal distribution of wealth and power in U.S. society. In this way, schools are an integral part of the societal social-class stratification system. They operate as social microcosms embodying the prejudice, oppression, and discrimination evident in larger society. According to Greer (1972), schools select individuals for opportunities according to a hierarchical schema that runs closely parallel to existing social-class patterns. The resultant social structure disadvantages working-class and poor students—weakening their academic achievement levels (Gans, 1995; Kao, 2003; Sennett & Cobb, 1972).

Educational researchers have documented a statistically significant relationship between working-class and poor student status and academic achievement. According to Wolf (1977), a poor child is roughly twice as likely to be a low academic achiever as a child who is not poor. Brookover, Beady, Flood, Schweitzer, and Wisenbaker's (1979) research with preadolescent students identified the presence of heightened academic futility among African American and working-class students. These students, perceiving weakened opportunities for future job attainment and economic success, also exhibited lower academic achievement than White and middle-class students. Brookover et al. (1979) found that students who exhibited higher levels of academic futility exhibited lower academic achievement. These researchers also noted, "[O]ur data indicate that high-achieving schools are most likely to be characterized by students' feeling that they have control, or mastery of their academic work and that the school system is not stacked against them" (p. 143).

When working-class students experience conflict between their desire to achieve and a sense of futility and anticipation of failure, they may develop coping strategies that negatively affect their academic achievement. One such strategy is simply to manifest a **not-learning** posture. "*Not-learning* is a strategy that makes it possible for them to function on the margins of society instead of falling into madness or total despair. It helps them build a small, safe world in which feelings of being rejected by school and society can be softened. Not-learning plays a positive role and enables them to take control of their lives and get through difficult times" (Kohl, 1991, p. 9). Other researchers (for example, Willis, 1981) have found that working-class students express opposition to oppressive school structures mainly through stylistic means. Willis found that working-class students performed acts of conspiracy almost ritualistically in rejecting the standards and cultural expectations of the dominant group. He also observed working-class male students pressuring other students into reducing their academic work output as a "massive attempt to gain informal control of the work process and output" (p. 53). While perhaps providing a sense of control, such actions also inhibit achievement.

Their limited privilege may lead working-class and poor students who want to achieve in school to believe that imitating middle-class student behavior while leaving social-class ties behind is perhaps their only option. Langston (1993) contended that because the physical conditions of working-class students' lives permit limited access to resources, "working class students seeking privilege and rewards must be willing to become middle-class impersonators" (p. 69). Unfortunately, when male working-class students engage in this form of cultural inversion, they risk being rejected by their peers. Both Eckert (1989) and Willis (1981) found that for working-class male students, compliance with teachers' wishes was registered with social-class peers as weak, acting "girlish," and lacking a backbone. The machismo persona that tends to dominate the working-class male code of conduct provides no tolerance for weakness or so-called "feminine" behavior.

## EXERCISE 13-1    Point of Reflection: Active and Passive Oppression

*Directions:*

1. In Column 1, list *active* acts of oppression and persons and groups who oppress (for example, Ku Klux Klan, tracking in school).
2. Note: Oppression requires stratification in that some groups are subordinate to a dominant group that has the power to carry out the subjugation of other groups. As in the case of tracking, middle-class students benefit from tracking while the middle class operates, sets standards for, evaluates, and doles out rewards and outcomes in schools.
3. In Column 2, list *active* acts, groups, and people who work against oppression (for example, Civil Rights Act, Dr. Martin Luther King Jr.).
4. In Column 3, list *passive* acts of oppression (for example, not speaking up when you hear a

sexist joke, not standing up when your coworkers refuse to hire a qualified candidate because he or she is a member of a minority group).

5. In Column 4, list *passive* acts that work against oppression. You probably have noticed that there are no *passive* acts of oppression to put in Column 4. The point of this exercise is to help you to realize that one must take action—even small action—to reverse the effects of stratification. Because oppression exists in the United States, in order to be a social-justice advocate, one must be proactive in fighting against it. All advocacy that you do within your spheres of influence makes you an advocate. If you have done anything in your life to *actively* work against oppression, place your name in Column 2. Keep this list and continue to add to your list of acts of advocacy throughout your teaching career.

| *Active* Acts of Oppression and Oppressors | *Passive* Acts of Oppression |
|---|---|
| *Active* Anti-Oppression Acts and Persons Who Work against Oppression | *Passive* Acts of Anti-Oppression |

*Source:* Adapted from Tatum, B. D. (1992). Talking about race, learning about racism: The application of racial identity development theory in the classroom. *Harvard Educational Review*, 62, 1–24.

Therefore, for working-class male students who wish to achieve in middle-class institutions, compliance may mean giving up ties to the working-class male community. For these working-class male students, to achieve is to be weak in the eyes of their male peers. Exercise 13-1 will introduce you to the concepts of active and passive oppression.

## HETEROSEXISM EFFECTS ON ACHIEVEMENT: TO ACHIEVE IS TO BE STRAIGHT

While lesbian, gay, bisexual, transgendered, and questioning (LGBTQ) individuals may experience joy and empowerment upon "coming out," the experience of embracing their sexual identities may be difficult for others who may experience less social support. And if LGBTQ individuals ingest heterosexism and negative stereotyping perpetuated in dominant culture, they may internalize this hate and rejection in ways that distance them from themselves, society, and schooling (Sayce, 1995). Anxiety, depression, self-harm, suicide, and attempted suicide have all been linked to the combined effects of the experience of prejudice, discrimination, and internalized negative feelings associated with heterosexism (Health Education Authority, 1998).

Addressing oppression that confronts LGBTQ students in schools is not easy. LGBTQ students may utilize a myriad of strategies to cope with their mistreatment. As with members of other minority groups, many gay and lesbian students may try to make themselves invisible (passing as dominant-culture others) in schools so their sexual orientation will not be detected, and as a result, they are distracted from their focus on schoolwork needed for effective learning and achievement. LGBTQ students, on the whole, tend to have a more difficult journey through adolescence than dominant-culture students because they feel more confined by the pressure to conform to society's sexual identity definitions and believe it is likely that they will be dismissed, despised, or deleted from school life (Khayatt, 1994). Along with these factors potentially interfering with their personal and academic development, gay and lesbian students' social and emotional needs and concerns often go unrecognized and unmet in schools. For LGBTQ students who feel they must pretend to be heterosexual in order to have opportunities to be accepted and an environment in which to succeed in schools, to achieve is to be straight.

## ABLEISM EFFECTS ON ACHIEVEMENT: TO ACHIEVE IS TO BE "NORMAL"

Because their disabilities are often emphasized in schools and may be seen as great deterrents to their education, students with disabilities may come to know that they will not be accepted for the strengths they have but rather for the ways in which they are able to overcome their disabilities and conform to expectations and standards for so-called normal students. Persons with disabilities often experience a lack of regard for contributions that develop from their differences. Schools instead tend to place a focus on finding ways for students with disabilities to perform in ways that "regular" students perform. They are taught to communicate, move, learn, and behave in ways that are as similar to dominant-culture students as they can manage. The message underlying such strategies is clearly that difference and disability equal deficiency. For students who attempt to meet these standards rather than being valued and respected for their unique contributions and being allowed to build on their different strengths within the school environment, to achieve is to be normal in as many ways as possible given their individual circumstances, therefore forsaking disability culture identification and values.

## REDUCING THE EFFECTS OF STRATIFICATION ON MINORITY STUDENT ACHIEVEMENT

One might argue that decreasing effects of societal stratification is beyond the mission and purpose of schools. Famed educator Horace Mann would disagree. Mann noted: "Education, then, beyond all other devices of human origin, is a great equalizer of conditions of men—the balance wheel of the social machinery" ("Horace Mann Quotes," 2006). If education is to function as "the balance wheel of the social machinery," it must ensure just and equal educational experiences for every student.

Some contend that access to just and equal educational conditions merely requires that minority students model the behavior and meet expectations of members of dominant culture. This view dismisses minority students' needs to maintain cultural integrity throughout their development. Others place blame on the schools for embodying the values and standards present in larger society while ignoring the values and perspectives of minority group members. Schools have always functioned to translate the values of dominant culture and produce conditions for students to take their parents' places in society.

One cannot blame minority students or schools for minority student underachievement. Instead, both minority students and their schools, when permitted opportunities through knowledge and resource appropriation to improve learning conditions, are key elements in the facilitation of minority student academic achievement (Takaki, 1993). However, both minority students and school officials lack significant direct power to make substantial structural changes in the larger sociopolitical economy that are essential for solid educational reform. Further, minority students and schools exist in adverse conditions in which they find themselves reacting to existing, sometimes conflicting mandates (legal, education reform, economic, accreditation, and so on), and therefore utilize often inefficient coping strategies that serve to distance both parties. Thus, decisions and actions made by minority students and school officials, when developed mainly to endure stressful times and conditions, further serve to divide schools and minority students and therefore hinder academic progress.

The process of allocating blame to one or the other is neither useful nor productive and is not the position taken here. Throughout this text, a number of strategies are presented in order to increase inclusion and to share availability of opportunity within the classroom with all students. These strategies will help to reduce school and classroom effects of stratification.

While it may seem that no one person, teacher, or school can change society—topple the heavily entrenched stratification system that steals our honor and punishes U.S. students—the opposite is actually true. We all have people who listen to us—people who look up to and admire us. They may be our own children or our family members, our students, or our friends. These people who like and want to be like us are within our different spheres of influence. As such, it is essential that you begin to think of yourself as a powerful person. Your personal power enables you to carefully choose what you do and say as you go about your daily activities. These carefully considered actions that you make (the schools to which you send your children, the friends you choose, the magazines to which you subscribe, the causes you support) are the makings of your social justice advocacy. But activism in larger society must take place as well (Darling-Hammond, French, & Garcia-Lopez, 2002; Downey, 2008; Gay, 2003).

Ogbu's (1992b) position that opportunity structures in society need to be changed so that subordinate minority students may have fair access to economic success is a guiding tenet in this approach. The opening of opportunity structures through

## EXERCISE 13-2    Think!

**Directions:** Ogbu advised that individual students can be helped when school officials and community members begin to think through an ideology that connects achieving with selling out. The goal is helping students realize that achieving in school is not an act of cultural betrayal.

1. Review the information for each cultural group presented in Chapters 5–12. Identify two unique characteristics, orientations, or behavioral styles for each cultural group that might come into play within a school setting and within the educational process and serve as barriers to their

academic achievement. For example, lower-income students may exhibit great proficiency in practical knowledge, arts, and skills as compared to theoretical knowledge and skills.

2. Take the list you created and discuss with a classmate, colleague, or instructor in a small group how these factors could be addressed in schools if they were perceived as differences rather than deficiencies. How might the qualities you identify be built upon to enhance school success for these students?

lobbying efforts and legislation for minority students would provide students with incentives for academic achievement. Minority communities must also strengthen their efforts to help minority children learn to disassociate achievement striving with denial of identity. It is essential for teachers and schools to support this notion and help minority students separate the idea of "rule following" from "the selling out" and loss of their identity (see Exercise 13-2). Further, it is essential that we become advocates for all students and the right to a just, free, and equal system of education (see Chapter 14).

## FROM CONCEPTS TO LIVED EXPERIENCE

Joshunda Sanders is an African American woman who describes her own personal journey through the U.S. educational system. Sanders's (n.d.) study brings Ogbu's adaptive strategies to life (refer to Table 13-1).

> **JOSHUNDA**
>
> When I first began kindergarten, I would sit at home and arrange my box of Crayola crayons so that they were in perfect order for the next school day. My mother tells me that I would actually pout when the weekend came because I wanted to be in school. I could never understand kids who I saw on television who *wanted* to stay home and even feigned sickness just so they wouldn't have to go to school. Later, I would realize that my love for education was the only source of organization and stability in my life, which is why I clung to it for dear life.
>
> The institutions where I have been educated are both numerous and distinct, some small and cozy, others large and impersonal. Wherever I was, whether it was a small suburban public elementary school in Pennsylvania or a large Catholic high school in the South Bronx, I often felt like a burden to the community. As a child, I was ashamed to be poor, because I knew others looked down on you if you were poor. So, I constantly worried about how the people in my school perceived me and I tried to behave as if there was nothing out of the ordinary happening in my life.

There was heat and food at school, normally. Those two factors only added to my enthusiasm about going to school. And while my mother and I lived a rather nomadic life, my enthusiasm for learning got me into schools that my family could never have afforded on our own. But those scholarships also landed me in some sticky circumstances. For instance, I often couldn't afford to buy lunch at the private schools I attended. I usually complained of sickness so that I would be in the nurse's office during lunchtime, not sitting with my peers. It was also rare that the winter coat I had was warm enough for me to bear the frigid temperatures of the winter months.

Despite my eagerness to be "normal," my poverty followed me into the classroom. When I attended a parochial school on the Lower East Side as a 4th grader, I owned one used uniform that I wore every day and I was sure that none of the other kids' parents needed to make use of our parish's pantry to make dinner for the evening.

I was very careful to disguise these setbacks and keep them from my classmates. I learned during my earliest exposure to education in the New York City public school system that being different was something that just was not accepted. It didn't matter that most of my peers were as poor as I was. The important thing was to look as if you were not poor (as if the problems that came with being poor stemmed from looking the part). If you looked poor, you got picked on. If you had on clothes that were too big, too small or (God forbid) out of style, you were ostracized as "the poor kid"—a stigma that usually meant you were also the kid without friends, since no one wanted to be associated with the poor kid.

My attempts at disguise didn't always work. Since I was doomed socially as the "poor girl," I found my salvation in books. I was never an "outcast" as far as literature was concerned. I became a part of whatever world I wanted to be a part of. And I decided that I wanted to be a part of every world I could find. I read everything from Judy Blume's *Are You There God? It's Me, Margaret* to Claude Brown's *Manchild in the Promised Land*. I would apply myself to every assignment I received so I could be done with my work and read whichever book I was consumed with for the day.

Unfortunately, my classmates were not enthused about the attention I received from my teachers. They found ways to tease me and discourage me from doing well, taunting me for being a "bookworm" and reminding me constantly that I wasn't "cool." Even though I loved to learn and I enjoyed reading, as I approached adolescence, I decided that being "cool" might be more exciting than doing my work and having the favor of my teachers. I tried on one occasion to be "cool" by not doing my homework. I was so ashamed by the disappointment on my teacher's face that I decided being "cool" wasn't worth it.

At home, my mother had her own issues to sort out. She had to find a way to pay the rent. She had to think about where we would go when we were locked out of our apartment. She never had time to express her pride in my diligence.

The one thing that she gave to me in abundance was her own love of learning. Although she never stayed at one school long enough to get a degree, she always made the attempt because she loved to learn new things. This may have been why she didn't see my interest in school as anything special.

Because she didn't treat my excellence in school as anything out of the ordinary, I didn't know that everyone wasn't performing the way I was. I didn't know that there was anything special about my love for books. I just knew that I had finally found something I could call my own: knowledge.

By the time I realized how education had transformed my life, I had graduated as valedictorian from 6th grade. I had become used to achieving. I began to understand that I could rise above my environment using my mind.

The most phenomenal part of my educational experience has been the teachers I have been blessed to come in contact with. They helped instill in me a sense of community. Every step of the way, people have given of themselves and their resources to me. In addition to material assistance, the encouragement and enduring confidence of these adults—teachers and others—led me through experiences I could not have overcome otherwise.

The gift of confidence in the ability of a child is one of the most powerful things in the world. Because of the gifts that each one of my teachers and mentors in my life have given me, I made a way for myself out of the ghetto. I attended a prestigious boarding school, which led me to Vassar College, where I am a full-time scholarship student.

Now I know that even when things seem darkest and we feel most alone, we are still a part of a community. That meant the world to me because I went through so much as a child that I could not have survived school were it not for the people who extended their support to me.

Each of us should understand how much power we have individually. Your mere presence in a child's life can make a world of difference. Giving of yourself and your resources is what helps strengthen society. These are the lessons that my short lifetime of education has given me. And I will pass these gifts of knowledge on to others.

# SUMMARY

**Cultural Deprivation Theory** Cultural deprivation theory blames minority student underachievement on minority students' cognitive or linguistic deficiencies, in effect blaming the victim for the discrimination she or he receives. Interventions stemming from a cultural deprivation model seek to supplement existing school curricula with often ineffective remedial education programming.

**Cultural Difference Theory and Social Stratification** Cultural difference theory explains minority student underachievement as a result of schools' failure to respond to the unique needs of a culturally diverse student population. Curriculum reform efforts based on this position have proven insufficient. Cultural difference and multicultural education approaches to curriculum reform fail to take into account the differential structure of opportunities that help to define minority relations to dominant-culture White groups and social institutions in the United States. Society is organized or stratified in hierarchies that disadvantage minority group members. Tracking (so-called ability grouping), grading, and ranking systems employed in our schools sort students in hierarchical, stratified ways that negatively affect all students except those enrolled in the highest tracks (honors and gifted programs).

**Ogbu's Oppositional Cultures Theory and Racial Stratification** Voluntary minority students are defined as persons whose ancestors came into this country by choice probably because they believed that the change would lead to better opportunities for success. Involuntary or subordinate minority students' ancestors were initially brought into U.S. society against their will, through slavery or conquest. Voluntary minority students are more willing to play by rules set by dominant culture in order to achieve. Involuntary minority students, having experienced an entire history of discrimination and injustice from dominant culture in the United States, often display distrust of traditional paths to success. Deculturalization is the educational process of destroying a people's culture and replacing it with a new culture. U.S. schools are a major part of this process.

**Gender Stratification Effects on Achievement** Gender is also a factor that contributes to a caste-like or subordinate minority positioning within U.S. schools. Research has documented inequitable expectations, insensitive or inadequate teacher-approval behaviors, and unfair patterns of teacher–student interaction to sustain functional sex-role stereotyping and disadvantage for female students in schools. In order to achieve, female students may, therefore, engage in gender passing by acting more like male students in order to be taken seriously.

**Social-Class Stratification Effects on Achievement**    U.S. society is stratified not only according to race and gender classifications, but also largely on the basis of social-class distinction. Educational researchers have documented that a statistically significant relationship exists between working-class student status and academic achievement, with poor children being more likely to be low academic achievers.

**Heterosexism Effects on Achievement**    Anxiety, depression, self-harm, suicide, and attempted suicide have all been linked to the combined effects of the experience of prejudice and discrimination and internalized negative feelings associated with living as a gay or lesbian person in U.S. schools. For these students, the stress and anxiety encountered inhibit their ability to learn. Perhaps one of the biggest barriers to a gay or lesbian student's learning and developing a facilitative relationship with a dominant-culture teacher is the teacher's potential lack of awareness and experience with diversity. Either through ignorance or denial, teachers are often unaware of the reality and experiences of gay and lesbian students within their classes. Further, once they are aware, they are often ill-prepared to respond in ways that create safe, facilitative learning environments.

**Ableism Effects on Achievement**    In addition to facing isolation, persons with disabilities may also find themselves treated like they are incompetent or with disdain. Initial attempts to include students with disabilities (mainstreaming in particular) were ill-conceived and ineffective and served to squelch efforts to improve conditions for students with disabilities because it appeared that their needs were being met. Despite the proliferation of research that dispels the myth that nondisabled students are disadvantaged by the inclusion of students with disabilities, some educators continue to resist full inclusion mandates.

**Reducing the Effects of Stratification on Minority Student Achievement**    Teachers and other individuals in society all have spheres of influence that can affect great change in working to reduce racial, gender, sexual orientation, and social-class stratification. Opportunity structures in society need to be changed so that subordinate minority students gain access to economic success. Subordinate minority communities need to strengthen their efforts to help subordinate minority children learn to disassociate achievement striving from denial of cultural identity.

## Questions for Review

1. How are cultural deprivation and cultural difference theory explanations of minority student achievement flawed?

2. How does Ogbu's oppositional cultures theory explain the achievement gap between subordinate minority and dominant-culture students?

3. What effects do racism, sexism, classism, heterosexism, and ableism have on academic achievement?

## Important Terms

cultural deprivation
   theory
cultural difference
   theory
tracking

deculturalization
gender passing
involuntary minority
multicultural
   education

not-learning
oppositional cultures
   theory
opportunity structures
social stratification

voluntary minority

## Field Experience Activities

As suggested throughout the chapter, stratification, or the creation of caste-like systems within society and schools, is detrimental to the academic achievement of those placed in the lower strata by definition of gender, sexual orientation, ability, socioeconomic condition, and race. The creation, maintenance, and impact of this stratification may be subtle yet have powerful ramifications.

The following are a series of field experience questions related to the topics covered within this chapter. Use them to guide a classroom observation. Share your experience with your teacher, your colleagues, or your classmates.

1. Interview teachers in a local high school and ask them for their opinions (both pro and con) on the process of tracking. How many cited the differential and detrimental treatment received by those in lower tracks? What criteria for placement are employed? Are these criteria valid?
2. Observe the various extracurricular activities in which the students of an elementary or middle school are engaged. This could include sporting activities, music, art, or even field trips (for example, trips to a museum or ski trips). List these activities and then identify the potential subtle barriers that may restrict the participation of students. For example, are activities segregated based on gender? Is there provision for students who cannot afford to buy the equipment needed or the bus fare required to participate?
3. Visit a school in a suburban area and a school in an inner city or rural setting. What differences, if any, did you find in terms of available classroom resources? Compare age and condition of textbooks, facilities, desks, and even the school building itself. Compare the presence of supplementary materials or instructional aids and technological support for teaching (for example, use of audio-visual aids or blackboard). How might the resource allocation impact curriculum? Instructional strategies? Academic achievement?

## Enrichment

Artiles, A. J. (2003). Special education's changing identity: Paradoxes and dilemmas in views of culture and space. *Harvard Educational Review*, 73(2), 164–202.

Beeghely, L. (2005). *The structure of social stratification in the United States* (4th ed.). Boston: Allyn & Bacon.

D'Amato, J. (1987). The belly of the beast: On cultural differences, castelike status, and the politics of school. *Anthropology & Education Quarterly*, 18, 357–382.

Ferri, B., & Connor, D. J. (2005). Tools of exclusion: Race, disability, and (re)segregated education. *Teachers College Record*, 107(3), 453–474.

Herrnstein, R. J. (1973). *The I.Q. in the meritocracy.* Boston: Little, Brown & Co.

Hooks, B. (1989). *Talking black.* Boston: South End.

Levine, D., Lowe, R., Peterson, R., & Tenorio, R. (Eds.). (1995). *Rethinking schools: An agenda for change.* New York: The New Press.

Lucas, S. R. (1999). *Tracking inequality: Stratification and mobility in American high schools.* New York: Teachers College.

Spring, J. (2004). *Deculturalization and the struggle for equality: A brief history of education of dominated cultures in the U.S.* New York: McGraw-Hill Higher Education.

Takaki, R. (1993). *A different mirror: A history of multicultural America.* Boston: Little, Brown & Co.

## Connections on the Web

http://www.childalert.co.uk/absolutenm/
templates/newstemplate.asp?articleid=35
&:zoneid=1

> This interesting site will help you answer the question: Is your school "girl-friendly"?

http://www.freshschools.org/whatisFRESH.htm

> This website is dedicated to focusing resources on effective school health (FRESH).

http://www.kl2.wa.us/equity/jointpohcy.aspx

> Prepared by the Washington State Human Rights Commission and the Washington State Superintendent of Public Instruction, this site offers information and resources for increasing education equity.

## References

Anyon, J. (1981). Schools as agencies of social legitimation. *International journal of Political Education*, 4, 195–218.

Apple, M. W. (1989). *Teachers and texts: A political economy of class and gender relations in education*. New York: Routledge.

Ausubel, D. P. (1964). How reversible are cognitive and motivational effects of cultural deprivation? Implications for teaching the culturally deprived. *Urban Education*, 1, 16–39.

Banks, J. A. (1987). *Teaching strategies for ethnic studies* (4th ed.). Boston: Allyn & Bacon.

Banks, J. A., & Banks, C. A. (Eds.). (1989). *Multicultural education: Issues & perspectives*. Boston: Allyn & Bacon.

Belenky, M. F., Clinchy, B. M., Goldberger, N. R., & Tarule, J. M. (1986). *Women's ways of knowing*. New York: Basic Books.

Bloom, B. S., Davis, A., & Hess, R. D. (Eds.). (1965). *Compensatory education for cultural deprivation*. New York: Holt, Rinehart & Winston.

Bowker, A. (1993). *Sisters in the blood: The education of women in Native America*. Newton, MA: The Women's Educational Equity Act Publishing Center.

Bowles, S., & Gintis, H. C. (1976). *Schooling in capitalist America: Educational reform and the contradictions of economic life*. New York: Basic Books.

Brookover, W. R., Beady, C., Flood, P., Schweitzer, J., & Wisenbaker, J. (1979). *School social systems and student achievement: Schools can make a difference*. Brooklyn: Praeger.

Brown, L. M. (1991). Telling a girl's life: Self-authorization as a form of resistance. In C. Gilligan, A. G. Rogers, & D. C. Tolman (Eds.), *Women, girls, and psychotherapy: Reframing resistance* (pp. 71–86). New York: Harrington Park.

Brown-Jeffy, S. (2010). School effects: examining the race gap in mathematics achievement. *Journal of African American Studies*, 13(4), 388–405.

Coleman, J. S., et al. (1966). *Equality of educational opportunity*. Washington, DC: U.S. Office of Health, Education, and Welfare.

Darling-Hammond, L., French, J., & Garcia-Lopez, S. P. (2002). *Learning to teach for social justice*. New York: Teachers College.

Debold, E., Wilson, M., & Malave, I. (1993). *Mother–daughter revolution: From betrayal to power*. New York: Addison Wesley.

Downey, D. B. (2008). Black/White differences in school performance: The oppositional culture explanation. *Annual Review of Sociology*, 34, 107–126.

Eckert, P. (1989). *Jocks and burnouts: Social categories and identity in the high school*. New York: Teachers College.

Fordham, S. (1982, December). *Cultural inversion and black children's school performance*. Paper presented at the annual meeting of the American Anthropological Association, Washington, DC.

Fordham, S. (1993). "Those loud black girls": (Black) women, silence, and gender "passing" in the academy. *Anthropology and Education Quarterly, 24,* 3–32.

Fordham, S., & Ogbu, J. U. (1986). Black students' success: Coping with the "burden of 'acting white.'" *The Urban Review, 18,* 176–206.

Gans, H. (1995). Deconstructing the underclass. In P. S. Rothenberg (Ed.), *Race, class, and gender in the United States: An integrated study* (pp. 51–56). New York: St. Martin's.

Gardner, S. (1993). What's a nice working-class girl like you doing in a place like this? In M. M. Tokarczyk & E. A. Fay (Eds.), *Working-class women in the academy: Laborers in the knowledge factory* (pp. 49–54). Amherst: University of Massachusetts.

Gay, G. (Ed.). (2003). *Becoming multicultural educators: Personal journey toward professional agency.* San Francisco: Jossey Bass.

Gilligan, C. (1982). *In a different voice: Psychological theory and women's development.* Cambridge, MA: Harvard University.

Goodlad, J. I. (1984). *A place called school: Prospects for future.* New York: McGraw Hill.

Greer, C. (1972). *The great school legend: A revisionist interpretation of American public education.* New York: Basic Books.

Health Education Authority. (1998). *Sexual identity.* World Mental Health Day.

Hirsch, E. D. (1987). *Cultural literacy: What every American needs to know.* Boston: Houghton Mifflin.

"Horace Mann quotes." (2006). *Brainy Quote.* Retrieved from http://www.brainyquote.com/quotes/authors/h/horace_mann.html

Hudley, C. A., & Graham, S. (1995, April). *Adolescents' perceptions of achievement striving.* Paper presented at the annual meeting of the American Educational Research Association, San Francisco.

Irvine, J. J., & Irvine, R. W. (1995). Black youth in school: Individual achievement and institutional/cultural perspectives. In R. L. Taylor (Ed.), *African-American youth: Their social and economic status in the United States* (pp. 129–142). Westport, CT: Praeger.

Jensen, A. R. (1969). How much can we boost IQ and scholastic achievement? *Harvard Educational Review, 39,* 1–123.

Kao, G, & Thompson, J. S. (2003). Racial and ethnic stratification in educational achievement and attainment. *Annual Review of Sociology, 29,* 417–442.

Keating, P. (1990). Striving for sex equity in schools. In J. I. Goodlad & P. Keating (Eds.), *Access to knowledge* (pp. 91–106). New York: College Board Publications.

Kerr, B. A. (1985). *Smart girls, gifted women.* Dayton: Ohio Psychology Press.

Khayatt, D. (1994). Surviving school as a lesbian. *Gender and Education, 6*(1), 47–61.

Kohl, H. (1991). *"I won't learn from you" and other thoughts on creative maladjustment.* New York: The New Press.

Kozol, J. (1991). *Savage inequalities: Children in America's schools.* New York: Harper Perennial.

Langston, D. (1993). Who am I now? The politics of class identity. In M. M. Tokarczyk & E. A. Fay (Eds.), *Working-class women in the academy: Laborers in the knowledge factory* (pp. 60–74). Amherst: University of Massachusetts.

Lever, J. (1976). Sex differences in the games children play. *Social Problems, 23,* 478–487.

McCarthy, C. (1990). *Race and curriculum: Social inequality and theories and politics of difference in contemporary research on schooling.* New York: The Falmer Press.

Meyer, J. W., & Rowan, B. (1977). Institutionalized organizations: Formal structure as myth and ceremony. *American Journal of Sociology, 83,* 340–363.

Miller, J. B. (1995). Domination and subordination. In P. S. Rothenberg (Ed.), *Race, class, and gender in the United States: An integrated study* (pp. 57–62). New York: St. Martin's.

Moll, L. C., & Diaz, S. (1987). Change as the goal of educational research. *Anthropology & Education Quarterly, 18,* 300–311.

Murray, C., & Herrnstein, R. J. (1994). *The bell curve: Intelligence and class structure in America life*. New York: Free Press.

Oakes, J. (1985). *Keeping track: How schools structure inequality*. New Haven, CT: Yale University.

Ogbu, J. U. (1974). *The next generation: An ethnography of education in an urban neighborhood*. New York: Academic.

Ogbu, J. U. (1992a). Adaptation to minority status and impact on school success. *Theory into Practice*, 31, 287–295.

Ogbu, J. U. (1992b). Understanding cultural diversity and learning. *Educational Researcher*, 21, 5–24.

Ogbu, J. U. (1994). Racial stratification and education in the U.S.: Why inequality persists. *Teachers College Record*, 96, 264–298.

Persell, C. H. (1977). *Education and inequality: The roots and results of stratification in America's schools*. New York: Free Press.

Pollard, D. S. (1989). Against the odds: A profile of academic achievers from the urban underclass. *Journal of Negro Education*, 58, 297–308.

Robinson, T., & Ward, J. V. (1991). "A belief in self far greater than anyone's disbelief": Cultivating resistance among African-American female adolescents. In C. Gilligan, A. G. Rogers, & D. L. Tolman (Eds.), *Women, girls, & psychotherapy* (pp. 87–104). New York: Harrington Park.

Rothenberg, P. S. (1995). *Race, class, and gender in the United States: An integrated study*. New York: St. Martin's.

Salend, S. J. (1994). *Effective mainstreaming: Creating inclusive classrooms*. New York: Macmillan.

Sanders, J. (n.d.). School as salvation and a ticket out of the ghetto. *Horizon Magazine* [Electronic version]. Retrieved from http://www.honzonmag.com/5/adversity.htm

Sayce, L. (1995). *Breaking the link between homosexuality and mental illness: Unfinished history*. Mind discussion document.

Sennett, R., & Cobb, J. (1972). *The hidden injuries of class*. New York: Vintage.

Spring, J. (1989). *The sorting machine revisited: National educational policy since 1945*. New York: Longman.

Spring, J. (2004). *Deculturalization and the struggle for equality: A brief history of education of dominated cultures in the U.S.* New York: McGraw-Hill Higher Education.

Takaki, R. (1993). *A different mirror: A history of multicultural America*. Boston: Little, Brown & Co.

Tatum, B. D. (1992). Talking about race, learning about racism: The application of racial identity development theory in the classroom. *Harvard Educational Review*, 62, 1–24.

Trueba, H. T. (1987). The ethnography of schooling. In H. T. Trueba (Ed.), *Success or failure? Learning and language minority student* (pp. 1–13). Cambridge, MA: Newburg House.

Uribe V., & Harbeck, K. M. (1992). Project 10 addresses needs of gay and lesbian youth. *Education Digest*, 58(2), 50–54.

Valentine, P., & Lloyd, A. (1989, March). *Living in Franklin Square: An exploration of black culture*. Paper presented at the American Educational Research Association Conference, San Francisco.

Willis, P. (1981). *Learning to labor: How working-class kids get working-class jobs*. New York: Columbia University.

Wise, A. E. (1979). *Legislated learning: The bureaucratization of the American classroom*. Los Angeles: University of California.

Wolf, A. (1977). *Poverty and achievement* (1991, No. 3). Washington DC: National Institute of Education.

*If we would have new knowledge, we must get a whole world of new questions.*
**Susanne K. Langer (2006)**

CHAPTER

**14**

# Transforming Knowledge

## A Primary Form of Teacher Advocacy

Educators are not only in the business of teaching what is known but they also reinforce and, in fact, present to students as *fact* what they value and what is valued in society. As such, it is important for teachers to question and scrutinize all that they have come to know because they will certainly pass it along to their students.

We live in the information era. Advanced technology permits rapid accumulation of information from various sources around the world. This is a time of growing research, ever-expanding information, and the potential for greater depth of understanding across all disciplines. But it is not simply new information emerging in every content area that should be of interest to educators. It is also the changing versions of "truth" and assumptions on which "truth" is built that require attention. Knowledge growth must be transformative as well as additive. **Transformative knowledge growth** occurs through teachers' integration of knowledge from marginalized groups who have heretofore been silenced or, at the very least, quieted by their oppression. This chapter explores what curriculum transformation is, why it is needed, and how to adopt this approach as an aspect of social justice education and advocacy.

## CHAPTER OBJECTIVES

1. Explain what transforming knowledge and curriculum transformation involve.
2. Describe ways in which knowledge in various disciplines is restricted and distorted to support and reflect dominant-culture perspectives.
3. Explain how prevailing modes of thought and standards of judgment serve to maintain curriculum bias.
4. Describe six stages of curriculum transformation.
5. Explain why it is important to challenge not only the content (*what* we know) but also the processes by which members of dominant culture *come* to know information in your field of study.

## A NEED FOR CRITICAL ANALYSIS OF SUBJECT CONTENT

In order to truly know, one must commit himself or herself to a continuous journey of curiosity, investigation, and critical analysis of what is presented as knowledge. Teachers stand before their classes as those who know and as those who wish to share and explore that knowledge with their students. But teachers who are knowledgeable about oppression theory and stratification effects on academic achievement must be more than simple depositories of information that has been gathered, organized, and packaged for their students' consumption. They must be aware that the best ways to actually engage students as scholars is by helping students develop skills that will allow them to construct their own knowledge through assimilation and critical analysis (Apple, 2004). Teachers and students alike must also come to understand that what is presented as "truth" cannot help but be reflective of dominant-culture values and biases of the time. Information embraced and promulgated in each field as worth knowing is always affected by the needs and wishes of the certified producers of knowledge in a given society. Because what has come to considered knowledge is necessarily incomplete and inaccurate due to the absence of minority voices, it must be replaced by knowledge that is informed by the full inclusion of the world's inhabitants (Takaki, 1993). It is incumbent on teachers to reflect upon what they know and teach, allowing their inquiries to lead them to their own critical analysis of what is known in their fields in order to refine and broaden the knowledge they teach.

The questioning and challenging of truths and knowledge described here are not part of the typical teacher's education curriculum. Understandably, it may be unsettling for teachers to criticize the very foundation on which their education rests. Content knowledge in one's field of study is knowledge believed to be solid and true. It is undoubtedly disconcerting to come to the realization it may be flawed by omissions, distortions, or inaccuracies. But as the Nigerian proverb reminds us, "Not to know is bad; not to wish to know is worse." Therefore, educators must endeavor to discover how to come to know what has been ignored and devalued in their fields (Darling-Hammond, French, & Garcia-Lopez, 2002). The time has come for a more inclusive and hence a more accurate knowledge (Takaki, 1993).

## TRUTHS THAT AREN'T: WHAT HAPPENS WHEN TEACHERS DO NOT QUESTION WHAT THEY KNOW AND TEACH?

When educators critically analyze knowledge in their own disciplines, they are likely to discover knowledge that has been lost or intentionally concealed in order to support dominant-culture perspectives and interests. The desire to support a particular perspective can be blatant and intentional, as in the case of many controversial topics in science and social studies curricula. Evolution, birth control, and various incidents in U.S. history are excluded from curricula in support of a particular set of values stemming from dominant-culture best interests. For instance, the example of African American soldiers in the Civil War is clear. "Even in the 1930s, evidence of their contributions was plain for all to see in the primary sources. Depression-era textbooks, however, omitted those facts, not because they were unknown but because including important acts by African Americans did not mirror the attitudes of [W]hite society" (Loewen, 1995, p. 286). Hidden "truths" that you will discover in your field are much more likely to result from less obvious and more insidious actions. Consider, the primary manner in which information, and therefore knowledge, is conveyed to students. For, "who controls the present, controls the past" (Orwell, 1949, p. 35). Knowledge in each discipline is legitimized by its presence in textbooks. In many instances, that which is not contained in textbooks is not transmitted as knowledge to students. Apple (1989) noted that curricula in most U.S. schools are not defined by teachers' "courses of study or suggested programs, but by one particular artifact, the standardized, grade-level-specific text" (p. 85).

You might be asking yourself why this would be a problem. There are at least two very good reasons. First, when teachers rely heavily on textbooks for instruction, they do not take responsibility for organizing their courses of study to carry out learning theories they endorse to effectively meet the pedagogical needs of their students. Therefore, someone else (the textbook author or editor) decides what and often how they teach subjects. Second, textbooks cannot help but reproduce perspectives that reflect dominant-culture views unless they actively seek (as this text does) to do so by challenging assumptions on which bodies of knowledge are based, and in so doing provide worldviews (voices) of marginalized others. Teachers cannot assume that textbooks are written as unbiased, comprehensive compendiums of information. What is included and what is excluded from textbooks often mirrors biases that permeate society. Consider the following process: Textbook companies seek to have their textbooks adopted by school districts, so they can sell large numbers of books to the biggest consumers. Textbooks are selected by school districts based on reviews from state and federal agencies that will pay a substantial amount of the textbook price for school districts that elect to use the textbooks they approve. Textbook publishers aim their efforts to meet with the approval of state and federal agencies. The result of these exchanges—one feeding into the next—is the production, distribution, and reception of textbooks that reproduce and inculcate dominant-culture values and views of what constitutes knowledge in every field of study (Apple, 1989). Standardized tests and mandated curricula that stem from texts approved for P-12 instruction provide another arena in which bias is sure to occur; when texts contain knowledge that omits and discredits minorities, standardized curricula and tests stemming from those texts will result in biased outcomes that further exclude and disadvantage minority students. One cannot blame textbook publishers for doing what is necessary to sell their products. They must utilize strategies that will garner the approval of those in power—their dominant-culture consumers.

Controlling the record of society's past is particularly important to members of dominant culture in stratified societies. (Stratification that exists in U.S. society is explained in Chapter 13.) In addition to other controls, maintaining a stratified system also requires control over ways by which citizens perceive the system. If dominant-culture members are depicted such that their privilege is historically unjustified, for example, they face embarrassment and a potential loss of status. As such, dominant culture has a vested interest in maintaining control of text materials that will contain the record of the times. Clearly, teachers must understand how knowledge presented in textbooks is affected by stratification (Apple, 1982) and take steps to critically analyze textbooks, frequently supplementing them with knowledge from other sources.

## WHAT DOES CURRICULUM TRANSFORMATION INVOLVE?

Effective educators are careful not to simply teach preset curricula conceived by someone else; instead, they engage in **curriculum transformation**. To do this, they recognize that what is accepted as knowledge in their disciplines was derived from a system of knowing that is influenced, for the most part, by the dominant-culture perspective. But they do not stop there. Beyond acknowledging the influence of dominant culture on curricula, they critically examine that curricula.

For example, the widespread use of the universal referent is another way in which dominant culture maintains control of knowledge. The universal referent puts the "man" in *mankind*—a term used to describe all the diverse women and men in the world. The problem with this type of false **universality** is that it has worked to perpetuate the widespread exclusion of women and people of color from U.S. curricula because it is the same exclusion that permits humanity (i.e., "man"kind) to be equated with maleness. Such partiality may seem benign, but it serves to endorse forms of thinking and knowledge embraced in the academy and society alike while discrediting the importance, contributions, thinking, and perspectives (for example, the Harlem Renaissance, Latino poetry, women's literature) of minorities—artists, researchers, and scholars. Teachers must begin to identify errors in thinking such as this, errors so familiar and subdued to be virtually invisible. Such awareness will lead to teachers' investigating and recognizing knowledge that has not been uncovered in their fields but that illuminates valued and important truths. For this kind of discovery (and ultimate transformation of knowledge) to take place, voices of marginalized groups who historically have been silenced must be heard and included (Minnich, 1990).

> As long as educators and scholars refrain from engaging in critique and correction of faulty assumptions in the thinking within curricula, the framework of meaning behind particular questions of what and how to teach will continue to be inhospitable to those who have been excluded from knowledge and knowledge-making. Marginalized groups will also systematically be excluded from effective participation in exercising power in dominant culture. These voices will continue to be excluded from curricula and will likely to be forgotten and to continue to be devalued. (Minnich, 1990, pp. 11–12)

## CURRICULUM TRANSFORMATION CHALLENGES

To transform curricula, educators must place emphasis not simply on *adding* to what is currently taught in schools but on *changing* it from the ground up. To merely add information about marginalized groups (women, minorities, gay and lesbian people) as a subset of or compliment to traditional knowledge is ineffective and inadequate (see Personal Narrative 14-1). Such an approach perpetuates a system built on conceptual errors that excludes meanings and content from others who exist outside dominant culture in the margins of society. The practice of simply including a member of a marginalized group (**tokenism**) in curricula reveals a profound lack of understanding of the nature and depth of the problem

## Personal Narrative 14-1    Understanding Moral Development: An Example of Ways to Expand What Is Known and Valued in the Fields of Education and Psychology

A good example of the impact of the influence of dominant-culture ways of knowing on knowledge is the treatment of the works of Lawrence Kohlberg and Carol Gilligan in the fields of education and psychology. Kohlberg's theory of moral development was, and still is, accepted as a universal theory for understanding all human moral development. When Gilligan (1982) researched and reported female moral development and outlined a model that has become highly respected knowledge about the way female moral decision making develops; it called into question Kohlberg's application of his model for understanding female moral development. Gilligan's theory posits that gender socialization in the United States has shaped the way women in U.S. society are required to think and act, and that therefore gender socialization affects women's moral decision making. Until Gilligan provided this knowledge, compiled using research methods qualitatively different from the traditional scientific methods used by Kohlberg and other dominant-culture researchers, women were disadvantaged by Kohlberg's theory that identified females as less moral than men. Using Kohlberg's theory,

women tended to be classified in Stage 3, at which their moral decisions were said to be based on pleasing others, while men were most commonly classified at Stage 4, at which moral decisions were said to be based on the need to conform to laws established in society for the sake of doing what is considered "right." Gilligan looked beyond traditional ways of thinking and reasoning to modify her research methods such that they met accepted standards of "making sense" in the behavioral sciences field while introducing a different way of knowing, thinking, reasoning, and perceiving that included the voices of adolescent girls and women to provide rich detail and insight into the thoughts and feelings that led to their moral decision making. Gilligan's model is now the standard, the accepted and highly regarded scholarship in the field of moral development. Yet, even today in most education and psychology textbooks, Kohlberg's theory is emphasized, often taking up most of an entire chapter on moral development, while Gilligan's theory is presented secondarily, often as a two-paragraph supplement to the knowledge on moral development that Kohlberg provides.

of exclusion. While tokenism provides evidence of an awareness of exclusion as a problem, it minimizes the extent and complexity of the problem. To add a few minority contributions to a course of study does not solve the problem. Ultimately, tokenism leaves the systems that produced and maintained exclusion and devaluation of minorities untouched. As Minnich (1990) points out:

> [D]iscoveries indicating the world is round did not merely supplement knowledge shaped by and supportive of the theory that the world was flat. Likewise, work by and about women, persons with disabilities, and people of color is not just missing from the academic canon: it is incompatible with some of the canon's basic founding assumptions. (p. 30)

Transforming curricula is, in fact, a radical political act. It is radical because it requires questioning all that one knows to be true and replacing it with information coming from nontraditional sources that are devalued and silenced in society and political in that it takes an important stance of advancing the rights and power of underrepresented individuals in society. When curriculum transformation is accomplished, advocacy occurs (Dee & Henkin, 2002; Swartz, 2003). In effect, by

**EXERCISE 14-1**   **Point of Reflection: Where Does What We Know Come From?**

*Directions:* Think about the most valued theorists, theories, texts, and ways of coming to know in your field.

**Ask Yourself:**

a.   Who in society do these aspects benefit?

b.   What are the effects of these aspects on knowledge development, the accumulation of facts, and practices based on these aspects in your field?

c.   How might endorsement of these aspects predispose a person to exclude different perspectives and approaches?

1.   Consider an adage or "truth" that is widely known in your field (for example, in the field of science: "Quantitative research is more credible than qualitative research."). Using the same three questions as examples, provide questions relevant to the adage you have identified from your field of study.

2.   Discuss your revelations with your classmates, colleagues, or your instructor.

listening to marginalized voices and integrating their teachings, minority groups are empowered—provided with opportunities to contribute evidence and reasoning that had previously been denied to them. Exercise 14-1 will help you begin this process for your particular field of study.

## How Established Modes of Thought Perpetuate Curriculum Bias

Major contributors to the problem of curriculum bias are the processes employed to construct knowledge (Apple, 2004). Scholarship that leads to the production of knowledge operates from an orientation in which only objective, rational scientific methods of inquiry are accredited. Because this requirement exists, it excludes thinkers who have not come to know in those ways. Using such criteria for the production of legitimate knowledge, content in slave diaries, for example, is excluded. When such knowledge is ignored, only a small part of a picture is considered. Loewen's (1995) *Lies My Teacher Told Me: Everything Your American History Textbook Got Wrong* retells U.S. history by replacing myths and misinformation contained in mainstream high school textbooks with a thorough presentation of documented events, enriched by plantation records, speeches, city directories, songs, photographs, newspaper articles, diaries, letters, and secondary works. This book is an excellent example of curriculum transformation and integration. The nontraditional sources featured throughout provide testimony that is not simply added to what was commonly known and called U.S. history. Instead, the previously ignored voices provide countless windows (each with a different vantage point) for peering into and challenging what is known to constitute U.S. history. The result is a new information, new knowledge, new truths. Exercise 14-2 will teach you how to examine content for bias.

## Limited by Standards of Judgment

Sometimes, even well-intentioned educators fall prey to standards reinforced by the status quo when attempting to include minority perspectives in their curricula.

## EXERCISE 14-2   Classroom Applications: Content Analysis

*Directions:* Go to a library and obtain a K-12 current textbook dealing with one of the following content areas: American history, biology, or health sciences. Then complete the following:

1. Focusing on only one chapter of the textbook you chose, answer the following:

   a.  What is the manner and extent to which Native American and other marginalized groups addressed?

   b.  In what ways are marginalized groups relevant to the discussion presented in the chapter even though they are not addressed (included) or sufficiently addressed (included)?

2. With your colleagues, classmates, or instructor, discuss who benefits from the knowledge presented in the textbook chapter you critically analyzed and who would benefit if what you identified in 1b was taken into account.

3. Now research and obtain Native American fables, African American poetry, and/or other typically excluded firsthand accounts and sources of knowledge. Write a reflection about what you learned that you would not have known if you had not read it in these works.

Consider, for example, the teacher who, while wishing to integrate minority voices and perspectives in her curricula finds herself frustrated by the fact that she can find no artists or writers who are people of color, women, or persons with disabilities to include. What this teacher fails to realize is that her inability to find minority voices to include is not a result of the absence of significant minority works but rather a result of an often unconsciously ingrained assumption and standard used to define "great" artists or writers worthy of inclusion. This teacher is operating with the assumption that in order for minorities to be considered worthy and fit for inclusion, they must meet existing standards for "greatness." Such judgments assume the centrality of White, middle-class men and "tradition" as it has come to be known as universal (Minnich, 1990), leaving little room for alternative approaches to knowing and associated values and standards.

If minorities create art, write, and think in modes that are not valued and accepted as those prescribed as reputable means for coming to know, then their contributions to the construction of knowledge are ignored and excluded. While amazingly inaccurate, this is a pervasive way of thinking among educators. Here is a case of victim-blaming at its worst—blaming minorities for not being talented artists, writers, and leaders worthy of inclusion in academia given the fact that they face enormous obstacles in their quests to achieve amid discrimination and oppression within the mis-education system and the awareness that modes of perceiving, interpreting, evaluating, and understanding are certain to be in conflict with dominant-culture modes of knowledge acquisition (as is noted in Parts 1 and 2 of the text). In essence, marginalized scholars are not given credit for their accomplishments because the system that judges them, that awards value, is so biased and slanted in favor of their own perspectives and goals, it does not see or hear their contributions to fields of study. Exercise 14-3 provides you with a means for recognizing curricular bias and misinformation.

**EXERCISE 14-3    Field Experience: Investigating Knowledge**

*Directions:* Research a gender topic (such as gender effects on communication or gender effects on learning). Find at least five research articles on the gender topic of your choice, then complete the following steps.

1. Read each article, identifying where the researchers agree and disagree about what is presented as knowledge on your topic (for example, does gender affect the way students learn? If yes, why and how do the different researchers explain their position?).

2. After summarizing four findings (the major positions with supporting evidence) from your research, think about who in society benefits from the different positions taken by each of the researchers featured in the articles.

3. Discuss with your classmates, colleagues, or your instructor how what you have uncovered and analyzed affects what you know about your topic. Decide, if you were to teach the material you researched, what you would teach as the truth about the topic and why.

## THINKING THROUGH CURRICULUM TRANSFORMATION

Curriculum transformation begins with questioning one's own discipline and assumptions about how knowledge comes to be in that field. Schuster and Van Dyne (1984) identified six stages of the curriculum transformation process:

*Stage 1:* The absence of the marginalized group is not noticed. There is neither knowledge of the need for nor the belief in curriculum transformation.

*Stage 2:* Teachers begin a search for missing voices in their curricula. Teachers believe their students need diverse role models at this stage and engage in a search of minority figures who are good enough to be included in their programs of study.

*Stage 3:* Teachers begin to question why they have trouble finding leaders, writers, artists, and so on who are members of marginalized groups to include in their curricula.

*Stage 4:* Teachers recognize that to document the experiences of the marginalized means documenting everything—for marginalized people have always been a part of human life. Instead of looking at the productions and outcomes of minority group member contributions to knowledge, teachers ask why marginalized groups and their perspectives are devalued and not included in their curricula. The answers to this question lead teachers to uncover biased processes and assumptions in their fields. It is during this stage that teachers may experience student resistance as classrooms heat up when discussions occur about oppression, subordination, and understanding the experiences of marginalized groups.

*Stage 5:* Teachers ask, "How valid are current definitions of standards of excellence, historical periods, and norms of behaviors within my discipline?" They reshape organizing questions in their disciplines to account for diversity.

Teachers, at this stage, give up the need for content that had seemed most stable, efficient, and free of personal values, to use gender, race, sexual

## EXERCISE 14-4    Classroom Applications: Questions to Guide Curriculum Transformation

*Directions:* The following are questions developed by Fiol-Matta (1994, p. 142) as a litmus test for educators to guide curriculum transformation. Your task is to select a lesson plan you have taught before or will teach at some point in your life. You can find published lesson plans in every field of education that you can use to some extent if you do not have lessons that you have created. Then, critically analyze the plan using the following questions.

1. What previously excluded groups have I included, and where in the course outline do they appear?
2. How often do I talk about these groups in class discussion instead of letting them speak for themselves? How much new knowledge by women and people of color have I included?
3. How often have I sought out colleagues who are more knowledgeable about women and people of color to critique concepts and discuss issues or concerns that are contained in the content of my course?
4. What tangible change can I see in my revised lesson/syllabus that reflects my new thinking? The new scholarship?
5. What are the race, gender, and class underpinnings of my course? Where are they manifested?

*Note:* You can use these same questions to analyze an entire curriculum or syllabus. Please consider doing just that before you begin to teach any body of knowledge.

---

orientation and social class as primary categories of analysis in order to transform perspectives on current data and concepts. This stage brings the classroom into a realization of the loss of old certainties. The gains at this stage include the recovery of meaningful historical and social context, the discovery of previously invisible dimensions of subjects, and access to tools of analysis that expose students to formerly suppressed material. (p. 425)

*Stage 6:* Process, instead of products, is emphasized. Courses taught at this stage include inquiries about how an awareness of race, gender, social class, ability status, and sexual orientation leads teachers and students to other sources of evidence.

A specific set of guiding questions that can help teachers begin the process of transforming curriculum is listed in Exercise 14-4. Clearly, transforming curricula results in fundamental change. It is a process that will result in changing what, how, and in what order one teaches. Curriculum transformation changes what is emphasized, what is valued, who is credited, and why the process of the construction of knowledge is important.

## FROM CONCEPTS TO LIVED EXPERIENCE

The following dialogue was an exchange between a first-grade teacher and Leigh Hall ("Ask the Literacy Teacher," n.d.). As you read the teacher's letter, see if you can identify how she has been influenced by dominant-culture values and why she is having trouble seeing things from her students' perspectives. Identify the knowledge that the first-grade teacher holds to be true about child development, literacy, and learning theory as you read.

Dear Literacy Teacher,

I have taught 1st grade for six years and in my short time of teaching things are getting worse! I teach in Texas where students in grades 3-12 are expected to pass state tests to pass to the next grade. My frustration is in the parents and dealing with beginning readers. What does one do when there is absolutely no reinforcement of reading skills outside of school? I have explained to parents the importance of my students being able to read on a 1st-grade level by May or they will be retained, but still I get no response.

To help these students, I tutor everyday after school for 45 minutes—they attend tutoring during school for 45 minutes—and I work with each child in a small group daily for 25 minutes (one-on-one) and still they make no progress. The body of children I work with is Hispanic, low socioeconomic children whose parents are on welfare and seem uninterested. I'm at my wits end to make these students successful, but I feel I'm getting nowhere. At this point in the year, I have seven children who are so far behind there's little hope for catching up. What can I do????? I've even considered leaving this profession because it's harder and harder every year. I use phonics programs, early literacy, whole language, and write-to-read programs with little results. The stress is baring [sic] down.

Signed,

Help

Dear Help,

As a former Texas teacher I understand what you are talking about! Your letter raises many issues, three of which I would like to deal with here: parent involvement, poverty and success.

The problem that you described around parent involvement is a common one that many teachers feel frustrated about. What solutions are out there? While there are no definitive answers, I do have some suggestions that could get you thinking about parent involvement in a new and different way. Consider these questions:

1.  What is your cultural background and what are your expectations? Many teachers are white, female and middle class. They tend to expect families that are not white and/or middle class to respond in the same manner that they would. Determine what your expectations for parents and families are. Think about why you hold these expectations and where they come from. Consider how your own cultural background and experiences with school as a child might play a part in these ideas.

2.  What is the background of the families that you serve? You already know that they are Latino. Do you know if English is spoken in the home? If the families do not speak English, then it would not be realistic to expect them to work with their children on English-only activities. In thinking about this question further, it would be helpful to know the stressors that affect the family, the schedules that they keep, the expectations for contribution to family economic stability. Do caretakers in the family work at night and sleep during the day? Once you have a solid understanding of the resources, strengths, and challenges confronted by your students' families, you can begin to consider strategies for getting them involved in school which is, of course, is only a beginning.

The second issue that you raised deals with poverty. You say that most of your students come from homes of low socioeconomic background whose parents are on welfare and

## EXERCISE 14-5    Classroom Applications: Identifying Steps for Transforming Curricula

*Directions:* Work with your instructor, your class-mates, or your colleagues to identify the knowledge transformation principles (discussed in this chapter) Leigh Hall suggests in her response. Use language from Schuster and Van Dyne's (1984) six stages of curriculum transformation to explain where in the stage theory the 1st-grade teacher is functioning and what steps that she must take to begin to transform her curricula.

seem uninterested. First, the term *low socio-economic background* is just that—a term. It is a way to sort and classify people. I encourage you to talk to the families whose children you serve. If you learn about what their lives were like in Mexico, you may find that they are not poor people. Poverty and what constitutes life riches and wealth are relative and viewed differently by different cultural groups. The idea that they "seem uninterested" is just that—an idea. Your attempts to connect with parents may have failed but that does not mean that these parents do not care about their children's education. I urge you to return to the two questions I stated earlier and begin to consider other routes that you can try to come to understand the families as they see themselves to better engage and involve them in your instructional efforts.

Finally you are worried about students who are not being successful. Consider your definitions for success? We live in a society that expects all students to be functioning at the same level in the same place at the same time that does not usually take into account that students have different barriers, challenges, and strengths. If your students are in the process of learning English, that would certainly affect their achievement. Likewise, if they had less time and attention to devote to schooling based on their family responsibilities, their achievement will be affected. Keep a careful record of specific progress made by your students. With all the hard work you do tutoring it sounds like they must have made some progress! Keep documentation that shows how they progress and the successes that they have made. Not only will this make you feel better, it can serve as a way to communicate to parents and administrators what your students have accomplished!

The Literacy Teacher

Now that you have read Leigh Hall's response to the first-grade teacher, see if you can identify various curriculum transformation steps she is recommending. Exercise 14-5 will help you apply what you have learned about curriculum transformation in this chapter.

## SUMMARY

**A Need for Critical Analysis of Subject Content**
Teachers must reflect upon what they know and teach. They must critically analyze and challenge what is known in efforts to refine and broaden knowledge. Teachers must question and challenge principles they have come to know to open themselves to new ways of knowing and different perspectives.

**Truths That Aren't: What Happens When Teachers Do Not Question What They Know and Teach** Knowledge continues to be lost or intentionally concealed in order to support dominant-culture perspectives and interests. The desire to support a particular perspective can be blatant and intentional, as in school districts that promote a creationist approach—excluding theories of evolution. Truth is more often distorted in less obvious and more insidious ways, such as allowing textbooks (which reflect dominant-culture bias) to dictate instruction.

### What Does Curriculum Transformation Involve?

The errors of exclusion and universality lead to the loss of knowledge. For example, assuming the issues of one group apply to all (such as equating humanity with maleness—putting the "man" in *mankind*) represents bias so deeply embedded that it is invisible to most educators. Educators who are concerned with transforming knowledge need to identify errors in thinking and investigate and recognize perspectives that have not been uncovered in their disciplines.

**Curriculum Transformation Challenges** To transform curriculum, educators must place emphasis not on adding to what is currently occurring in schools but on changing it. Simply adding knowledge about marginalized groups (women, minorities, gay and lesbian people) as a subset of or compliment to traditional knowledge is ineffective and inadequate because it continues to rest within a system built on conceptual errors

that exclude meanings and content from others outside dominant culture. Transforming curriculum is a radical political act. It is radical because it requires questioning all that we have known to be the whole truth and replacing it with information coming from sources that have for centuries been devalued and silenced.

**Thinking through Curriculum Transformation**
In Stage 1 of Schuster and Van Dyne's (1984) six stages of curriculum transformation, there is neither knowledge of the need for nor the belief in curriculum transformation; during Stage 2, teachers begin a search for missing voices in their curricula; in Stage 3, teachers begin to have trouble finding members of minority groups who are leaders, writers, and artists that they can include in their curricula; when they reach Stage 4, teachers ask why marginalized groups and their perspectives are devalued in their curricula; at Stage 5, teachers give up the need for content that had seemed most stable, efficient, and free of personal values to use gender, race, sexual orientation, and social class as primary categories of analysis in order to transform perspectives on current data and concepts; and finally in Stage 6, process, instead of products, is emphasized. Courses taught at this stage include inquiries about how an awareness of race, gender, social class, and sexual orientation suggest other sources of evidence.

## Questions for Review

1. How might typical knowledge construction processes, including the use of textbooks at the center of instruction, create bias?

2. What do the stages of curriculum transformation entail?

3. Why is it important for teachers to critically analyze content and knowledge construction processes in their fields of study?

## Important Terms

| | | | |
|---|---|---|---|
| curriculum transformation | tokenism | transformative knowledge growth | universality |

## Field Experience Activities

Observe a teacher in action and assess the degree to which he or she integrates curriculum transformation strategies. Use the following questions as your observation guide. When finished, discuss your observations with your classmates, colleagues, or instructor. For all those items to which the answer is "no," brainstorm ways you could create a more generative learning environment:

1. In the classroom you observed, were the students:
   a. exposed to examples and experiences that are relevant to their lives and represent opportunities for authentic problem solving?
   b. contributors in the knowledge construction process carried out in the classroom?

2. Did the teacher:
   a. use instructional materials that included different cultural perspectives, issues, truths, and ways of knowing?
   b. encourage students to question content presented?
   c. teach students to develop and practice critical analysis skills?

## Enrichment

Adams, M., Bell, L. A, & Griffin, P. (Eds.). (1997). *Teaching for diversity and social justice: A sourcebook for teachers and trainers.* New York: Routledge.

Chenoweth, T. G., & Everhart, R. B. (2002). *Navigating comprehensive school change: A guide for the perplexed.* Larchmont, NY: Eye on Education.

Gay, G. (1986). Multicultural teacher education. In J. Banks & L. Lynch (Eds.), *Multicultural education in western societies* (pp. 154–177). New York: Praeger.

Gilligan, C. (1977). In a different voice: Women's conception of self and morality. *Harvard Educational Review, 47,* 481–517.

Loewen, J. (1995). *Lies my teacher told me: Everything your American history textbook got wrong.* New York: The New Press.

Mayberry, J. J. (1996). *Teaching what you're not. Identity politics in higher education.* New York: New York University.

Melnick, S., & Zeichner, K. (1995). *Teacher education for cultural diversity.* East Lansing, MI: National Center for Research on Teacher Learning.

Sarason, S. (1990). *The predictable failure of educational reform: Can we change course before it's too late?* San Francisco: Jossey Bass.

Sparks, L. D., & Phillips, C. B. (1997). *Teaching/learning anti-racism: A developmental approach.* New York: Teachers College.

## Connections on the Web

http://www.diversityweb.org/Digest/W97/advice.html

This site provides educators with approaches and resources to successfully transform their curricula.

http://www.edchange.org/multicultural/curriculum.html

This site provides resources and links to inform the integration of cultural diversity in curricula.

http://wise.fau.edu/~ecou1533/politics.htm

This site contains examples of curriculum transformation efforts and their effects.

## References

Apple, M. W. (1982). *Education and power.* Boston: Routledge & Kegan Paul.

Apple, M. W. (1989). *Teachers and texts: A political economy of class and gender relations in education.* New York: Routledge.

Apple, M. W. (2004). *Ideology and curriculum* (3rd ed.). New York: Routledge Falmer.

"Ask the literacy teacher." (n.d.). Retrieved from http://teachers.net/gazette/MAR02/hall.html

Darling-Hammond, L., French, J., & Garcia-Lopez, S. P. (2002). *Learning to teach for social justice.* New York: Teachers College.

Dee, J. R., & Henkin, A. B. (2002). Assessing dispositions toward cultural diversity among pre-service teachers. *Urban Education,* 37, 22–40.

Fiol-Matta, L. (1994). Litmus tests for curriculum transformation. In L. Fiol-Matta & M. Chamberlain (Eds.), *Women of color and the multicultural curriculum.* New York: New York Press.

Gilligan, C. (1982). *In a different voice.* Cambridge, MA: Harvard University.

Loewen, J. (1995). *Lies my teacher told me: Everything your American history textbook got wrong.* New York: The New Press.

Melnick, S., & Zeichner, K. (1995). *Teacher education for cultural diversity.* East Lansing, MI: National Center for Research on Teacher Learning.

Minnich, E. (1990). *Transforming knowledge.* Philadelphia: Temple University.

Orwell, G. (1949). *1984.* New York: Harcourt Brace.

Schuster, M., & Van Dyne, S. (1984). Placing women in the liberal arts: Stages of curriculum transformation. *Harvard Educational Review,* 54(4), 413–419.

Susanne K. Langer quotes. (2006). *ThinkExist .com quotations.* Retrieved September 2006, from http:// einstein/quotes/susanne_k._langer/

Swartz, E. (2003). Teaching White preservice teachers: Pedagogy for change. *Urban Education,* 38(3), 255–278.

Takaki, R. (1993). *A different mirror: A history of multicultural America.* Boston: Little, Brown & Co.

*Transformative pedagogy turns the lens on social realities. These are, in turn, critically analyzed by students through a process of collaborative dialogue. Using the cultural capital of the students, classrooms become a forum in which students are able to voice opinions which have been silenced within practices of traditional pedagogy. This process can be both validating and empowering as students come to learn that their actions can enable change.*

**Ena Lee and Caterina Reitano (n.d.)**

"A Critical Pedagogy Approach: Incorporating Technology to De/Reconstruct Culture in the Language Classroom"

CHAPTER

15

# Moving from *Knower* to *Doer*

## Advocacy for Educators

So far in this text, you have experienced the richness of diversity in classrooms, schools, and society. It is clear that understanding diversity will become more and more important as the population of minority students grows to make up more than 46 percent of the nation's student population by the year 2020 (Pallas, Natriello, & McDill, 1989). In examining oppression theory and diversity concepts, we understand why educators are charged to enrich the lives of all students by integrating diversity into their curricula. From our exposure to the lives and circumstances of diverse peoples—hearing their firsthand accounts of their experiences in schools and society—we realize that teachers must become advocates for their students, helping to make significant academic and social changes in the lives of all students. In our exploration of research and principles of transformative pedagogy, we have found that teachers can validate and empower their students within equitable learning environments. This approach and these insights and strategies create pieces of the dream of social justice.

After reading this text, which explores the various struggles and challenges that minority students confront, it is easy to become discouraged—feeling that the problems of oppression, stratification, and inequity are too large for any individual to affect. And, while most educators are keenly aware of the existence and impact of oppression, they are often stymied by the breadth and depth of the problem and the way it is reinforced and maintained through various structures, policies, and practices carried out in schools. In an effort to do something about the problem of oppression and associated disadvantages for students, many educators address diversity by adding information about diverse peoples in their lessons. Teaching students about different cultural groups is not a bad idea; it is, however, inadequate. Raising students' awareness of diverse cultures is necessary but not sufficient for advancing social justice advocacy. Because oppression thrives on ignorance and inaction, work to decrease the impact of oppression in schools and society requires action—proactive steps taken to advocate for all students and especially for those whose voices have been silenced. Educators must act, and act with a precision that is informed by a thorough understanding of diversity issues and dynamics. In order to *walk the talk* of the missions they promise to fulfill, educators must take their own steps to increase educational opportunities and equity. To do so, they must become advocates who know and effectively integrate diversity.

This chapter examines qualities and tools of educators who are advocates for educational equity for all students—seeking to reverse overt and covert forces of oppression within their classrooms, their schools, and their communities.

## CHAPTER OBJECTIVES

1. Describe the need for educators to become advocates for integrating diversity.
2. Identify reasons for system resistance to change.
3. Describe characteristics of allies.
4. Describe principles to be followed when working as agents of change.
5. Identify forms of advocacy in classrooms.
6. Identify forms of advocacy in schools.
7. Create a personal **activism plan** for helping members of marginalized groups.

## WHY ADVOCATE?

Because oppression is such a complicated and unpleasant topic—layered with issues that exert extreme discomfort and sometimes anger and resentment, it is understandable that educators tend to ignore it in their classrooms, schools, and society. However, when educators ignore oppression created by the *isms* in larger society, outcomes are not benign. Failure to advocate for equality within classrooms and schools not only negatively affects those oppressed by the *isms* but it also disadvantages all students, all individuals, and the enlightened production of knowledge worldwide as it diminishes the significance of inclusion and pluralism and therefore supports the continuance of suppression of knowledge informed by diverse experiences and perspectives. Educators cannot simply take a passive stance. To **advocate**, they must do more than merely have an awareness of the issues concerning minority students in schools; they must actively confront the oppressive forces that interfere with their students' academic achievement.

Many educators, while recognizing the need to be proactive, exhibit real anxiety about that possibility. Often, this anxiety is rooted in their perceptions about what it means to be an advocate (see Exercise 15-1). For many, the thought of acting as an advocate conjures images of conflict, hostility, and an "us vs. them" encounter. This need not be the case. Social justice educators are advocates for

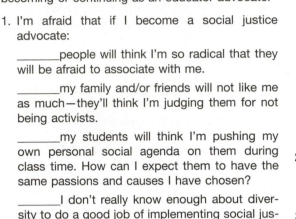

# EXERCISE 15-1    Point of Reflection: Extreme Challenge

*Directions:* Consider the following list of statements that educator allies and advocates have made in the past as they began their journeys to become effective social justice advocates. Mark those that fit with the way you currently feel about becoming or continuing as an educator advocate.

1. I'm afraid that if I become a social justice advocate:

    _____people will think I'm so radical that they will be afraid to associate with me.

    _____my family and/or friends will not like me as much—they'll think I'm judging them for not being activists.

    _____my students will think I'm pushing my own personal social agenda on them during class time. How can I expect them to have the same passions and causes I have chosen?

    _____I don't really know enough about diversity to do a good job of implementing social justice education in my classroom/school—I don't know all the facts, statistics, and theories.

    _____my students might ask me questions about diversity that I can't answer. I'll feel uncomfortable talking about racism and the other isms, and my students might even start experiencing conflict with each other if I bring these topics up in class/school.

    _____I haven't experienced enough diversity in my life and been exposed to enough difference to be a good advocate. I might insult marginalized groups when I try to interact with them, and I'll be seen as someone who doesn't "walk the talk"—I'll be found out as a fraud who doesn't really know what he/she is talking about in terms of diversity.

    _____I'm not sure if I really believe in social justice. I kind of think everyone should just be treated equally and we shouldn't call attention to differences among students.

2. After you have indicated which statements you agree with, discuss your feelings with your instructor, your classmates, or your colleagues in small-group discussion.

3. Write a reflection that explains what would make becoming or continuing as a social justice advocate difficult for you, then list actions you believe you need to take to move you one step closer to becoming a better social justice advocate.

equality. They seek to fulfill schools' missions to effectively educate all students within equitable learning environments (see Exercise 15-2). And while the fulfillment of school missions might seem to be something all school officials should routinely pursue, that is not the case. So, if social justice advocacy is good for all and not meant to be adversarial, why does it divide groups of people?

Advocacy, by definition, necessitates change. Schools, like all organizational systems, are known for their tendencies to resist any change, particularly significant change, in the ways they operate (Argyris, 1970; Benms, 1969; Blake & Mouton, 1976; de Jager, 2001; Wickstrom & Witt, 1993). Change is viewed as a threat not just to the organization's stability but to its very identity—its very existence. Much in the same ways family units seek **homeostatsis**—the tendency for a system to seek stability and equilibrium or balance; school staff members frequently fend off change in order to feel stable and balanced within their work environment. New behaviors and ideas about how to go about doing things that would change and therefore eradicate the old and known unit and modes of acting are often fought tooth and nail or squelched through both passive and aggressive means.

**EXERCISE 15-2**    **Classroom Applications: Advocacy and School Mission**

***Directions:*** Using the tenets listed by the San Francisco Unified School District's mission, identify what an individual educator could do (consistent with the state's mission) to advocate for minority students (as they have been defined and explored in this text).

- All individuals are treated with respect and dignity.
- All individuals are given the opportunity to learn in many different ways and at varying rates.
- All individuals are given recognition for their achievements.
- All individuals are recognized as both potential learners and potential teachers.
- The learning process includes cognitive, creative, and affective dimensions.

- The learning environment is characterized by interdependence and cultural diversity.
- Instruction is focused and subdivided into a number of specific, concrete competencies.
- All teachers must accept responsibility for student failure and take appropriate instructional and other supportive actions.
- Parents want their children to attain their fullest potential as learners and to succeed academically.
  1. After you compile a list of at least 10 potential acts of advocacy, put a check mark next to those that you (if you were that educator) would be willing and able to do.
  2. Reflect on the items you checked and evaluate your current strengths and weaknesses as a potential advocate.

To change, even if change is for the better, also requires school staff members to expend a great deal of energy that would be exerted in addition to the work they are already doing to keep what are considered primary school functions in operation. If change is to occur, schools must redefine their processes, structures, and ways of doing things. Such actions are time-consuming and threatening because they result in imbalance and uncertainty throughout the search for new ways of being and acting and increased work for members of the school community. No one likes to feel lost or unsure about how to do one's work. Seeking change, especially significant change that would reassign rewards and status, is highly precarious because the stakes are high and potential outcomes, perhaps, unsettling for school community members who do not know whether their rights will be protected and where they will fall in the newly created systemic hierarchy. Because social justice advocacy is designed to elevate and include minority groups that are devalued and excluded, a change in the way power in the system is distributed is broached. Whenever power is at stake, resistance is inevitable. Raising social justice issues leads individuals to question their worldviews—unsettling both unconscious and deeply held beliefs about society, self, and social relations. This disequilibrium can create **resistance**, as familiar ground shifts, and individuals encounter uncertainty, doubt, and fear about what will result if change occurs (Griffin, 1997, p. 292). Personal Narrative 15-1 shows this in action.

## BECOMING AN ALLY

An **ally** is an individual who purposefully and proactively works to help secure social justice and equality for oppressed groups of individuals in society. Becoming an ally involves a development process progressing through four basic stages.

## Personal Narrative 15-1    Why Do We Have to Know This?

In their paper on Multicultural teaching in a mono-cultural school, Sandra Lawrence and Heather Krause (1996), share their frustrations with attempting to introduce multicultural perspectives into the curriculum.

> The biggest roadblock that I have faced ... is that unfortunately, in this community, there's a lot of parents that are really prejudiced and there's almost a stereotype of (this community) as white upper middle class. Parents, at times, will balk if you try to share different things with their children, and it's like, "Well, we don't have a lot of black kids, we don't have a high proportion of Latinos in this community ... Why do we have to teach the kids about it?" (p. 33)

For Reflection

1. Identify the source and nature of the fears experienced by the various school constituents referenced in the quote.
2. Describe the nature of power redistribution that is suggested in the suggested curricular change.
3. With the help of your teacher, colleagues, or classmates, identify two strategies you could employ to reduce the fears and resistance and facilitate the curriculum adjustment desired.
4. Answer the following questions: What makes the suggested changes unsettling to some? What is the reason, as you see it, for their resistance?

*Stage 1*  *Awareness*—Individuals know they are different from and similar to members of oppressed groups. During this stage, individuals seek out information on members of oppressed groups, may attend workshops, and engage in self-examination.

*Stage 2*  Knowledge/Education—Individuals research and explore policies, laws, and practices that negatively affect members of oppressed groups. During this stage, individuals educate themselves to gain a better understanding of diverse cultural perspectives and values as well as discriminatory institutional laws, policies, and practices.

*Stage 3*  Skill Development—Individuals communicate their newfound awareness to others. During this stage, practice occurs through workshop attendance, role-playing activities, talking with peers, family, and friends, and in joining forces with others who share similar advocacy goals.

*Stage 4*  *Action*—Individuals interact in familiar and unfamiliar settings as advocates for members of oppressed groups proactively keeping a focus on marginalized groups' rights and challenging biased actions and perspectives contained in policies and practices. During this stage, individuals may attend events in support of oppressed group members' rights, learn to use inclusive language; display representations that make them known as allies; and confront oppression when it occurs.

Overall allies (1) have worked to develop an understanding of oppression and diverse cultural perspectives and issues; (2) choose to align with members of oppressed groups in support of their rights; (3) believe it is in their best interests to become an ally; (4) are committed to personal growth in spite of the probability of discomfort; (5) expect to make mistakes as they begin to advocate but do not use mistakes as excuses for non-action; (6) are aware that they are responsible for their responses to oppression; (7) are aware that when in both oppressed and non-oppressed roles, it is their responsibility to initiate personal and institutional changes responding to oppression and can expect support from other allies; and (8) are responsible for playing an empowering humanizing role in society in seeking social justice and advocacy for oppressed groups (West Chester University, LGBT Ally Manual, 2005, p. 27).

# BECOMING AN ADVOCATE AND AGENT FOR CHANGE IN SCHOOLS

## School Advocacy Strategies

Change within schools often comes at the hands of major sociopolitical initiatives. Consider the changes that influenced the U.S. educational system following the launching of Sputnik and the resulting National Defense Education Act of 1958, or the changes experienced as a response to PL 94-142, and No Child Left Behind legislation.

Rogers and Shoemaker (1971) suggested a number of principles, which serve as practical directives for educators who want to become advocates for change. These principles suggest that educators seeking to introduce a change in curricula, procedures, structures, and even composition of schools should plan change with an eye toward tying the change to the fundamental mission of the school. Thus, they need to articulate and amplify the mission of the school and demonstrate how the changes they suggest will bring the school more closely in line with the fulfillment of that mission.

Because change involves imbalance and requires expenditures of great energy and resources, it will most probably meet with resistance, especially when the anticipated positive effects of such change have yet to be proven and experienced. It is prudent that innovation be presented in small gradual steps and in ways that help members of the system take ownership in the proposed changes. Weick (1984, p. 43), for example, found that a sequence of well-articulated small wins (that is, measurable outcomes of moderate importance) set a pattern that can "attract allies, deter opponents and lower resistance" to system change.

Systems, like people and families, resist change if it appears that the current way is working. Privilege, among those in power in schools and school districts, works to disguise the enormous and widespread problems that result from institutionalized discrimination. Given this reality, it is helpful for educators attempting to initiate change, be it in classrooms or in their schools or wider communities, to tie that change to a need—an ill—recognized and experienced by others in the system. Initiating strategies as a way of helping the organization more effectively meet its goals can create the best paths to successful change (Stephan, 1999). Similarly, administrators who feel pressure from federal, state, and community forces tend to be more receptive to suggested change geared to relieve these pressures. Consider the speed and willingness to incorporate safety measures (including expensive and inconveniencing security systems) within U.S. schools following dramatic incidents of school violence. When a need is perceived to be greater than the cost of the innovation, change is more likely to be embraced. Exercise 15-3 will help you find ways to suggest change that fall in line with the school's needs.

# EXERCISE 15-3    Field Experience: Assessing the Need for Advocacy

**Directions:** While it may be easy for us to detect the stereotyped images presented in text materials or the clear void of information supporting the contributions and values of minority group members, the subtle ways schools convey devaluing of others are, by definition, harder to detect.

1. Spend a day in a school observing and talking to teachers, students, and administrators. Use the following questions as your guide to assess the degree to which subtle biased attitudes and beliefs may exist within the school you visit. An alternative may be to conduct the observation at your own or the local university or college.

   a. What do you notice about how teachers, administrators, and staff verbally and nonverbally interact with students from different racial/ethnic groups?

   b. What do you notice about how teachers, administrators, and staff respond to languages and dialects of students from different ethnic and racial groups?

   c. What cultural groups are represented among administrators, teachers, cooks, bus drivers, and maintenance workers? Are there power differential distinctions in terms of which cultural groups occupy which positions?

   d. Are students grouped based on ability? What is the criterion for grouping them? Are students essentially in the same groups that the previous teacher put them in? Are marginalized students mostly in lower "ability" groups?

   e. Ask teachers to identify five students they trust enough that they would direct a substitute teacher for assistance in their classrooms. Are these students similar to the teacher in terms of race, social class, gender, ability, sexual orientation, and so on?

   f. Do teachers have trouble relating to certain students? Are these students dissimilar to the teacher in terms of race, social class, gender, ability, sexual orientation, and so on?

   g. Is more instructional time spent with high achievers?

   h. Have the teachers and/or the administration evaluated test materials for bias? Do they feel they have a sufficient background in tests and measurement to do so?

   i. Do marginalized students tend to perform more poorly on standardized and classroom teachers' tests than do dominant-culture students?

   j. Do teachers assume responsibility for their students' failures and successes?

   k. Are comparisons of students' performance on display? What do they reflect?

   l. Do instructional materials treat oppressed groups accurately and respectfully?

   m. Does the curriculum help students learn to function effectively as intercultural communicators?

   n. Does the curriculum include positive and negative aspects of minority group member experience?

   o. Has the faculty and administration evaluated textbooks and other curriculum materials for bias?

   p. Does the faculty make an effort to get to know the students and their families? Do they know about their cultural backgrounds, values, and ways of thinking? Do they use this information to improve their teaching methods?

   q. Do teachers provide students with many opportunities to contribute to the focus and emphasis of instruction?

   r. Do teachers deal sufficiently with the concept of oppression in their curricula?

   s. Do teachers spend time helping students become critical thinkers so that the students can learn to question, challenge, and critically analyze what they have been taught?

2. Share your observations with your teacher, colleagues, or classmates in small-group discussion and talk about ways that you might combat such bias. For example, are there specific workshops or training experiences that would be helpful? Would curriculum and instructional materials be needed? Perhaps more parental involvement and collaboration are needed? These are examples of strategies that could be implemented to advocate for all students.

## Classroom Advocacy Strategies

Studies (Johnson, 1966; Litcher & Johnson, 1969; Trager & Yarrow, 1952) have suggested that children's racial attitudes can be modified by school experiences (materials, curricula, and pedagogy) that are specifically designed for that purpose. As such, teachers must clearly define their objectives and strategies to target reduction of prejudice, discrimination, and oppression in order to be effective. School administrators need to review not only school curricula but also all formal and informal structures and processes that work to maintain the status quo. Within individual classrooms, teachers need to examine their learning environments, content, and instructional strategies to be sure that each reflects support for **pluralism**—support for oppressed groups' maintenance of their unique cultural identities within larger society and the promotion of educational equity and social justice.

While it is important to decorate the walls and provide visual reminders of varying cultures, family compositions, and gender models of achievement, the equitable classroom is also one in which teachers actively model and teach a value of and respect for diversity. Teacher advocates create a learning environment in which the teacher and students know one another, trust one another, and are encouraged to express opinions and feelings. To do this, teachers must utilize structured and unstructured activities to help themselves and their students gain an understanding of class members' perspectives, values, worldviews, and concerns of their students. Teacher advocates demonstrate flexibility and creativity in organizing their classrooms and designing their instructional activities to reflect a pluralistic approach to joining as a group. Teacher advocates' classrooms are cohesive, warm, and collaborative environments that are organized in ways that invite student expression and participation that result in students' positive feelings about their contributions and worth within that classroom.

In studying classroom organization, Lloyd and Duveen (1991) found that some teachers used gender to organize classroom activities. For example, teachers often formed lines of boys and girls or even had seating arrangements based on gender. And while it could be argued that the teachers were not necessarily discriminating based on gender, the practice of separate organization, or at least subgroup identification, might continue to reinforce gender distinction in the minds of the students and increase the chances that their own gender biases might operate more strongly in interacting with classmates (Eder, Evans, & Parker, 1995). Research indicates that a simple way to encourage gender-fair classrooms, or at a minimum help to reduce gender stereotypes, is to create work and play groups that include both sexes (Pellegrini & Perlmutter, 1989). These groups can be formal, as in organizing mixed-gender and cultural groups for cooperative learning activities, or more informal, such as simply encouraging spontaneous interaction as would occur when students mingle and check work against that of others in class.

In U.S. schools, the typical social organization of learners, or the structure that organizes classroom functions, is characterized by mainly whole-group, direct instruction. Students typically are seated in individual seats arranged in rows or in small groups around tables. Children listen to a teacher explain and demonstrate, engage in some type of independent practice, and then are tested. Many have suggested that such organizational structures are unsatisfactory for encouraging effective diverse student interaction (Cushner, McClelland, & Safford, 1992; Franklin, 1992). Tharp (1989) noted that Hawaiian and Navajo children, for example, grow up with social organization structures that are characterized by small-group cooperation and collaboration. Native American, Latino, and African American, female students and students with disabilities may prefer to work with the support of other students, especially when academic tasks link to their prior personal experiences (Brown & McGraw-Zoubi, 1995; Morales-Jones, 1998). Such preferences would be frustrated in a classroom that promotes mostly individual and competitive achievement. A similar dissonance is created for African American students, who experience a mutually supportive, process-oriented environment at home but find themselves in classrooms that encourage academic competition, formality, and task-completion rather than relationship-oriented learning (Clark, 1991). Mismatch between home and school values and organizational structures can lead to students' failure to achieve.

## INSTRUCTIONAL TASKS AND SOCIAL INTERACTION STRATEGIES

Whereas dominant-culture approaches tend to emphasize task completion (product), many minority cultures, instead, emphasize process—focusing on how one works to accomplish tasks, including fostering effective social interaction and communication, critical thinking, and problem-solving skills. It is important to understand that students from different cultures may differ in their attitudes toward what constitutes an appropriate balance between task and social functioning. Students coming from a process-oriented cultural background (social-functioning orientation) may find themselves being disciplined for talking during class work or penalized when the quantity of their product is not equal to those who focused strictly on the assigned task.

A strategy that helps students maintain a positive social identity while interacting cooperatively with others students is the use of jigsaw instruction (Aronson, Stephan, Sikes, Blaney, & Snapp, 1978). Not only does this technique facilitate the development of positive social identities but it also provides positive, equitable contact between members of different groups, which in turn can effect positive change in intergroup relationships (Johnson & Johnson, 1992a, 1992b; Stephan & Stephan, 1996). Jigsaw activities involve the teacher dividing materials into as many parts as there are students in the group. Each student then learns his or her own part of the material and presents this piece of the instructional puzzle to the other members of the group. Using this strategy, students in each group are dependent on one another to learn all the material. The groups do not compete with one another, and each student is graded individually on his or her performance. The groups usually work together for four to six weeks and then new groups are formed. Research on this technique suggests that the benefits for students include higher self-esteem, greater liking for school and classmates, and improved performance on tests (Aronson & Gonzalez, 1988).

Teachers must be mindful of how and with whom they interact in the classroom (Palmer, 2002). They must be aware of whom they call upon and ask themselves: Do I ask more questions of students from one group or another? Do I tolerate, discipline, or applaud behaviors differentially? Do I use gender-based illustrations and examples? Do I provide more support, affirmation, or approval for achievement to one group of students than to another? Do I listen more intently, teach more directly, and reward more often one group of students over another? These are questions that teachers must ask if they are to become social justice advocates.

## Texts and Lesson Content

Textbooks from the early 1960s, presented what appeared to be "happy, neat, wealthy, [W]hite people whose intact and loving families live only in clean, grassy suburbs" (Fantini & Weinstein, 1968, p. 133). When culturally different peoples were finally added to textbooks, they were typically depicted in full stereotype. People of color were presented only in stories about their native lands or as foreigners to U.S. soil. Women were relegated to careers as mothers or nurses or teachers. And issues of disability, religious diversity, or sexual orientation were rarely, if ever, included. Textbooks largely presented a monocultural view of society.

While textbooks today tend to provide a more diverse and broader view of society, it is important for teachers to critically review the materials they use, noting biased content, and narrow views when present and integrating diverse perspectives in inclusive instructional materials that will help students expand their knowledge of the world. Teachers need to evaluate curriculum materials to identify linguistic bias, stereotyping, invisibility, omission, imbalance, inaccuracy, and fragmentation.

Multicultural education strategies are typically designed to teach students about the characteristics of various ethnic groups, their histories, their current experiences, and the ways they are similar and different to other ethnic groups. It is geared to help facilitate students' ability to function more competently in intercultural interactions (Banks, 1997). Beyond this approach, teachers must take steps to ameliorate students' negative attitudes toward oppressed groups and provide them with the opportunity to experience life (through firsthand content and instructional design) from the perspectives of diverse groups.

**Critical pedagogy** involves teachers' commitment and methods used to engage in critical reflection, dialogue, and social activism with students as a part of their curricula (Freire, 1996; McLaren & Fischman, 1998; Shor, 2000). Teachers engaging in critical pedagogy implement curricula that teach and encourage their students to develop critical consciousness, think critically about what is presented to them as fact, pose questions, and become socially and politically active (Edelsky, 1999). At a minimum, teacher advocates expose their students to the processes of oppression and subjugation as they are enacted through texts and other curriculum materials used in the classroom. Instead of focusing on increasing students' awareness of diversity alone, they also invite students to challenge educational and social biases presented in instructional materials and found within their schools and communities. Ayers (2001) explained that it is important for teachers to be "both dreamers and doers, to hold onto ideals but also to struggle continually to enact those ideas in concrete situations" (p. 126). Thus, teacher advocates are involved in transformative social activism within their own classrooms and schools and extending to their communities at large (Montano, Lopez-Torres, DeLissovoy, Pacheco, & Stillman, 2002). Critical pedagogy helps learners process and reflect on their own experiences and the experiences of members of oppressed groups, while awakening in them the motivation to work toward social change.

Teachers must not only infuse their curricula with minority voices and oppression theory, but they must also employ instructional strategies that facilitate social justice education. To do this, they must (1) balance the emotional and cognitive components of the learning process, paying attention to safety, respect, and valuing behaviors; (2) acknowledge and support their students' individual experiences while illuminating the realities of institutional discrimination; (3) create opportunities for meaningful social relationships and group cohesion to form in their classrooms; (4) utilize reflection exercises and other student-centered learning strategies, including problem posing and self-reflection; and (5) value personal growth, awareness, and change for themselves and as outcomes of the learning process while taking into account student interest and readiness (Adams, 1997). Such strategies require cooperative, interactive teaching that engages students as active coinvestigators who learn to explore and synthesize multiple perspectives throughout the learning process (Maher, 1985). Through these methods, students will come to know that oppression is not the natural order but rather the result of socially constructed forces that can be changed. The goal of critical pedagogy is to help students experience education as something they *do* instead of as something *done to them* (Freire, 1996). Exercise 15-4 will help you come up with a plan for instituting this in your classroom.

**EXERCISE 15-4**

## Classroom Applications: Creating a Personal Activism Plan

**Directions:** Keeping in mind your own spheres of influence (see Chapter 13), create a personal activism plan for your own family, classroom, school, neighborhood, or larger community.

1. The first step requires that you identify a person or a group within your family, classroom, school, or local community who is marginalized. This may be an elderly family member who is discounted because of age or loss of sensory abilities (for example, physically impaired, deaf, or blind), a student who is ostracized because of his or her sexual orientation, or a group that is shunned by the community (for example, a group of Muslims living in your neighborhood or who attend your local YMCA).

2. Identify one way in which this person or group has had their needs frustrated or restricted in terms of the means and degree to which their needs can be satisfied. For example, the student who has been ostracized due to his or her sexual orientation may feel alone and may develop a negative self-concept because of peer isolation.

3. Identify specific actions that could enable the person or group to function better as a more included and valued part of your family, classroom, school, neighborhood, or larger community. For example, perhaps a teacher could have a group-sharing activity during which students shared times when they have felt isolated and alone. Such an activity may help your identified student recognize the feelings of the isolation of others and begin to express her or his feelings of isolation. Or perhaps a teacher could place the student in a role, such as small-group project reporter, which would by its nature increase interaction and in turn allow for the development of personal relationships.

4. Decide what you are willing and able to do to be a part of the solution in making the changes stated in #2 happen (for example, learning sign language so you can communicate with a deaf relative or beginning a book group that enrolls a lesbian student so she can interact with her peers and you in the discussion of meaningful topics found in books read).

5. Enact your activism plan.

Congratulations! You are an advocate. You have changed society for the better by taking one step at a time. Celebrate your courage and success!

# FROM CONCEPTS TO LIVED EXPERIENCE

The first story in this section is of one teacher's "awakening" to the need and opportunity to become an advocate. It is the reflection of Alice G., a White ninth- and tenth-grade social studies teacher who describes her experiences with system resistance to social justice advocacy.

The second story describes Kay Toliver's teaching career, spanning 34 years at the elementary and middle school levels. Teaching in East Harlem, she had students with diverse levels of interest, motivation, knowledge, and skill. It was a career guided by a singular principle: All students can learn at high levels.

### DOMINANT-CULTURE ADVOCACY: AN ADVOCATE'S STORY

It seemed benign. We are sitting at the faculty meeting, one of the last for the year and most everyone was talking, well actually complaining, about this child or that child. Everyone seemed to be looking forward to the end of the school year—and most were hoping to get out of the meeting ASAP and enjoy what had become a beautiful spring day.

Well, the principal started the meeting by announcing that "this should be a brief meeting (to which everyone applauded), but there were a few pieces of information that needed to be discussed." She began by highlighting upcoming events in the school calendar, then passed out a district report on anticipated enrollments for the next year, and finally proceeded to congratulate the baseball team for going to the district championship.

As everyone was talking about the baseball team I began looking at the enrollment sheets. I noticed that, because of redistricting, we are going to have a large number of children from a predominately Latino area of our school district. Prior to this redistricting our student composition was 95 percent Caucasian, 3 percent African American, 2 percent defined as other. If there were one or two Latino children in our school, they were included in the "other" category.

As the faculty chatted about the great baseball season, I raised my hand. When recognized, I asked the simple—or at least what I thought was simple—question. "I see from the redistricting statistics that we will be adding over 80 students from Southside. My assumption is that most of these students are Latino. Are we making any provisions for insuring that our school is welcoming and supportive?" Wow! People chuckled and made comments like "[O]kay bleeding heart Alice!—let's get movin'." Even the principal snickered! I tried to clarify—and said "No, seriously—do we have any bilingual teachers? Or will we receive any in-service training on developing curriculum and teaching strategies to increase our knowledge of Latino culture and values?" Understanding that I was serious, the principal responded by saying that she "was sure that central office will be addressing these issues" and then she moved on to the last item: the faculty picnic.

I left that meeting feeling like I had rocked the boat—or in some way said something I shouldn't have. It was not at all comfortable, and I really kind of wished I had kept my mouth shut. It concerns me that I was the only one to bring up these issues. I wonder—Am I so right? Or is everyone else in my school so wrong?

### MINORITY GROUP MEMBER ADVOCACY: AN ADVOCATE'S STORY

I was born and raised in East Harlem and the South Bronx. I am a proud product of the New York City public school system, graduating from Harriet Beecher Stowe

Junior High, Walton High School and Hunter College (AB 1967, MA 1971) with graduate work at the City College of New York in mathematics.

Becoming a teacher was the fulfillment of a childhood dream. My parents always stressed that education was the key to a better life. By becoming a teacher, I hoped to inspire African American and Hispanic youths to realize their own dreams. I wanted to give something back to the communities I grew up in.

For more than 30 years, I taught mathematics and communication arts at P.S. 72 East Harlem Tech in Community School District 4. Prior to instructing 7th- and 8th-grade students, I taught grades 1 through 6 for 15 years.

My educational philosophy is simple: All students can learn. It is a teacher's job to expand minds and take children from the known to unknown.

I have made my classroom a place where students can talk without fear, write, manipulate ideas, and listen. I focus upon integrating math with other curriculum areas, for I want students to begin to see that mathematics goes beyond numbers and computation.

Over the years I have shared my knowledge and skills primarily with students. Over the past few years, I began working with teachers as a staff developer for my school district. I am also acting as a panelist and a speaker at educational conventions, when my school schedule permits.

At East Harlem Tech, with the support of my principal, I established the "Challenger" program. Challengers are students who can face any problem in life.

The program, for grades 4–8, presents the basics of geometry and algebra in an integrated curriculum. This is a program for "gifted" students, but following my belief that all children can learn, I accept students from all ability levels. ("Kay Francis Tolliver," n.d.)

## SUMMARY

**Why Advocate?**   Failure to advocate for equality within the classroom and within the school not only negatively affects those oppressed by *isms* and results in less attention, and thus achievement, within the schools, but it can also be seen as, at a minimum, trivializing such oppressive forces or, worse yet, supporting them. Teachers need to do more than simply understand the issues concerning minority students; they must actively confront the issues and the forces oppressing minority students and interfering with their academic achievement. When advocating for our students, we are by definition advocating for change. Schools, like all organizational systems, are known for their ability to resist significant change in the ways they operate.

**Becoming an Ally**   An ally is an individual who purposefully and proactively works to help secure social justice and equality for oppressed groups of individuals in society. Becoming an ally involves a development process progressing through four basic stages.

**Becoming an Advocate and Agent for Change in Schools**   In schools, it is helpful to link advocacy to school mission. Introduce change in small steps (shaping). Tie change to felt need. When a need is experienced as greater than the cost of the innovation, change is more likely to be embraced.

In classrooms, teachers must review and address barriers associated with classroom climate, content, and processes that do not value and integrate diversity and the promotion of educational equity. Such actions will lead to the encouragement of positive student social identities. It is important to understand that students from different cultures may differ in their attitudes toward what constitutes an appropriate balance between task completion and social functioning. Teachers must be mindful of how and with whom they interact in the classroom.

Teachers need to evaluate curriculum materials for bias—linguistic, stereotyping, invisibility, imbalance, omission, inaccuracy, and fragmentation.

Teachers engaging in critical pedagogy implement curricula that encourage students to become socially and politically active—exposing their students to the processes of oppression and subjugation as they may be enacted through texts and other curricular materials.

## Questions for Review

1. What are qualities that allies share?

2. What does critical pedagogy involve?

3. How is it that teachers can act as advocates for oppressed groups and still have time to teach necessary content in their classes? Explain.

## Important Terms

| | | | |
|---|---|---|---|
| activism plan | ally | homeostatsis | resistance |
| advocate | critical pedagogy | pluralism | |

## Enrichment

Adams, M., Bell, L. A, & Griffin, P. (Eds.). (1997). *Teaching for diversity and social justice: A sourcebook.* New York: Routledge.

Bartunek, J. M. (2003). *Organizational and educational change: The life and role of a change agent group.* Mahwah, NJ: Lawrence Erlbaum.

Darling-Hammond, L., French, J., & Garcia-Lopez, S. P. (2002). *Learning to teach for social justice.* New York: Teachers College.

Delpit, L. (1995). *Other people's children: Cultural conflict in the classroom.* New York: The New Press.

Fine, M., & Powell, L. (Eds.). (1997). *Offwhite: Critical perspectives on race.* New York: Routledge.

Gay, G. (Ed.). (2003). *Becoming multicultural educators: Personal journey toward professional agency.* San Francisco: Jossey Bass.

Palmer, P. J. (1993). *To know as we are known: Education as a spiritual journey.* New York: Harper & Row.

## Connections on the Web

http://www.lessonplanet.com/search?grade=All&keywords=critical+pedagogy&rating=3&search_type=narrow

This site provides lesson plans for all K-12 age groups that employ critical pedagogy.

http://www.centerfortransformativeeducation.org/

The Center for Transformative Education website features educational program guidelines to help transform schools and society.

http://safezonefoundation.tripod.com/id27.html

This site provides guidelines and resources to help organizations create their own safe zones to support the inclusion of and advocacy for oppressed groups.

# References

Adams, M. (1997). Pedagogical frameworks for social justice education. In. M. Adams, L. A. Bell, & P. Griffin (Eds.), *Teaching for diversity and social justice: A sourcebook*. New York: Routledge.

Argyris, C. (1970). *Intervention theory and method: A behavioral science view*. Reading, MA: Addison Wesley.

Aronson, E., & Gonzalez, A. (1988). Desegregation, jigsaw and the Mexican-American experience. In P. Katz & D. Taylor (Eds.), *Eliminating racism* (pp. 301–304). New York: Plenum.

Aronson, E., Stephan, C., Sikes, J., Blaney, N., & Snapp, M. (1978). *The jigsaw classroom*. Beverly Hills, CA: Sage.

Ayers, W. (2001). *To teach: The journey of a teacher* (2nd ed.). New York: Teachers College.

Banks, J. A. (1997). *Educating citizens in a multicultural society*. New York: Teachers College.

Benms, W. G. (1969). *Organizational development: Its nature, origins and prospects*. Reading, MA: Addison-Wesley.

Blake, R. R., &; Mouton, J. S. (1976). *Consultation*. Reading, MA: Addison Wesley.

Brown, G., & McGraw-Zoubi, R. (1995). Successful teaching in culturally diverse classrooms. *The Delta Kappa Gamma Bulletin*, 61(2), 7–12.

Clark, M. L. (1991). Social identity, peer relations and academic competency of African American adolescents. *Education and Urban society*, 24, 41–52.

Cushner, K., McClelland, A., & Safford, P. (1992). *Human diversity in education: An integrative approach*. New York: McGraw Hill.

de Jager, P. (2001). Resistance to change: A new view of an old problem. *Futurist*, 35(3), 24.

Edelsky, C. (1999). On critical whole language practice: Why, what and a bit of how. In C. Edelsky (Ed.), *Making justice our project: Teachers working toward critical whole language practice* (pp. 7–36). Urbana, IL: National Council of Teachers of English.

Eder, D., Evans, C., & Parker, S. (1995). *School talk: Gender and adolescent culture*. New Brunswick, NJ: Rutgers University.

Fantini, M. D., & Weinstein, G. (1968). *The disadvantaged: Challenge to education*. New York: Harper & Row.

Franklin, M. E. (1992). Culturally sensitive instructional practices for African-American learners with disabilities. *Exceptional Children*, 59, 115–122.

Freire, P. (1996). *Education for critical consciousness*. New York: Continuum.

Johnson, D. W. (1966). Freedom school effectiveness: Changes in attitudes of Negro children. *The Journal of Applied Behavioral Science*, 2, 325–330.

Johnson, D. W., & Johnson, R. T. (1992a). Positive interdependence: Key to effective cooperation. In R. Hertz-Lazarowitz & N. Miller (Eds.), *Interaction in cooperative groups* (pp. 174–199). New York: Cambridge University.

Johnson, D. W., & Johnson, R. T. (1992b). Social interdependence and cross-ethnic relationships. In J. Lynch, C. Modgil, & S. Modgil (Eds.), *Cultural diversity in the schools* (Vol. II, pp. 179–190). London: Falmer.

"Kay Francis Tolliver." (n.d.). Retrieved from http://www.thefutureschannel.com/kay_toliver.php

Lawrence, S. M., & Krause, H. E. (1996). Multicultural teaching in a multicultural school: One cooperating teacher's personal and political challenges. *Equity & Excellence in Education*, 29(2), 30–36.

Lee, E., & Reitano, C. (n.d.). A critical pedagogy approach: Incorporating technology to de/reconstruct culture in the language classroom. Retrieved from http://mingo.info-science.uiowa.edu/-stevens/critped/otherdefs.htm

Litcher, J. H., & Johnson, D. W. (1969). Changes in attitudes toward Negroes of White elementary school students after use of multiethnic readers. *Journal of Educational Psychology*, 60, 148–152.

Lloyd, B., & Duveen, G. (1991). Expressing social gender identities in the first year of school. *European Journal of Psychology of Education*, 6(4), 437–447.

Maher, F. A. (1985). Pedagogies for the gender-balanced classroom. *Journal of Thought*, 20(3), 48–64.

McLaren, P., & Fischman, G. (1998). Reclaiming hope: Teacher education and social justice in the age of globalization. *Teacher Education Quarterly*, 25(4), 125–133.

Montano, T., Lopez-Torres, L., DeLissovoy, N., Pacheco, M., & Stillman, J. (2002). Teachers as activities: Teacher development and alternate sites of learning. *Equity & Excellence in Education*, 35(3), 265–275.

Morales-Jones, C. (1998). Understanding Hispanic culture: From tolerance to acceptance. *The Delta Kappa Gamma Bulletin*, 64(4), 5–12.

Pallas, A. M, Natriello, G, & McDill, E. L. (1989). The changing nature of disadvantaged population: Current dimensions and future trends. *Educational Researcher*, 18(5), 16–22.

Palmer, P. J. (Ed.). (2002). *Stories of the courage to teach: Honoring the teacher's heart*. San Francisco: Jossey Bass.

Pellegrini, A. D., & Perlmutter, J. C. (1989). Classroom contextual effects on children's play. *Developmental Psychology*, 25(2), 289–296.

Rogers, E. M., & Shoemaker, F. F. (1971). *Communication of innovations*. New York: Free Press.

Shor, I. (2000). (Why) education is politics. In I. Shor & C. Pan (Eds.), *Education is politics: Critical teaching across differences, postsecondary* (pp. 1–14). Portsmouth, NH: Heinemann.

Stephan, W. (1999). *Reducing prejudice and stereotyping in schools*. New York: Teachers College.

Stephan, W. G., & Stephan, C. W. (1996). *Intergroup relations*. Boulder, CO: Westview.

Tharp, R. G. (1989). Psychocultural variables and constants: Effects on teaching and learning in schools. *American Psychologist*, 44, 349–359.

Trager, H. G., & Yarrow, M. R. (1952). *They learn what they live*. New York: Harper.

Weick, K. E. (1984). Small wins. *American Psychologist*, 39(1), 40–49.

West Chester University, LGBT Ally Manual, (2005). LGBT Services, LGBT Concerns Committee, and LGBTA. West Chester University, West Chester, PA.

Wickstrom, K. F., & Witt, J. C. (1993). Resistance within school-based consultation. In J. E. Zins, T. R. Kratochwill, & S. N. Elliot, *Handbook of consultation services for children* (pp. 159–178). San Francisco: Jossey Bass.

# Index